AF607980

THE *DECAMERON* EIGHTH DAY IN PERSPECTIVE

The *Decameron* Eighth Day in Perspective

Volume Eight of the *Lectura Boccacci*

EDITED BY WILLIAM ROBINS

UNIVERSITY OF TORONTO PRESS
Toronto Buffalo London

Toronto Buffalo London
utppublishing.com

ISBN 978-1-4875-0690-2 (cloth)
ISBN 978-1-4875-3513-1 (EPUB)
ISBN 978-1-4875-3512-4 (PDF)

Toronto Italian Studies

Library and Archives Canada Cataloguing in Publication

Title: The Decameron eighth day in perspective / edited by William Robins.
Names: Robins, William Randolph, 1964– editor.
Series: Toronto Italian studies. | Toronto Italian studies. Lectura Boccaccii ; v. 8.
Description: Series statement: Toronto Italian studies | Lectura Boccacci ; volume 8 | Includes bibliographical references and index.
Identifiers: Canadiana (print) 20200207504 | Canadiana (ebook) 20200207520 | ISBN 9781487506902 (cloth) | ISBN 9781487535131 (EPUB) | ISBN 9781487535124 (PDF)
Subjects: LCSH: Boccaccio, Giovanni, 1313–1375. Decamerone.
Classification: LCC PQ4287 .D42 2020 | DDC 853/.1–dc23

University of Toronto Press acknowledges the financial assistance to its publishing program of the Canada Council for the Arts and the Ontario Arts Council, an agency of the Government of Ontario.

Canada Council for the Arts **Conseil des Arts du Canada**

Funded by the Government of Canada | Financé par le gouvernement du Canada | Canada

Contents

Acknowledgments

I would like to express my deep thanks to Victoria University in the University of Toronto, my home institution, for providing an unparalleled environment for studying pre-modern literary cultures, and for helping to fund this volume's publication.

I owe a great debt to Jeff Espie, whose attentive comments on matters of substance and whose thoughtful editorial advice have strengthened every page of this volume; he deserves huge thanks from me on behalf of all of the contributors. This collection and the essays within it have also benefited from judicious comments made by two anonymous reviewers, for which the contributors and I are grateful.

I very much appreciate the support this volume has received, from inception through completion, from the officers of the American Boccaccio Association, under whose auspices the Lectura Boccaccii series is produced. Similar thanks are due to Suzanne Rancourt and the editorial staff of the University of Toronto Press for shepherding this book through the publication process so expertly.

THE *DECAMERON* EIGHTH DAY IN PERSPECTIVE

Introduction

WILLIAM ROBINS

The *Beffe* of Day Eight

Day Eight of the *Decameron* features stories about *beffe*, practical jokes.[1] Lauretta, the queen for the day, proposes the subject: "dico che ciascun pensi di dire di quelle beffe che tutto il giorno o donna a uomo o uomo a donna o l'uno uomo all'altro si fanno" [I want each of you, instead, to think up a story about the tricks that women are always playing on men, or men on women, or men on other men (VII.Concl.4)].[2] Stories told about pranks, *novelle di beffa,* have enjoyed a long tradition in Italian culture, especially in Florence, and Boccaccio's tales constitute an important codification of basic patterns for the genre.[3] In Boccaccio's hands, *novelle di beffa* tend to celebrate the triumph of cleverness and wit over gullibility and folly. In the tales of Day Eight, the target of the prank, the *beffato,* typically possesses an overblown sense of self-importance, revealed in traits such as hypocrisy, conceit, greed, or

1 I would like to thank Jeff Espie for reading through several drafts of this Introduction and for providing his helpful advice on matters of structure and style. This Introduction owes much to his contributions.

2 Excellent overviews of Day Eight and its most salient interpretive issues include Cottino-Jones, *Order from Chaos,* 135–55; Grimaldi, *Il privilegio di Dioneo,* 277–98; Forno, "L'amaro riso"; Wallace, *Giovanni Boccaccio: Decameron,* 84–98; Picone, "L'arte della beffa"; and Alfano, "Giornata VIII: Scheda introduttiva." The text of the *Decameron* is cited from Boccaccio, *Decameron,* edited by Quondam, Fiorilla, and Alfano. English translations are from Boccaccio, *Decameron,* translated by Rebhorn.

3 On *beffe* in the *Decameron,* see Fontes-Baratto, "Le thème de la *beffa*"; Di Maria, "Structure of the Early Form of the *Beffa*"; Segre, "La beffa e il comico"; Ferroni, "Sulla struttura della beffa"; Mazzotta, *The World at Play,* 186–212; Ferme, "*Ingegno* and Morality"; Arend, *Lachen und Komik,* 209, 318–54; Zunino, "*Florentini, trufatores maximi*"; and Holmes, "Trial by *Beffa*."

overzealousness (Savelli, "Riso"). The tricksters who perform the prank, the *beffatori*, bothered by the arrogance they observe, cleverly devise a way to undercut it through an act of mockery or deceit. The resulting prank often involves irreverent physicality, and frequently brandishes a cruel malice even when laughter is the ostensible aim. Unlike the pranks recounted in Day Seven, most of which deal with matrimionial comeuppance and turn upon avoiding or dealing out punishment, the *beffe* of Day Eight are mostly gratuitous in nature (Fontes-Baratto, "Le thème de la beffa"). Most of these pranks are performed by an in-group made up of two or more *beffatori*; as they shame and scapegoat an outsider, they reinforce their collective identity and strengthen the codes that they share for judging others (Holmes, "Trial by *Beffa*"). Occasionally they perform their jest as a spectacle to be enjoyed by neighbours and other bystanders, extending the in-group to embrace these sympathetic audiences. Similarly, at an extradiegetic level those who listen to or read a *novella di beffa* are implicitly expected to relish the lampooning of the dupe, to sympathize with the tricksters, and to join the spirit of in-group solidarity. The antics of the pranks which so delight the pranksters and their accomplices continue to provide amusement when recounted as a *novella di beffa*.

A *beffa* can be deployed as a method of critique by those who lie outside of systems of power, permitting them to communicate their contempt for oppressive forms of authority. But a *beffa* can just as easily be employed by the powerful to direct hostility toward the weak and vulnerable. The resulting laughter at times may be corrective, altering the behaviour of the dupe; at other times it may be cathartic, an outlet for repressed desires and feelings of revenge; and at yet other times it might serve to reduce the friction of potentially violent social conflict. But a prankster does not necessarily aim for such noble ends: the prankster is distinguished by situation-specific ingenuity, an "absorption in the theatrical moment of the spectacle he creates" (Williams, *Tricksters*, 21), as he, or indeed she, works to bring down the overblown pretensions of some irritating fool.[4] Usually the *beffa* acts as an adequate corrective and a fitting spectacle, but sometimes it misses the mark and gives rise to a retaliatory prank, as the dupe learns from experience, transforms vulnerability into aggression, and tricks the original

4 Studies of laughter and performative comedy in the *Decameron* include Baratto, *Realtà e stile* (for Day Eight see 260–4, 309–22, 377–9, 393–9); Cottino-Jones, "Comic Modalities"; Picone, "Gioco e/o letteratura"; Savelli, "Riso"; as well as the works cited in the previous note.

trickster. Day Eight's tales range from schematically simple jests to more elaborate plots of *beffa* and counter-*beffa*.[5]

In the *Decameron,* the eighth day rounds out a tryptich of three days devoted to manifestations of cleverness. Day Six with its tales about *motti* (clever ripostes) presents tales of clever wit exhibited through words. The next two days recount *beffe*, which are instances of clever wit exhibited in plotted actions. After Day Seven's focus on tricks played by women upon men, Day Eight explores the *beffa* freed from the previous day's thematic specificity, making the day "a sort of treatise on the art of the *beffa*, with ten examples of concrete application."[6] This series of three days begins mid-way through the *Decameron*'s one hundred tales, a moment that strikes many readers as a "new beginning" for the entire collection.[7] Barolini speaks of the second half of the *Decameron* as manifesting an increasing "turn toward reality" which includes a "continued insistence on Florence" ("Wheel of the *Decameron,*" 234). In this respect the transition from Day Seven to Day Eight is significant: during the seventh day when the *brigata* relaxes in the idyllic Valle delle Donne they are at their furthest distance from Florence, while for Day Eight they return to their previous villa, beginning to trace their journey back toward the city, which will be completed two days later. Before they begin the storytelling of Day Eight, the ten storytellers attend a divine service at a nearby church, "una chiesetta lor vicina" (VIII.Intro.2), moving outside their private sanctuary in what is "the only public, social action of the storytellers recorded in the *Decameron*."[8] In this fashion Day Eight begins with the *brigata* drawing back from their idealized escapism, directing their attention to what is contiguous in space and time, to what is located "lor vicina" [nearby] and what happens "tutto il giorno" [always].

Day Eight showcases repetition and amplification. When Lauretta proposes her topic for the day, she enlarges upon Dioneo's topic for Day Seven. Where Dioneo called for stories about the tricks which

5 The form of the *beffa* is accommodating enough even for Dioneo, who on this day declines to exercise his privilege of departing from the proposed topic.

6 "una sorta di trattato sull'arte della beffa, con dieci casi di applicazione concreta" (Sanguinetti, *Lettura del Decameron*, 228).

7 On this new beginning, and on the place of Days Six, Seven, and Eight in the overarching structure of the *Decameron*, see Stewart, "La novella di Madonna Oretta"; Barolini, "The Wheel of the *Decameron*"; Paden, "Elissa: La ghibellina"; and Bevilacqua, *Leggere per diletto*, 11–17.

8 "È l'unico atto sociale, pubblico, dei novellatori registrato nel D[ecameron]" (Boccaccio, *Decameron*, ed. Branca 1980, 889n3).

wives have played upon their husbands, Lauretta expands the topic's range: "quelle beffe che tutto il giorno o donna a uomo o uomo a donna o l'uno uomo all'altro si fanno" [the tricks that women are always playing on men, or men on women, or men on other men (VII.Concl.4)]. This is the only time in the *Decameron* when the new theme enlarges that of the preceding day. Other days with paired themes involved reversal instead: the tales portraying determination in the face of Fortune in Day Three countered those about human subjection to Fortune in Day Two, while the happily ending love stories of Day Five balanced the tragic loves of Day Four. Lauretta acknowledges that she could easily devise a theme more directly antithetical to Dioneo's by focusing specifically on tricks played by men against women. But overcoming any inclination to "vendicare" [retaliate (VII.Concl.3)], she resists sharp distinction and opts instead for a more capacious logic of accumulation, reinforced even in her polysyndeton of substitutable alternatives, "o … o … o … " In expanding Dioneo's frame of reference, Lauretta tempers its sexual underpinning, suggesting that her day's *novelle* might or might not entail gendered violence.[9] From her vantage, *beffe* can happen to any person at any moment as part of "the open-ended bedlam and chaos of unexpurgated life" (Barolini, "Wheel of the *Decameron*," 242).

Lauretta follows the declaration of her theme with another gesture of repetition. Recognizing that the next two days will be Friday and Saturday, Lauretta proposes that the *brigata* copy the practice of the previous week and suspend storytelling for two days. When Neifile recommended such a pause prior to Day Three, she worried about "dilungandomi dalla maniera tenuta per quelle che davanti a me sono state" [depart[ing] from the ways of my predecessors (II.Concl.4)]. By contrast, Lauretta acknowledges that she is performing an act of repetition: "volendo il buon essemplo datone da Neifile seguitare" [since I want to imitate the excellent example Neifile has given us (VII.Concl.17)]. When the storytelling finally begins on Sunday morning, it also continues past practice, returning "al novellare usato" [to tell stories as usual (VIII.Intro.3)]. Calling the day's tale-telling *novellare usato*, the narrator poses an oxymoronic puzzle: what is novel is also time-worn.

At the end of the day, the preoccupation with clever tricks is brought to a close by Emilia, who proposes that the next day's storytelling be free of any constraint. Even Emilia's professed eagerness for change

9 On the misogyny that persists in the tales of Day Eight, see Migiel, "The Untidy Business"; Wallace, *Giovanni Boccaccio: Decameron*, 85.

involves an act of repetition, for she copies the unrestricted freedom of the very first day of storytelling. She then extends the mode of repetition further when she affirms that the next ruler will once again constrain the storytellers within their "usate leggi" [customary laws (VIII. Concl.5)]. They do not know it yet, but that day of storytelling will turn out to be their last. As the eighth day comes to a close, the tale collection enters its final laps.

Boccaccio's Geographic Imagination

When introducing the tales of the eighth day, the members of the *brigata* characteristically measure the geographical proximity of their stories to the villa where the storytelling takes place. Varlungo is a "villa assai vicina di qui" [a village not very far from here (VIII.2.6)]. The hilltown of Fiesole "noi possiamo di quinci vedere" [we can clearly see from here (VIII.4.4)]. Calandrino's farm lies "non guari lontan da Firenze" [not very far from Florence (VIIII.6.4)]. For the tales set in the city of Florence itself, proximity is expressed as a matter of shared civic identity, with events occurring "nella nostra città" [in our city (VIII.3.4, VIII.5.4)]. Some of the storytellers provide temporal orientation in relation to their present moment as well, noting that the events occurred "ancora non è gran tempo" [not so very long ago (VIII.3.4)], "non sono ancora molti anni passati" [not so many years ago (VIII.7.4)], or "non ha gran tempo" [not all that many years ago (VIII.9.5)].[10] Lauretta delimits an even narrower period of time for the action of VIII.9 when she describes the arched tombs of Santa Maria Novella as new but the feces ditch by San Jacopo a Ripoli as a thing of the past, implying that her story is set in the not-too-distant past (the signposts point to the first quarter of the fourteenth century).

Boccaccio also announces temporal coordinates by mentioning actual historical figures in his stories. The tales associated with Calandrino and his friends should evoke the first two decades of the fourteenth century, when the painter Calandrino (Nozzo di Perino, d. 1318) was active.[11] The naming of the notary Bonacorri da Ginestro in VIII.2 conjures up an even more recent period, anytime between about 1320 and

10 These kind of indications, by no means limited to Day Eight, are an important feature of Boccaccio's manner of introducing tales: see Forni, "Realtà/verità," 316–17.

11 Calandrino can be identified with the painter Nozzo di Perino, who died in 1318. Buoanamico di Martino Buffalmacco died in 1336, and Bruno di Giovanni

Table 1. Geographic Organization of the Tales of Day Eight

Novella	Main Setting	Region	Coordinates	Movement
VIII.1	Milan	Trading City	Northern Italy	Genoa
VIII.2	Varlungo	Contado	East	Florence
VIII.3	Florence	Florence	San Giovanni	Contado
VIII.4	Fiesole	Contado	North	
VIII.5	Florence	Florence	Santa Croce	
VIII.6	Contado	Contado	?	Florence
VIII.7	Florence	Florence	?	Contado
VIII.8	Siena	Tuscany	South	
VIII.9	Florence	Florence	S. Maria Novella	
VIII.10	Palermo	Trading City	Southern Italy	Naples

the date of the *brigata*'s storytelling. The events of VIII.10 are said to have occured "in quei tempi" [at that time (VIII.10.42)] when Boccaccio's friend, Pietro dello Canigiano, served as treasurer to the Empress of Constantinople, and so in the 1330s (Mallet, "Canigiani, Piero," 94). Although the remaining tales don't provide comparable temporal signposts, they all depict worlds whose customs and physical features are nearly contemporaneous with each other, with the *brigata*, and with Boccaccio's implied audience: "sì come noi veggiamo tutto il dì" [just as we see every day (VIII.9.4)].[12]

The fictional worlds of Day Eight are carefully orchestrated through Boccaccio's geographical imagination (see Table 1). The first and last tales are set in Italian trading cities to the north and south, with VIII.1 taking place in Milan and VIII.10 in Palermo; these two *novelle*, with their outlier locations, serve as bookends for the remaining tales, which all take place in Florence and its environs, and through which the city is "scenographically conjured up."[13] The eight local tales alternate neatly between those set primarily in the city of Florence itself (VIII.3, VIII.5, VIII.7, and VIII.9) and those set in the surrounding countryside or nearby towns (VIII.2, VIII.4, VIII.6, and VIII.8).

d'Olivieri is mentioned in documents from 1301, 1320, and 1340 (Boccaccio, *Decameron*, ed. Branca 1980, 906n2 at VIII.3.4; Watson, "The Cement of Fiction," 44).

12 Rebhorn's translation has been modified.

13 "scenograficamente evocata" (Forno, "L'amaro riso," 133).

Map 1. Locations in Novellas VIII.3, VIII.5, and VIII.9

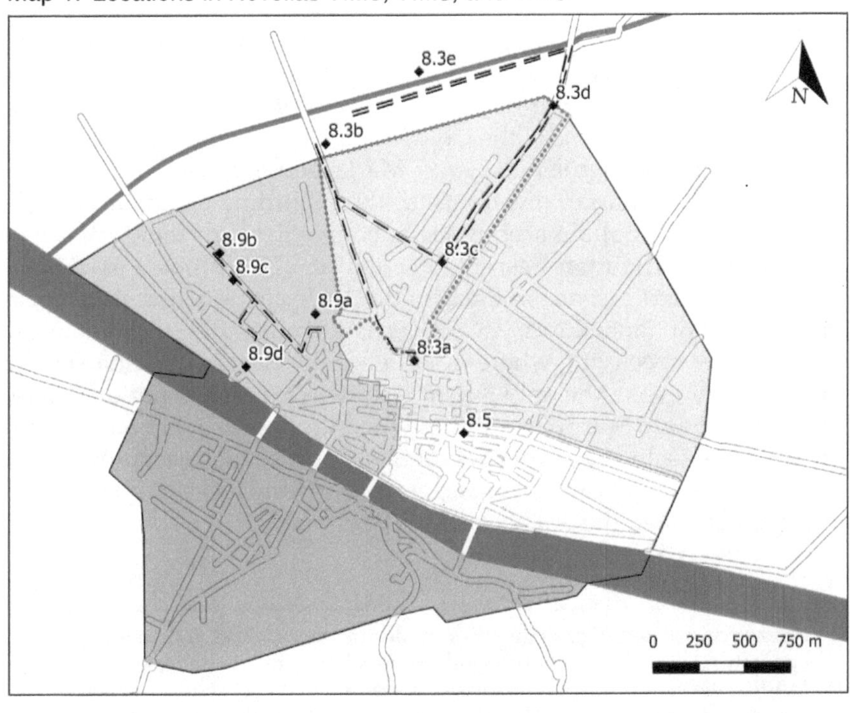

Quartieri

- S. Croce
- S. Giovanni
- S. Maria Novella
- S. Spirito

...... Gonfalone of Leon d'Oro

_ _ Journeys Described in *Decameron* VIII.3 and VIII.9

Locations

8.3a Battistero di S. Giovanni
8.3b Monastero delle Donne della Beata Umilità di Faenza
8.3c Canto alla Macine
8.3d Porta San Gallo
8.3e Mugnone River
8.5 Palazzo del Podestà
8.9a Santa Maria Novella
8.9b San Jacopo a Ripoli
8.9c Santa Maria della Scala
8.9d Ognissanti

Credit: Artemisia Robins

The four tales that begin and end in Florence seem to respect the administrative division of the city into four *quartieri*, at times even calling to mind the further subdivision of *quartieri* into neighbourhood *gonfaloni* (see Map 1).[14] The *quartiere* of San Giovanni provides the setting

14 The four *quartieri* were introduced to replace an earlier division of the city into six *sestieri* as part of a major reform of city government in 1343, just after Boccaccio's return to Florence (Carocci, "Le antiche divisioni"). Florentines identified closely with their *quartieri* and *gonfaloni* both as communities of neighbourhood sociability

for VIII.3, which begins its action in the baptistery of San Giovanni, from which the quarter takes its name, and then follows Calandrino as his movements trace the perimeter of one of the *quartiere*'s neighbourhoods, the *gonfalone* of the Golden Lion.[15] The central *beffa* of VIII.9 transpires in the *quartiere* of Santa Maria Novella; beginning in the piazza of Santa Maria Novella itself, the nighttime escapade of Simone, Bruno, and Buffalmacco plots its course through the *gonfalone* of the Unicorn.[16] The more restricted action of VIII.5 unfolds as characters come in and out of the Palazzo del Podestà, which is situated in the *quartiere* of Santa Croce. By contrast, Novella VIII.7 is deliberately vague, never specifying where in Florence the *palazzo* of Elena stands; this tale may evoke the only *quartiere* in which a *beffa* is not otherwise set, namely Santo Spirito. For critics who interpret VIII.7 in an autobiographical key, a hidden evocation of Santo Spirito may seem fitting, for this was Boccaccio's own *quartiere*, his house being located in the parish of Santa Felicità in the *gonfalone* of the Seashell.[17]

---

and as decisive partitions of the city's adminsitrative, juridical, and political apparatus (Eckstein, "The Neighbourhood as Microcosm").

15 In VIII.3 the named locations of the action are, in order: the baptistery of San Giovanni, the monastery outside the Porta di Faenza, the Porta San Gallo, downstream along the Mugnone River, upstream along the Mugnone, the Porta San Gallo again, and Calandrino's house near Canto alla Macine. Canto alla Macine (now the intersection of Via Guelfa and Via San Gallo/Via Ginori) was named after a mill that had been on this spot when the Mugnone stream ran here, prior to being rechannelled to the north when the city walls were constructed in 1333; the road from the Canto alla Macine to Porta San Gallo was built along the old course of the stream; by walking from his house here to the Mugnone's new location, Calandrino physically traces the history of Florence's urbanistic expansion.

16 Simone and Buffalmacco meet in the piazza of Santa Maria Novella, pass by the churches of Santa Maria della Scala and San Jacopo a Ripoli, reach the sewer ditches near Porta al Prato, and return past Santa Maria della Scala and the field of the church of Ognissanti back to the piazza of Santa Maria Novella. Santa Maria della Scala, San Jacopo a Ripoli, Porta al Prato, and Ognissanti are all in Unicorno; the Piazza of Santa Maria Novella is split between Unicorno and Leon Bianco, with the "avelli rilevati" (whether this term indicates the six arches in the façade or the raised tombs along Via degli Avelli) in Leon Bianco. The novella also sets action in Simone's house in Via del Cocomero (now Via Ricasoli), which lies in the quarter of San Giovanni; interestingly, his "bottega … in Mercato Vecchio alla 'nsegna del mellone," mentioned in IX.3.17, lies in Santa Maria Novella.

17 Autobiographical approaches to VIII.7 include Moravia, "Boccaccio," 145–7; Muscetta, *Giovanni Boccaccio*, 265; and Leone, "Tra autobiografismo reale e ideale." For an important critique, see Marcus, "Misogyny as Misreading." On Boccaccio's house in Santa Felicità, see Branca, *Giovanni Boccaccio: Profilo biografico*, 53, 79n45, 85–6, 183.

In a comparable manner, each of the tales set in the surrounding regions aligns with one of the four cardinal directions. They take place in Varlungo to the east (VIII.2), in Fiesole to the north (VIII.4), and in Siena to the south (VIII.8). Extrapolating from this pattern, the remaining regional novella, which occurs at Calandrino's farm not far from Florence, might be correlated with the fourth cardinal direction, west of the city.[18]

Such a neat "cartographic" arrangement of tales is unique to Day Eight.[19] Through it, Boccaccio tries out a new basis for linking the *novelle* told within a single day of storytelling, with tales connected not only through the variations they perform upon a literary genre or theme but also through coordinates of nearness and distance, through parameters of orientation and movement, which differentiate and at the same time unify the narrative worlds in which the stories occur.

Spatial demarcations and contiguities are also explored through the movement that occurs within each of the tales. The traversing of different *quartieri* of Florence has already been mentioned. Even more notable, in half of the eight local tales characters move back and forth between the city of Florence and its *contado* (countryside). The story of Calandrino and the heliotrope in VIII.3, which begins and ends in the city, stages its memorable *beffa* during a Sunday outing beyond the city gates along the the Mugnone stream. The tale of Elena and Rinieri, VIII.7, likewise begins and ends in Florence, but the characters travel far into the *contado* for the culminating scene of cruelty at a "podere verso il Valdarno di sopra" [farm in the upper valley of the Arno (VIII.7.60)]. Those movements out of the city find their mirror image in journeys into the city in other tales. From Varlungo, just outside the city walls, the peasants of VIII.2 traipse to the city and back, while in VIII.6 Bruno and Buffalmacco run in and out of Florence from Calandrino's country farm. Journeys of much grander geographical scope characterize the

18 Boccaccio had previously employed the four cardinal directions to divide the narrative action that occurs in the "valle non molto spaziosa, / di quattro montagnette circuita" described in the *Caccia di Diana*. There Diana divides the ladies who have joined her into four groups, sending them to hunt on the four surrounding mountains "a meriggio … al ponente … a tramontane … verso l'oriente" (*Caccia di Diana* 2.1–48, pp. 16–17). This episode constitutes, as Branca notes, "una opaca ma diretta anticipazione della scena" of the Valle delle Donne in the *Decameron* (*Caccia di Diana*, p. 287, note to 2.1).

19 Analyses of geospatial representation in the *Decameron* include Cottino-Jones, "The City/Country Conflict"; Celli-Olivagnoli, "Spazialità nel *Decameron*"; Marcozzi, "Raccontare il viaggio"; Alfano, *Introduzione alla lettura del Decameron*, 110–13; Bolpagni, *La geografia del Decameron*; and Papio, "Geospatial Visualizations."

two non-Tuscan tales, with the merchant Guasparruolo of VIII.1 travelling from Milan to Genoa on business, and with Salabaetto in VIII.10 sailing to Naples after each of his mercantile adventures in Palermo. Rather than linking a city to its hinterland, the merchants' journeys in these tales belong to the ever-widening connections of medieval commerce and trade.

Boccaccio's attention to geographical demarcations reinforces his exploration of the insider/outsider dynamic at stake in the genre of the *novella di beffa*. His *beffe* are often triggered by tensions between Florentine patterns of behaviour and intrusive foreign habits, especially in the many tales that feature a character who arrives from elsewhere. The Podestà and his judge, Niccolo da San Lepidio, come from the Marche, bringing to urbane Florence the bumbling self-importance of rustic lawyers. Master Simone hails from Bologna, dressing up his asinine behaviour with the airs of a doctor. The scholar Rinieri, although a Florentine, has cultivated an intellectual arrogance during his time studying in Paris. In these three cases, foreignness is aligned with a conceited attitude that has been moulded through professional formation. Foreignness and pretension are equally targeted by the *beffe* played against these professed experts. The final tale reverses this dynamic, as the Florentine Salabaetto arrives in Sicily, where the local Iancofiore takes advantage of his naivety; after he turns the tables, enacting his revenge with the aid of a fellow Florentine, the sympathetic Florentine narrator sums up the moral of the tale with a rhyme, "Chi ha a far con tosco, non vuole esser losco" [If with Tuscans you vie, / Don't you dare close your eye (VIII.10.67)].

A *Brigata* of Tricksters

As Boccaccio explores a poetics of repetition, accumulation, and contiguity in Day Eight, his most striking innovation is the interpolation of a group of *novelle* in which some of the same protagonists reappear. Up to this point Boccaccio "has led us to expect that each story of the *Decameron* will be unique, employing its own *dramatis personae*, and its own interplay of personalities" (Marcus, *Allegory of Form*, 91). But this changes after VIII.3, during which the narrator Elissa introduces a tale involving several historically identifiable Florentine jokesters from the city's recent past:

> Nella nostra città ... fu, ancora non è gran tempo, un dipintore chiamato Calandrino, uom semplice e di nuovi costumi. Il quale il più del tempo

con due altri dipintori usava, chiamati l'un Bruno e l'altro Buffalmacco, uomini sollazzevoli molto ma per altro avveduti e sagaci, li quali con Calandrino usavan per ciò che de' modi suoi e della sua simplicità sovente gran festa prendevano. Era similmente allora in Firenze un giovane di maravigliosa piacevolezza in ciascuna cosa che far voleva, astuto e avvenevole, chiamato Maso del Saggio; il quale, udendo alcune cose della semplicità di Calandrino, propose di voler prender diletto de' fatti suoi col fargli alcuna beffa o fargli credere alcuna nuova cosa. (VIII.3.4–5)

[Not so very long ago, there lived in our city … a painter named Calandrino, a simpleminded man with some strange habits. He used to hang out with two other painters named Bruno and Buffalmacco, a pair who were very merry, but who, being quite perceptive and shrewd, spent time with Calandrino because they often found his antics and his simplicity really funny. At the same time there also lived in Florence a marvelously entertaining, astute, and capable young man named Maso del Saggio, who having heard tales of Calandrino's simplicity, decided to go and amuse himself at Calandrino's expense by playing a practical joke on him or by getting him to believe some far-fetched notion.]

Bruno and Buffalmacco spend time with Calandrino because his behaviour provides them with continual episodes of amusement. Stories of his simple-mindedness circulate among their fellow citizens, prompting one of them, Maso del Saggio, to instigate yet another episode. This dynamic, in which stories about an individual figure multiply and cluster together into a repertoire, is soon replicated at the level of the frame tale, with Maso del Saggio no longer the creator of a new story but a figure about whom new stories are told.[20]

When it is Filostrato's turn to narrate, he announces that Elissa's mention of Maso del Saggio has spontaneously prompted him to relate another anecdote about him: "il giovane che Elissa poco avanti nominò, cioè Maso del Saggio, mi farà lasciare stare una novella la quale io di dire intendeva, per dirne una di lui e d'alcuni suoi compagni" [the young man Elissa mentioned just a short while ago, that is, Maso del Saggio, has prompted me to pass over a story I intended to tell you in order to recount another one about him and some of his companions (VIII.5.3)]. Filomena, the next storyteller, prompted by Elissa's mention of Calandrino and imitating Filostrato's accumulative poetics, adds a

20 Maso del Saggio is also mentioned in Frate Cipolla's speech in VI.10.42.

further link to the chain: "come Filostrato fu dal nome di Maso tirato a dover dire la novella la quale da lui udite avete, così né più né men son tirata io da quello di Calandrino e de' compagni suoi a dirne un'altra di loro" [just as Filostrato was led by the mention of Maso's name to rehearse the story about him you just heard, I, too, have been led in exactly the same way by the one concerning Calandrino and his buddies to tell you another (VIII.6.3)]. Finally Lauretta, the queen of the day, adds her tale about Master Simone and the "due dipintori de' quali s'è oggi qui due volte ragionato, Bruno e Buffalmacco" [Bruno and Buffalmacco, the two painters about whom we have already told two stories today (VIII.9.7)].

The principle of repetition at work here is a striking facet of Boccaccio's emphasis in Day Eight on repetition and accumulation. After all, Boccaccio could have told these exact stories but given the characters different names and kept the story-lines separate. He chooses instead to link them by having characters reappear. This way of gathering discrete humorous anecdotes around familiar characterological identities calls to mind the narrative mode of trickster cycles, in which tricksters remain tricksters, forever unreformed and always poised for yet another adventure (the stories of Reynard the Fox constitute a prime medieval example).[21] Boccaccio's introduction of such an accumulative procedure into the *Decameron* no doubt owes something to the circulation in Trecento Italy of repertoires in which the jests and witticisms of individual entertainers were collected, of which the *Novellino*, an earlier tale collection, gives us a glimpse.[22] In Boccaccio's handling, one tale prompts another here not because they both exemplify the same abstract moral (this is a common reason given by narrators elsewhere in the *Decameron* for transitioning to a new tale) but because these trickster figures and their familiar dupes exercise upon the storytellers themselves a force of attraction: "come Filostrato fu dal nome di Maso

---

21 Branca suggests, unconvincingly, that "un vago raffronto può essere stabilito" between an episode from Branch XV of the *Roman de Renart* and the tale of Calandrino and the pig (Boccaccio, *Decameron*, ed. Branca 1980, 934n6, at VIII.6.1). Any apparent resemblance between the *Roman de Renart* and the *Decameron*'s cycle of tales probably hinges more upon the shared narrative mode of trickster cycles than any specific influences in plot or idiom.

22 Anecdotes about individual *giullari* circulated orally before emerging into textualized collections such as the *Novellino* and, later, Franco Sacchetti's *Trecentonovelle* and Poggio Bracciolini's *Facetiae*. Considering that some tricksters in the *Decameron* cycle probably were actual entertainers, such as Ribi and Maso del Saggio, Boccaccio likely had such repertoires loosely in mind as he introduced into the *Decameron* this new manner of connecting *novelle*.

tirato … così né più né men son tirata io" [just as Filostrato was led by the mention of Maso's name … I, too, have been led in exactly the same way to tell you another (VIII.6.3)]. The *novelle di beffa* involving these figures "bespeak the pleasure inherent in the impulse to repeat" (Mazzotta, *World at Play*, 193), a pleasure in a poetics of accumulation. For Boccaccio and his readers, such pleasure is further enhanced by the fact that these characters are characteristically Florentine and occupy well-known coordinates of time and space. These *novelle* coalesce with each other not only because of the topic proposed by Lauretta but also because there are contiguities in the lived reality of the pranksters themselves.

There are six tales in this cycle, four in Day Eight (VIII.3, 5, 6, and 9) plus two in Day Nine (IX.3 and 5). Each features local pranksters who belong to a loose confederacy of *uomini sollazzevoli*, "amusing men," who always work in teams. Membership of this *brigata* of pranksters is in continual flux: Maso del Saggio, Bruno, and Buffalmacco (and, in Day Nine, Nello) act in more than one of the tales, Maso's accomplices Ribi and Matteuzzo appear just once. Calandrino provides this cluster of *novelle* with a centre of gravity, for he is the pranksters' most frequent, although not their only, dupe. Because Calandrino does not feature in all of these stories, it can be limiting to designate this cluster as a "Calandrino cycle," as is frequently done. If our focus were to fall less on the dupes and more on the tricksters, then we would say that the *brigata* of *uomini sollazzevoli* is what holds the cycle together. Popping up in various situations, this troupe of pranksters comes to seem like an inescapable element of the *Decameron*'s depiction of Florence, embodying the city's energy and epitomizing the image Florentines have of themselves as smart and cunning. Readers are led to sense that a character could turn a corner in this city and encounter Bruno and Buffalmacco (as indeed happens to Master Simone in VIII.9) just as easily as any architectural landmark, as the streetscape becomes "a civic stage, all set to release from every corner a gag, a trick, a bizarre act of the imagination, an adventure instigated by a spur-of-the-moment inspiration."[23]

Throughout Day Eight the ingenious schemes staged by *beffatori* echo the narrative inventiveness both of the *Decameron*'s ten storytellers and

23 "Firenze va interpretata come contemporaneità, nel senso teatrale del termine, come scena cittadina pronta a sprigionare da ogno angolo un lazzo, una beffa, un'invenzione bizzarra, un'avventura dovuta a un estro improvviso" (Baratto, *Realtà e stile*, 261).

of Boccaccio as author. Similarly, the gullibility of the dupes mirrors the credulity of listeners and readers as they suspend disbelief in fictional worlds. In this respect Day Eight, as Picone puts it, "represents a complete novelty within the panorama of medieval narrative: the *beffa* here has become a personal creation, almost a double of literary invention; and the creator of the *beffa* is placed in the same class as the narrators of the frametale and the author of the work."[24] Compared to the *Decameron*'s *brigata* of aristocrats who amuse themselves with storytelling, the working-class, male *uomini sollazzevoli* constitute a coarse anti-*brigata*, enmeshed in the vibrant social life of Florence, on the look-out for fun, entertaining each other by concocting practical jokes.

The tales which feature Bruno, Buffalmacco, and Calandrino especially bring to the fore notions of illusionistic representation, for these characters are all painters. The narratives at times even present them in the act of creating or contemplating paintings. Evoking the mimetic illusionism which Trecento Florentine painting aspired to, Bruno and Buffalmacco at one point paint their faces to look as if they have been bruised in order to lend even greater believability to the trick played on Master Simone the night before. In these ways, the eighth day is animated by metafictional concerns about illusion, verisimilitude, and the ethics of deception, even as Boccaccio experiments with how to establish the coordinates of time and space that lend a sense of lived reality to his own tales.[25]

Self-deluding fantasies are also a part of this, particularly when dupes are led to believe that their desires will be satisfied magically.[26] Calandrino, cajoled by Maso del Saggio into believing in a fantasy land where mountains are made of Parmesan cheese and rivers flow with

24 "rappresenta una novità assoluta nel panorama della narrativa medievale: la beffa è qui diventata una creazione personale, quasi un duplicato dell'invenzione letteraria. E il regista della beffa si pone allo stesso livello dei narratori della cornice e dell'autore dell'opera" (Picone, "L'arte della beffa," 206).

25 Boccaccio's fascination with the correspondence between verbal and visual arts surfaces elsewhere in the *Decameron*, as in the novella about Giotto (VI.5) and, more explicitly, in the authorial comment at the work's conclusion: "Sanza che alla mia penna non dee essere meno d'auttorità conceduta che sia al pennello del dipintore" (Concl.Aut.6). On Boccaccio's tales about painters and on his own interests in the visual arts, see Kirkham, "Painters at Play"; Watson, "The Cement of Fiction"; Battaglia Ricci, *Ragionare nel giardino*; Ciccuto, "Il novelliere *en artiste*"; Gilbert, "Boccaccio's Devotion to Artists"; Martinez, "Calandrino and the Powers of the Stone"; Land, "Calandrino as Viewer"; and Legassie, "The Lies of the Painters."

26 On the role of magic in the *Decameron*, see Giardini, *Tradizioni popolari nel Decameron*; and Cottino-Jones, "Magic and Superstition."

wine, accepts as true that stones from the local stream will make him invisible and thus rich (VIII.3). Master Simone believes Bruno's claims that through an elaborate magic ritual he will be initiated into a secret society of men who continually enjoy decadent feasts and erotic satisfactions (VIII.9). An extreme credulity about magic also affects Elena, who so desires the return of her lover that she recklessly trusts Rinieri's magic ceremonies to bring it about (VIII.7). An analogous although non-magical enchantment distinguishes the day's final tale, as Iancofiore stokes the naïve credulity of Salabaetto with the seductive and intoxicating ceremonies of the bathhouse (VIII.10). The tricksters of these tales elicit the yearnings of their victims, captivating them in their own fantasies, priming their gullibility, making them willing to believe even the unbelievable.

The Eighth Day in Perspective: The Individual Essays

Vittore Branca held that the *novelle* of Day Eight were derived more or less directly from local, oral, "municipal anecdotes."[27] One implication of Branca's claim would seem to be that Boccaccio here sidesteps any serious grappling with previous literary traditions and urgent sociopolitical concerns. The essays in this volume contest such a conclusion, exploring how Boccaccio, drawing on fabliaux, epic, philosophy, exempla, *facezie*, Dante's *Commedia*, and scripture, even while meditating on the dynamics of civic engagement in Trecento Florence, develops in these *novelle di beffa* a self-consciously literary representation of the Florentine social imaginary. Accordingly, these contributions analyse both the literary sources that his comic narratives transform, and the political, legal, and ethical contexts with which they engage. Following the format of the *Lectura Boccaccii* series, each contributor to the volume tackles a single tale, yet their separate essays also register major themes and concerns that recur throughout Day Eight, making for many diverse connections among the essays.

Florentine polity. The tale of Calandrino and the heliotrope (VIII.3), Justin Steinberg argues, turns a traditional dream of invisibility into a representation of Florentine politics, satirizing both Calandrino's obsession with private gain and his disregard for the common good. In the context of Florence's growing surveillance against anti-social behaviour, the tale functions as a kind of internalized police force, censuring

---

27 "anedotti municipali fiorentini" (Boccaccio, *Decameron*, ed. Branca 1980, 905n4 and 934n6).

Calandrino's failures as a citizen. Poised against Calandrino's self-interest are the members of the *brigata*; they reconstitute a sense of the commonweal in their stories, finding there a remedy for a plague-ridden Florence bereft of its collective fictions. The tale of the judge from the Marche (VIII.5), as William Robins and Leah Faibisoff explain, similarly engages the Florentine civic sphere, creating in literature an imaginative space in which all Florentines can participate in communal governance. Its *beffa* carries out by different means the business conducted in the evaluation known as the *sindacato*. Whereas the *sindacato* unmasks poor performance by foreign magistrates and preserves the viability of the republican commune, the *beffa* of the Florentine pranksters unmasks inflated pretensions and forms a community around the shaming of an outsider judge.

Parody and obscenity. The tale of the adulterous Sienese couples (VIII.8), Olivia Holmes shows, transposes the question of justice into a parodic key. In its sexualized exchange this novella registers a Tuscan concern with retribution, legality, and judicial process. Representing both transgression and its comic correction, Boccaccio outlines a harmonious symmetry that ensures suitable civic punishment, but that doesn't insist upon ethical or narrative closure. Equally parodic and obscene, as Maggie Fritz-Morkin demonstrates, the tale of Monna Belcolore and the priest of Varlungo (VIII.2) explores justice within an Aristotelian framework. While the protagonists' botched exchange reveals the insufficiency of a structure of material reciprocity such as the *Nicomachean Ethics* envisages, at the end of the tale the lovers develop a creative partnership that mirrors an Aristotelian model of true friendship; in their euphemistic wordplay they create a bond that is just as essential as justice in preserving a sense of community.

Aristotelian ethics. The tale of Monna Piccarda and the provost of Fiesole (VIII.4), as Katherine Brown explains, likewise translates Aristotelian ethics into the mode of a *beffa*, representing through its rhetoric the connections among excess, measure, and lack. Part bed trick, part metafictional meditation, the novella suggests for Brown the necessity of balancing physical and mental pleasure in order to attain the good. The tale of the widow Elena and the scholar Rinieri (VIII.7), as Teodolinda Barolini argues, exemplifies the violation of all Aristotelian measure, representing Rinieri as a failed philosopher incapable of mediating his own excesses or properly applying the ethical lessons of his university education. By transforming medieval tropes of the intellectual-lover, the novella extends Boccaccio's abiding interests in the relationship between the sexes and in his own role as an intellectual and artist.

Intertextuality. The tale of Master Simone (VIII.9), Elisa Brilli maintains, develops intellectual traditions with equal sophistication, refiguring in its *beffa* material familiar from religious exempla and Petrarchan invective. More than a "municipal anecdote," the novella spans a wider world of textuality, harnessing its precedents in identifying the three grievous faults of master Simone. The tale of Salabaetto and Iancofiore (VIII.10), Roberta Morosini suggests, transforms similarly established discourses in its treatment of the Mediterranean, absorbing motifs from ancient epic and orientalist portrayals into a narrative of mercantile mobility, representing Iancofiore as a modern Siren or Circe. Mapping the structure of the plot onto the back-and-forth rhythms of the Mediterranean, this novella takes place on land but harnesses motifs and character types that in earlier literature belonged at sea.

Resonance and reception. The tale of Calandrino and the stolen pig (VIII.6), as Rhiannon Daniels demonstrates, takes its literary precedent from the *Decameron* itself, constructing through the Calandrino cycle of tales a self-conscious intratextuality that encompasses both orality and writing. Bocaccio here balances clashing strategies of contemporary cultural production – the performative and the literary – creating a hybrid mode of reception that distinguishes his work from prior storytelling collections. The tale of Gulfardo and Ambruogia (VIII.1), K.P. Clarke argues, generates a reception history beyond the *Decameron*, establishing in its monetization of sex a moral problem revisited in the fourteenth and fifteenth centuries. Despite, or perhaps because of, its unsatisfying resolution and flat tone, this novella goads its readers – among them Giovanni Sercambi and Geoffrey Chaucer – to respond creatively to a narrative that doesn't quite work.

The essays in this volume register the fact that some of the tales of Day Eight are remarkably short and skeletal in their narrative framework, close to a "degree-zero" expression of the *beffa* structure, while others are more complex, involving tricks and counter-tricks, including the longest novella in the entire *Decameron*, the tale of Elena and Rinieri (VIII.7). Not so much a theme as a narrative structure, the *beffa* as a form is capacious enough for numerous variations, and these variations lie at the heart of the investigations in these essays.

The Tale of Gulfardo and Ambruogia (VIII.1)

K.P. CLARKE

Tricks (*beffe*) played by women on their husbands, the theme of Day Seven, prompts the theme for the following day, which is now widened to include tricks more generally played by men on women, women on men, or men on other men.[1] The result is a day of stories frequently marked for their humour and wit, such as the three stories featuring Bruno and Buffalmacco (VIII.3, 6, and 9), or the story of the three young friends who pull down the trousers of a judge (VIII.5). Neifile opens Day Eight with a tale of a wife who – having sought a large sum in exchange for sex – is tricked into thinking she is being paid for her favours; the money, rather, is being repaid to her moneylender husband.[2] The theme of this first story of Day Eight recalls the tricks of the previous day, and it will also be echoed in several stories to come, such as the tricks played between the scholar and the widow (VIII.7), as well as the tricks played between Salabaetto and the courtesan Iancofiore (VIII.10). The theme of love coming at a price is explored elsewhere in the *Decameron*, for example in VI.3, where a Catalan nobleman, Dego della Ratta, sleeps with the wife of a Florentine for an agreed price, but pays him in falsified coin. The story of the priest and Monna Belcolore (VIII.2) is also very closely related in theme and plot to VIII.1. Despite these similarities, Neifile's story is unusual in the way it treats of its theme. *Beffe* in the *Decameron* are sites of intelligence, of quickness, and are often executed to comic effect. As Alberto Asor Rosa has noted, the *beffa* can be an "instrument of punishment and of just correction, that is, set up as a norm of social and moral sanction (the intelligent punish

1 On Day Eight, see Holmes, "Trial by *Beffa*"; Picone, "L'arte della beffa"; Forni, "L'amaro riso"; and Ceruti Burgio, "Annotazioni."

2 See Ferreri, "Madonna Ambruogia"; this is the only single article dedicated entirely to the tale. See also Geninasca, "I contratti e la beffa."

the foolish for their conceited stupidity)."[3] But the *beffa* in VIII.1 is neither clever nor funny: rather, it is bitter, unsettling, and unresolved. In VI.3 the trick perpetrated upon the greedy husband forms a context for Monna Nonna de' Pulci's witty and sharp retort about the dishonesty of the noble Catalan, and the trick in VIII.2 ends up being humorously resolved to the (sexual and monetary) satisfaction of all parties. *Decameron* VIII.1, by contrast, shows no such *brio*, and nowhere in the *Decameron* does a story strike such an oddly flat note.

This essay will explore these problems of tone. The fourteenth-century reception history of the tale provides a valuable interpretive perspective, throwing into high relief its ethical and narrative co-ordinates. Four responses to Boccaccio's tale reveal, each in its own way, a reader who sees the story as not quite working. Two of the responses are adaptations of the story incorporated into new story collections; one is a set of copyist's annotations in the margins of the tale; and one is a line drawing included in a manuscript of the *Decameron*. The two adaptations contrast in their own way, not least because one was written in vernacular Italian by the Luccan writer Giovanni Sercambi and the other written in Middle English by Geoffrey Chaucer.

~

Boccaccio's story is brief, the shortest of all those told during Day Eight. Gulfardo, a German mercenary in Milan, is in love with Madonna Ambruogia, the wife of his friend Guasparruolo Cagastraccio, a rich merchant. The German begs her to grant him her favour, to which she agrees, but on condition that he keep their liaison a secret and that he give her two hundred gold florins. Disgusted at this venality (*'ngordigia*, "greed" or "covetousness"), and finding his love turned to hatred, Gulfardo proceeds to borrow this sum from Guasparruolo. He then goes (with a witness) to Madonna Ambruogia, giving her the sum and asking that it be given to her husband. She understands this remark to be intended to hide the real motive for giving her the money in front of his *compagno*. He enjoys sexual relations with her for the duration of her husband's absence, and upon the husband's return Gulfardo reveals, in the presence of Ambruogia and his *compagno*, that the money had not

3 "strumento di punizione e di giusta correzione, cioè essere adottata come norma di sanzione morale e sociale (gli intelligenti puniscono gli sciocchi della loro tronfia stupidità)" (Asor Rosa, "*Decameron*," 545; see also 542–5, on *beffe* in the *Decameron*).

been needed after all and had been returned while Guasparruolo was away in Genoa. Thus the wise Gulfardo tricks the greedy Ambruogia.

After Neifile concludes her story, it is met with an unusually coherent response by the rest of the *brigata*, where both its male and female members *equally* praise and commend the behaviour of Gulfardo and agree that Ambruogia was greedy and covetous: "Commendavano *igualmente* e gli uomini e le donne ciò che Gulfardo fatto aveva alla 'ngorda melanese" [Both the gentlemen and the ladies were *equally* applauding Gulfardo's treatment of the covetous Milanese lady (VIII.2.2, emphasis added)].[4] That reference to Ambruogia being *'ngorda* – in the eyes of the *brigata* – echoes the description of Gulfardo's sense of the wife's *'ngordigia*. The word *ingordo*, meaning "avaricious," "greedy," or "covetous," is unusual in the *Decameron*, and only appears once again, in Dioneo's story at the end of Day Eight, and with reference to the exorbitance of Iancofiore's rate of interest, "pregio ingordo" (VIII.10.61).[5] This rare vocabulary of avarice further connects the stories that open and close Day Eight, already similar in terms of theme, and invites comparison between the liveliness of Dioneo's story and the off-key tone of Neifile's. Indeed, Dioneo's story is exceptional in adhering to the day's theme, while Neifile's story is exceptional in its vehement denunciation of the female protagonist.[6]

Neifile considers her story as rather straightforward: Ambruogia, who conducted herself for financial gain – "per prezzo si conduce" (VIII.1.3) – should be punished by being burned at the stake. She prefaces her story by asserting that the kind of judicial leniency encouraged and applauded in Filostrato's story of Madonna Filippa (VI.7) has no place here. Madonna Filippa is driven to adultery not by personal gain but "per buono e per pefetto amore" [on account of the deep and perfect love (VI.7.13)] which she has for her lover. And yet the story chosen by Panfilo to follow Neifile is in many respects a variation of the story of Gulfardo and Ambruogia. A priest tricks a lover, the married

4 Reference to the *Decameron* will be to the text edited by Maurizio Fiorilla in Boccaccio, *Decameron*, ed. Quondam, Fiorilla, and Alfano. Reference will also be made to Giancarlo Alfano's introductory *scheda* for VIII.1 in this edition (Alfano, "Giornata VIII: Scheda introduttiva," 1179–81), and to Branca's valuable notes in Boccaccio, *Decameron*, ed. Branca 1992. All translations will be those in Boccaccio, *Decameron*, trans. McWilliam 1995, though here the translation has been modified to give a more literal rendering.

5 On *avarizia* as a theme in Day Eight, see Ceruti Burgio, "Annotazioni."

6 On the different ways that VIII.1 and VIII.10 focus on money, see Duranti, "Le novelle di Dioneo," 20.

Monna Belcolore, out of the sum requested. He does this by leaving his cloak as payment while at the same time borrowing from her a mortar, and then returns the mortar in front of the husband, claiming the cloak had been left as a surety. The wily priest thus tricks the greedy lady, but this is not how the tale ends. Both parties come to a resolution – without a pestle, a mortar is not much good – and thus they enjoy continued sexual relations. Even though Monna Belcolore asks for money in exchange for sex, she is not subject to the opprobrium reserved for Madonna Ambruogia. Indeed the ladies of the *brigata* laugh heartily at Panfilo's story: "le donne avevano tanto riso che ancora ridono" [the ladies laughed so heartily over Panfilo's tale that they are laughing yet (VIII.3.2)].

The tales of the *Decameron* are best read in the wider context of their telling, that is, as a dialogic response to the set theme as well as to the stories already told.[7] The first two stories of Day Eight are intended to be read in such productive dialogue with each other. Their striking similarities highlight how it is the differences between the two stories, in the end, that make all the difference. The setting of VIII.2 is rustic, with peasant characters from a low social class; Gulfardo, Guasparruolo, and Ambruogia, by contrast, are wealthy and have pretensions to a superior social class (Surdich, *Boccaccio*, 173). The rustics pose no threat to the courtly code since they are entirely excluded from it, whereas the rich merchants are accessing, negotiating, and renegotiating the terms of membership of elite society.

The witty lightness that marks the end of the story of the priest and Monna Belcolore, turning as it does on an outrageous double entendre of the pestle and mortar, emphasizes the troubling tone of the tale of Gulfardo and Ambruogia. The latter's brevity recalls the short tales told during Day Six, but those stories are often resolved in wit and compression. By contrast, VIII.1 ends with no such comedy, and the trick does not result in laughter or humorous appreciation but rather in bitterness and regret. The few critical responses to the story all grapple with its troubling tone. Carlo Muscetta, for example,.descibes VIII.1 as "a simple story, and a little grey and mean," while Anna Ceruti Burgio refers to its "oppressive meanness."[8]

Gulfardo's *beffa* is directed at the greedy wife, but her husband Guasparruolo is drawn into the trick as an unintended target. While

7 See Bragantini, "Dialogo"; and Bragantini, "Premesse sull'ascolto decameroniano."

8 "un racconto modesto e un po' grigio e meschino" (Muscetta, *Giovanni Boccaccio*, 261); "plumbea meschinità" (Ceruti Burgio, "Annotazioni," 168).

a gullible – and cuckolded – husband is frequently the butt of a joke in the *Decameron*, Guasparruolo is nowhere condemned in the story as deserving of such retribution. The *beffa* is facilitated not so much by Gulfardo's intelligence as by the trust built up between him and Guasparruolo. Cheating Madonna Ambruogia out of free sex is the point of the *beffa*, but cheating Guasparruolo out of free money – in not paying the interest owed – appears as a gratuitous act by Gulfardo. As Mario Baratto has asserted, both "love and the trick have been equally degraded by money."[9]

Money not only touches the lives of everyone in the story of Gulfardo and Ambruogia, it also taints them. The Lombard city was an important financial nexus in medieval Europe, and the German Gulfardo (i.e., Wolfard) was evidently attracted to Milan's international reputation for trading in arms.[10] Mercenaries were in high demand, and a German mercenary could earn as much as four hundred florins a year. The circulation of cash and credit was essential to the making of war and peace, and those who dealt in the exchange of money were crucial players in the statecraft of the period. Despite the nervousness around the morals of moneylending, and in particular of charging interest on loans, the practice had been (and still is) firmly established as a necessary evil for the smooth economic running of society. It led to some remarkable concentrations of wealth: men of relatively low birth who were gifted with business acumen found themselves enjoying many of the material trappings of an aristocratic life. It is in such a context that we can see the substantial sum of money in circulation in the tale: two hundred florins is approximately six months' wages for Gulfardo, and Guasparruolo can disburse it without difficulty;[11] Ambruogia is used to the transaction of large volumes of cash, and appears comfortable in setting her "price." She feels confident the market can sustain such a huge figure, and given the ease with which Gulfardo can access the credit to acquire the sum, Ambruogia appears to have read the market correctly.

The brevity of VIII.1 puts considerable pressure on the lexicon deployed, so that key terms are frequently powered by doubleness. The language of commerce is established from the very beginning as guiding the story with words like *investire* (to deserve, but also to invest) (§2), and *merito* (value, and interest) (§3). Ambruogia is described as one who "per prezzo si conduce" [conducts herself for money

9 "l'amore e la beffa sono stati ugualmente degradati dal denaro" (Baratto, *Realtà e stile*, 397).

10 See Wallace, *Giovanni Boccaccio: Decameron*, 85–6.

11 See Caferro, *Petrarch's War*, 120 (Table 2.4), and cf. p. 130: "The wage of an ordinary German cavalryman was about the same as the Florentine chancellor."

(VIII.1.3)], which strongly echoes how Gulfardo is described as "un tedesco al soldo" [a German mercenary (VIII.1.5)], a German who sells his loyalty to whoever will pay. Boccaccio goes out of his way to set up manifest parallels between Gulfardo and Ambruogia and how money drives them both. Specialist verbs such as *dannare* (§15) and *acconciare* (§17), meaning "to clear an account," create an atmosphere of technical moneymaking and exchange, while mercantile terms such as *ragione* (account) (§15) and *utile* (interest) (§10) resound ambivalently, since the same words also mean "reason" and "utility," further layering the ethical concerns at stake in the tale.[12] An anxious attention to the meaning of words may be detected in the way that Neifile glosses certain terms with a more precise definition, such as her reference to Ambruogia as "la donna," only to specify "anzi cattiva femina" [the lady, or strumpet rather (VIII.1.9)], a judgment which is reiterated when Neifile refers to "sua cattività" [her depravity (VIII.1.18)], or suggests that the "beffa" [deception] should rather be considered "merito" [a reprisal (VIII.1.3)]. The terms of the tale are difficult to untangle.

In the minutely careful construction of his book of stories, Boccaccio left nothing to chance, and he composed a rubric, or short summary, for the beginning of each tale.[13] Finding rubrics in medieval narrative texts is very common, but it is rare to be able to attribute them so securely to a specific author.[14] The rubric Boccaccio devised for VIII.1 also expresses some of this anxious concern over terms, and carefully attending to it primes the reader for what is coming. The story is summarized thus:

> Gulfardo prende da Guasparruolo denari in prestanza, e con la moglie di lui accordato di dover giacer con lei per quegli sì gliele dà; e poi in presenza di lei a Guasparruol dice che a lei gli diede, e ella dice che è il vero. (VIII.1.1)
>
> [Gulfardo borrows from Guasparruolo a sum of money equivalent to the amount he has agreed to pay the latter's wife in return for letting him sleep with her. He gives her the money, but later tells Guasparruolo, in her presence, that he has handed it back to his wife, and she has to admit it.]

---

12 Hollander, "*Utilità* in Boccaccio's *Decameron*." On the financial terms in the tale, see Ferreri, "Madonna Ambruogia."

13 On rubrics in the *Decameron*, see Usher, "Le rubriche del *Decameron*"; D'Andrea, "Le rubriche del *Decameron*"; and Milanese, "Affinità e contraddizioni."

14 For further theoretical reflections on the rubric, see Clarke, "Sotto la quale rubrica," esp. 149–53. More generally on Boccaccio and rubrics, see Clarke, "Boccaccio and the Poetics of the Paratext," esp. 76–86; and cf. Daniels, "Where Does the *Decameron* Begin?" esp. 53–7.

Stark in its compression, this is a rubric that does not express wit or a quickness of plot. It sets up a rhythmic taking and giving in the verbs *prendere* and *dare*, while the alliterative repetition of forms of *prendere* (take), *prestanza* (loan), and *presenza* (presence) adds a sense of tight, even claustrophobic, circularity. The giving of money to Ambruogia, who is not yet named, is repeated twice, "sì gliele dà" and "a lei gli diede," with the verb *dare* deployed both in a present tense, suggesting the immediacy and perhaps a certain urgency of the transaction, and a past, suggestive of a definitive end to this arrangement. The deal reached by Gulfardo and Ambruogia is expressed in the verb *accordare* (to agree), which gives a technical, contractual flavour to their relations. The rubric implies that sex has taken place because the money has been paid. In the rubric, sex and money are one and the same. It is Gulfardo's word, his *dire* (saying), that resolves the narrative, revealing the *giving* of the two hundred florins to Ambruogia, which she, through her own word (the verb *dire* is repeated), confirms as *vero* (true). The rubric does not present the story of Gulfardo and Ambruogia as a *beffa*, but states their exchange as a fact. It is simply the truth, *il vero*.

Two orders of value clash in the tale. As Olivia Holmes has said, "love and lucre are anathema to each other in courtly rhetoric, but maintaining their distance can be difficult in a mercantile setting" ("Trial by *Beffa*," 368). Rather than maintaining a distance, it is precisely the interweaving and overlayering of love and lucre in the tale that constitutes its key moral concern. The aristocratic currency of courtly love, a love freely and generously given, is set up against a currency of mercantile commodities, in which everything is for sale and has a price, acquired with cash or on credit.[15] Thus, Gulfardo sends word to Ambruogia "che le dovesse piacere d'essergli del suo amor cortese e che egli era dalla sua parte presto a dover far ciò che ella gli comandasse" [imploring her to grant him the sweet reward of his devotion, and affirming that he, for his part, was prepared to do whatever she might ask of him (VIII.1.6)], suggesting a cashless exchange based on honour and service. Ambruogia's reply echoes the language of Gulfardo, but is deployed with a very different sense. She informs him that "ella era presta a far ciò che Gulfardo volesse" [she was prepared to comply with his request], but only on condition of secrecy and gold, the latter because "ricco uomo era" [he was well off], and, having been given the money, "sempre sarebbe al suo servigio" [she would always be at his service (VIII.1.7)].

15 See Mazzotta, *The World at Play*, 190–2.

The contrast, then, is between gift and commodity, where, in Marxist terms, a gift is an inalienable object exchanged between two "reciprocally dependent transactors," while a commodity is an alienable object exchanged between two transactors "enjoying a state of mutual independence."[16] The status of credit lies somewhere in between gift and commodity. Credit is both an exchange of "goods" (cash) that comes at a price, but its circulation is also dependent on mutual trust and creditworthiness, and so has an inherent moral dimension. While Gulfardo is paying the usual rate of interest for his loan from Guasparruolo, it is his worthiness as a man of trust that affords him such ready access to credit. Neifile is at pains to specify that while as a soldier he is "assai leale" [extremely loyal], in respect of money, and more precisely repaying his loans, he is "lealissimo" [*most* loyal (VIII.1.5; translation modified, emphasis added)]. His priorities are clear. The unmeasurable qualities of fidelity and trust are commodified and assigned a price.

The corresponding currency of trust for a woman is based on her worthiness, *onestà*, and chasteness, *castità*, established by Neifile at the outset of the tale as that which should be guarded by *every woman* more than her own life: "con ciò sia cosa *che ciascuna donna* debba essere onestissima e la sua castità come la sua vita guardare" (VIII.1.3, emphasis added).[17] The use of the superlative form *onestissima* (most honourable) echoes the superlative used to describe Gulfardo, who is *lealissimo* (most loyal), placing both values in apposition. Like credit, *onestà* and *castità* are a matter of trust and reputation, always delicately poised between the public and private spheres. A woman's *onestà* will impact

16 Gregory, *Gifts and Commodities*, 12. On the gift, see Mauss, *The Gift*.

17 The critical edition prepared by Vittore Branca, based on the Berlin autograph (Berlin, Staatsbibliothek Preussicher Kulturbesitz, MS Hamilton 90), omits "che ciascuna donna" (Boccaccio, *Decameron: Edizione critica secondo l'autografo Hamiltoniano*, 506); in the commented edition Branca includes a note explaining that the subject, *la donna*, is implied (Boccaccio, *Decameron*, ed. Branca 1992, 890n5). For the autograph, see also Boccaccio, *Decameron: Facsimile dell'autografo*, ed. Branca; Boccaccio, *Decameron: Edizione diplomatico-interpretativa dell'autografo*, ed. Singleton; as well as the description prepared by Cursi, *Il Decameron*, 161–4 (Cat. 1). Maurizio Fiorilla, however, opts for the reading in the Paris manuscript (Paris, Bibliothèque nationale de France, MS Italien 482, discussed further below), where the clarification serves to specify and emphasize that *each woman* is tasked with being *onestissima*. A good deal of textual work has been carried out on the Berlin autograph (B) and the Paris manuscript (P), and Vittore Branca in particular has argued that, while B represents the author's last will in respect of the text of the *Decameron*, P witnesses an earlier authorial version of the collection of stories. The differences are set out and discussed in Vitale and Branca, *Il capolavoro del Boccaccio*; for *Decameron* VIII.1 see 2:131–2.

upon her own reputation as well as that of her husband and the rest of the household.

The injunction to maintain *onestà* is repeated often in the *Decameron*, and frequently describes the manner in which the members of the *brigata* tell their stories,. but here the term *onestà* enters into uncomfortable proximity with issues of credit, money, and sex.[18] A woman who would commodify this honesty is worthy only of a death sentence. The difference between a woman who would make financial profit from the credit accrued in terms of *onestà* and a mercenary who has built up a credit rating with a moneylender must, at all costs, be kept separate. If a woman in her fragility finds herself unable to resist the forces of love, then leniency is to be observed, since resistance is futile. For this reason the forces of love are frequently represented in the *Decameron* as bringing its victims into a kind of morally neutral sphere. Madonna Filippa, in VI.7, is a case in point. While she is technically guilty of adultery, the virtue of her lover and the ennobling influence of love both take over from her guilt and render her innocent. One often hears the forces of the market described as neutral, but when Ambruogia attempts to negotiate this market, she is sharply excluded. Virtue, honesty, and chastity, while her responsibility to guard and maintain, are not hers to sell. But ultimately Ambruogia, and women like her, deserve to be burned alive, according to Neifile (VIII.1.3), precisely *because* she resembles the mercenary so patently, both selling their bodies, both selling virtue and loyalty, both exposing the real behind the ideal.

From a narrative perspective there is no way out of this moral impasse, and this is perhaps one reason the story is so problematic in its peculiar directness and flatness. In a sense it is a *beffa* without the twist, without the story.[19] In respect of Guasparruolo it is not his gullibility that sets the story in motion but rather the fact that Gulfardo takes advantage of his own creditworthiness, a value in the masculine world of commerce which is the equivalent of *onestà* for a woman. As such, the *beffa* is much less a demonstration of his intelligence as of his desire to do an injury to Ambruogia. The final clause of the tale neatly expresses how Gulfardo's *beffa* is not aimed at moral sanction but at getting what he wants without paying: "così il sagace amante senza costo godé della sua avara donna" [and thus the sagacious lover had enjoyed the favours of his rapacious lady free of charge (VIII.1.18)].

18 On *onestà*, see Cherchi, *L'onestade*, esp. 85–121.

19 Mario Baratto calls it "una beffa inutile" (*Realtà e stile*, 397).

Responding to the Tale in the Fourteenth Century

The critical tradition surrounding the story of Gulfardo and Ambruogia is not extensive, with scholars only briefly referring to it, if at all, generally before turning to longer and more entertaining stories told during Day Eight. In contrast to this modern critical silence, there are four fourteenth-century examples of compelling responses to the story that in their own way suggest how the story was read and received. In chronological order they are: first, the line drawing that accompanies the story in Paris, Bibliothèque nationale de France, MS Italien 482, fol. 151r, representing three key scenes in the tale; second, the scribal intervention in the margins of the tale as copied in Florence, Biblioteca Medicea Laurenziana, MS Pluteo 42.1, fol. 119v, a famous copy of the *Decameron* transcribed by Francesco d'Amaretto Mannelli; third, a version of the story as adapted and incorporated into Geoffrey Chaucer's framed collection, *The Canterbury Tales*, told by the Shipman; and finally, the version of the story adapted for Giovanni Sercambi's collection of *Novelle*. In these responses it is possible to identify how each reader has identified a particular problem in the tale and made alterations accordingly. The problem of VIII.1, that is, its greyness, its tonal heaviness, its narrative flatness, is recognized in each of the four responses discussed below.

Visualizing the Tale in Paris, Bibliothèque nationale de France, MS Italien 482

A cycle of simple, though lively and energetic pen drawings illustrates Paris, Bibliothèque nationale de France, MS Italien 482 (often assigned the sigil P).[20] The manuscript, known as the *codice Capponi* after its scribe, Giovanni d'Agnolo Capponi, dates to the 1360s and is unusual not just in being the only early *Decameron* to be on vellum with a text copied in a *mercantesca* script but also, especially, for its program of illustrations. While single-scene illustrations are more typical in Tuscany in the mid-fourteenth century, MS P opts for a series of drawings comprising multiple scenes, echoing Angevin manuscripts

20 On the manuscript, see Cursi, *Il Decameron*, 31–6 and 217–19 (Cat. 44). See also Branca, *Boccaccio visualizzato*, 2:66–72 (Cat. 7, entry by Maria Cristina Castelli). The manuscript can be consulted online at http://gallica.bnf.fr/ark:/12148/btv1b10509038z.

of chivalric texts.[21] The images depict scenes from the first story from each day of storytelling (except Day Six, where the second story is illustrated instead, on fol. 122v). A number of other "non-canonical" scenes are also included, such as that representing Guinevere and Lancelot, at the opening of the Proem (fol. 5r), or the "extra" story of Filippo Balducci from the Introduction to Day Four (fol. 79v), as well as a scene representing the argument between Licisca and Tindaro, at the opening of Day Six (fol. 122v).[22] Given the high quality of the text in MS P, and the rather unusual program of illustrations, several scholars, such as Vittore Branca and Maria Grazia Ciardi Dupré dal Poggetto, have attributed these drawings to the hand of Boccaccio himself. Though such an attribution cannot be ruled out with complete certainty, more recent work would suggest that it is now far from secure.[23] Whatever the specific doubts, it is generally accepted that Boccaccio had some form of supervisory role in the confection of MS P.[24] The early date of the iconographic program, and possible influence by Boccaccio himself, render the image accompanying VIII.1 an important visual response to the tale, offering an alternative interpretation of the story.[25]

The story of Gulfardo and Ambruogia is depicted at the top of fol. 151r, where the narrative unfolds in three scenes, read from left to right. In the left-hand scene Gulfardo is seen on one side of a counter, while Guasparruolo is on the other, handing over the loan. In the centre panel Gulfardo is again on the left-hand side of the scene, standing with a companion who acts as a witness, while Ambruogia stands on the other side of a table, receiving the proferred cash. Each table suggests its sphere of use, the first mercantile, the second domestic. The right-hand scene depicts Gulfardo and Ambruogia in the foreground in an amorous embrace, while a bed in the background visually echoes those two pieces of horizontal furniture upon which the first parts of the transaction have taken place. A chest sits on the floor between the bed in the background and the two figures in the foreground, perhaps suggestive of a marriage chest containing the bride's dowry and used

21 See Mazzetti, "Boccaccio e l'invenzione del libro illustrabile," esp. 147–51.

22 On Lancelot and Guinevere, see Delcorno Branca, "'Cognominato Prencipe Galeotto.'"

23 See Battaglia Ricci, *Scrivere un libro di novelle*, esp. chapter 3.

24 See Cursi, *La scrittura e i libri*, 113–28; see also Cursi, "Il Parigino Italiano 482."

25 See Mazzetti, "Boccaccio e l'invenzione del libro illustrabile," 147: "alcune delle miniature propongono una lettura precisa della novella, alternativa o liminare a quella proposta nel narrato decameroniano."

for valuables (such as gold florins).[26] The gestures of the three principal characters also echo each other. The outstretched arms of Gulfardo and Guasparruolo, the former accepting the money being handed over by the latter, echo the outstretched arms of Ambruogia and Gulfardo in the central scene, one offering money and the other accepting it. This is then echoed once again in the final, right-hand scene, where outstretched arms now indicate an amorous embrace. The subtle patterning of the gestures suggests a paralleling of money and sex, both represented as transactions. The image condenses the key moral problem of the tale, that in her greed Ambruogia exchanges sex for money.[27]

The image representing VIII.1 in MS P is placed at the top of the page (fol. 151r) and ranges the width of the page, across both columns of text. The story itself begins immediately after the image. Thus, one's reading of the story in MS P is conditioned by the image. It is also worth noting that in P the image is preceded by the text of Boccaccio's rubric to the tale (discussed above), which appears at the end of the previous folio (fol. 150v). Thus in P the rubric conditions the image, which in turn conditions our reception of the tale. The starkness noted above in respect of the rubric finds several echoes in the simple lines and almost naïve directness of the drawing, with its blatant parallels of the financial transaction between Gulfardo and Guasparruolo and the sexual transaction between Gulfardo and Ambruogia. The drawing omits the final scene between Gulfardo and Guasparruolo, perhaps because such a scene is already implied in the first three scenes. But the artist's avoidance of this scene also draws attention to it: the final "revelation" is neither dramatic nor funny. The *beffa* is left as a transaction, money for sex. Like the rubric, one is left with this as *il vero*, the truth of the story.

Glossing the Tale in Florence, Biblioteca Medicea Laurenziana, MS Pluteo 42.1

In August 1384 a Florentine named Francesco d'Amaretto Mannelli added a colophon declaring completed his task of copying the *Decameron* and the *Corbaccio* in a manuscript now in the Biblioteca Medicea Laurenziana, MS Pluteo 42.1.[28] The text of the *Decameron* has long been recognized as authoritative, but the margins of the manuscript

26 For more on these chests, see Clarke, "Marrying Word and Image."

27 See Barsella, "La parola icastica," 99–101.

28 On the figure of Mannelli, see Clarke, *Chaucer and Italian Textuality*, 113–28; Clarke, "Leggere il *Decameron*"; and Clarke, "Author-Text-Reader." On Mannelli's marginal responses to the *Corbaccio*, also copied in the manuscript, see Clarke, "Taking the

are host to a whole range of responses in the form of brief annotations, sometimes exhortative appeals to a particular character, sometimes a Latin quotation, sometimes a comment on style or syntax. Of these much under-studied glosses, four are found in the margins of the story of Gulfardo and Ambruogia.

The first gloss is simply "Nota" [Note], and it occurs *ad* VIII.1.5, where Neifile asserts that it is rare to find an honest German, and highlighting, importantly, that Gulfardo is just such an honest foreign mercenary. This gloss will resonate powerfully with the final gloss on this story, *ad* VIII.1.17: "O non sapevi tu che egli aveva nome Gulfardo?" [Did you not realize that he was called *Wolfard*?]. Here, Mannelli is responding to Guasparruolo's assurance to Gulfardo that his account has now been cleared to the former's satisfaction: "Gulfardo, io son contento: andatevi pur con Dio, ché io acconcerò bene la vostra ragione" [That settles it, then. Don't worry, Gulfardo, I shall make quite sure that it's entered up in the books (VIII.1.17)]. The gloss is in a vocative mode, the voice of this reader directed at Guasparruolo, wondering how he could have been so trusting and so blind to Gulfardo's national stereotype. It is noteworthy how Mannelli has become so personally involved in reading the tale, directly addressing a character, exasperated at Guasparruolo's naïvety.[29] In this gloss there is not a little sympathy for the Italian who has been cruelly tricked by the German. It is also a gloss that focuses attention on the figure of Guasparruolo, highlighting the extent to which *he* has been deceived. None of this would have happened had he been more suspicious of the German. The premise of this gloss, that Gulfardo is in fact typical of Germans in being untrustworthy to those whom they serve, directly resists the description in the tale of Gulfardo being very loyal, "assai leale" (VIII.1.5), and wise, "sagace" (VIII.1.18). Amongst the univocal responses by the *brigata* praising Gulfardo and blaming Ambruogia, this gloss strikes a discordant note.

Mannelli expresses a sensitivity to names not just in his gloss wondering why "Gulfardo" wasn't a sufficiently clear clue as to the German's trustworthiness, but also when Neifile reveals in her story the full name

---

Proverbial." The manuscript may be consulted online at http://mss.bmlonline.it. Translations of Mannelli's glosses are my own.

29 Compare Mannelli's gloss *ad* X.10.61, when Gualtieri reveals that he has been testing Griselda and that the time has come for her to reap the rewards of her patience, a gloss that is in the voice of an alternative Griselda: "Pisciarti in mano Gualtieri! chi mi ristora di dodici anni? le forche?" [Go piss on your hand Gualtieri! Who'll give me back twelve years? The gallows? (fol. 170r)]. For a discussion of this extraordinary gloss, see Clarke, *Chaucer and Italian Textuality*, 122–3.

of the merchant husband: Guasparruolo Cagastraccio. Carlo Muscetta has described this name as sounding "ridiculous and mocking,"[30] and it is surely invested with a certain comic dimension. This lies behind Mannelli's gloss *ad* VIII.1.6: "Nota gentil nome" [Note the noble name]. The irony is unavoidable. Drawing attention to the name as *gentile*, "noble," adds another layer to a contemporary reader's sense of the courtly code clashing with the mercantile ethic.

It is, however, in the fourth gloss on the tale that Mannelli reveals his most intriguing response to the story. When Ambruogia sets two hundred gold florins as the price of her love (or rather as the price of access to her body), Mannelli, *ad* VIII.1.7, places a Latin gloss in the margins, "Non emo tanti unum penitere" [I would not buy regret at so high a price], drawn ultimately from the *Attic Nights* of Aulus Gellius, where the philosopher Demosthenes is speaking to the *grande horizontale* Lais, and thus responds to her demand of an almost unimaginably large sum for her professional services.[31] Mannelli need not have read the *Attic Nights* directly to have encountered this quip, for it had achieved a certain notoriety and was included in several medieval anthologies and *florilegia*.[32] The anecdote was included in John of Salisbury's *Policraticus* (1159), and Walter Map included it in his widely copied *Dissuasio Valerii ad Rufinum*, which was in turn incorporated into his *De nugis curialium* (1180–3). Boccaccio copied the text of the *Dissuasio*, along with other popular anti-matrimonial and misogynist literature, in the so-called Zibaldone Laurenziano.[33] The gloss serves to parallel Gulfardo and Demosthenes, with the latter choosing not to engage in any negotiations with Thaïs, while the former manages to trick sex out of Ambruogia at no cost. But the gloss does not share in the opprobrium of the *brigata* in respect of selling love; rather, it focuses attention on something much more practical, much more of interest to a mercantile readership: the

30 "caricaturale e canzonatorio" (Muscetta, *Giovanni Boccaccio*, 261).

31 Gellius, *The Attic Nights*, 1.8.

32 Francesco da Buti in his commentary on the *Commedia* (1385–95) includes this quotation during a discussion of the lustful in *Inferno* 5, to illustrate his claim that regret after sex is a well-established phenomenon; see Buti, *Commento sopra la Divina Commedia, ad Inf.* 5.25–45. The prostitute Thaïs (Laïs) appears in *Inferno* 18.133–6, there represented as a figure of flattery. See too Pastore Stocchi, "Taide"; and more generally Barchiesi, *Un tema classico e medievale.*

33 Florence, Biblioteca Medicea Laurenziana, MS Pluteo 29.8, fols. 53r–54r. On this manuscript, see De Robertis et al., *Boccaccio: Autore e copista*, 300–13, esp. 307n28 (Cat. 56, entry by Stefano Zamponi). See too Zamponi, Pantarotto, and Tomiello, "Stratigrafia dello Zibaldone." For a digital facsimile of the manuscript, see www.autografi.net/dl/resource/2796.

price demanded. Regret, that is, might be bought at a lower price, and Ambruogia made the same mistake as Thaïs.

Reading Boccaccio's tale in parallel with Mannelli's marginal glosses disorients the reader. Mannelli has not had a "canonical" response, and does not wholly accept the moral premise of the story. That is, his reading is marked by many resistances, which are directed at both the author and his characters. It is a potent reminder that it is easy to take for granted how a medieval text was received, that the response of a real reader will not always be in sympathy with what we theorize as the text's *implied* reader.[34] Mannelli reads the story of Madonna Ambruogia and Gulfardo as a tale of a husband with a ridiculous name, dealing with a German who cannot be trusted, who in turns deals with a wife who charges too much for sex.

Retelling the Tale: Chaucer's Shipman

Chaucer adapts the story of Ambruogia and Gulfardo and includes it amongst those told by the group of pilgrims on the way to the shrine of Saint Thomas Becket in Canterbury.[35] While evidence suggests that it was originally told by a different pilgrim, perhaps the Wife of Bath, the tale is assigned to the Shipman in the Ellesmere manuscript (San Marino, California, Huntington Library, MS El 26 C 9). It is entirely possible that the change was a recognition of a perceived match between the story's financial theme and the world of international trade so familiar to the Shipman.

Chaucer makes a number of important alterations whose cumulative effects significantly change both the narrative dynamic and the tonal range of the story. Chaucer makes the husband guilty of *avarizia*, and his stinginess finds expression in respect of his wife both financially and sexually. Thus, unlike Ambruogia, this wife is a woman (doubly) wronged by her husband. The lover is a monk rather than a soldier, a detail Chaucer may have incorporated from *Decameron* VIII.2, and which draws a comic tone into the story. The dynamics of the trick remain largely unchanged: the wife's lack of access to cash prompts her to acquire it through selling sex to the monk, which he pays for

34 For the notion of the implied reader, see Iser, *The Implied Reader*.

35 The *Shipman's Tale* is cited from Chaucer, *The Riverside Chaucer*, ed. Benson, 203–8. On the tale, see Cooper, *The Canterbury Tales*, 278–86; and Pearsall, *The Canterbury Tales*, 209–17. On the sources of the tale, see Scattergood, "The Shipman's Tale." For some other, debatable hypotheses on the sources of the *Shipman's Tale*, see Biggs, *Chaucer's Decameron and the Origin of the Canterbury Tales*.

using a loan from the husband. When all is revealed, the wife responds with a self-possession reminiscent of Madonna Filippa in *Decameron* VI.7: she defends herself by saying that she believed the money had been intended for her own use – and that it has now been spent, in any case – and proposes to repay her husband by keeping a tally of her conjugal rights with him. The clash of courtly and mercantile values drives the story of Ambruogia and Gulfardo, where Ambruogia is sharply excluded from navigating the "market" so deftly managed by Gulfardo. The wife in Chaucer's tale, on the other hand, returns to the notion of a "market," but this time with the authority of biblical precedent: the conjugal debt, the sexual obligations contractually undertaken in marriage, affords the wife a formal mode for resolving the narrative. In the tale, everyone gets what he or she wants, and money seems to have made it possible. Lee Patterson asserts that "The *Shipman's Tale* describes the process by which the circulation of a hundred franks among three people generates, as if by magic, a profit for all of them" (*Chaucer and the Subject of History*, 349).

If linguistic ambivalence powers the story of Gulfardo and Ambruogia, in the *Shipman's Tale* there is also an acute attention to the doubleness of mercantile language. Puns and double entendres feature prominently. The connection between sex and money is signalled with the rather outrageous rhyme *flankes*:*frankes* (groin and coin) (*Shipman's Tale* 7.201–2).[36] The breach of trust between the kinsman monk and the husband is also signalled in a series of puns on *cosyn* (deceive) and *cosynage* (kinship). And the wife's proposal that her husband keep an account of her repayments is expressed with a pun on *taille* (tally stick and sexual member) (7.416).[37] The pun is repeated in the final couplet of the tale, with the Shipman auguring that God send us as much credit as we need all the days of our lives: "Thus endeth my tale, and God us sende / Taillynge ynough unto oure lyves ende" (7.433–4). While the murkiness of the tale must be admitted, leading Donald Howard to characterize it as "an immoral tale told by an immoral man" (*Idea of the Canterbury Tales*, 273), the contrast between VIII.1 and the *Shipman's Tale* is even more striking. That Chaucer should choose to resolve the narrative as he does, with the wife asserting herself and ultimately being vindicated, is a clear indication that he is dissatisfied with the flatness of Boccaccio's story and did not see it as *quite* working.

36 The *franc a cheval* was a unit of currency introduced in 1360 and would become a common French gold coin.

37 For *tail*, see also the *Wife of Bath's Tale* 3.466 (*The Riverside Chaucer*, 111).

Sercambi's *Novelle*

When Giovanni Sercambi came to compile the 155 stories that comprise his *Novelle* (begun ca 1399), he made use of no fewer than 24 stories from Boccaccio's *Decameron*, including the tale of Madonna Ambruogia and Gulfardo (Novella 32).[38] Like the *Decameron*, the *Novelle* are interleaved with lyrics, some apparently composed by Sercambi but many written by the Florentine musician and poet Niccolò Soldanieri. Unlike the *Decameron*, however, where entire days are closed with a lyric, Sercambi places these lyrics at the beginnings of individual stories. Novella 32 is introduced by a stanza excerpted from Soldanieri's canzone that begins "Colei non è donna, ben che donna / dimostri per sua vesta" [She is not a lady even though she looks dressed as a lady], which turns on the difference between *donna* (lady) and *femina* (female), on *onestà* and *disonestà*.[39] The tale is then rubricated in Latin and vernacular: "De avaritia et luxuria. Di Pierozzo e monna Suffía in Perugia" [On Avarice and Luxury. On Pierozzo and Monna Suffia in Perugia], which further emphasizes the moralizing stance of Sercambi. Many of the key details in Boccaccio's story are included in Novella 32. Pierozzo is a moneylender, specializing in lending to foreign mercenaries, such as Messer Bernardo. His wife, Monna Suffia, has a reputation for adultery, motivated by money rather than love. She sets a price of two hundred florins for her favours with Bernardo, who in turn borrows this amount from Pierozzo, using it as payment for a night of pleasure with Suffia. When Pierozzo returns from a business trip to Ancona, Bernardo visits to let the moneylender know that, since he has not in the end needed the money, the sum has been returned to Monna Suffia. A trusted servant has witnessed this return, and is present to verify events as described by Bernardo.

Sercambi's tale makes several striking innovations to Boccaccio's story, and these innovations go to the heart of the problem explored by Boccaccio. Firstly, the courtly language with which Boccaccio describes the love of Gulfardo for Madonna Ambruogia is absent in Sercambi. Bernardo thinks that Monna Suffia's propensity for adultery increases his own chances of success with her: "s'innamorò di lei, pensando se costei con altri ha fatto fallo, agevolmente doverne aver diletto" [he

38 Rossi, "Sercambi e Boccaccio," esp. 163; Bec, *Cultura e società*, 59–79. All references will be to Sercambi, *Novelle*, ed. Sinicropi. See also Sercambi, *Il novelliere*, ed. Rossi, 1:lv–lvi and 196–201. Translations are my own.

39 For the work of Soldanieri, see *Rimatori del Trecento*, ed. Corsi, 717–77, esp. 735–6 and 770–4 for the canzone opening Sercambi's Novella 32.

fell in love with her, and thought that if she were unfaithful with others, he would easily have some pleasure (*Novelle* 32.7)]. Gulfardo is horrified that Madonna Ambruogia would ask for money at all, an act that turns his love for her to hatred. Bernardo, in contrast, is struck not so much by Monna Suffia asking for money but rather, like Mannelli's own response to the tale, by what he perceives to be the excessive amount of money requested and wonders if her *quintain* smells of rare and expensive musk: "Troppo dè aver odorifera la sua guintana, che sarè' vasto fusse moscato volerne tanti fiorini" (32.9).[40] The attention to female smell is a staple of the misogynist repertoire, and in Boccaccio's *Corbaccio* the Spirito recounts the insatiable amatory exploits of the widow in testing the skills of male relatives in bearing arms and hitting the *quintain* (*Corbaccio* 252, 265, pp. 486–7).

The reference to the *guintana* (or *quintana*) is to a jousting game in which a rider aims a lance at a dummy set up on a rotating base; the dummy holds a ring – the *quintana* (quintain) – at the end of an outstretched arm, with a club or shield on the other. The aim is to get the lance into the ring without being hit by the dummy's other arm. While Boccaccio's tale makes little direct mention of sex – Neifile merely says that Gulfardo and Ambruogia enjoyed sexual relations on repeated nights – Sercambi goes to considerable lengths to describe both the sexual prowess of Bernardo, who is likened to a jouster, and the particular qualities of Monna Suffia's *quintana*. If Monna Suffia's motivation is money, she is also skilled in the joust, and the following morning her *quintana* is described as having done greater honour than any other in Perugia.

This jousting addition creates an atmosphere of burlesque sexual excess, drawing the story into a tone more reminiscent of the comico-realist poetry of Rustico Filippi, or perhaps the more risqué stories of the *Decameron*. These are not minor alterations but utterly transformative. For Sercambi it has not been possible simply to include the story of Gulfardo and Ambruogia; he has had to make it *more* Boccaccian. The end of Boccaccio's story is somewhat flat and bitter, but the end of Sercambi's tale is most unexpected. Monna Suffia has learned a lesson, but it is not moral in nature. Rather, it is practical: "Monna Soffía, vedendosi cosí esser beffata, pensò di non cadere in tal fallo mai con persona che per quel modo riabia quello che dato l'avesso. E cosí oservò

40 For use of the image of the *quintana* in anatomical terms, see Rustico Filippi, "No riconoscereste voi l'Acerbo," v. 10 (*Sonetti satirici e giocosi*, 104); and Sacchetti, Novella 226.3 (*Le Trecento Novelle*, ed. Zaccarello, 600–2).

poi" [Monna Soffia, seeing herself tricked in this way, resolved never to make such a mistake again with someone who can take back that which they have given. And she did so (*Novelle* 32.23)]. Monna Suffia realizes her mistake: trusting someone like Bernardo. Her fault is not that she wants money in exchange for sex, it is that she is a poor judge of character.

Conclusion

Boccaccio constructs with care the stark similarities between Gulfardo and Ambruogia, but he has Neifile condemn Ambruogia ultimately at the expense of a good story. No clever or funny *beffa* can be allowed to obscure a message that is grounded on the morally bankrupt reality that everything is for sale, whether you think you are on the market or not. In responding to the tale, there can be no disagreement amongst the members of the *brigata*, and no other story in the *Decameron* can be allowed to come to Ambruogia's aid. The clearest evidence that something in the story does not "work" is to be found in the four fourteenth-century responses, which in their own way conspicuously diverge from, "rewrite" even, the original story, especially its ending. Boccaccio answers the problem of VIII.1 with the following story, of Monna Belcolore and the priest of Varlungo: they, in the end, resolve their disagreement over the cost of sex not in a cash settlement but a new skin for her tambourine – "rincartare il cembal suo" (VIII.2.47) – to which he adds a little bell. Sex here leads to continued play, to music, to artistic expression. The reference is clearly intended to be sexually suggestive, but that word *rincartare* (to re-skin), used only this once in the *Decameron*, suggests also a "re-paging," both an ethical and a narrative resolution in respect of the bleak barrenness of Gulfardo and Ambruogia, looking ahead with new "pages" to the stories that follow.[41]

41 This paper was delivered at the Renaissance Society of America Annual Meeting in Boston, in March 2016, under the auspices of the American Boccaccio Association. My gratitude is extended to the Department of English and Related Literature at York, and the Danish National Research Foundation (DNRF102ID).

Obscene Exchanges (VIII.2)

MAGGIE FRITZ-MORKIN

Now and then we encounter a Boccaccian novella that seems to exist for the sole purpose of setting up a good punch line (Todorov, *Grammaire*, 37). Just such a tale is *Decameron* VIII.2, whose plot of sexual negotiation advances through a series of verbal and material references to grinding. These culminate in a priest's meticulously staged double entendre that describes sexual escapades in terms of kitchen grinding.[1] When his lover Monna Belcolore sends word that the priest of Varlungo "non pester[à] mai più salsa in suo mortaio" [will never pound any more sauce in her mortar again (VIII.2.44)], he retorts that "s'ella non ci presterà il mortaio, io non presterò a lei il pestello; vada l'un per l'altro" [if she won't lend us her mortar, I'm not going to let her have my pestle; the one is no good without the other (VIII.2.45)].[2] The mortar and pestle stand out as the material emblems – "radiant synecdoches," or "memorial objective correlatives" that can reveal "the genetic secrets of the texts in which they appear" (Forni, *Adventures in Speech*, 60). This essay will follow the novella's cues to take the mortar and pestle as its interpretive key, the structural hinge on which turn both its plot and its meaning.

1 Forni includes the mortar and pestle of VIII.2 among "the book's memorable thematic objects, the objects that make the stories, the vectors of the *novum* without which there would not be *novella*" (*Adventures in Speech*, 60). Cf. Paul Heyse's 1871 *Falkentheorie* ("falcon theory") recognizing the emblematic objects that emerge organically and come to represent Boccaccio's most gemlike novellas, as does Federigo degli Alberighi's falcon in *Decameron* V.9 ("Einleitung," xx).

2 All Italian citations of the *Decameron* are taken from Vittore Branca's edition included in *Tutte le opere*, and English citations are taken from Wayne A. Rebhorn's translation. Rebhorn renders "vada l'un per l'altro" (VIII.2.45) as "And so, it'll be tit for tat," which I have modified above in order to emphasize the inseparability of the mortar and pestle conveyed in the Italian.

Critical approaches informing the present study of this novella have focused extensively on the prank's social function of reinforcing unspoken moral codes by punishing the excesses and deficiencies of group members.[3] Trickery amounts to an extrajuridical tool in what Olivia Holmes has described as the Florentine "beffocracy," a responsive and democratic "kind of meritocracy and system for enacting justice" outside of juridical institutions ("Trial by *Beffa*," 356). Through this lens, *Decameron* VIII.2 has appeared as a reproof of female venality, in which Belcolore is punished by the priest for attempting to commodify their amorous relationship. But their negotiations are somewhat problematic given their status inequality: Panfilo himself warns of the structural advantage of priests who can forgive their own sins and thus have no qualms about lying (VIII.2.3–4). The priest's abuse of his moral and spiritual authority in his dealings with Belcolore (detailed more fully in the summary below) thus injects the tale with a vein of anticlerical satire. Finally, the novella is also credited for its contribution to the idea of "Florentinity" that emerges in the *Decameron* and especially in the tales of Day Eight. The lively tableau of peasant life in the peripheral town of Varlungo achieves a sense of realism through historically authentic details (names of real people; allusions to legal principles and juridical practice) and rustic dialogue.[4] Florentine *ingegno* (wit) gives rise to the dramatic *beffe* that supply the plots for these tales, but also to the dazzling (and often obscene) wordplay that permeates the speech of characters and narrators alike.

Belcolore and the priest's climactic verbal exchange regarding the mortar and pestle crystallizes a point of intersection between two of the most pervasive themes in the *Decameron*, and especially in Day Eight's tales of *beffe*: the poetics of obscenity and the problems inherent in negotiating with friends. The first part of this essay will argue that the inability of Belcolore and the priest to settle on fair terms of economic exchange reveals the insufficiency of a justice of structural reciprocity described in Aristotle's *Nicomachean Ethics* 5.5. Portions of

3 Indispensable readings on the pranks of Day Eight include Holmes, "Trial by *Beffa*"; Picone, "L'arte della beffa"; Forno, "L'amaro riso"; Ferroni, "Sulla struttura della beffa"; Segre, "Funzioni, opposizioni e simmetrie"; Porcelli, "*Dec.* VIII.2"; Mazzotta, *The World at Play*; and Kirkham, "Painters at Play."

4 On the tale's peasant language, distortions of juridical terminolgy, and playful neologisms, see Holmes, "Trial by *Beffa*," 360); Porcelli, "*Dec.* VIII.2"; Branca's notes to the tale in Boccaccio, *Decameron*, ed. Branca 1992; and Getto, *Vita di forme*, 193. Picone credits the novella's rustic stylings with the inauguration of the *letteratura rusticana* of the Florentine and Venetian Renaissances ("L'arte della beffa," 203).

their dialogue in fact seem to translate key passages of economic theory in the *Ethics* into their own idiom. The second part of this essay demonstrates that the protagonists' increasing investment in euphemistic wordplay marks a dialectic shift in their relationship toward collaborative poetic engagement. Their failure to negotiate a trade deal gives way to a creative partnership which mirrors the true, stable friendship of *Ethics* Books 8–9, held by Aristotle to be even more essential than the justice of *Ethics* 5.5 in preserving a community.[5] Furthermore, their obscene poetic collaborations are additionally ennobled by literary longevity: the peasants' novel euphemisms are memorialized by the Author in the *Decameron*'s Conclusion. I will ultimately argue that an important source for Boccaccio's novella is the biblical story of Tamar, who overcomes thwarted fertility via an unseemly trick that enables her exceptional family's genealogical longevity. *Decameron* VIII.2 fashions medieval theories of obscenity into a case for economic, sexual, and poetic promiscuity, where all kinds of exchange can prove fertile in unexpected ways.

The following summary of *Decameron* VIII.2 up to the point of that pivotal exchange between Belcolore and the priest privileges the threads of economic and artistic negotiation between the two protagonists. The priest of Varlungo begins to lust after a parishioner, the lively peasant Belcolore, whom Panfilo describes as "atta a meglio saper macinar che alcuna altra" [knew the art of grinding at the mill better than any other girl around (VIII.2.9)]. Since she is also known as a talented musician and dancer, he attempts to woo her by singing loudly in church, and by bringing her aphrodisiac gifts of leeks, scallions, beans, and garlic from his garden.[6] When he discovers that her husband is headed to Florence on an errand, the priest pays her a visit and offers to service her sexually,

5 On the importance of the *Nicomachean Ethics* (and Thomas Aquinas's reception of it) in shaping Boccaccio's moral system, see Cesari, "L'*Etica* di Aristotele del codice Ambrosiano"; Bausi, "Gli spiriti magni"; Kirkham, *The Sign of Reason*, 10–13; and Sherberg, *The Governance of Friendship*, 1–5. Lianna Farber underscores the importance of trade in fostering cohesive community in medieval commentaries and treatises in response to *Ethics* 5.5. Rather than taking the *Ethics* as a dialectic text in which friendship surpasses justice (as Boccaccio read it), Farber argues that in the thirteenth and fourteenth centuries Aristotle's theory of economic value (*Ethics* 5.5–10) was primarily in tension with Augustine's system of "natural" value (*De civitate dei* 11.16) in which God's living creations outranked the non-living, such that fleas were by nature more valuable than money (*An Anatomy of Trade in Medieval Writing*, esp. 39–42).

6 The Hippocratic tradition maintains that alliums (including garlic, leeks, and scallions) are humorally hot, laxative, diuretic, and good for the body (Sanguineti White,

noting that priests are better lovers than other men "perché noi macini-amo a raccolta" [because we only do our grinding when the millpond's full (VIII.2.23)]. But Belcolore prefers monetary compensation, and since the priest has no cash on him, they settle that he will leave his cloak with her as a pledge until he can come back with the agreed-upon price. After the priest tenderly makes love to her, he goes home and immediately regrets having left a pledge worth far more money than what he owed – so he devises a con to get it back without paying her a cent.

First, the priest sends a neighbour boy the next morning to borrow a mortar from Belcolore, under the guise that he needs it to prepare a sauce for his brunch guests. Having secured the mortar, the priest then has his clerk bring it back to Belcolore at mealtime, when he guesses that she will be sitting down to eat with her husband, now back from Florence. The priest carefully scripts the message for his clerk to deliver: "'Dice il sere che gran mercé, e che voi gli rimandiate il tabarro che il fanciullo vi lasciò per ricordanza'" ["The Reverend Father says thank you very much and asks you to send him back the cloak the boy left with you as security" (VIII.2.41)]. Unable to refuse the request without revealing her sexual infidelity to her husband, Belcolore is forced to hand over the valuable cloak. But thinking quickly, she scripts her own encoded line for the clerk to say to the priest – the above-cited oath that the priest shall never again grind sauce in her mortar (VIII.2.44). This gives the priest a good laugh and sets him up to deliver his final quip via the clerk, that in that case he'll deny her his pestle and both will suffer equally (VIII.2.45).

The economic negotiations between the priest and Belcolore offer a parodic illustration of Aristotle's discussion of just exchange that binds communities together.[7] For while the priest initially attempts to play the game of courtly love with Belcolore, offering to serve her with

Seduzione e privazione, 85); Trotula's regimen lists these vegetables as augmenting and generating semen, as well as menses (Green, *The Trotula*, 69, 87).

7 Cf. Farber's reading of Chaucer's *Shipman's Tale*, in which the commodified sexual encounters and tricky deals between a monk, wife, and shipman reflect the economic values ritualized in trade practices. She argues that the wife only finds balance once she can recognize that "natural" pleasures (sex) and "economic" ones (money) are always already inextricably connected for her; such is marriage (*An Anatomy of Trade*, 68–79). Along with Day Eight's first tale, *Decameron* VIII.2 is widely acknowledged as Chaucer's source for *The Shipman's Tale* – but Chaucer ends his version of the infidelity story with reinforced marital pacts (prompting Farber's interpretation), while Boccaccio never shifts his focus from the developing rapport between the priest and Belcolore.

love and pleasure, he readily assents to her request to count her sexual favours as a commodity for monetized exchange. Venality may tarnish the gleam of eros, but the political philosophy underpinning communal Florence values currency as useful for the good of social cohesion. Money, the philosopher tells us, is an exchangeable representative of the need that holds communities together.[8] And when Belcolore reorients their negotiation toward monetary transaction, she articulates the need that motivates her request:

> Egli mi conviene andar sabato a Firenze a render lana che io ho filata e a far racconciare il filatoio mio: e se voi mi prestate cinque lire, che so che l'avete, io ricoglierò dall'usuraio la gonnella mia del perso e lo scaggiale dai dí delle feste che io recai a marito, ché vedete che non ci posso andare a santo né in niun buon luogo. (VIII.2.28)

> [I've got to go to Florence on Sunday … so that I can deliver some wool I've spun and get my spinning wheel fixed. Now, if you'll lend me five *lire* – and I know you've got them – I'll be able to go the pawnbroker's and get back my dark skirt and my Sunday-best waistband, the one I brought as part of my dowry, because you see, without them, I can't go to church or anywhere decent in public.]

Belcolore defends her asking price by embedding it in a comprehensive economic autobiography. We hear the details of her wool work: production and distribution, equipment maintenance, and even evidence of a loan that she secured by independently managing the dowry that purchased her marriage. She presents herself as an industrious person with economic compentence and agency. And she shows notable savvy in the way she frames her need. Her narrative anticipates and refutes the potential accusation of venality: she sees money and fine clothes as merely instrumental to her enjoyment of the shared life and festival rites of her community.

Aristotle addresses exchange and community under the rubrics of justice (*Nicomachean Ethics* 5.5) and friendship (Books 8–9); the first discussion is concerned with the problem of commensurability of goods and services in the discrete exchanges of an impersonal marketplace, while the second discussion addresses fair exchange in the context

8 "All things, therefore, must be measured by some one thing … This thing is, in truth, need, which holds all things together … money has become, by agreement, a kind of exchangeable representative of need" (Aristotle, *Nicomachean Ethics* 5.5, 1133a25).

of ongoing personal relationships.[9] The plot-making conflict between Belcolore and the priest arises from confusion over which of Aristotle's two codes governs their transactions. Careful justification for their appraisals of their goods and services on offer (as seen above in Belcolore's defence of her five-*lire* price, but also in the priest's long testament to his cloak's high quality and great worth) suggests that both parties desire the precision and fairness of a quid-pro-quo marketplace exchange: the province of *Ethics* 5.5. But there are also rhetorical gestures at friendship that undermine their commitment to an equal and self-contained transaction. Belcolore's request that the priest lend rather than pay her the five *lire* ("se voi mi prestate ...") may seem an artful way to diminish the magnitude of her request, but for Aristotle at least, the presence of debt "bears the mark of friendship because of the deferral of the payment to the seller."[10] In other words, Belcolore's turn of phrase also establishes their relationship as a friendly one in which it is reasonable to ask favours. The tenor of their friendship seems to warm even further after their sexual encounter: she is readily willing to lend a kitchen appliance – this time without anything in pledge – still unsuspecting that the mortar she sends him will become the token of his swindle.

Of course, the priest's deceptive intent undercuts these subtle traces of friendship. But their problem is not merely that they fail at trusting each other enough to defer repayment – even their discrete, quid-pro-quo exchange agreements fall apart. The priest initially estimates his sexual need to be equal to the five *lire* requested by Belcolore, only

9 Even in his introduction to fair marketplace exchange, Aristotle looks ahead to Books 8 and 9 and privileges relationships of reciprocal giving, "for this belongs to gratitude: one ought to serve in return someone who has been gracious, and ought oneself, the next time, to take the lead in being gracious" (*Nicomachean Ethics* 5.5, 1133a5). Giuseppe Mazzotta cites this passage as the basis of Boccaccio's elevation of gratitude as the most laudable virtue – and the one that prompts him to compose the *Decameron* – noting that the term is nonetheless "couched in the discrete language of commercial transactions" (*The World at Play*, 247). Michael Sherberg's project connects Aristotelian theory of gratitude and friendship as presented in the work's Proem with Boccaccio's training in legal theory and governance (*The Governance of Friendship*, 2).

10 *Nicomachean Ethics* 8.13, 1162b25. Aristotle here refers to "legal" friendships governed by specific contractual terms, rather than higher-order "moral" friendships where contracts are unnecessary. If Belcolore is truly offering to repay the priest over time, then she won't get anything in return for her sexual favours other than the priest's service as her loan officer; this literal reading makes her out to be either a terrible negotiator (improbable) or a rather willing lover (more probable).

to devalue it drastically once that need is satisfied.[11] Buyer's remorse then prompts his attempt to secure a full refund; and when he succeeds with his mortar-and-pestle shell game, Belcolore's oath regarding her mortar threatens an embargo on all future transactions between them. Yet it is catastrophic for a community if people do not trade one good for another, for then "there is no mutual exchange, and people stay together through mutual exchange" (Aristotle, *Nicomachean Ethics*, 5.5, 1133a). The priest's obscene joke around which the whole novella turns – "s'ella non ci presterà il mortaio, io non presterò a lei il pestello; vada l'un per l'altro" [if she won't lend us her mortar, I'm not going to let her have my pestle; the one is no good without the other (VIII.2.45)] – thus translates the Aristotelian idea that exchange among "those who are different and not equal" is an efficient cause of community. Where Aristotle explains that socio-economic cohesion arises not "out of two doctors but rather out of a doctor and a farmer" (5.5, 1133a 15), the priest assigns that task to an overdetermined mortar and pestle. His jovial protest at his impasse with Belcolore illustrates that principles of fair trade alone will ultimately be insufficient to negotiate their relationship; the novella's climax demands that characters and readers alike search for alternative principles guiding their social intercourse.

Turning from the tale's economy of goods and services to the characters' verbal economy, creative, aestheticizing impulses shape the priest and Belcolore's interactions as they match wits. The governing logic of their verbal exchanges is independent of and sometimes at cross-purposes with their economic self-interest. The above summary of the novella (minus its denouement, addressed below) emphasized two phenomena within the novella that contribute to its portrait of the creative process. One is the protagonists' increasing treatment of reality as plastic and manipulable, particularly evident in their quasi-theatrical scripting of lines to be delivered by third-party actors; the deployment of these obscene messages requires a real sense of stagecraft. The other phenomenon is that the protagonists' repetition of grinding euphemisms and instruments acquires intentionality over the course of the novella. The mortar and pestle are narrative drivers, "vettori della narrazione" (Segre, "Funzioni, opposizioni e simmetrie," 82), that are also purposefully incorporated into the grinding leitmotif. The

11 Aristotle acknowledges that desperately felt need inflates the price one is willing to pay, but nonetheless concludes that the value of aid should be measured according to the recipient's perceived need in the moment of need, rather than according to the giver's estimation of its value (*Nicomachean Ethics* 8.13, 1163a).

narrator Panfilo plays with the image in his description of Belcolore, and grinding will find an important reprise at the macrotextual level in the Author's Conclusion.

While critics have often described the sexual metaphors built on *macinare* and *pestare* as obvious and commonplace, historical dictionaries actually cite *Decameron* VIII.2 as the first attestation of such innuendo in vernacular Italian.[12] The evidence is, of course, insufficient to prove whether Boccaccio coined or merely recorded this colourful vernacular expression, but its novelty seems compelling to the characters, narrator, and Author, all of whom experiment with the poetic possibilities of this whimsical set of symbols. Without them, there's no joke – and no story. The narrative structure of the *Decameron* displaces the origin of grinding wordplay from the Author or narrator onto the novella's characters. Furthermore, Belcolore and the priest are among the rare characters who play with shifts between literal and metaphorical levels of the objects in their world; such self-reflexivity is more common to the narrators and the Author (Forni, *Adventures in Speech*, 66). Their explicit rhetorical equivalence of the mortar and pestle to their own sex organs allows Boccaccio to argue that he is only writing what people actually say to one another, shifting the blame for turning everyday objects into sexual symbols to another author. But no matter their origin, the repetition of grinding images and objects at each of the novella's narrative levels – character dialogue, Panfilo's narration, authorial paratext – suggests that Boccaccio conceptualizes the novella at least in part as a space to study the generation and transmission of a pleasing new coinage, as Forno has suggested ("L'amaro riso," 143).

The metaliterary work done by grinding in the novella becomes clearer in the Author's Conclusion, where Boccaccio twice invokes

12 Branca directs us to read *macinare* "nel tradizionale senso equivoco, sessuale" [as sexual, in its traditional equivocal sense] (Boccaccio, *Decameron*, ed. Branca 1992, note to VIII.2.9, p. 896n9); cf. Forni's "everyday sexual metaphor" (*Adventures in Speech*, 73). These glosses are accurate and useful aids for a modern reader's comprehension, but they also obscure the freshness and novelty of Boccaccio's metaphors at time he was writing. Battaglia, *Grande Dizionario della Lingua Italiana*, offers "dedicarsi ai piaceri sensuali" (to dedicate oneself to sexual pleasures) as a figurative definition of *macinare*, citing *Decameron* VIII.2 as its earliest example; Battaglia's definition further includes the priest's variant *macinare a raccolta* indicating that the act is done "con particolare energia" (with particular energy). The *Tesoro della lingua Italiana delle Origini* also cites this novella as the earliest recorded vernacular use of the metaphor. Ziolkowski notes a distant classical cousin of the figurative uses of *macinare* and *pestare*: a Ciceronian letter recording *battuit* (the verb associated with a mortar and pestle) as a possible sexual euphemism ("The Latin Grammatical and Rhetorical Tradition," 43).

the grinding instruments and innuendo of *Decameron* VIII.2 to defend the licence he has taken in writing the *Decameron*.[13] Arguing that no deed or story is so "disonesta" [unseemly] that it cannot be told "con onesti vocaboli" [in seemly language (Concl.Aut.3)], he begs to be excused if he has written

> alcuna paroletta piú liberale che forse ... non si conviene ... non si dee a me esser disdetto d'averle scritte che generalmente si disdica agli uomini e alle donne di dir tutto dí "foro" e "caviglia" e "*mortaio*" e "*pestello*" e "salsiccia" e "mortadello," e tutto pien di simiglianti cose. (Concl.Aut.5, emphasis added)

> [some little word, that is freer than might seem appropriate ... it was no more improper for me to have written them than for men and women generally to go around all day long saying "hole" and "rod" and "*mortar*" and "*pestle*" and "sausage" and "mortadella" and lots of other things like that.]

First of all, this subtle reference to *Decameron* VIII.2 via its emblematic objects confirms that Boccaccio sees the novella as an exemplary specimen of those tales whose sexual content and innuendo are most likely to draw fire from his moralizing critics. The passage also strikes at the role of unseemly expressions, as described by Leslie Dunton-Downer, in critiquing the inadequacy of available language to say what needs to be said: with no way to speak directly about sex and desire, people must resort to inventing figurative language that, while it is not merely referential, is neither fully poetic nor figurative.[14] Reading the same passage with a focus on the reader's reception of unseemly language (rather than authorial expression), Giuseppe Mazzotta extracts the Boccaccian aesthetic of not naming sexuality directly, noting that Boccaccio's argument for the moral neutrality of all texts shifts the burden of morality entirely to the audience while also providing a moral alibi for

---

13 Bàrberi Squarotti argues that all symbols are, in some sense, metaliterary: "Il simbolo ha, insomma, sempre una tradizione: è un motivo che contiene in sé elementi metaletterari, cioè è anche un discorso della letteratura sopra se stessa, in quanto creatrice e istrutrice di simboli, che, poi, variamente vengono modificati, interpretati, utilizzati, sistemati in diverse catene e strutture ("Qualche dubbio sulla metafora," 229).

14 Dunton-Downer, "Poetic Language," 23–5. Cf. Porcelli on the ambiguity of euphemisms, which can be both obscene and not obscene at the same time ("*Dec.* VIII.2," 86).

the text's erotic pleasures.[15] Marilyn Migiel emphasizes that even when the *brigata* reveals how a novella might be received – at Belcolore's tale, for example, "le donne avevano tanto riso che ancora ridono" [the ladies laughed so hard that they have not stopped laughing about it to this very day (VIII.3.2)] – it is nonetheless up to the reader to interpret their response. Do the women laugh beyond measure about sex? Or is their understanding subtler, more nuanced, beyond male comprehension and thus beyond even the Author's ken?[16]

The Conclusion's second reference to *Decameron* VIII.2 repeats the priest's whimsical boast of his industrial-strength grinding – "noi maciniamo a raccolta" (VIII.2.23) – which is the origin of the grinding meme in the *Decameron*.[17] The Author coyly hints that any women piously objecting to his portrayal of clerics who "macinano a raccolta" [do their grinding when the millpond is full] do not really believe clerics to be celibate, but rather know that they merely "nol ridicono" [never blab about it afterward (Concl.Aut.26)]. The unique expression's migration across the *Decameron*'s narrative strata – from the direct discourse of a novella's character, through Panfilo's mediating narration, to the Author's metaliterary commentary on the entire work – illustrates one possible model of poetic generation that dignifies popular sources of aesthetic inspiration. In reproducing the priest's metaphor verbatim, Boccaccio subtly casts his Author persona as a receptive member of the novellas' audience – one sensitive to the rhetorical features that make each tale original and particular, who can then improvise new expressions with those same features. Of course, it is structurally impossible for news of the Author's riff on *macinare a raccolta* to filter back to the world of the novella. No real dialectic of creativity can emerge between the character-priest and Author who imitates his style. Yet this kind of creative collaboration is exactly what develops within the world of the novella in the aestheticized back-and-forth negotiation between the

---

15 Especially relevant is Mazzotta's comparison of pornography to allegory, both of which require an integument of moral myth to travel, or an alibi to hide their fruits (*The World at Play*, 116–19). Ziolkowski notes that Quintilian argues in a similar fashion for the inherent moral neutrality of words ("The Latin Grammatical and Rhetorical Tradition," 42). Marchesi finds the same defence in Ovid's *Tristia*, and argues that Boccaccio's use of Quintilian in his self-defence is done to style himself after that ancient *praeceptor amoris* (*Stratigrafie decameroniane*, 23).

16 Migiel, *A Rhetoric of the Decameron*, 140–1. I have modified Rebhorn's translation in the citation of *Decameron* VIII.3, which gives "made the ladies laugh so hard."

17 Chronologically, that is, as the action of the individual novellas precedes the narrator's presentation, which in turn precedes the Author's interventions; Panfilo's introduction of Belcolore as an expert grinder is sequentially first in the *Decameron*.

priest and Belcolore. These macrotextual engagements with grinding objects and metaphors confirm that these symbols do not simply point to the exchange of sexual favours in *Decameron* VIII.2 but also comment on the role of obscenity in artistic reproduction.

Perhaps the most enduring conception of obscenity, and the one that makes it obviously applicable to the novella of the priest and Belcolore, is that it has to do with illicit sex. Isidore of Seville, for example, defines "obscene" as the kind of love one has for prostitutes, rather than for a wife or child (*De differentiis verborum*, 10a). Other etymologists derive the term from a theatrical context, and obscenity understood in this vein is especially relevant to *Decameron* VIII.2, where protagonists script innuendo to be delivered by other characters. In his thirteenth-century lexicon, Giovanni Balbi proposes that the term is a compound of the Latin *ob* and *cena* (filth) or *scena* (stage) (*Catholicon*, s.v. "obscenus"). Going further back, Varro (d. 27 BCE), derives *obscaenum* (foul) from *scaena* (stage), and "quare turpe ideo obscaenum, quod *nisi in scaena* palam dici non debet" [thus anything filthy is called obscene, because it ought not to be said openly *except on the stage*].[18] Similarly, Horace charges tragic actors with eloquently narrating the gruesome acts of violence that must occur offstage (*Ars poetica* vv. 182–4, pp. 464–7); comic actors should refrain from "immunda ... ignominiosaque dicta" [obscene and vulgar jests (v. 247, pp. 470–1)] that will chafe at a well-bred audience's sense of decorum. The stage becomes a repository for the language that conveys the unmentionable obscene, where actors may describe what people self-censor, and where a community might encounter its taboos. If obscene speech belongs to the stage, it implies

18 Varro, *De lingua latina* 7.96, 1:350–1; I have gently modified Kent's translation for clarity, and added emphasis. Compare a similar prohibition of unseemliness/obscenity from the oratorical tradition, which identifies it as speech that provokes an involuntary aesthetic experience of ugliness, repugnance, or disgust: "fugienda est omnis turpitudo earum rerum, ad quas eorum animos, qui audient, trahet similitudo" (Cicero, *De Oratore* 3.163, 2:128); see also Quintilian, *Institutiones oratoriae* 8.39, 3:362–3; both of these passages emphasize the speaker's responsibility for the mental images transmitted to the audience. Ziolkowski notes that for Cicero and Quinitilian the unseemly and the obscene were also often associated with theatrical performers ("The Latin Grammatical and Rhetorical Tradition," 44). See also Barański, "Scatology and Obscenity" and *Language as Sin and Salvation*, 10–11, on Dante's combination of sexual obscenity and excremental filth in the manner of Scripture's *sermo humilis*. For a thorough discussion of the medieval rhetorical theories of obscenity, see especially Ziolkowski, "The Latin Grammatical and Rhetorical Tradition." Alastair Minnis, "From *Coilles* to *Bel Chose*," and Dunton-Downer, "Poetic Language," give special attention to the varying hermeneutic demands of obscene words, texts, actions, and objects.

the speaker's awareness of participating in a spectacle, and the presence of an audience – a structural configuration not unlike that of the *beffa*, where a prankster targets a victim before a real or implied audience.[19] Tracing the grinding obscenities in *Decameron* VIII.2 from their point of origin in the priest's first sexual overture to Belcolore through their climactic exchange, one can observe the protagonists' transition from using a utilitarian sort of obscenity that signifies illicit sex (as in Isidore) to using it with self-aware, aestheticized theatricality (as in Varro).[20] This shift occurs in incremental phases.

The priest's initial boast of grinding like a well-powered mill does not seem governed by the norms of the stage. He has carefully chosen a private moment – Belcolore's husband has gone to town – when they can best avoid an audience: "non c'è persona, e forse quand'io ci tornassi ci sarebbe chi che sia che c'impaccerebbe: e io non so quando e' mi si venga cosí ben fatto come ora" [nobody's around. By the time I got back, there might be someone or other who'd mess up our plans, and I don't know when it would work out as well as it would right now (VIII.2.31)].[21] He can, however, be minimally credited with the ability to recognize something like a Bakhtinian chronotope – that particular moment in time and space where characters meet and things can happen.[22] A sense of timing is a prerequisite for improvisational theatre or

19 Even without explicit connection to the stage, obscenity produces "a curiously engaged reflectivity that efficiently captures the human paradox of being at once a subject within and a self critical of language" (Dunton-Downer, "Poetic Language," 26). Picone describes the *beffa* as a "forma mentis": a creative act that duplicates the process of literary invention ("L'arte della beffa," 206). See also Ferroni, "Sulla struttura della beffa," 73; and Mazzotta, *The World at Play*, 188.

20 Picone observes an analogous shift in performance of Ciappelletto, another of Panfilo's characters, in *Decameron* I.1: the dying sinner begins his improvised false confession for the utilitarian purpose of sparing his friends' reputation, but he exceeds what is necessary by delivering his saintly confession with consumate histrionic ability ("Gioco e/o letteratura," 64–5). The case of Ciappelletto is different from that of Belcolore and the priest in that he works alone, rather than collaboratively.

21 *Nota bene* that, given the mere fifty-minute walk along the old Via Aretina from Varlungo to Santa Reparata, the risk of being caught *in flagrante* by Belcolore's husband cannot be entirely eliminated. Many thanks to Don Vittorio Menestrina, who tends to the parish of Varlungo seven centuries after Boccaccio's priest once did, for his generosity in offering a tour of the Church of San Pietro and a rich historical portrait of Varlungo along the old Via Aretina, just upstream of Santa Reparata.

22 Mikhail Bakhtin, "Forms of Time and Chronotope," 98; Forno mentions the importance of chronotope in Day Eight tales ("L'amaro riso," 142). An elm in front of a church (as featured in *Decameron* VIII.2.6 and VIII.6.41) historically marked a

performance art. His next strategic move incorporates the stage direction of other players: the neighbour boy and his clerk, whose actions and words accompany the series of transfers involving the cloak and mortar. In other words, he works out a grammatically coherent plot before setting his drama in motion (Todorov, *Grammaire,* 10). In this phase, there is no apparent obscenity; his selection of the mortar seems arbitrary, and unrelated to mill grinding; any object will do for his shell-game. The conclusion of this phase also introduces the rhetorical complexity of dramatic irony. The priest directs the clerk to speak a precise expression, reported by Panfilo in direct discourse, that will mean one thing to Belcolore and something else to her husband: "Dice il sere che gran mercé, e che voi gli rimandiate il tabarro che il fanciullo vi lasciò per ricordanza" [The Reverend Father says thank you very much and asks you to send him back the cloak the boy left with you as security (VIII.2.41)]. Belcolore recognizes the discrepancy between her husband's (and the clerk's) understanding of the scene and her own, and is forced to concede the loss, at least in their economic exchange.

Had the novella ended at the completion of the priest's trick, one could read it as unambiguous anticlerical satire, or as a moral lesson punishing feminine venality that disrupts courtly love dynamics. But Belcolore takes up the priest's tools of stagecraft and dramatic irony, and adds the additional rhetorical flourish of an obscene metaphor to the mix. The line of dialogue that she crafts for the clerk – "voi non pesterete mai più salsa in suo mortaio" [you'll never pound any more sauce in her mortar again (VIII.2.44)] – whose true referent is knowable only to its intended audience, is evidence that she too has begun operating with a playwright's theory of mind. She manipulates the sequence of real-life events while keeping track of the other players' individual perceptions of reality. In one important way, Belcolore's success as a dramaturge supersedes the priest's: his obscene words have at this point always been in the service of deeds. Belcolore's reprisal and variation of the priest's grinding metaphor – his *macinare* with an implied mill becomes *pestare* with a mortar and pestle – shows her interest in creating a sense of aesthetic unity in their story. The priest's laughter signals his recognition of the aesthetic value that she adds to the plot. He expresses his appreciation through imitation, adding his final obscene double entendre to their co-authored script. When Panfilo, who holds the entire tale in his mind as he tells it, introduces Belcolore as an expert

space for meeting and even conducting official community business; see Davidsohn, *Storia di Firenze,* 1:474–5.

grinder, he is therefore referencing her authorial intervention, which was an effort to unite the sequence of events under a single aesthetic umbrella. As the priest and Belcolore turn Varlungo into a theatre of the obscene, they become collaborative authors whose influence ripples outward not only to Panfilo's stylistic choices but even to the macrotext Author, whose conclusion features multiple references to the poetic process of these humble characters.[23]

The priest's punch line concludes neither the novella nor their friendship. To summarize the tale's problematic happy end: Belcolore remains cross with the priest, who cheated her of five *lire* "insino a vendemmia" [right up to the grape harvest (VIII.2.46)], and although he extorts her into renewing friendship under the threat of damnation, authentic and mutual fondness seems to ensue: "col mosto e con le castagne calde si rappatumò con lui, e piú volte insieme fecer poi gozzoviglia" [she … made peace with him over some new wine and roasted chestnuts. From then on, they had more than one good guzzle together (VIII.2.46)] In lieu of her five *lire*, "le fece il prete rincartare il cembal suo e appiccovi un sonagliuzzo, e ella fu contenta" [the priest not only had her tambourine re-covered with a new skin, but had a little bell hung on it, and then she was happy (VIII.2.47)]; thus ends the tale.

Several obvious blights degrade the happiness of this ending: the priest's abuse of his spiritual authority, the gluttonous and probably lustful instincts that are indulged in their fellowship, and the fact that Belcolore remains deprived of the five *lire* she should have had according to their verbal contract. The novella risks portraying a "male fantasyland in which women bestow their gifts freely when asked without paying the requested price" (Holmes, "Trial by *Beffa*," 359). But it is also worth considering that Panfilo, who will select the theme of liberality for the final day of storytelling and is thus associated with the work's dominant virtues of gratitude and generosity, is neither ironic nor scornful in the three little words that end his novella.[24] The vintage season suggests a festive atmosphere; the convivial scene with wine and chestnuts is the fruition of a long-cultivated rapport.[25] For

23 The audience of a *beffa* can be its perpetrators, as it is here; such an exercise in self-pleasure is implicitly erotic (Forno, "L'amaro riso," 134; Mazzotta, *The World at Play*, 192).

24 On Panfilo and gratitude, see Mazzotta, *The World at Play*, 247; and the final chapter of Sherberg, *The Governance of Friendship*, 191–232.

25 Chestnuts were considered especially nourishing and a known aphrodisiac, suggesting a continued sexual relationship (Sanguineti White, *Seduzione e privazione*, 86).

Aristotle, mature friendship is exercised in shared life: company and conversation.[26] The small favour that the priest substitutes for his debt – repairing and improving Belcolore's tambourine – is actually a quite thoughtful gift, if we recall that Belcolore is initially presented as a lively woman skilled at singing, playing music, and dancing. Panfilo tells us that these are the very things that caught the priest's fancy in the first place.[27] The priest's gesture acknowledges her artistic range and facilitates her creative expression. The Varlungo spectacle thus impresses upon its audience a sense of *Gesamtkunstwerk* or a Horatian satyr-play by weaving many art forms together: instrumental music, song, dance – alongside the plotting of tricks, and the drama of scripted obscenity.[28] If *Decameron* VIII.2 relates to the macrotext through its grinding images, it also replicates at a smaller scale the work's incorporation of multiple and multisensory artistic forms. Once Belcolore and the priest have rendered money useless between them,[29] they may come together to enjoy the pleasure of each other's company and stimulate one another's artistic expression.[30]

---

26 Aristotle, *Nicomachean Ethics* 9.9, 1170b10–15; Sherberg, *The Governance of Friendship*, 5.

27 "era quella che meglio sapeva sonare il cembalo e cantare *L'acqua corre la borrana* e menar la ridda e il ballonchio, quando bisogno faceva, che vicina che ella avesse, con bel moccichino e gente in mano. Per le quali cose messer lo prete ne 'nvaghì sì forte" [when it came to playing the tambourine, singing "The water runs down the ravine," and taking the lead in a round or a jig, while holding a fine, dainty little kerchief in her hand, she had no equal among the women in the village. All of these things made Messer Priest desire her so much (VIII.2.9–10)].

28 See Kuhns on the appeal of multiple sensorial registers in the Decameron: "*Gesamtkunstwerk* seems to be a natural cultural enactment realized in performance, because performance makes natural demands on each sense modality and on bodily movement and rests on a synesthesia in which all senses contribute to each other" ("The Creation of a Total Work of Art," 126). See also Mazzotta on the repertory of rhetorical forms and traditions of play present in the *Decameron* (*The World at Play*, 9).

29 Money "exists not by nature but by law, and it is up to us to change it or render it useless" (Aristotle, *Nicomachean Ethics* 5.5, 1133b30).

30 Picone's rule for Day Eight, that whatever amorous affection exists between prankster and victim is ultimately subordinated to the prankster's skill (*virtù*) or the victim's credulity in the course of erotic pranks ("L'arte della beffa," 208), seems in fact not to apply in this case, where erotic attraction threatened by the prank is carefully repaired, preserved, and developed into deeper affection; to read *Decameron* VIII.2 as a case of a cunning priest prevailing over Belcolore's "sana ma ingenua avidità (non solo sessuale)" does not adequately account for her complicated negotiation involving the pledge or the apparent happiness of both parties at the end.

The reverberating obscenity of *Decameron* VIII.2 illustrates a sad truth of poetic generation and literary genealogy: that poetic innovators can never know the fate of their works beyond their temporal and spatial horizons.[31] The priest and Belcolore are unaware that their ephemeral dramatic scene will ever be reproduced or known to future audiences. They cannot know that Panfilo will pass on their story, that Boccaccio will set it down in writing, and that both will reproduce the grinding metaphor whose birth we seem to witness at a Varlungo kitchen table. That obscene euphemisms also stake out an undercurrent of anxiety regarding biological – in addition to poetic – generation that moves through the tale seems barely to have been noticed. Recognizing it here, and reading its two components closely, reveals a possible biblical source for the tale that further dignifies the protagonists' unseemly words and actions. Those two components are, first, a clear allusion to pregnancy as a risk of prostitution; and second, a subtle reference to the withdrawal method of contraception (also known as onanism after its first practitioner).

Well into their negotiation for Belcolore's sexual favours – they have just settled on five *lire* but have not yet worked out that the priest will leave his cloak as a pledge – she objects that she does not want to end up like the priest's former fling Biliuzza, "che se n'andò al ceteratoio" and "n'è divenuta femina di mondo pur per ciò" [who had quite a bit to complain about ... that's what turned her into a streetwalker (VIII.2.30)].[32] The obscure *ceteratoio* has been glossed by critics as a distortion of the "et ceteras" dotting the legal prose of lawsuits, or, alternatively, as a derivation of *cetera*, a guitar with a rounded belly.[33] Either way, Biliuzza's fate shows that her encounter with the priest resulted in greater damage than lost earnings, and the most logical explanation is that she became pregnant while unwed and took on sex work for income. The stakes for Belcolore should not be so high. Already married, she could easily pass off a child fathered by the priest as the product of the union with her husband – a welcome addition at that, since

31 This is not to suggest that authors did not adopt complex strategies to ensure the enduring fame of their works. Here I merely state the obvious: that Boccaccio can only enjoy his fame during his lifetime; he may imagine and boast that future generations will savour his work, but centuries of canonicity are never guaranteed. See Bourdieu, *Language and Symbolic Power*, 58.

32 I have modified Rebhorn's translation, which gives "who went off empty-handed."

33 In his notes, Branca credits Fiacchi and Piovano Arlotto with the juridical glosses, and Pézard with the derivation from *cetera* (Boccaccio, *Decameron*, ed. Branca 1992, note to VIII.2.30, p. 901n7).

the couple appears to be childless.[34] Belcolore's fretting over Biliuzza's fate may simply be a rhetorical strategy in her negotiation: by inflating the measure of her risk, she can demand higher compensation. But perhaps she simply rejects biological reproduction and the passive role in procreation assigned to women.[35]

In fact, Belcolore's handling of seeds early in the novella hints more obliquely at a popular form of contraception, one that connects the novella to the story of Onan and Tamar and is therefore consequential for the moral orientation of the tale. When the priest comes to pay his visit, she is up in the loft, and he calls up that he has stopped by because he knew her husband was gone away to Florence. Coming down to greet him, "si pose a sedere e cominciò a nettare sementa di cavolini che il marito avea poco innanzi trebbiati" [she took a seat and began picking over some Brussels sprouts seeds that her husband had threshed just a little while before (VIII.2.19)].[36] The singular form *sementa* is unusual for plural seeds; more commonly it refers to the action of planting, or to semen.[37] But subtle morphological distinctions are not even necessary to understand her husband's just-threshed seeds as a surrogate for his semen: the semantic fields of vegetable and human generation thoroughly overlap in biblical literature, and the *Decameron* has already trained us to see "sex organs masquerad[ing] as vegetables" (Migiel, "Figurative Language," 231). Belcolore's careful cleaning and managing of her husband's seeds hints at an attempt to control and defer conception through *coitus interruptus*, as Onan did with his widowed

34 For Aristotle, the point of marriage is both begetting children and dividing the tasks of a household's economic activities: childless couples are also more likely to separate (*Nicomachean Ethics* 8.12, 1162a15–30). In his commentary on the passage, Aquinas privileges procreation and de-emphasizes home economics (Thomas Aquinas, *On Aristotle's Love and Friendship*, 52).

35 Aristotle's *De generatione animalium* begins with the theory that male semen acts by imputing form on the passive matter of women's menstrual blood; Camille underlines the common analogy of coitus and writing, procreation mirrored in the creative act in which a man pens an idea on a blank page ("Manuscript Illumination," 80–4). Boccaccio subverts the active-male/passive-female model of procreation in *Decameron* IX.3, in which Calandrino is tricked into believing himself pregnant, and then concludes that his wife Tessa is to blame for preferring to be on top during intercourse.

36 Rebhorn translates *cavolini* as "cabbages," but the testicular size and shape of Brussels sprouts makes accuracy in this case seem especially important.

37 In medieval Italy, *sementa* was also used figuratively for humans as a product of divine creation, for the act of fertilization, and for progeny; by the sixteenth century, *scialaquare la sementa* meant "to have frequent sexual encounters" (Battaglia, *Grande dizionario della lingua italiana*, s.v. "sementa").

sister-in-law Tamar: "introiens ad uxorem fratris sui semen fundebat in terram" [when he went in to his brother's wife, he spilled his seed upon the ground (Vulgate Bible, Genesis 38:6)].[38]

If such a reading appears to overinterpret a minor mimetic detail of agrarian realism, a closer look at the story of Tamar reveals so many narrative parallels to *Decameron* VIII.2's plot and theme of creative generation that it may well be Boccaccio's source for the novella.[39] After Onan's disappointing performance, Tamar orchestrates a sexual encounter with Judah, the father of her dead husband, by veiling herself as if she were a harlot. Without recognizing her, Judah asks to lie with her. Tamar asks in turn what he will offer her in exchange for enjoying her company. He proposes to send her a kid from his herd of goats, but she requests a pledge guaranteeing the debt before agreeing to sleep with him. He leaves her his ring, bracelet, and staff, and they sleep together. Judah promptly sends his shepherd to deliver the promised payment and retrieve his pledged items (Genesis 38:16–20). Despite the notable structural similarities between the two narratives, one crucial difference is that Tamar – Belcolore's gender analogue who, like her, negotiates pledged sex – is the one to plan a complicated trick (cf. *Decameron* VIII.2's priest) that involves seduction and, as we shall see, cheating on a verbal contract. However, Tamar's unseemly and morally ambiguous actions are ultimately deemed just by Judah.

Tamar's chances to bear fruit for Judah's line are initially undermined at several turns: her first husband, Judah's eldest son, is struck down by God for his wickedness; Onan refused Judah's command to provide his seed; Judah's youngest son Sela was at first too young to marry. Tamar finally takes matters into her own hands, and plans to seduce Judah himself: "quod crevisset Sela et non eum accepisset maritum" [because Sela had grown up, and she had not been married

38 The description of Onan's technique becomes a well-known shorthand for the withdrawal method; see Cherubino da Siena's fifteenth-century admontion of those who practise "quella cosa, la quale è ordinata per ingravidare, la fanno andare per modo che non può generare, come colui che lavora il terreno e poi getta le sementa sopra le pietre" [that action which is designed for impregnating, they do in such a way that it cannot generate anything, like one who tills the earth and then throws his seeds over stones (my translation)]; note here as well that *sementa* is used for plural seeds (cited in Pinto, "Matrimonio e sessualità coniugale," 159).

39 Branca cites a few distant echoes in the fabliaux tradition but prefers popular tales as Boccaccio's source (Boccaccio, *Decameron*, ed. Branca 1992, note to VIII.2.3, p. 895n3). To my knowledge, Genesis 38 has not been previously suggested as a source for this novella, but Wendy Doniger proposes it as inspiring the recognition-by-token topos in *Decameron* III.9 ("Pregnant Riddles," 155–9).

to him (Genesis 38:14)]. That the scriptural passage includes this detail about her purpose suggests that she feels a proprietary right to Judah's seed, something like the conjugal debt that Paul would later describe as binding spouses.[40] Indeed, Tamar conceives in that single encounter with Judah, and then uses her father-in-law's pledged items as identifying evidence of his paternity; the patriarch ultimately declares "iustior me est quia non tradidi eam Sela filio meo" [she is juster than I: because I did not give her to Sela, my son (Genesis 38:26)].

Tamar's procreative impulse prompts her to embrace morally marginal strategies – falsification of identity, apparent prostitution, quasi-incest, deceptive negotiation – that paradoxically result in great communal benefit (to borrow Aristotelian terms) when one of her twin sons from Judah produces the line of kings down to David. She is the first woman recorded in Matthew's genealogy of Jesus (Matthew 1:3), and in veiling herself to seduce Judah, she is read typologically in medieval commentaries as a figure of the nascent Christian church at the moment of mystical union with Christ (represented by Judah).[41] Even in light of her revealed Christian significance, Boccaccio cannot help but have noticed Tamar's mastery of the art of the *beffa*, her skill at forging a coherent plot that achieves its happy end, unhindered by – and indeed enabled by – the unseemliness of its structural devices. In the tale of Belcolore and the priest, Boccaccio dismantles and reconfigures the causes, effects, intents, and tools of Tamar's story.[42] He begins with procreative anxiety rather than impulse; unseemly acts and trickery are initially motivated by self-interest; artistic impulse (which replaces the

40 For general background on conjugal debt, see Makowski, "The Conjugal Debt." Rudolph Bell notes that where Paul articulates spouses' reciprocal and equal ownership of each other's body, medieval commentaries (including those of Augustine, Jean Gerson, and Bishop Antoninus of Florence) suppress the wife's proprietary claim over the husband's body (*How to Do It*, 30). See also Michael Camille on how the visual representation of disputes over a husband's failure to pay the conjugal debt in illuminations accompanying Gratian's *Decretum* attest to the tyrannized male body, manifesting here through performance anxiety ("Manuscript Illumination," 71–3).

41 Early and medieval Christian commentaries distinguish Tamar's compliance with marriage law and custom (in which widows were married to kinsman of their defunct husbands, and resulting offspring were counted as the first husband's seed) from her appearance of harlotry; under her new veil she is read typologically as a figure for the nascent gentile church, Christ's bride (Balthasar, "The Tamar Motif").

42 "Medieval narratives are often restructured for effect precisely to undermine our expectations of linear coherence, and this goes as much for sexual as for other stories" (Camille, "Manuscript Illumination," 71).

drive for biological reproduction) only matures in the process of spontaneous collaboration.

The Christian figural interpretation of Tamar implies her prophetic understanding of her place in Christ's family tree: Tamar's extraordinary determination to carry Judah's child signals her anticipation of the Messaiah's eventual birth. But even in her own lifetime, Tamar's twin sons Phares and Zara represent the fullfilment of her zealous efforts. They are the tangible signs and rewards of Tamar's commitment to "increase and multiply" the human family (Genesis 1:28). In Boccaccio's novella, Tamar's fulfilment is paralleled by Belcolore and the priest's fullfilment of an Aristotelian model of friendship, characterized by shared life and cycles of collaboration and pleasant repose. It is not by chance that the protagonists' negotiations are put aside for the sake of pleasure in the vintage season, "for the ancient sacrifices and gatherings appear to take place after the harvest ... because people used to have leisure especially in these seasons" (*Nicomachean Ethics*, 8.9, 1160a 25–8). Such moments to enjoy the fruits of shared labour are set aside because "community aims not at the present advantage but at that pertaining to life as a whole" (8.9, 1160a 22–3). But just as Tamar's story has its typological afterlife, so too does the scope of Belcolore and the priest's happy ending extend beyond their temporal horizon. Their poetic intervention leaves its aesthetic mark on the Author's Conclusion, and even the lexical record beyond Boccaccio's authorial control.

The Artist and the Police (VIII.3)

JUSTIN STEINBERG

Introduction

At the beginning of Plato's *Republic*, one of Socrates's interlocutors, Glaucon, tells a story about Gyges, the king's shepherd who discovers a ring of invisibility and uses it to seduce the queen, murder the king, and treacherously ascend to the throne. For Glaucon, this tale proves that men act justly only when it is expedient, only when they know others are watching. Socrates spends the remaining books of the *Republic* refuting this thesis.

Boccaccio didn't read Plato, of course, but he would have found the tale of Gyges excerpted in Cicero's widely circulated *De officiis*. In that work, Cicero uses the *fabula* of Gyges's invisibility to pose the ethically loaded hypothetical: "if nobody were to know or even to suspect the truth, if for the sake of riches or power or sovereignty or sensual gratification you could do something which would remain forever hidden from the knowledge of both gods and men, would you do it?"[1] While Gyges's actions lead to rape, treason, and ultimately tyranny, Cicero recognizes that a host of lesser crimes – such as corruption, forgery, and embezzlement – similarly proliferate when citizens are willing to act unlawfully provided they remain unseen. In the tradition of Plato and Cicero, Boccaccio uses Calandrino's fantasy of invisibility in *Decameron* VIII.3 to explore why we should act lawfully when there is no one around to see.

Calandrino's schemes lack both Gyges's ambition and effectiveness. Nonetheless, Calandrino too aims to steal and cheat as soon as he

1 "... si nemo sciturus, nemo ne suspicaturus quidem sit, cum aliquid divitiarum, potentiae, dominationis, libidinis causa feceris, si id dis hominibusque futurum sit semper ignotum, sisne facturus" (Cicero, *De officiis* 3.9.39, pp. 306–7).

learns about the magical powers of the heliotrope. His thoughts while "invisible" demonstrate that this "new citizen" is physically but not psychologically integrated within the city; he views obedience to the law as an act of submission rather than as a duty. While many critics have recognized Calandrino's obsessive focus on private gain, I argue that it is his disregard for the public good, such as when he believes he has given the slip to the customs agents at the Gates of San Gallo, that Boccaccio deems the more urgent problem. Behind the folly of this would-be thief lies a serious predicament for the Florentine government: how to persuade its citizens to pay taxes even when it becomes possible to evade them.

~

In the third tale of the eighth day of the *Decameron*, the narrator Elissa tells the story of an elaborate *beffa*, or prank, played on the Florentine painter Calandrino (Nozzo di Pierino).[2] The structure of the tale can be divided into two parts: the preparation for the prank and its execution. In the first part, Maso del Saggio, upon finding Calandrino gazing at the newly decorated tabernacle in the Baptistery of San Giovanni, entices Calandrino by expounding on the virtuous stones that are to be found in the far-off land of Bengodi, where the mountains are made of Parmesan cheese and the rivers run fresh with Vernaccia wine. Having whetted Calandrino's appetite with this fantasy of instant gratification, the broker-turned-mineralogist Maso ably redirects Calandrino's desire toward a marvel closer to home, one found no further than the Mugnone River outside of Florence: the legendary heliotrope stone, which has the power to render its holder invisible.

In the second part of the tale, the painters Bruno and Buffalmacco (Bruno di Giovanni d'Olivieri and Buonamico di Martino) accompany Calandrino to the banks of the Mugnone in order to find the heliotrope. At the river's edge, Calandrino fervently stuffs his shirt full of rocks, hoping that at least one of them will turn out to be the elusive stone. When the folds of Calandrino's clothing reach capacity, Bruno and Buffalmacco suddenly pretend that they do not see him anymore, that he has become invisible. "Where is Calandrino?" they ask. Tricked

2 The *Decameron* is cited from the Italian text edited by Maurizio Fiorilla in Boccaccio, *Decameron*, ed. Quondam, Fiorilla, and Alfano; all English translations of that text are my own.

into believing he has discovered the heliotrope, Calandrino decides to return to the city to exploit his invisibility. His friends, still pretending not to see him, follow him home, pelting him with rocks the entire way. Evading the customs officials at the Florentine gates (who are in on the joke), Calandrino makes it home undetected, only to be upbraided by his wife Tessa for coming home late for lunch – a markedly domestic disenchantment. Enraged at his wife for robbing him of his newfound power (she both sees him and sees through him), he proceeds to beat her mercilessly; only the timely intervention of Bruno and Buffalmacco prevents the tale from taking a darker turn. After listening to him recount the day's events, Bruno and Buffalmacco convince Calandrino that he alone was at fault for not taking precautions against encountering women while in possession of the heliotrope, since their spell-breaking powers are well known. At the end of the tale, the pair leaves Calandrino dejected and defeated in a house full of useless rocks.

The novella of Calandrino and the heliotrope is one of the most memorable and felicitous in the *Decameron*. Showcasing the elaborate artistry of the painters as they manufacture a perfectly self-contained fictional universe, Boccaccio uses this tale to reflect upon his own artistry and fictions. In this respect, the novella recalls other key metaliterary tales that feature talented con artists, such as those of Ser Ciappelleto and Frate Cipolla.

The novella also signals a turning point in the collection as the *brigata* prepares to return from the spiritual recreation of storytelling in the countryside to the social realities of the city. In this tale, for the first time, Boccaccio introduces characters who will reappear in other stories (VIII.3, VIII.5, VIII.6, VIII.9, IX.3, IX.5), breaching the walls of the singular novella as well as the formal containers of the discrete days.[3]

---

3 The influence of the novella of Calandrino and the heliotrope exceeds even the confines of the *Decameron* itself; no other novella has enjoyed as rich an afterlife. In Novella 67 of Franco Sacchetti's *Il Trecentonovelle* (composed shortly after the *Decameron* at the end of the fourteenth century), the "elitropia di Calandrino" makes an important appearance within a novella that highlights the violence of the *beffa*. In the masterful Renaissance novella *Grasso legnaiuolo* (Fatty the Woodworker), the main character, having lost his identity and been transformed into another, asks himself, "Sarei io mai Calandrino?" In fact, the ways in which the superior artists Filippo Brunelleschi and Donatello manipulate the humbler craftsman Manetto (the eponymous "Fatty") as if he were pure material owe much to Boccaccio's novella. Finally, Bruno and Buffalmacco's management of space and perspective in the performance of their masterful prank contributed to the novella's enduring influence on sixteenth-century comic theatre, including Bibbiena's *La Calandra* and Machiavelli's *La Mandragola*. For more on "Fatty the Woodworker," see Albert Ascoli's wonderfully suggestive essay, "The History of a Story."

Moreover, the tales featuring Calandrino and the painters are all set in and around a Florentine locale, referred to repeatedly by the storytellers as "nostra città" [our city (VIII.3.4 and VIII.5.4; and cf. VIII.6.4, VIII.9.3, IX.5.6)], and the frequent passage of characters between city and countryside calls attention to the similar movements of the *brigata*. The characters in these tales, drawn from the urban and artisanal classes, are based on local historical figures from the recent past with whom the storytellers, and presumably contemporary readers, would have been familiar.[4] As the "wheel of the *Decameron*" turns homeward, fact and fiction begin to merge and the relation between them assumes new urgency.[5]

Because of its particular resonance across the *Decameron*, critics have long singled out *Decameron* VIII.3 as an exemplar of Boccaccio's artistry, and some of the most incisive criticism on the *Decameron* is dedicated to this novella. Among these rich and varying approaches, two fundamental lines of inquiry emerge: one focused on the problem of representation and the other on that of justice. Critics in the first category grapple with the contending realistic and fantastic aspects of the tale, the novella's engagement with visual culture, and how the story self-reflectively explores the nature of fiction and poetic language.[6] In the second category belong those critics who explore Calandrino's moral failings, the *beffa* as both a means for maintaining social consensus and a form of Dantean retaliatory punishment, and the gender politics between Calandrino and his wife.[7] My aim in this chapter is to put these

4 Biographical information on the painters is found in Bacci, "Gli affreschi di Buffalmacco"; Bellosi's chapter "Buffalmacco, pittore girovago," in *Buffalmacco e il Trionfo della Morte*, 68–73; Gilbert, "La devozione di Giovanni Boccaccio per gli artisti e l'arte"; and Battaglia Ricci, *Ragionare nel giardino*.

5 See Barolini, "The Wheel of the *Decameron*."

6 Giuseppe Mazzotta and Millicent Marcus brilliantly underline the metaliterary component of the tale, the status of the painters as masters of illusion, and the dangers inherent in believing too literally in fictions, including the fictions of the self. See Marcus's chapter "Mischief and Misbelief: The First Tale of Calandrino (VIII.3)," in *An Allegory of Form*, 79–92; and Mazzotta, "Games of Laughter." Creighton Gilbert, Norman Land, and Paul Watson have focused instead on the historical painters and painting in the tale, the implications of Calandrino's viewing of the ornate and illustrated tabernacle in the Florentine baptistry at the beginning of the novella, and the question of the relationship between literary and visual representation (*ut pictura poesis*). See Gilbert, "La devozione di Giovanni Boccaccio per gli artisti e l'arte"; Land, "Calandrino as Viewer"; and Watson, "The Cement of Fiction." See also Auerbach's chapter "Farinata and Cavalcante," in *Mimesis*, 174–202; and Baratto's chapter "La commedia," in *Realtà e stile nel Decameron*, 271–322.

7 For Giulio Ferroni and Michelangelo Picone, the first tale of Calandrino is an exemplary illustration of the social mechanisms of the *beffa*. See Ferroni, "Sulla struttura della beffa"; and Picone, "L'arte della beffa." Observing Calandrino

two strands of criticism in dialogue with each other by contextualizing the issues of representation raised by the tale in light of contemporaneous innovations in the "art" of policing.

Historians of crime describe a major shift in fourteenth-century Florence as its government moved from a communitarian form of policing to a more centralized model. Over the course of the century, surveillance and repression became crucial components of the Florentine city-state's ability to maintain social control.[8] Before 1350, it was still the responsibility of villages, parishes, and local corporations and guilds (who salaried their own security forces) to investigate, denounce, and even arrest their own. By the beginning of the fifteenth century, however, the Florentine police force was significantly enlarged and centralized, transformed into a professionalized standing army under the sole jurisdiction of the *Signoria*. In addition to this standing police force, the city appointed functionaries for each neighbourhood (*denuntiatores*) to spy and report back on local misdeeds and affixed special boxes (*tamburi*) to prominent public buildings into which secret, anonymous accusations could be deposited.[9]

In the *Decameron*, we find evidence for this more robust and expansive surveillance, which manifests itself in the ever-present city guards who populate the urban tales, conditioning characters' choices and affecting the outcomes of plotlines. For Calandrino, this surveillance

---

ritualistically and sadistically humiliated, transformed by the omnipotent tricksters Bruno and Buffalmacco into a thing – or rather, in this case, a no-thing – constitutes the viewing public (first those in on the prank, then the company of storytellers, and finally, implicitly, the readers as well) as a cohesive social group which identifies with the perpetrators and distances itself from the victim. Carlo Muscetta identifies the moralizing and satirical elements of the tale, in particular its condemnation of Calandrino as an avaricious social climber who cannot help but embody all the stereotypes of the rustic despite his desire for instant cosmopolitanism ("Boccaccio e la commedia dei cafoni"). Ronald Martinez teases out the network of allusions to Dante's poetry implicit in the martyrdom of Calandrino, especially to the disturbing vengeful fantasies of the *Rime petrose* (stony rhymes) (Martinez, "Calandrino and the Powers of the Stone"). On the *contrapasso*, see Holmes, "Trial by *Beffa*."

8 I recognize the anachronism of speaking of late medieval cities as "states" – since these governments lacked the centralization, sovereignty, and biopolitics that we generally associate with the modern state – but I also believe it remains the best word we have to convey their public nature and that more is lost than gained when we reach for a safer, anodyne substitute.

9 On shifting forms of policing in Trecento Italy, see Becker, "Changing Patterns of Violence and Justice"; Bowsky, "The Medieval Commune and Internal Violence"; Samuel Cohn, "Criminality and the State in Renaissance Florence"; Manikowska, "Il controllo sulle città"; Manikowska, "Polizia e servizi d'ordine a Firenze"; Zorzi, "Ordine pubblico e amministrazione della giustizia"; and Zorzi, "The Judicial System in Florence in the Fourteenth and Fifteenth Centuries."

is a persistent fact of life, as demonstrated when he announces that he has remarkably eluded the customs agents who usually want to *see* everything: "sapete quanto esser sogliano spiacevoli e noiosi que' guardiani a volere ogni cosa vedere" (you know how these tedious and bothersome guards usually want to see everything [VIII.3.60]). Indeed, Calandrino's first thought when he hears of the heliotrope's powers – to steal florins from the moneylenders in the public square, unobserved – can be seen as a psychological response to the new "scopic regime" that Marvin Trachtenberg identifies as dominating Florentine urbanism in the Trecento (Trachtenberg, *Dominion of the Eye*, 177). In this sense, Calandrino's adventure in invisibility participates in the wish-fulfilment that fuels Boccaccio's entire collection: to see and not be seen.

Despite its focus on discovering crime, the Florentine authority was still far from realizing the panoptic surveillance state that Michel Foucault famously describes in his analysis of post-Enlightenment policing. The shift toward centralization was a slow and gradual one, and medieval Florence still largely relied on a rotating security force drawn from individual neighbourhoods whose per capita numbers were modest compared to modern figures.[10] The *Decameron* is accordingly full of characters who elude detection. When the prostitute Fiordaliso studies the actions of Andreuccio in the market square without the latter ever realizing it, or when King Agilulf's stable boy secretly observes the sovereign's nightly habits so as to sleep with the queen (thereby coming dangerously close to reproducing the subversive actions of Gyges), they are effectively invisible to the police forces of their respective states (*Decameron* II.5.4–9, III.2.12).

Boccaccio and his readers would have been attuned to the zones of potential invisibility that still remained within the city, especially given the disintegration of civic order wrought by the plague. The *Decameron* opens, in fact, with an extended nightmarish vision of what happens to public order when the repressive forces, the ministers and executors of

10 It is not surprising, then, that whenever a character in the stories of the *Decameron* encounters a member of the local police force, Boccaccio feels the need to justify the encounter. His explanations include that the guards had been summoned by the noise of the crowd, that they happened to be around the corner because they were lying in ambush to catch a known criminal, and that, by pure chance, "per caso" (IV.6.31), they were walking by just at that time. Apparently, within the collective Florentine imagination, a police presence was not yet assumed as a constant, unexceptional reality, but instead was something fortuitous, novel even. On the actual numbers of the police in late medieval Florence, see especially the essays by Halina Manikowska cited above.

the law, are no longer vigilant. Because of the state's weakened condition, criminals and exiled outlaws can walk the city streets in broad daylight, in front of everyone's eyes, while remaining for all intents and purposes legally invisible.

The capacity of the sovereign state to oversee its entire citizenry turns out to be an elaborate fantasy – a fantasy that Boccaccio would have thoroughly absorbed reading Dante's *Commedia*. The sinners of Dante's infernal city are all relentlessly on display, trapped by the panoramic vantage point afforded to Dante's character (and subsequently to the Poet's readers). This point of view is nowhere more evident than in the episode in Cantos 24–5 of the *Inferno*, which describes the punishment of the thieves in the seventh pouch of Malebolge. Here, the naked sinners are bound and sexually violated by ghastly reptilian creatures, after which the sinners are themselves turned into the snakes and lizards with which they have just copulated. These humiliating bestial metamorphoses take place right before our eyes thanks to one of Dante's most ostentatious displays of ekphrasis. The terrified former thieves truly have no place to hide – or, as Dante memorably puts it, they are "sanza sperar pertugio o elitropia" [without hope of crevice or heliotrope (*Inf.* 24.93)].[11]

In medieval Florence, the threat of a panoptic inferno was no doubt an effective means for discouraging citizens from attempting to exploit any political invisibility. Boccaccio, however, by having his artist characters paint the would-be thief on the walls of readers' imaginations, prefers to showcase a less centralized form of imaginative deterrent. Like Emilia when narrating the novella of Simona and Pasquino (IV.7), Boccaccio is concerned with the afterlife of reputation, with *fama* and *infamia* and the image of oneself that the community preserves even after one's death. Rather than reminding his readers of the all-seeing eye of a sovereign God,[12] he reminds them of the decentralized, collective, and mobile eyes of their fellow citizens. As both producers and consumers of Calandrino's image, the participants in the *beffa* extend the reach of the surveillance apparatus with a brilliantly conceived and expertly executed shaming portrait, thereby dooming the invisible Calandrino to always be seen. (Indeed, we are given a bird's-eye view of the protagonist as he moves throughout the city – a perspective we retain even

11 Text and translations from the *Commedia* are from Dante, *The Divine Comedy*, translated by Robert Durling.

12 This all-seeing eye makes an appearance in the form of the all-seeing sun of *Decameron* VIII.7, in which the tyrannical scholar reappropriates this Dantean fantasy of panoptic control as revenge on the widow for spurning him.

after he enters his home at the end of the tale.) For their participation in fixing this portrait in the collective imaginary, the painters Bruno and Buffalmacco, the narrator Elissa, and the author Boccaccio can all be seen – each in their own way – as fulfilling the role of the *denuntiatores*.

If the judicial universe of Dante's otherworld can be seen as a cultural anticipation of centralized policing in Trecento Italy, Boccaccio opts for an alternative, primarily cooperative model. The successful implementation of the prank against Calandrino depends on a collaboration between two painters and two customs agents. It is only through the complicity of the guards, who conspire together with the artists to entrap a common victim, that Calandrino is definitively convinced that he did, in fact, become invisible. Moreover, Calandrino's hostility toward the guards and glee at escaping the gate tax expose the potential political-historical ramifications of his avarice. In addition to his unwillingness to share the stone or his riches with his fellow guildsmen, his tax evasion disrespects the common good in its manifestation as the *fiscus*, or public treasury. It is ultimately for neglecting this public good that Calandrino is publicly punished, in front of as many characters and readers as possible.

I will return to Calandrino's lack of interest in the *res publica* later in this chapter, when I analyse more closely his interaction with the customs agents. But first, to better understand how Boccaccio views the public role of art, we need to examine the most likely source for the tale's interwoven treatment of art, ethics, and mineralogy: Pliny the Elder's *Natural History*. To my knowledge only Paul Watson has explored the final books of Pliny's encyclopedic work as a source for the tales featuring Bruno, Buffalmacco, and Calandrino.[13] Yet not only does Boccaccio draw on Pliny's anecdotes about ancient painters in his portrayal of modern painters, as Watson has amply demonstrated, but he also adopts Pliny's moralizing perspective on the contrast between the use-value and the exchange-value of art. Above all, Boccaccio is influenced by Pliny's conception of the potential normativity of images, in particular how ancestral portraiture shaped behaviour both by reminding its viewers of their clan's dignity and reputation and by encouraging them to take care for their own future image. For Pliny, this primarily public

13 See Watson, "The Cement of Fiction," 51–5.

role of art had been replaced in his time by private decoration and the commodification of images in both painting and sculpture. In the next section, we will see how Boccaccio revives this lost normative art in a comic vein and for a popular audience.

From Roman *Imago* to Florentine *Beffa*

We have direct evidence of Boccaccio's interest in Pliny's *Natural History*: he both annotated and illustrated Petrarch's copy of the *Natural History* (Paris, Bibliothèque nationale de France, MS Latin 6802) and copied sections of the text into his private handbook known as the *Zibaldone Magliabechiano*.[14] Boccaccio probably did not see Petrarch's copy of Pliny before meeting with Petrarch in Milan in 1359, after the composition of most of the *Decameron*. Because of this, studies on Pliny's influence on Boccaccio have been limited to the latter's mature Latin works (*De casibus, De mulieribus, Genealogie deorum gentilium, De montibus*), after Boccaccio's supposed "conversion" toward Petrarchan humanism and away from vernacular writing.[15] Recently, scholars have begun to question the directionality of influence between Petrarch and Boccaccio, rejecting the notion of a one-way transmission from preceptor to disciple and reimagining the engagement instead as a series of exchanges between friends.[16] This understanding seems especially appropriate in the case of the *Natural History*, given that Pliny was one of the most popular authors of the Middle Ages rather than one of the ancients Petrarch claims to have rediscovered. Boccaccio, moreover, appears to have had access to at least one other manuscript of the *Natural History* in addition to Petrarch's copy. He drew materials from this other manuscript for various entries in *De montibus*. More significantly for our purposes, it has recently been confirmed that the

14 The manuscript is now Florence, Biblioteca Nazionale Centrale, MS Banco Rari 50. See Kirkham, "A Visual Legacy," 334–6; McHam, *Pliny and the Artistic Culture of the Italian Renaissance*; and especially Perucchi, "Boccaccio geografo lettore del Plinio petrarchesco."

15 See Barkan, *Unearthing the Past*, 91–102; Billanovich, "Nuovi autografi del Boccaccio," in *Petrarca e il primo umanesimo*, 142–57; and Cachey, "Between Text and Territory," 276–8.

16 For a refiguring of the relationship between Boccaccio and Petrarch and for Boccaccio's humanism in the *Decameron*, see Filosa and Flora, "Tracce di Seneca (e Giovenale) nel *Decameron*"; Rico, *Ritratti allo specchio*; Santagata, *Per moderne carte*, 246–70; Velli, "Il rapporto Petrarca-Boccaccio"; Velli, "La poesia volgare del Boccaccio e i *Rerum vulgarium fragmenta*"; Velli, *Petrarca e Boccaccio*; Velli, "Seneca nel *Decameron*"; and Zak, "Boccaccio and Petrarch."

sections from the *Natural History* he copied in his *Zibaldone* from 1350 to 1355 derive from a different textual tradition than that of Paris MS Latin 6802.[17] In light of these findings, it now seems prudent to consider the influence of Pliny on Boccaccio as a series of encounters rather than as one single, discrete contact. As I hope to show, the novella of Calandrino is one of the most important of these early encounters.

At least in the case of the heliotrope, scholars grant that Pliny's encyclopedia was a plausible source for Boccaccio,[18] typically referencing the following passage from the *Natural History*: "Here, moreover, we have quite the most blatant instance of effrontery on the part of the Magi, who say that when the heliotrope plant is joined to the stone and certain prayers are pronounced over them the wearer is rendered invisible."[19] These same scholars rarely quote this passage in its entirety, however, and almost never discuss it in depth. When we consider fully the tone and context of this source, we can see how Pliny's description of the heliotrope takes on new life in Boccaccio's novella.

Pliny is not neutrally reporting common lore about the heliotrope in this passage but specifically attacking the claims of the magicians (*magi*) – one of the most frequent targets of Pliny's ire in the *Natural History* – for their effrontery (*inpudentia*).[20] He considers their false notions about the heliotrope the ultimate, culminating example (*manifestissimum … exemplum*) of their perverse art, which he regards as always, at base, a ploy for their own enrichment. This outburst against the magicians occurs in the final book of the encyclopedic work, Book 37, which is entirely dedicated to gems. Here, and in the three previous books dealing with minerals, Pliny launches his most vehement attacks against contemporaries for their conspicuous consumption and addiction to precious metals and jewels. Because minerals provide the raw materials for paintings, sculpture, tableware, and jewellery, these books also contain long digressions on the history of ancient art, focusing on its decline from public utility to mere commodity. Deeply influenced by classical Stoicism, Pliny combines a critique of the abuses of nature

---

17 See Petoletti, "Boccaccio e Plinio il vecchio"; and Reeve, "The Text of Boccaccio's Excerpts from Pliny's *Natural History*."

18 See, most indicatively, Vittore Branca's note on the heliotrope in Boccaccio, *Decameron*, ed. Branca 1992, 905n2. See also Marcus, "Mischief and Misbelief," 86–7; Martinez, "Calandrino and the Powers of the Stone," 6–8; and Watson, "The Cement of Fiction," 51–2.

19 "Magorum inpudentiae vel manifestissimum in hac quoque exemplum est, quoniam admixta herba heliotropo, quibusdam additis precationibus, gerentem conspici negent" (Pliny, *Natural History* 37.60.165, 10:298–9).

20 On Pliny and magi, see Graf, *Magic in the Ancient World*, 49–56; and Janowitz, *Magic in the Roman World*, 13–16.

with an account of the decadence of art within contemporary Roman society.

Throughout the *Natural History*, Pliny contrasts the simplicity of the Age of Augustus with the decadence that has overtaken Roman life under the emperors Tiberius, Caligula, and Nero. At the beginning of each book, he draws a sharp distinction between *dignitas* and *luxuria*. According to his nostalgic ideology, everything was better when there was less.[21] Pliny reserves his most extreme attacks for those whose lust for gold and gems leads them to plunder the land. He describes mining as an almost sexual violation of Mother Earth, as men "penetrate her inner parts" [imus in viscera (33.1.2, 9:2–3)] in order to "seek a jewel merely to be worn upon a finger" [ut digito gestetur gemma petitur (2.63.158, 1:292–3)].

When it comes to art, this contemporary decadence manifests itself as a triumph of private decoration over the originally public functions of painting and sculpture. In his own time, Pliny laments, the prestige of public art has been overtaken by private collection and the fetishization of expensive materials. He especially objects to his generation's fervour for marble interiors, which he depicts graphically as bringing the "entrails" of the earth into the bedroom (36.1–4). In previous times, by contrast, the visual arts served to memorialize great men and deeds. Julius Caesar promoted the representation of public subjects in public spaces, and artists like Apelles and Protogenes "did not decorate walls merely for the owners of property." Rather, through their art they "kept watch [*excubabat*] over cities." As a consequence of his social utility, the painter was considered a "res communis terrarum" [the common property of the world].[22]

The chief cause of art's decline, as we see in Pliny's polemical introduction to the history of painting at the beginning of Book 35, is that the practice of ancestral portraiture – the transmission of a "living effigy" – has fallen into disuse:

> And first we shall say what remains to be said about painting, an art that was formerly illustrious, at the time when it was in high demand

21 "Omnia ergo meliora tunc fuere, cum minor copia" (Pliny, *Natural History* 35.50, 9:298).

22 "Sed nulla gloria artificum est nisi qui tabulas pinxere. eo venerabilior antiquitatis prudentia apparet. non enim parietes excolebant dominis tantum nec domos uno in loco mansuras, quae ex incendiis rapi non possent. casa Protogenes contentus erat in hortulo suo; nulla in Apellis tectoriis pictura erat. nondum libebat parietes totos tinguere; omnium eorum ars urbibus excubabat, pictorque res communis terrarum erat" (Pliny, *Natural History* 35.37.118, 9:348–9; Rackham's translation has been slightly modified).

> with kings and nations and when it ennobled others whom it deigned to transmit to posterity [*posteris tradere*]. But at the present time it has been entirely ousted by marbles, and indeed finally also by gold, and not only to the point that whole party-walls are covered – we have also marble engraved with designs and embossed marble slabs carved in wriggling lines to represent objects and animals … The painting of portraits, used to transmit through the ages extremely correct likenesses of persons, has entirely gone out. Bronze shields are now set up as monuments with a design in silver, with a dim outline of men's figures; heads of statues are exchanged [*permutantur*] for others (for some time now sarcastic epigrams have even circulated about this phenomenon): so universally is a display of material preferred to a recognizable likeness of one's own self. And in the midst of all this, people tapestry the walls of their picture-galleries with old pictures, and they prize likenesses of strangers, while as for themselves they imagine that the honor only consists in the price for their heir to break up the statue and haul it out of the house with a noose. Consequently, nobody's likeness lives and they leave behind them portraits that represent their money, not themselves [*itaque nullius effigie vivente imagines pecuniae, non suas, relinquunt*].[23]

No longer do Romans preserve the likenesses of their ancestors or concern themselves with the posthumous lives of their own images. In lieu of this ancient genealogical practice, in which accurate mimesis was highly valued because of the real connection between person and portrait within the collective memory of aristocratic Roman families, images are treated as any other commodity. Since the rich fill their houses with images of strangers, it no longer matters whether the portraits are accurate or not. Similarly, the body parts of sculptures can be amputated and then exchanged at will, since no one remembers who these statues – indifferently Greek or Roman – were originally meant to be.

---

23 "primumque dicemus quae restant de pictura, arte quondam nobili – tunc cum expeteretur regibus populisque – et alios nobilitante, quos esset dignata posteris tradere, nunc vero in totum marmoribus pulsa, iam quidem et auro, nec tantum ut parietes toti operiantur, verum et interraso marmore vermiculatisque ad effigies rerum et animalium crustis … imaginum quidem pictura, qua maxime similes in aevum propagabantur figurae, in totum exolevit. aerei ponuntur clipei argentea facie, surdo figurarum discrimine; statuarum capita permutantur, volgatis iam pridem salibus etiam carminum. adeo materiam conspici malunt omnes quam se nosci, et inter haec pinacothecas veteribus tabulis consuunt alienasque effigies colunt, ipsi honorem non nisi in pretio ducentes, ut frangat heres forasque detrahat laqueo. itaque nullius effigie vivente imagines pecuniae, non suas, relinquunt" (Pliny, *Natural History* 35.1.2–2.5, 9:260–3).

The difference between then and now in Pliny's historiography can be summarized as the difference between *tradere* and *permutare*, between art as a vehicle for transmitting memory and art as commerce.[24] It is worth pointing out before returning to Boccaccio's treatment of contemporary painters and painting that Pliny's positive account of public art contrasts with the views of Stoic philosophers, such as Seneca and Juvenal, who explicitly mock the aristocracy for its attachment to ancestral images and portraiture. For Pliny, however, the collective imaginary is sustained by that attachment and cannot be wished away without serious political harm. Within his highly Ciceronian adaptation of Stoicism, focused on the public good, images remain fundamental because they are normative.[25] They stare down at you from the walls, reproaching you while simultaneously inspiring a "love of virtue" out of concern for your own depiction in posterity. Ultimately it is this loss of a *ius imaginum* that most preoccupies Pliny – the fact that we no longer have images "keeping watch" over us.

~

From the outset of the Calandrino tales, Boccaccio raises the question of what gives art value. When we first encounter Calandrino, he is staring in rapt attention at the painted shutters (executed by Lippo di Benevieni) and marble inlay supporting the tabernacle in the Baptistery of San Giovanni.[26] Commissioned by the wool guild of the Calimala, this ornate devotional artifact resides at the intersection of a complex network of religious, artistic, and economic discourses.[27]

---

24 On the art of memory in Pliny, see Sorcha, "Imaging Memory." For the tension between art as commodity and art as genealogy, see Uberman, "The Molding Image."

25 For the condemnation of images by Seneca and Juvenal in contrast with the more accommodating stance of Cicero and Pliny, see Citroni Marchetti, "Iuvare mortalem," esp. 133–4; and Citroni Marchetti, *Plinio il Vecchio e la tradizione del moralismo romano*, 242–55.

26 On the significance of Calandrino's gaze, see Land, "Calandrino as Viewer"; Marcus, "Mischief and Misbelief," 86–90; Martinez, "Calandrino and the Powers of the Stone," 12–21; and Mazzotta, "Games of Laughter," 120–4.

27 On the painting and marble decorating the tabernacle, see Gilbert, "La devozione di Giovanni Boccaccio per gli artisti e l'arte," 145–63; Land, "Calandrino as Viewer"; Sapori, *Una compagnia di Calimala ai primi del Trecento;* Neri Lusanna, "L'antico arredo presbiteriale e il fonte del Battistero"; Valentier, "Tino di Camaino in Florence"; and Watson, "The Cement of Fiction."

As a result of this confluence, readers are temporarily left to wonder at the source of Calandrino's absorption. Is he mesmerized by the miraculous powers of the Eucharist housed within the tabernacle, the perspectival illusionism of the painting and bas-reliefs, or the precious materials used in the construction of these adornments? To put it in the terms employed to depict Giotto's rediscovery of ancient verisimilitude: is Calandrino evaluating the tabernacle with "lo 'ntelletto de' savi" [the mind of the learned] or with the vulgar "occhi degl'ignoranti" [eyes of the ignorant (*Decameron* VI.5.6)]?[28] Judging from his subsequent reaction to Maso's account of the two virtuous stones that can be found outside of Florence, it is likely that Calandrino belongs to the latter category of undiscerning viewers, that his appreciation of the tabernacle is limited to its brilliant, material surface. (It is no coincidence that the name *Calandrino* derives from the diminutive of *calandro* [pipit]; he is a small bird dazzled by shiny appearances.) As we come to see, Calandrino shows no interest in how the mineral world might be fashioned to create a socially useful form of art, but instead values nature's marvels only as opportunities for private gain.

Although it is often overlooked in the scholarship, the first virtuous stone Maso describes to Calandrino is not the heliotrope but a variety of sandstone found in the neighbouring hills of Settignano and Montici.[29] This stone was known as *macigno* because it was primarily used to fashion millstones, *macine*. In fact, once *macigno* has been transformed into a *macina*, Maso explains, it possesses the "magical" property of being able to grind wheat into flour. Despite its social utility, *macigno* is ubiquitous around Florence and thus undervalued, "poco prezzata" (VIII.3.19), for the same reason that emeralds are said to be undervalued in Bengodi (or in Pliny's India).[30]

---

28 The portrait of Calandrino dazzled before the tabernacle can be seen as a forerunner to Petrarch's depiction of a personified Gaudium, who is similarly bewitched by the surface appearance of art objects, in *De remediis utriusque Fortunae*, a work in direct dialogue with Pliny's writing about art. See Giulia Perucchi's important introduction in *Petrarca e le arti figurative*.

29 The millstone makers in Montici were regarded enough to have formed their own guild, with statutes and elected consuls. In this light, Calandrino's rejection of millstone can be seen as his first rejection of corporatism. On the millstone makers, see Najemy, *A History of Florence*, 41.

30 According to Pliny, there is a greater demand for copper and lead in India than there is for emeralds and pearls because of India's abundance of precious stones: "India neque aes neque plumbum habet gemmisque ac margaritis suis haec permutat" (*Natural History* 34.163).

The other locally available virtuous stone discussed by Maso is of course the heliotrope, which has the power to make one not seen where one is not: "non è da alcuna altra persona veduto dove non è" (VIII.3.20). Although this one-sentence description is both nonsensical and scant, especially compared to Maso's excursus on millstone, Calandrino is instantly enthralled. Grasping at once the commodity-value of the heliotrope, he cannot wait to privatize the shared magic of Bengodi by possessing the stone for himself and putting it in his money-purse ("mettercela nella scarsella"). His lip service to the powers of both stones notwithstanding, it is clear that Calandrino cares only about the heliotrope: "Gran virtù sono queste: ma questa seconda dove si truova?" [These stones have marvelous powers, but where does one find this second one? (VIII.3.21)].

The harnessing of *macigno* for a socially beneficial purpose exemplifies the ideal relationship between nature and art as conceived by Pliny. It also recalls the elaborately constructed garden described in the introduction to Day Three, where a stream of water originating in an engraved marble fountain finishes its course by spinning two water mills. But for Calandrino, the ready availability of sandstone renders it practically worthless. Even after listening to a very Plinian contrast between, on the one hand, the harmonious alignment of Nature's gifts with Man's needs and, on the other, the senseless capriciousness of the marketplace, Calandrino still opts for exchange-value over use-value. When, at the end of the tale, Bruno and Buffalmacco find Calandrino with a house full of rocks, their quip "Che è questo, Calandrino? Vuoi tu murare?" [What's all this, Calandrino? Are you going to build a wall? (VIII.3.55)] is thus both sardonic and telling. Calandrino's scarce commodity has undergone a tragicomic conversion back into common utility.

Despite his apparent disregard for *macine*, we learn later in the tale that our protagonist lives right next to Canto alla Macine, a street corner named after an ancient mill that stood on the banks of the Mugnone (at the modern-day intersection of via San Gallo and via Guelfa). Calandrino's street address would thus have reminded Boccaccio's readers of Florence's recent urban past, before the Mugnone was diverted to make way for new, more encompassing walls, thereby greatly expanding the city's perimeter into the neighbouring suburban countryside. As a new immigrant himself, Calandrino is one of the "nuove genti" [new peoples (VIII.3.4)] who made that expansion necessary. Just like the "gente nuova" [new people] Dante criticizes in the *Inferno*, with their "sùbiti guadagni" [immediate gains (*Inf.* 16.73)], Calandrino believes his newfound status depends on "arricchire subitamente" [getting rich immediately (*Decameron* VIII.3.29)] rather than on civic duty.[31] Finally, the whole reason Calandrino wants to get rich quick is so he can quit painting, an art which he compares to sliming the walls all day like a snail, "senza avere tutto dí a schiccherare le mura a modo che fa la lumaca" (ibid.). For Calandrino, painting is not creative work intended for posterity and for the benefit of his community; it is merely labour for hire.

Enlarging our purview to include the other tales featuring Bruno and Buffalmacco, it is easy to discern the moralizing influence of Pliny (and other Roman Stoics, especially Seneca) in these other *novelle* as well. The painters, despite their poverty, have achieved a degree of Stoic or at least Epicurean detachment: they care nothing for the world and thus live happily, "meno che alcuni altri del mondo curassero e più lieti vivessono" (VIII.9.8).[32] The victims of Bruno and Buffalmacco's pranks, on the other hand, display all the decadent traits of Pliny's contemporaries, and are thus easily seduced by materialism and false magic.[33] Calandrino is a greedy would-be thief, entranced by exotic gems and focused on expanding his private property. Another victim, Master Simone the doctor, believes in his inherent superiority because he wears scarlet robes and expensive furs; he is swayed by verbal descriptions of luxuriance, by gold and silver and expensive tableware, delicate victuals, and the lure of faraway lands.[34] He commissions the painters to decorate his house with

31 On the connection between paying taxes and citizenship (especially for immigrants from the countryside) and the seriousness with which the Italian cities policed and punished tax evaders, see Vallerani, "Fiscalità e limiti dell'appartenenza alla città in età comunale"; and Vallerani, "La cittadinanza pragmatica." For the specific case of Florence, see Tanzini, "I forestieri e il debito pubblico."

32 In this respect, they are both true heirs of Pliny's golden-age painters, who are described as living simply despite their fame and public service, and true disciples of Giotto, whose inner character and talent are deliberately contrasted in *Decameron* VI.5 with his humble outward appearance and worldly possessions (ugliness, old horse, peasant clothes).

33 The exotic medical and magical concoctions, abortifacients, the "gibberish" of incantations, writing as a charm, and of course, the marvellous virtues of certain gems that Pliny derides appear to provide source material for various set-ups instigated by Bruno and Buffalmacco and are reappropriated as instruments of deception in the Calandrino tales. On magic in the Calandrino stories, see Cottino-Jones, "Magic and Superstition in Boccaccio's *Decameron*."

34 Just as Pliny at once amasses an encyclopedic universe of wondrous lore while strategically interjecting his personal scepticism and sardonic disapproval, Boccaccio's metanarrators luxuriate in Plinian depictions of Bengodi and *andare in*

private frescoes – a decadent practice Pliny abhors – yet lacks the discernment to recognize the illusory wounds that Bruno and Buffalmacco cunningly paint on their own bodies. In this, Simone is not unlike the animals who cannot tell a painting from the real thing in Pliny's famous anecdotes about ancient art.[35]

Pliny's critique of a largely private, decorative, consumer-driven experience of art is revisited in the tales involving the painters. But what about his more positive assessment of art's public role and the painter as a "common good"? Does Boccaccio provide any modern analogies in the Calandrino tales that would correspond to the ethical uses of painting in ancient Rome? At first glance it would appear not. For Pliny, the decline of public art in Rome was directly related to the neglect of mimetic representation in his time. Once the worth of an art object was located in its value as a commodity, the accuracy of its likeness no longer mattered. In *Decameron* VI.5, Boccaccio celebrates Giotto for having revived the ancient art of pictorial verisimilitude, which had been buried for centuries under the errors of an ignorant public enamoured with mere surface appearances. Yet this renaissance is only partial: in the novella's depiction of the recovery of ancient mimesis, no mention is made of its original educative function. In contrast with the philological reconstruction of Roman *imagines* that we find in the Sala Virorum Illustrium in Padua – perhaps directly influenced by Petrarch – or even in the lost cycle of famous men and women that Giotto himself painted for King Robert of Anjou's palace in Naples, the iconoclastic mercantile milieu of the Florentine novella has no use for exemplary images of heroic ancestors.[36]

At the same time, the *beffa* executed by the painters is itself a masterful work of art, whose canvas is the entire Florentine cityscape. As such, it can be viewed as Boccaccio's civic and comic answer to Pliny's aristocratic and heroic *ius imaginum*. The normative power of the prank operates on two levels. First, it supplements the punitive function

---

corso while using comic discourse (double negation, nonsense words, estrangement of the mundane) to telegraph their mastery over the content of their own speech.

35 In one example, Pliny gives an account of a horse-painting competition, judged by horses, who only react to Apelles's image (*Natural History* 35.95). See also *Natural History* 35.23 and 35.65–6 for further examples of animals deceived by painted representations of nature.

36 See McHam, *Pliny and the Artistic Culture of the Italian Renaissance*, 71–6; and di Simone, "Giotto, Petrarca e il tema degli uomini illustri." Fera, "I *fragmenta de viris illustribus*," is sceptical about Petrarch's influence on the Paduan cycle, which was destroyed by a fire and completely redone in the sixteenth century.

of the state by retributively shaming Calandrino in front of an ever-expanding audience. Second, the prank serves as a deterrent for those who observe it. While laughing at Calandrino exposed may provide a momentary release from one's own vulnerability, it ultimately reaffirms the compass of an internalized police force. As a vernacularized reinvention of a Roman *imago*, the portrait of Calandrino keeps watch over us.[37]

Calandrino is the ideal target for Bruno and Buffalmacco because, even when he is not being actively pranked, his performance of citizenship is risible. In his superficial playacting, the urbanized rustic believes that the external trappings of a bourgeois lifestyle – wealth, household management, and a country estate – make for a convincing portrayal of the citizen. Like a pre-Giottesque painting, his self-portrait lacks vitality, relying too heavily on stereotyped compositions and showy appearances (in stark contrast with Boccaccio's portrait of Giotto himself in VI.5). To put this social aspirant back in his place, Bruno and Buffalmacco merely need to accentuate his personality tics by providing him a venue for his bumbling performances.[38] Ultimately, the *beffa* only reproduces on a grander scale Calandrino's first action in the novella, when he eavesdrops on Maso's discourse about virtuous stones while erroneously believing he is invisible.

As a form of violence perpetrated against one's persona, the *beffa* has several essential characteristics in common with the Italian communal tradition of *pittura infamante*, in which the city-state commissioned humiliating portraits of accused criminals to be painted on public buildings and city walls, accompanied by the subjects' real names. These defaming portraits were intended to injure the image of a culprit who was otherwise unavailable in the flesh, most often because he or she simply refused to show up for court. In other words, the portraits compensated for, or at least supplemented, the state's limited ability to physically oversee its citizens – a role similar to that of the *beffa*.

---

37 Compare *Decameron* I.8 and Guiglielmo Borsiere's proposed portrait of *Cortesia* for Erminio de' Grimaldi's house, which shames the nouveau riche Erminio into changing his ways and combines the shaming portrait with the comic normativity of the novella. Similarly, Bruno and Buffalmacco's satirical paintings of personified Lent and the Battle of the Cats and Mice in Maestro Simone's dining room in VIII.9 can be seen as reproducing the social poetics that underlie their prank.

38 On the pranks perpetuated against Calandrino as a form of social conservatism, see Ferroni, "Sulla struttura della beffa," 72–9.

Critics have long noted that the darkly humorous poetics of Dante's *contrapasso* appear influenced by the state-commissioned irony of *pittura infamante*.[39] In turn, many scholars have observed that the logic of the *beffa* in the Calandrino tales owes a substantial debt to the poetic justice of the *contrapasso*.[40] Yet rather than simply being influenced by the *contrapasso*, Boccaccio re-secularizes its retaliatory art by creating an animated, three-dimensional variant of *pittura infamante*. The moving panels of this living theatre are populated by fellow citizens, and the infamy it portends belongs wholly to the mechanisms of worldly justice as actually practised in Boccaccio's time. Just as the city of Florence hired artists to paint embarrassing depictions of its disgraced citizens on the city walls, Bruno and Buffalmacco's public deconstruction of Calandrino is a normative portrait that will remain in the collective memory. In this respect, the artists can be seen as collaborating with the state by proactively policing their own.

This collaboration is most evident in the painters' partnership with the customs agents. Calandrino's interaction with the customs guards at the Florentine gates is crucial for bringing out both the public nature of the prank and the political consequences of his anti-social behaviour. In the next section, we will examine Calandrino's illegal border crossing within the context of rampant tax fraud in Boccaccio's time. Only once we comprehend the threat that this widespread practice posed to Florence's financial solvency can we fully appreciate the anxieties that the novella raises about what happens when citizens stop believing in their own fictions.

The Guards and the Gabelles

In a novella characterized by proper nouns and direct dialogue, the customs guards at the gates are never named and never speak. They are identified by their office, by what they do, rather than by who they are, and critics have largely ignored them on account of this facelessness. Yet the role of these police officers within the narrative is as vital as their function within the Florentine bureaucracy.

---

39 Defendants accused of graft, for example, were typically depicted with money-bags hanging prominently around their necks. See Milani, *L'uomo con la borsa al collo*, 219–40; Ortalli, *Pingatur in palatio* and Steinberg, *Dante and the Limits of the Law*, 28–40.

40 Holmes, "Trial by *Beffa*," 361–2; Martinez, "Calandrino and the Powers of the Stone," 14–18.

When Calandrino arrives at the Gates of San Gallo, the guards pretend not to see him, and let him through. They are in on the joke and play along, having been previously informed about it by Bruno and Buffalmacco. Without their assistance, the *beffa* would have been immediately foiled, just as it risks being unmasked when Calandrino reenters the domestic sphere and Tessa sees him.

After Calandrino passes through the gates, the narrative effectively splits into two independent, concurrent scenes. In one of these, Calandrino continues on home, supposedly still invisible, until he is discovered by his wife. In the other, Bruno and Buffalmacco unload the rocks they were carrying and tarry with the guards, laughing together with them at Calandrino's expense. This shared, celebratory laughter at a would-be thief is a striking – and rare – moment in the *Decameron* of total complicity between population and police. By temporarily allowing the surveillance apparatus they implement to be employed for collective amusement, the guards humanize the institution while lending an official endorsement to the shaming punishment it helps effect.

The institutional stamping of the prank gets replayed at the end of the tale, when Bruno and Buffalmacco, having entered Calandrino's house, accuse him of abandoning them down by the river as part of a practical joke that *he* perpetrated against *them*. To prove that he did indeed become invisible and thus was not playing a trick on them, Calandrino describes how he passed through the gates undetected by the guards:

> E dicovi che, entrando alla porta con tutte queste pietre in seno che voi vedete qui, niuna cosa mi fu detta, ché sapete quanto esser sogliano spiacevoli e noiosi que' guardiani a volere ogni cosa vedere. (VIII.3.60)

> [And I'll tell you another thing: as I was coming in at the city gate, loaded up to the eyebrows with all these stones you see here, nobody said a word to me, and you know for yourselves what those customs men are like, with their tedious and offensive manner of demanding to see everything.]

For Calandrino, it is the city guards' inaction that seals his faith in the powers of the heliotrope. They didn't see or say anything. This wondrous suspension of state power renders Calandrino's invisibility finally and definitively real for him. At this point, there is no turning back for our protagonist; consecrated by the guards' performance, art has overtaken nature. His wife's deflating remarks may break the spell, but they cannot reveal the con.

While Bruno and Buffalmacco view the guards as willing collaborators, Calandrino perceives them as a hostile, repressive force – or "spiacevoli e noiosi" [tedious and offensive (VIII.3.60)], as he puts it. He especially resents their surveillance: they always want to see everything, "ogni cosa vedere" (ibid.). Indeed, in many ways, Calandrino's greatest victory is that he walked through the gates without being stopped by the customs officers, and yet nowhere else in the story does the magic of the heliotrope come closer to resembling common fraud. In light of the vital importance of direct taxes for the Florentine economy, many of Calandrino's neighbours would have considered his avoidance of the gate tax a serious offence. It turns out that Calandrino is not simply a grasping friend and abusive husband; he is also, and maybe even foremost, a bad citizen.

To learn why not paying the gate tax was such a dire charge, we need first to understand the absolutely vital role that indirect taxes played in Florentine finances. The primary role of the "guardie dei gabellieri" was to ensure collection of the *gabelle*, duties levied on consumption and exchange.[41] The gabelles were the commune's major source of income, accounting for 75 to 85 per cent of all revenue after the abolition of the *estimo*, or direct assessment on property, in 1315. The most lucrative gabelle was the gate tax on all imports and exports. To give an idea of how crucial this tax was for the city's finances, the chronicler Giovanni Villani estimated that nearly one-third (90,000 florins) of the city's total annual income (300,000 florins) derived from this gate tax alone (Villani, *Nuova cronica* 12.92).

The Florentine government depended on funds from the gabelles for a range of activities, most notably the financing of its military campaigns and the repayment of its creditors. In times of economic crisis, it thus needed to raise the prices of the gabelles; during the course of the Trecento, rates of the gabelles fluctuated wildly. Tariffs reached an all-time high at mid-century when the gate gabelles more than doubled. Not surprisingly, these increases were fiercely resented by the impoverished populace, especially since they were often accompanied by an increase in the prices of wine and other goods. The nearly intolerable burden imposed on the more humble members of Florentine society by the shift from direct to indirect taxes was one of the primary sources of social unrest throughout the fourteenth century and culminated in the Ciompi revolt.[42] Given that the injustice of the gabelles was one of

41 On direct taxes, the gabelles, and the gate tax, see Franceschi, "Medici Economic Policy"; Molho, "Communal Income"; Ronciere, "Florence in the Fourteenth Century"; and Sapori, "La gabella delle porte di Firenze."

42 On the gabelles as a source of social tension and political change, see Najemy, *History of Florence*, 118–23, 132–9, 157–60; and Ronciere, "Florence in the Fourteenth Century."

the rallying calls of the minor guildsmen and unincorporated workers, contemporary readers of this tale may well have perceived Calandrino's rumblings about the bothersome guards as distinctly more consequential than we do.

Despite continual increases in tariffs throughout the fourteenth century, overall receipts for Florence's communal budget remained stagnant. The problem was one of arrears. Genuine poverty, negligence, and fraud made collection a constant preoccupation of the Florentine government. The most prevalent and damaging instances of fraud occurred at the city gates, where citizens invented a myriad of devices for avoiding the onerous import and export taxes. Others sought alternative ways into the city to circumvent the legal routes into the urban centre. The busiest and most lucrative of these trade routes was the one that led from the northern gate, Porta San Gallo, directly into the Mercato Vecchio, the same road Calandrino traverses while supposedly invisible.

Boccaccio himself would have had first-hand knowledge of this financial crisis from his experience of working for the Florentine government. Recently discovered archival documents have revealed that Boccaccio's political and diplomatic activity was much more extensive than previously believed. We now know, for example, that in 1348, the fictional date of the *Decameron*, Boccaccio served a four-month turn as supervisor over all indirect taxes for his district.[43] In his capacity as *dominus gabellorum*, the author-turned-civic-official would no doubt have had frequent dealings with the *gabellieri* and would have been familiar as well with those who tried to trick these agents and defraud the state. One of the primary concerns of the Florentine commune at this time was how to police and punish fiscal evasion.

Although played for laughs, Calandrino's illegal border crossing is in fact a serious crime that civic authorities, Boccaccio included, would have recognized as part of a systematic threat to Florentine financial solvency. On the most literal level, Calandrino walks through customs without paying for what he believes is a cartload of precious stones. (Precious stones and gems are explicitly mentioned by the Florentine statutes as being subject to taxation.) But Boccaccio is concerned not so much with the transgression itself as with the attitude that makes such a transgression possible: the lack of belief in and subsequent

43 See Armstrong, Daniels, and Milner, "Boccaccio as a Cultural Mediator," 6–15; and also the "Elenco dei documenti" in Regnicoli, "Documenti su Giovanni Boccaccio," 394–402.

disobedience to the fictions of state. Because he is so focused on enriching his private wealth and property, his *res propria*, Calandrino shows no interest in the commonweal, the *res publica*.

Scholars typically identify Calandrino's gullibility as the moral flaw for which he ends up the butt of the practical jokes in Days Eight and Nine, but in truth Calandrino believes both too much and too little. Calandrino credits Maso's depiction of fantastical Bengodi and the magical heliotrope simply because it is recounted to him with a straight face. But the "simplicità" (VIII.3.4) that makes Calandrino such an easy mark for Bruno and Buffalmacco signifies more than mere credulousness. He utterly fails to appreciate the human capacity to remake reality through language, the very power Bruno and Buffalmacco exploit when they pelt him with rocks *as if* he were not still in front of them. Even though as a newly minted citizen he would himself have been considered an *as if* citizen (*tamquam*, *velut*, or *sicut civis* according to the jurists), Calandrino lacks the sophistication necessary to play along *as if* the abstractions of state were real. In the end, he is punished for a *failure* of imagination and, in particular, for not trusting in the reality of what medieval jurists called fictive persons.

According to these jurists, any collective – from minor guild to the entire populace – could be represented as a fictive person. This "living corpus" was variously identified as a *persona ficta*, *persona imaginaria*, *persona representata*, or even, most interestingly in the present context, a *persona invisibilis*.[44] In our novella, the customs guards derive their authority from and protect the rights of a personified *res publica*, especially in its manifestation as the public treasury, the immortal and inalienable body of the *fiscus*.[45] But Calandrino does not see this invisible person looming behind the individual city guards, who remain for him nothing more than a nuisance. He can imagine himself instantly transformed into an invisible man, but not represented by an invisible person; he believes in the materialism of magic, not in the abstraction of a corporate body. It is because of this scepticism in the "public thing" that Calandrino can blithely boast about sneaking across the Florentine border under the nose of the municipal police, unconcerned, or at least unaware, of the harm he potentially causes the corporate body of the *fiscus*.

---

44 On fictive persons, see Kantorowicz, "The Sovereignty of the Artist"; and Thomas, *Fictio legis*.

45 See Kantorowicz's chapter "Christus-Fiscus" in *The King's Two Bodies*, 164–92.

Calandrino as a *res nullius in bonis*

The punitive element of the prank against Calandrino is fully intelligible only when we take into consideration his indifference toward the common good. The ironic logic of his punishment depends on a legal distinction between two types of ownerless goods, *res nullius* (no one's things) and *res nullius in bonis* (things in no one's property). Calandrino is fixated on the heliotrope because he views it as a *res nullius*, a still-to-be-owned good that he longs to be the first to seize, to occupy. Obsessed with becoming a first taker, he ignores, even while he takes advantage of, those other unowned goods (*res nullius in bonis*) that the state has set aside for the enjoyment of all, including the city streets, gates, and walls. In an especially apt *contrapasso*, Calandrino is himself fated to be enjoyed collectively as a public good – first by the other characters in the tales, then by the storytellers of the *brigata*, and eventually by the readers of the novella.

Although Roman law was primarily concerned with private, individual ownership, jurists recognized that not everything useful for human life could be bought and sold. Following a longstanding philosophical tradition, they allowed, for example, that air, flowing water, the seas, and the shores were by natural law "common to all men."[46] Pliny is certainly playing on this concept of universal access when he depicts the ancient painters as "res communis terrarum" [the common property of the world (*Natural History* 35.118, 9:348–9)].

More important from a legal perspective were those goods that the law actively subtracted from the marketplace and "sanctified." The Roman jurist Gaius divides all goods into two essential categories: "Some things are subject to divine right, others to human. Those subject to divine right are, for example, sacred things and religious

46 In addition to Justinian's *Digest* 1.8 and *Institutes* 2.1, Boccaccio could have found the concept of *res communes* in Cicero, *De officiis* 1.16.51–2, pp. 54–7, where Cicero criticizes the refusal to share those common goods which cost nothing to give. It is especially suggestive for our understanding of collective storytelling as a shared good that, in addition to water and fire, Cicero includes honest counsel (*consilium fidele*) among the common goods Nature orders to be given freely (*De officiis* 1.16.52, pp. 56–7). For the vexed history of the natural rights of *res communes* in potential opposition to civically ordained *res publicae*, see Perruso, "The Development of the Doctrine of *Res Communes*"; and Robbe, *La differenza sostanziale tra "res nullius" e "res nullius in bonis."*

things. Sanctified things [*res sanctae*], such as the city walls and gates, are in a certain degree subject to divine right. For what is subject to divine right is not anyone's property [*nullius in bonis*]."[47] The emperor himself created these *res nullius in bonis* when he consecrated them to the gods; these unownable goods could be "sacred" and "religious" things, such as churches and burial grounds, but also, by analogy, the "sanctified" resources of the city's common infrastructure. These venerable civic structures were inalienable not as a form of corporate property (under certain circumstances the state's assets could in fact be bought or sold), but because they were deliberately set aside for public use, *usibus publicis relictae*. Since they belonged to no one, everyone could use them.[48]

As the civic equivalent of the sacred, *res sanctae* were inviolable. According to the Roman jurist Ulpian, the reason they were considered "sanctified" was that violating them resulted in a "sanction": "Properly speaking, we use the term 'sanctified' [*sancta*] of objects which are neither sacred nor profane but which are confirmed by some kind of sanction."[49] The classic illustration of this form of sanctity was the city walls; any attempt to transgress them by scaling them or entering or exiting the city other than through the gates was considered an "abomination" punishable by death. Indeed, it was said that no less a figure than Remus was killed when he tried to climb over the city walls. This oft-repeated foundational myth was a favourite of medieval jurists who

47 "summa rerum diuisio in duos articulos deducitur: nam aliae sunt diuini iuris, aliae humani. diuini iuris sunt ueluti res sacrae et religiosae. sanctae quoque res, ueluti muri et portae, quodammodo diuini iuris sunt. quod autem diuini iuris est, id nullius in bonis est" (Justinian, *Digest* 1.8.1, 1:24, translation slightly modified). Citations and translations from the *Digest* are based on *The Digest of Justinian*, edited by Mommsen and Kreuger, translated by Watson. In Justinian's *Institutes* 2.1, the potential *res* not held by private persons were further divided into *res publica, res communes, res universitatis*, and *res nullius*. There is some ambiguity between the passage in the *Digest* and that of the *Institutes* that was compounded by the medieval commentary and gloss. At the level of generalization necessary for this essay, however, the important point is that Roman law doctrine provided for a concept of goods that could not be seized, sold, or possessed privately. For a diachronic history of these tangled set of descriptors, see the accounts in Perruso, "The Development of the Doctrine of *Res Communes*"; and Robbe, *La differenza sostanziale tra "res nullius" e "res nullius in bonis."*

48 For the concept of *res nullius in bonis*, see Thomas, "La valeur des choses."

49 "Proprie dicimus sancta, quae neque sacra neque profana sunt, sed sanctione quadam confirmata" (*Digest* 1.8.9.3, 1:26).

sought to valorize the public majesty of, and duties owed to, their wall-enclosed city-states.[50]

While sacred, religious, and sanctified things can never be owned, *res nullius* (without the qualifier *in bonis*) are unowned only because they have not *yet* been seized and taken into possession.[51] From their inception, the *res nullius* await their proper owner; in this way, they are the exact opposite of *res nullius in bonis*, which are decreed exempt from possession in perpetuity. Examples of these unowned, rather than unownable, goods include wild animals, fish, buried treasure, and, most notably for our purposes, stones and gems found along the shoreline, which, in accordance with natural law, enter into one's ownership immediately (*statim*) after being seized.[52]

Calandrino is on a single-minded mission to be the *first* to possess the heliotrope, which he clearly views as a precious *res nullius*. This is why he frantically pesters his friends to seek out the heliotrope with him before anyone else does – "prima che alcuno altro n'andassero" (VIII.3.26), "prima che altra persona v'andasse" (VIII.3.28) – why he then agrees to wait until Sunday morning so that no one else will see

50 See *Digest* 1.8.11, 1:26: "It is an offence punishable with capital punishment to violate city walls, for example, by moving up ladders and climbing over or by any other means. It is unlawful for Roman citizens to use any other egress than the portals; for to do so is a hostile act and an abomination. Indeed, the tradition is that Romulus's brother Remus was slain on the very ground that he tried to climb out over the city wall" [si quis uiolauerit muros, capite punitur, sicuti si quis transcendet scalis admotis vel alia qualibet ratione. nam ciues Romanos alia quam per portas egredi non licet, cum illud hostile et abominandum sit: nam et Romuli frater Remus occisus traditur ob id, quod murum transcendere uoluerit]. See also *Institutes* 2.1.10, p. 54: "Sanctified things, such as city walls and gates, are also in a certain sense under divine law and thus in no one's property [*nullius in bonis*]. We call the walls sanctified because anyone who offends against them faces a capital penalty" [Sanctae quoque res, veluti muri et portae, quodammodo divini iuris sunt et ideo nullius in bonis sunt. Ideo autem muros sanctos dicimus, quia poena capitis constituta sit in eos, qui aliquid in muros deliquerint (translation slightly modified)].

51 On the distinction between *res nullius in bonis* and *res nullius*, see Thomas, "La valeur des choses," 1447–8; and Robbe, *La differenza sostanziale tra "res nullius" e "res nullius in bonis."*

52 See *Digest* 1.8.3, 1:24: "Pebbles, gems, and so on which we find on the shore forthwith become ours by natural law" [item lapilli, gemmae ceteraque, quae in litore inuenimus, iure naturali statim fiunt]; see also *Digest* 41.2.1.1, 4:502: "Things captured in war, islands arising in the sea, and gems, and stones, and pearls found on the seashore become the property of him who first takes possession of them" [item bello capta et insula in mari enata et gemmae lapilli maragaritae in litoribus inuentae eius fiunt, qui primus eorum possessionem nanctus est].

them, and also why he refuses to share the magic stone with his friends. Viewing the accumulation of natural resources as a zero-sum game, he fantasizes not simply about finding the heliotrope but specifically about putting it in his own pocket.

Blinded by his impatient, arriviste desire to acquire a *res nullius* for himself, Calandrino does not realize that throughout his journey he continually benefits from *res nullius in bonis*. His quest for the heliotrope takes him from a civic church through recently paved and straightened thoroughfares to the open access of a shoreline, and then on to the sixth, ultimate circle of defensive walls between Porta Faenza (which stood adjacent to the monastery Bruno and Buffalmacco are painting when he finds them) and Porta San Gallo. The choice to set much of the action of the tale at the city's outer perimeter is especially striking because the expansion of the walls to reach Porta Faenza and Porta San Gallo had only recently been completed when Boccaccio wrote the *Decameron*. Initiated in 1284 as part of a comprehensive urban plan under the supervision of Arnolfo di Cambio (whose appointment was subsequently passed on to Giotto and Andrea Pisano), the construction of these massive, fortified walls (8.5 kilometres long, 14 metres high, 2 metres wide, interspersed with 63 towers at strategic locations and 12 massive gates) remains one of the great engineering feats in Florentine history, encompassing not only the building of the actual walls but also the deviation of the Mugnone river to encircle the walls as a moat. The project's final completion in the 1340s was capped by Porta San Gallo's elaborate decorative program of sculpture, frescoes, architectural flourishes, and bas-reliefs, whose simultaneously patriotic and religious content (lions, lilies, the red cross of the *popolo*, patron saints, the Virgin as protectress) made this primary entryway into the city a privileged site of civic self-representation.[53]

Despite their vital contribution to the defence of the city, it took over fifty years to finish the last circuit of walls because the city often lacked adequate tax revenue. Frequent wars, the ensuing financial crises, and the continuous hijacking of public projects by factional interests made it intermittently impossible to find the funds necessary for both labour and materials. The challenge for the Florentine public authority was thus both practical and conceptual: how to convince the populace

53 See Cardini, "Le mura di Firenze"; Manetti and Pozzana, *Firenze, le porte dell'ultima cerchia di mura*; Mantini, "Un recinto di identificazione"; Tanzini, *Firenze*, 1–16 and 192–9; and Sznura, "Appunti sull'urbanistica fiorentina tra XIII e XIV secolo."

to shoulder the substantial financial burden of paying for the walls (through both direct and indirect taxes) based on their allegiance to an abstract *res publica*. Citizens needed to be willing to sacrifice for and feel committed to a collective undertaking that was not only super-individual but also transgenerational. Medieval jurists, in fact, justified the perennial, rather than *ad hoc*, nature of the *fiscus* by invoking the continued need to finance the city walls; both the walls and the *fiscus* were in some sense immortal, extending beyond the natural lifetime of any particular individual or ruling party.[54] Boccaccio himself participated in this collective project of "immortalizing" one's private belongings when he bequeathed in his will ten soldi in small florins for the construction of the city walls of Florence.[55]

Although the population would soon drop precipitously because of the plague, the walls' expansion was initially prompted by the rapidly growing Florentine populace, many of whom had, like Calandrino, recently immigrated from the countryside. Just as Cavalcanti's brief promenade from Orsanmichele to the original Roman gate of Porta San Giovanni maps out the symbolic space of aristocratic Old Florence, Calandrino's trek from San Giovanni to Porta San Gallo delineates the sprawling Florence of the "new people" [nuove genti (VIII.3.4)].[56] Nonetheless, even when passing through the imposing gates of "his" walls, Calandrino fails to connect them with the collective financial sacrifice required to build and maintain such public structures. Essentially a free rider, he does not appreciate the "magic" of open access, bragging instead that, like a modern-day Remus, he has violated the city walls by not registering with the customs agents. And yet these same "magical" resources would have allowed him to experience collectively a measure of the free plenitude of Bengodi that he instead seeks to own

54 For the close connection in legal doctrine between the *fiscus* and the city walls, see the contributions of Sara Menzinger, specifically "Verso la costruzione di un diritto pubblico cittadino" and "Mura e identità civica in Italia e in Francia meridionale."

55 The fact that Boccaccio left the same amount for both the maintenance of the Church of Santa Maria Reparata and the construction of the city walls shows that he viewed them as complementary incarnations of the civic body. On Boccaccio's will, see Papio, "An Intimate Self-Portrait."

56 In *Paradiso* 15.97, Cacciaguida similarly characterizes the socioeconomic transformation of Florence in terms of its ever-expanding walls. He declares that life was simpler and nobler before recent immigration, when citizens still dwelt "dentro dalla cerchia antica" [within the ancient circle] of its walls.

for himself. Behind the comedy of Calandrino's antics at the gates is a tragedy of the commons.

The more valuable the more he is shared, Calandrino turns out to be himself exactly the type of alternative commodity he fails to comprehend. Not only does he unwittingly provide his friends with a ready supply of free capons – one of the primary enticements of Bengodi – but his endless gullibility serves as a kind of miraculous, communal meal. The "gran festa" (VIII.3.4) derived from fooling him succeeds not in spite of but because of its being divided among many parts. That is why it needs to be Bruno *and* Buffalmacco who prank Calandrino, and why each new tale involves more co-conspirators than the last (Maso, the customs agents, the priest, the painter Nello, Master Simone, the merchant homeowner, the prostitute, and her pimp).

Calandrino's status as a Eucharistic meal is made explicit by the storytellers when they remark upon his exceptional properties as raw source material for their *novelle*. In Day Nine, Filostrato justifies telling another story about Calandrino, despite the fact that he has been the subject matter for various *novelle* on the previous day, by exclaiming that *anything* one says about Calandrino can't help but increase the festivities ["multiplicar la festa" (IX.3.3)]. Similarly, Fiammetta, while recognizing that the company has already talked about the "fatti" [deeds] of Calandrino "assai volte" [many times], explicitly agrees with Filostrato – "come poco avanti disse Filostrato" [as Filostrato pointed out a little earlier] – that tales about the urbanized rustic will always continue to delight, even when repeated "mille volte" [a thousand times (IX.5.4–5)]. Moreover, she justifies the telling of one last story about Calandrino by locating the material about him – once again echoing Filostrato – within an exceptional festive space: "che per aver festa e buon tempo e non per altro ci siamo, stimo che ogni cosa che festa e piacer possa porgere qui abbia e luogo e tempo debito" [since we are gathered here for no other purpose than to be festive and have a good time, I consider this a suitable time and proper place for any subject that will promote our pleasure and festiveness (IX.5.4)].[57] Finally, Fiammet-

57 It is worth noting, in this context, that Calandrino seeks the heliotrope on a Sunday because, since Sunday is a day of *festa* and rest from commerce, he knows he will

ta's categorical statement that, given the appropriate context, "niuna cosa è di cui tanto si parli, che sempre più non piaccia" [everything is more pleasurable the more you talk about it" (IX.5.3)] even echoes Virgil's explanation in *Purgatorio* that heavenly goods, in contrast with worldly goods, only increase in value with sharing: "quanti si dice più lì 'nostro' / tanto possiede più di ben ciascuno" [the more say "our" up there, / the more good each one possesses (*Purg.* 15.55–6)].[58] These seemingly ancillary reflections on the pleasure derived from re-utilizing the same source material signal in actuality a radical change from the economy of storytelling that has prevailed up until this point, in which narrators jockeyed to lay claim to content that was considered valuable precisely because it was rare and new.

As the *brigata* prepares to leave the idealized feudal countryside and re-enter the city, they remain committed to an alternative "festive" economy, one founded on the community's collective memory rather than on competition for scarce narrative resources. In fact, once back inside the city's sanctified walls, the storytellers will again be able to take advantage of its roads, waterways, and plazas – public goods not unlike the tales of Calandrino in their ability to continuously replenish. The *brigata* must be prepared, then, not only to re-adapt to the concrete realities of the city, but also to reconstitute its fictions, which have suffered under the brutal, self-interested realism brought about by the plague. As practice, they pool their resources of Calandrino tales in order to consecrate a "nobody's property" that gains in value the more it is shared (but not possessed). In this respect, Calandrino resembles Pliny's ancient painters in spite of himself; he is a "common property of the world."

The designation of Calandrino as ownerless is the final irony visited upon his posthumous image. For his scepticism in the *res publica* (in contrast with his overweening faith in the *res propria*), he earns a very Dantean punishment: to be transformed from the subject Nozzo di Pierino into the object Calandrino, a new emblematic *thing*, a "nuova cosa" (VIII.3.5). In his quest to be the first to possess a *res nullius*, he is remade for posterity into a *res nullius in bonis* – a public good for us to enjoy over and over again.

---

not find anyone working down by the river. Day Eight also takes place on a Sunday and is the only time the company attends Mass before settling in for their daily ritual of storytelling.

58 In contrast, see Aquinas's comments about worldly goods in his definition of avarice: "[avaritia] est directe peccatum in proximum, quia in exterioribus divitiis non potest unus homo superabundare nisi alter deficiat, quia bona temporalia non possunt simul possideri a multis" (Thomas Aquinas, *Opera omnia*, *ST* II.II. Q.118 A.1 *ad* 2).

Monna Piccarda, Ciutazza, and the Provost of Fiesole: An Absence of Beauty (VIII.4)

KATHERINE A. BROWN

Nestled between VIII.3, the tale that introduces Calandrino and his search for the heliotrope, and VIII.5, the story of three young Florentine men who pull down the breeches of the unsophisticated judge from the Marches, Emilia's novella of the lustful provost of Fiesole and the widow, Monna Piccarda, who tricks him into bed with her unsightly *fante* (servant), Ciutazza, seemingly lacks the comic and thematic novelty that characterizes these other tales and that, among other qualities, has drawn the attention of scholars.[1] Emilia's tale is the only one of Day Eight referred to as a *ragionamento*: "Fatto aveva Emilia fine al suo ragionamento" [Emilia had brought her story (argument) to an end (VIII.5.2)]. The designation of the tale as an argument, rather than a novella, underscores it as it also sets it apart from the rest of the tales on Day Eight.[2]

In his edition, Branca connects the word "ragionamento" to a verse in *Purgatorio* that marks the conclusion of one of Virgil's speeches to Dante and signals their transition from the third terrace of the wrathful to the fourth terrace of the slothful: "Posto avea fine al suo ragionamento / l'alto dottore" [The lofty teacher had made an end of his discourse (*Purg.* 18.1–2)].[3] The lexical and syntactical similarities that link VIII.4 to *Purgatorio* 18 point toward a larger, conceptual debt, as

1 The *Decameron* is cited from the text edited by Maurizio Fiorilla in Boccaccio, *Decameron*, ed. Quondam, Fiorilla, and Alfano; translations are from Boccaccio, *Decameron*, trans. McWilliam, unless otherwise noted.

2 Not all of the *novelle* of Day Eight are referenced in generic terms, but those that do have a designation are called either a "novella" (VIII.5, VIII.6, and VIII.9) or a "novelletta" (VIII.2, VIII.3, VIII.8, and implied in VIII.7).

3 See Branca's note in Boccaccio, *Decameron*, ed. Branca 1976, p. 1422 (698n2); he also notes that the same phrase is used at the beginning of VII.5 to refer to Lauretta's tale,

Virgil's two speeches in Cantos 17, 18, and 19 of *Purgatorio* collectively inform the notions of absence and aesthetics in *Decameron* VIII.4.[4]

Before discussing the Dantean intertext, this reading of Novella VIII.4 will consider the critical history, examine how the tale coordinates with other *novelle* in the *Decameron*, and then analyse the play of lack and surplus among the tale's characters. The contrast of absence and excess is mapped onto an Aristotelian distinction between deficiency and excess, with virtuous behaviour existing at the mean between these poles. In thematizing these concepts, VIII.4 subverts the comic and escapist cast of the other tales narrated on Day Eight by bringing to the fore questions of morality and aesthetics as mental activities, as it also meditates on the nature of storytelling as reliant on a balance of narrative absence and excess, thought and action. Ultimately, VIII.4 undermines a moral reading in favour of an aesthetic one, where "aesthetic" implies a relation both to the study of beauty and to sensory perception.[5]

Previous Scholarship

Novella VIII.4 has not been the focus of many sustained critical analyses but tends instead to be mentioned only in passing in the critical tradition of the *Decameron*. Most commentaries on the tale analyse its intertextual relationships with other *novelle* and evaluate the characters' virtue or lack thereof. Baratto argues that the novella, along with VIII.1, contributes to a stylistic turn in the *Decameron* toward a satiric and even cruel typology of characters. Whereas the lustful provost's awkward speech to the widow underscores the reason he deserves punishment, Baratto considers the description of the *fante*'s ugliness to be grotesque to the point of brutality.[6] In spite of the long description

---

VII.4. Dante's *Commedia* is cited from *La Commedia secondo l'antica vulgata*, edited by Petrocchi, with translations from *The Divine Comedy*, translated by Singleton.

4 Indeed, Boccaccio had earlier cited this line in its entirety in his *Ninfale Fiesolano*, at the point when Girafone tries to warn his son Africo about the dangers of falling in love with one of Diana's nymphs: "Posto avea fine al suo ragionamento / il vecchio Girafone lagrimando" (*Ninfale Fiesolano* 96.1–2, p. 317). While the provost of Novella VIII.4 is something of a buffonic rewriting of Africo, the widow succeeds in remaining chaste where the nymph Mensola had failed. Both stories are underscored by lack – though with comic and tragic outcomes respectively – and both ultimately take their cue from Dante's text.

5 For the medieval use of "aesthetic" as related to sensory perception, see Lehmann et al., *Mittellateinisches Wörterbuch*, s.v. "aestheticon."

6 Baratto, *Realtà e stile*, 397–8. Baratto contrasts the description of Ciutazza with that of Nuta in VI.10, which he considers a limit case in a cultivated world of entertainment; the description of Ciutazza, on the other hand, he finds "feroce."

of her physical hideousness, Ciutazza has otherwise not merited much critical scrutiny.

In his study of anticlericalism in the *Decameron*, Ó Cuilleanáin eliminates Novella VIII.4 from consideration because he finds the widow's strictures not severe enough to constitute anticlericalism, even though the provost is guilty of concupiscence (*Religion and the Clergy*, 81). In Smarr's reconsideration of clergy in the *Decameron*, she cites the bishop as a praiseworthy member of the "upper clergy" who serves as a counterpoint to the unseemly jokester bishop in VI.3, though she does not mention the provost ("Clergy in the *Decameron*," 59). Indeed, within the novella the bishop serves as a moral counterpoint to the provost, balancing the latter's vices with judiciousness.

Though Novella VIII.4 ostensibly offers subtle additions to the theme of anticlericalism in the *Decameron*, these are ultimately mitigated. The use of a widow rather than a married woman to spurn the advances of a provost instead of a priest or bishop or abbot constitutes the main innovation in relation to previous anticlerical tales. As Ó Cuilleanáin points out, a provost is the highest ecclesiastical rank among the clerical lovers in the *Decameron* (*Religion and the Clergy*, 110–11). However, the provost's ego and position in society, more than his position within the church, are wounded upon the revelation of the lady's deception, for "il proposto, conosciuto lo 'nganno della donna, sì per quello e sì per lo vituperio che aver gli parea, subito divenne il più doloroso uomo che fosse mai" [what with his discovery of the lady's deception, and the disgrace that he felt he had suffered, the Provost was instantly transformed into the saddest man who ever lived (VIII.4.35)]. The anticlericalism of the tale is ambiguous at best, in part because the bishop is not hypocritical in punishing the provost, and more pointedly because the provost is a character of excess who deserves to be tricked; his flaws are merely intensified by his ecclesiastical rank.

The widow has also been the subject of some attention, especially from Migiel, who offers a mixed review of Monna Piccarda. On the one hand, she praises the widow's use of intelligence to avoid what she does not want (*Ethical Dimension*, 169n40).[7] Yet she also posits that Novella IX.1 is something of a feminist response to VIII.4, since the heroine of IX.1 manages to rid herself of the attention of two unwanted suitors without having to "degrade" another woman in the process, as Monna Piccarda ostensibly does to Ciutazza in VIII.4 (*A Rhetoric of the*

7 In this assertion, Migiel is opposing Lino Pertile's classifications of characters who use their intelligence to achieve what they desire. See Pertile, "Dante, Boccaccio e l'intelligenza."

Decameron, 59). Migiel's reading of VIII.4 presumes that a sexual act is a degradation for Ciutazza and that her honour and social status are wounded. However, it can be argued that Ciutazza appears to profit in multiple ways from her exchange with her mistress without compromising her standing, perhaps because her status was already too low to be in jeopardy.

The sources for Novella VIII.4 have also not helped it garner much critical attention. Almansi has argued that VIII.4 is linked to VII.8 and III.2 because all present versions of the cycle of the *gageure* or wager, as identified by Gaston Paris (Almansi, *Il ciclo della scommessa*, 7). In his brief remarks on this novella, Almansi insists on the substitution of a servant for her mistress in bed as a core element of the *gageure* narrative tradition, and argues that Boccaccio's contribution to this theme in VIII.4 is his emphasis on the extraordinary ugliness of the servant Ciutazza. According to Almansi, the deformed servant is a variation on the mutilation theme associated with the *gageure* cycle, whereby some man punishes the seduced woman by beating her or otherwise altering her appearance after the seduction. In this instance, however, Boccaccio describes Ciutazza's deformity before the sexual encounter as a way to heighten the provost's dishonour and disappointment in spending the night with her (*Il ciclo della scommessa*, 8–9). This reversal of the mutilation theme nullifies the consequences of the sexual encounter for the woman, since in VIII.4 Ciutazza cannot be made any more physically deformed, nor is she obviously harmed in any way. The device of an inferior taking another's place in bed seems to be the only thematic element that VIII.4 shares with the other *gageure* tales in the *Decameron*.

Lee cites an Old French fabliau, "Le Prestre et Alison," attributed to Guillaume le Normand, as a convincing antecedent owing to the similarities of their plots (*Decameron: Sources and Analogues*, 254–5).[8] In the Old French text, however, Alison is a prostitute hired by a virtuous woman to take the place of her daughter in bed with a lecherous priest. Alison's counterpart in the *Decameron* is Ciutazza, one of the least attractive women described in the collection. Boccaccio's transformation of the Old French text's woman of questionable morals into a physically repulsive woman reinforces a reading of Novella VIII.4 that implicates the relationship between aesthetics and morality.

8 For the fabliau, see the *Nouveau recueil complet des fabliaux*, 8:183–206.

Decameronian Intertexts

In addition to the intertextual links established by previous scholarship, the fourth novella of Day Eight may be considered a response to the second novella of the same day, in which a priest is both the lover and trickster of a married woman. On the level of anticlericalism, Novella VIII.4 is a corrective rewriting of VIII.2, since the provost in VIII.4 receives his just punishment, both publicly and within the Church hierarchy, whereas the priest-lover in VIII.2 is acquitted of his financial debt and continues to enjoy the company of Monna Belcolore. Despite the economic mechanism of the trick in VIII.2, where the woman is duped out of the money the priest promised her for sex (usually considered a variation of that in VIII.1), the result is that she acquiesces to the priest's sexual desire as much for her own pleasure as for the fear of damnation with which the priest threatens her, and not for money. In VIII.4, there is no threat of damnation and the financial transaction happens instead between the widow and her servant, who is the satisfied recipient of a sexual encounter with the provost, and more importantly, who "guadagnò la camiscia" [won herself a smock (VIII.4.37)]. While Novella VIII.2 subtly condemns the exchange of sexual favours for money by women even as it tolerates the sexual exploits of a witty priest, Novella VIII.4 tacitly valorizes sex acts for personal gain, at least among ugly, non-noble women, when performed in the service of a mistress and as punishment for a lusty cleric.

Emilia underscores the thematic repetitiveness of her tale when she introduces the narrative of VIII.4: "Valorose donne, quanto i preti e' frati e ogni cherico sieno sollecitatori delle menti nostre in più novelle dette mi ricorda esser mostrato; ma per ciò che dire non se ne potrebbe tanto che ancora più non ne fosse, io oltre a quelle intendo di dirvene una d'un proposto" [Dear ladies, it has already been shown, as I recall, in several of the stories we have heard, that priests and friars and clerics of all descriptions will stop at nothing to force themselves on our attention. But however much we may discuss this particular subject, more will remain to be said; and I therefore propose to tell you a story about a provost (VIII.4.3)].[9] Her comment implies an inexhaustible supply of anticlerical stories, with such tales ostensibly begetting more of the same. Moreover, her use of polysyndeton – a device echoed in the tale – to enumerate the types of clerics subject to licentiousness ("i

9 McWilliam's translation has been slightly modified.

preti e' frati e ogni cherico") signals a certain thematic staleness. The novelty of her *ragionamento* is not to be found in its treatment of clerical figures, but rather in its thematization of excess and lack. Although Emilia introduces her tale with an anticlerical diatribe, the novella itself offers a balanced view of the clergy. In this way, Emilia's novella seems to undermine her stated intentions.[10] The real focus of the tale is not its role in the anticlerical current of the *Decameron*, but rather its presentation of two comically unappealing characters, the provost and Ciutazza, and their interaction as orchestrated by the widow.

Absence and Excess among Characters in VIII.4

From the beginning of the tale, the widow, Monna Piccarda, is associated with virtue and moderation. As she lacks a husband and financial means, "e per ciò che la piú agiata donna del mondo non era" [and since she was not the wealthiest of women (VIII.4.5)], she lives year-round in her *podere* near the main church in Fiesole with two of her brothers. In spite of her vulnerable social and financial position, the widow is described favourably by Emilia: "*e* essendo ancora assai giovane *e* bella *e* piacevole" [and since she was still a very beautiful and charming young woman (VIII.4.6)], a generic statement that nonetheless underscores her virtues. This description with its repetition of the conjunction *e* – the device of polysyndeton will be repeated throughout the tale, particularly in relation to the provost and Ciutazza – does little to make her a remarkable heroine within the *Decameron*, but it explains her superficial appeal to the provost. Polysyndeton is a stylistic feature that permeates the *Decameron*, but it is particularly noteworthy in moments of both comic excess and irony. For example, when Panfilo describes the delight Ser Cepparello takes in sowing discord among others, the passage makes use of the device of polysyndeton to highlight the extreme depravity of his ways: "Aveva oltre modo piacere, e forte vi studiava, in commettere tra amici *e* parenti *e* qualunque altra persona mali *e* inimicizie *e* scandali, de' quali quanto maggiori mali vedeva seguire tanto più d'allegrezza prendea" [He would take particular pleasure, and a great amount of trouble, in stirring up enmity *and* discord *and* bad blood between friends *and* relatives, *and* anybody else; the more calamities that ensued, the greater would be his rapture

10 Emilia narrates another anticlerical novella, I.6, about a greedy inquisitor whose gluttony is brought to light by the comment of an inebriated man. Hers is the fourth anticlerical novella of Day One.

(I.1.12)].[11] The Author's Conclusion, on the other hand, demonstrates the deployment of polysyndeton as a defence against critics of the salty language of some tales: "dico che più non si dee a me esser disdetto d'averle scritte che generalmente si disdica agli uomini e alle donne di dir tutto dì 'foro' *e* 'caviglia' *e* 'mortaio' *e* 'pestello' *e* 'salciccia' *e* 'mortadello', *e* tutto pien di simiglianti cose" [I assert that it was no more improper for me to have written them [i.e., such words] than for men and women at large, in their everyday speech, to use such words as *hole*, and *rod*, and *mortar*, and *pestle*, and *crumpet*, and *stuffing*, and any number of others (Concl.Aut.5)]. The irony is that all of these words were used with a sexual connotation in various tales, their *copulatio* here only adding to the force of the irony. Though the use of polysyndeton is not unique to Novella VIII.4, its deployment here emphasizes excess and irony where the provost and Ciutazza are concerned, whereas for the widow, it conveys her many virtues.

Meanwhile, the widow's own words of discouragement to the provost, "io non son fanciulla, alla quale questi innamoramenti steano oggimai bene" [I am not a young girl, able to take affairs of this sort in her stride (VIII.4.8)],[12] use litotes – "not young" – to underscore her age as one of the reasons she cannot reciprocate the provost's love. The delicacy of her speech fails to deter him, owing as much to the provost's arrogance as to the widow's discretion and restraint in not revealing her true dislike for the man. The trick she devises for her suitor, however, calls for him to deprive himself of voice and vision during their rendezvous – "a modo di mutolo senza far motto o zitto alcuno e al buio a modo di ciechi" [completely silent, like deaf-mutes, without saying a word, and [to] move about in the dark, as though ... blind (VIII.4.16)] – and for her servant, Ciutazza, who takes her place in bed, not to speak, "non far motto" [not to utter a single word (VIII.4.25)]. The widow's speech in these instances is marked by repetition ("a modo di ... a modo di ...") more than in her previous verbal rejection of the provost, because her strategy to rebuff him has changed; her newfound verbal repetitions meet the provost on his level in order to convince him of her sincerity and thereby trick him.

11 I have slightly modified the translation of McWilliam, who sidesteps the polysyndeton of this passage by using commas to replace the conjunction *and*. This device is also echoed in the holy friar's high praise of San Ciappelletto near the end of Novella I.1 as a means to augment the comic irony of the sinner revered as a saint.

12 McWilliam's translation has been slightly modified.

While all tricks in the *Decameron* arguably depend upon some lack, especially a lack of understanding among the victims of the mechanisms of the ruse, the widow's trick emphasizes sensory deprivation as an ironic counterpoint to the provost's sexual zeal, for her stratagem announces her restraint, a restraint which appears both in her absence from the bedroom and in her absence from the delivery of the provost's humiliation at the end of the novella. After planning this trick for the provost and promising a "camiscia" [smock (VIII.4.23)] as reward to Ciutazza, the widow effectively disappears from the narrative, since her brothers take over the role of trickster, and the bishop, along with the children of Fiesole, metes out punishment and humiliation. The widow's disappearance reflects her character; whereas her moderation, honour, and moral decency are registered through her ultimate absence, the trick she plays links the provost and Ciutazza by their respective excesses. Indeed, despite being the trickster, the widow is completely missing from the denouement, being doubly replaced by her brothers and her servant, further accentuating absence as one of the thematic keys to understanding the novella.

As a counterpoint to the virtuous widow, the provost is a figure of excess. Although old, the provost is described in exaggerated terms as "di senno giovanissimo, baldanzoso e altiero, e di sé ogni gran cosa presummeva, con suoi modi e costumi pien di scede e de spiacevolezze, e tanto sazievole e rincrescevole, che niuna persona era che ben gli volesse" [[having] the mentality of a small child, being haughty and presumptuous, and possessing a mighty high opinion of himself. He was forever picking holes in people and making himself generally unpleasant, and was so pompous and tedious that he was disliked by everybody (VIII.4.7)]. The superlatives and multiple, nearly synonymous adjectives in this description distinguish the provost as extravagant, while the use of *baldanzoso*, a rare adjective in the whole of the *Decameron*, hints at not only his arrogance but also the fact that he is sexually charged.[13] The heavy use of the conjunc-

13 Markulin has counted eight occurrences of nominal, adverbial, and adjectival forms of *baldanzoso* in the *Decameron*, where he claims they are overwhelmingly suggestive of courage, especially courage in sexual curiosity ("Emilia and the Case for Openness"). While Emilia, who narrates this novella, begins her first tale on Day One "baldanzosamente," Markulin argues that the term fits poorly with her character and the story, and that it serves instead as a marker of some unusual trait to her tale, namely interpretive openness (185–6). Within the context of Day Eight, however, the adjective *baldanzoso* aptly describes the aggression and sexual desire of the provost. In this instance, Ciutazza is the character most open to interpretation. Even though Boccaccio's *novelle* are open to interpretation, the argument of this

tion *e* supports the exaggeration as it adds detail to his character – the audience arguably knows more about him than about the widow. The provost carries over his excessive self-love in his desire for the widow, "usando la sua trascutata prontezza" [with his habitual arrogance and effrontery], in order to solicit her favours "molte volte *e* con lettere *e* con ambasciate *e* ancora egli stesso quando nella chiesa la vedeva venire" [repeatedly by means of letters and messages, as well as by word of mouth whenever he saw her coming into the church (VIII.4.9)]. Here another deployment of polysyndeton highlights the provost's relentless and excessive pursuit of love. In this way, repetition to the point of excess is associated with the provost's lust, to such a degree that he is incapable of recognizing the widow's initial rejection for what it is: "non fece come sbigottito o vinto al primo colpo" [the Provost was not the sort of man to be discouraged or defeated by a single rebuff (VIII.4.9)].

His final act of excess in love occurs, fittingly, in the bedroom with Ciutazza, where before being discovered he "s'era affrettato di cavalcare e era … cavalcato già delle miglia più di tre" [had been riding at a furious pace, and already … he had covered at least three miles (VIII.4.32)]. The riding metaphor renders the provost a parody of the chivalric lover, tying him to a tradition of Old French fabliaux in which non-noble characters (clerics or laymen) are often described in courtly terms.[14] If the implication of the provost as an ironic courtly lover reveals yet one more level on which he may be judged an inappropriate suitor for the widow,[15] the repetition in "cavalcare … cavalcato," and the mention of the substantial distance he has covered in his efforts, strengthen his ties to comic exaggeration.

---

essay is to suggest that Boccaccio also offers his readers aesthetic principles to help them interpret works, in this case, balance and the harmony in language, structure, and action.

14 For example, the fabliau *La damoisele qui ne pooit oïr parler de foutre* uses an extended metaphor of a chivalric quest to avoid naming genitalia and the sexual act (*Nouveau recueil complet des fabliaux*, 4:57–89 and 374–9). Most studies of the sources for the *Decameron* tales indicate the significant influence of the fabliaux tradition. See, for example, notes to each story in Boccaccio, *Decameron*, ed. Branca 1992; as well as Lee, *The Decameron: Its Sources and Analogues*, 254–7.

15 The widow's first speech establishes the irony of appealing to the rules of courtly love in this context, for not only is she a widow, not particularly wealthy, and somewhat too old to be an ideal *domna*, but the provost is both a cleric and too old to be a courtly lover, all of which contradicts the precepts of courtly love, as outlined by Andreas Capellanus in his *Art of Courtly Love*.

Although the trick serves, as so many others do in the *Decameron*, to call out the provost's behaviour in regard to the widow, it has a more deleterious effect on his self-love:

> Questo peccato gli fece il vescovo piagnere quaranta dí ma *amore* e *isdegno* gliele fecero piagnere più di quarantanove; senza che, poi a un gran tempo, egli non poteva mai andar per via che egli non fosse da' fanciulli mostrato a dito, li quali dicevano: "Vedi colui che giacque con la Ciutazza"; il che gli era sì gran *noia*, che egli ne fu quasi in su *lo 'mpazzare*. (VIII.4.37, emphasis added)
>
> [The Provost was forced by his bishop to do forty days' penance for his sin, but love and indignation prolonged his suffering to forty-nine days at the very least, to say nothing of the fact that for a long time afterwards, he was unable to walk down the street without being pointed at by small boys, who would taunt him with the words: "There goes the man who went to bed with Ciutazza." And this riled him so much that he was almost driven out of his mind.]

The taunting of the children as a form of public humiliation is felt excessively by the provost, bringing him near the point of insanity. Indeed, he still suffers from the sin of excess, even lamenting his fate longer than the forty-day punishment imposed by the bishop. Nevertheless, the bishop's final remark echoes Emilia's initial comment about the justness of the punishment – "il trattò sì come egli era degno" [she treated him according to his deserts (VIII.4.3)] – when he commends the widow and her brothers, "che, senza volersi del sangue de' preti imbrattar le mani, lui sì come egli era degno avean trattato" [who, not wishing to soil their hands with the blood of a priest, had treated the Provost as he deserved (VIII.4.36)]. That the trick was a fitting corrective measure to the provost's vices in the Dantean sense of *contrapasso* shows the narrative harmony of the tale, with the very word "degno" bookending the novella. The provost, however, remains a figure connected to extremes, his excess transformed to absences – of love, of dignity, and of mental composure – but otherwise morally unimproved.

Perhaps the most notable absences and excesses in the story converge in the person of the *fante*, Ciutazza, and, more pointedly, in the striking failure of the other characters or the *brigata* to address her honour or even humanity. The description of Ciutazza borders on the grotesque in its presentation of her extreme ugliness:

> Aveva questa donna una sua fante, la quale non era però troppo giovane, *ma* ella aveva il più brutto viso *e* il più contrafatto che si vedesse mai:

ché ella aveva il naso schiacciato forte *e* la bocca torta *e* le labbra grosse *e* i denti mal composti *e* grandi, *e* sentiva del guercio, né mai era senza mal d'occhi, con un color verde *e* giallo che pareva che non a Fiesole *ma* a Sinagaglia avesse fatta la state, *e* oltre a tutto questo era sciancata *e* un poco monca dal lato destro; *e* il suo nome era Ciuta, *e* perché così cagnazzo viso aveva, da ogni uomo era chiamata Ciutazza; *e* benché ella fosse contrafatta della persona, ella era pure alquanto maliziosetta. (VIII.4.21–2, emphasis added)

[Now, this lady had a maidservant, who was none too young and had the ugliest and most misshapen face you ever saw. She had a huge, flat nose, wry mouth, thick lips, big teeth, which were unevenly set, and a pronounced squint; moreover, she was always having trouble with her eyes, and her complexion was a sort of yellowy green, so that she looked as though she had spent the summer, not in Fiesole, but in Senigallia. Apart from this, she was hipshot on the right side, and walked with a slight limp. Her name was Ciuta, but because she was so ugly to look at, everyone called her Ciutazza. And although her body was so misshapen, she was always prepared for a spot of mischief.]

A model of polysyndeton with approximately a dozen conjunctions, this description of one of the ugliest people in the *Decameron* is laden with superlatives of hideousness,[16] as if to counterbalance the superlatives of beauty normally attributed to the ladies of courtly romance, but also to contrast with the minimalist description of the widow's attractiveness. Ciuta's ugliness perfectly suits the punishment of the provost, since it most tarnishes his vanity. Moreover, the ugliness of the subject matter is set in opposition to the beauty of the form; the rhetorical symmetry and cohesion of this description make it apt and thus aesthetically pleasing.

While the description of Ciutazza, whose nickname highlights her ill qualities, is excessive in its focus on her looks, her physique is characterized by asymmetry and lack. Not only is she likened to an outsider, as if she summered in Sinagaglia, thus explaining her barely human greenish-yellow complexion, but she is deformed to the point of being "monca." Derived from the Latin word *mancus*, which signifies "maimed" because of imperfection, *monca* is also etymologically connected to the verb *mancare*, meaning "to be missing."[17] The image

16 Even the descriptions of the ugly maid Nuta in VI.10 and Messer Forese da Rabatta in VI.5 barely compete with the one of Ciutazza in length and detail, not to mention in the use of superlatives and the device of polysyndeton as a form of exaggeration.

17 Panigiani, *Vocabolario etimologico*, s.v. "mancus"; accessed 27 June 2016.

of missing body parts is intimately tied to the idea of *malum* and specifically to hell for Dante in Canto 32 of *Inferno*, where some of the sinners are missing body parts. It is also here that the word *cagnazzo*, used to describe Ciuta's face, is found in a description of the traitors in the ninth circle of hell: "Poscia vid' io mille visi cagnazzi / fatti per freddo" [After that I saw a thousand faces made purple by the cold (*Inf.* 32.70–1).[18] The implication is that ugliness is a sign of moral corruption – the absence of beauty in the body and soul.

Yet Ciutazza's deformity, that she is missing physical completeness and perfection, seems to contrast with her character, "e benché ella fosse contrafatta della persona, ella era pure alquanto maliziosetta" [And although her body was so misshapen, she was always prepared for a spot of mischief (VIII.4.22)]. In spite of the word's etymological connection to *malum*, "maliziosetta" with its diminutive ending denotes a harmless mischievousness that offsets the harshness of Ciutazza's looks and name, conveyed by the pejorative suffix *-azza*. Indeed, Ciutazza is a character of contrasts and, in many respects, of uncertain interpretation.

Her speech, though limited in the text to two lines, evidences this same ambivalence. She indicates that she is willing to sacrifice her honour, even her life – "Madonna, se voi mi date una camiscia, io mi gitterò nel fuoco, non che altro" [If you give me a smock, ma'am, I'll go through fire for you (VIII.4.24)] – but it is unclear if the exaggerated expression is an empty rhetorical gesture or if it signifies a real desire of some sort, whether that be her desire to serve her mistress or rather a greedy wish to obtain a shift at any cost. Similarly, her second offer – "Sì, dormirò io con sei, non che con uno, se bisognerà" [if need be … I would sleep with half-a-dozen men, let alone one (VIII.4.26)] – which is ultimately executed when she sleeps with the provost, may contribute to a sense of her magnanimity in serving the widow, or else it may reveal an excessive lust. Both responses, however, are exaggerations and out of proportion with the favour the widow has asked of her, with the reward promised, and with the stakes of the ruse, but Ciutazza seems impervious to moral concern. As a figure of excess, Ciutazza can hope for balance only through her economic transaction with the widow. In this, Novella VIII.4 undermines the sexual exchange orchestrated by a man in VIII.2 (and by proxy in VIII.1).[19] In terms of Ciutazza's morality, the

18 See Branca's note, Boccaccio, *Decameron*, ed. Branca 1976, 694n11, p. 1420.

19 While for Migiel VIII.4 shows one "woman's triumph from the degradation of other women" (*A Rhetoric of the Decameron*, 59), the degradation of Ciutazza is arguably

tale and the *brigata*'s reaction to it are deficient, for the novella seemingly traffics in a moral system where the poles of excess and lack are sinful and punishable and where moderation is prized, but Ciutazza's role undermines this because she is rewarded for her extremes. Indeed, the description of Ciutazza's hideousness is one of the highlights of the novella and one of the keys to understanding the tale's role in Day Eight and in the *cento novelle*.

There is no mention that Ciutazza's soul or even social standing is mutilated, so to speak, for apparently selling herself for the price of a shift. The interpretation of the act depends on the interpretation of Ciutazza herself – whether she is selflessly serving her mistress no matter the personal cost or whether she is satisfying her greed and lust in one economic gesture, or perhaps both. The incongruity of the form, Ciutazza's ugly body, and its meaning, her ambiguous morality, leads to the question of aesthetics and morality which Dante's text elucidates.

Absence and Aesthetics

In the first *ragionamento* that Virgil tells the pilgrim Dante in Canto 17 of *Purgatorio*, he explains that there are two types of love: natural love and mental love. While natural love is without error, "l'altro puote errar per malo obietto / o per troppo o per poco di vigore" [the other may err either through an evil object, or through too much or too little vigor (*Purg*. 17.95–6)]. In *Decameron* VIII.4, the provost comically exemplifies the error of excessive love, both for himself and in his desire for the widow. Clearly, the licentious provost has turned too much of his attention away from God and toward earthly appetites. The real objective of Virgil's speech sheds light on the stakes of Boccaccio's novella. Virgil explains the nature of love and how it may be the origin of vice and virtue:

> Mentre ch'elli è nel primo ben diretto,
> e ne' secondi sé stesso misura,
> esser non può cagion di mal diletto;
> ma quando a mal si torce, o con più cura
> o con men che non dee corre nel bene,

---

an open question. Her ultimate enjoyment of the "camiscia" implies that she herself does not feel degraded, and the issue is not addressed in the story or by the *brigata*. As the economic exchange is limited to the domestic sphere of the widow, however, Migiel's position that the tales on Day Eight "delimit the power that women might yield" (149) is justified.

contra 'l fattore adovra sua fattura.
Quinci comprender puoi ch'esser convene
amor sementa in voi d'ogne virtute
e d'ogne operazion che merta pene. (*Purg.* 17.97–105)

[While it is directed on the Primal Good, and on secondary goods observes right measure, it cannot be the cause of sinful pleasure. But when it is turned awry to evil, or speeds to good with more zeal, or with less, than it ought, against the Creator works His creature. Hence you can comprehend that love must needs be the seed in you of every virtue and of every action deserving punishment.]

Virgil does not define the "mal" or that which is punishable as an absence in Thomistic terms, nor does he attribute a substance to evil because he plainly states that love is the source of both virtue and vice. In this respect, Virgil's *ragionamento* in *Purgatorio* 17 does not contradict scholastic philosophy, but it does highlight the importance of *misura* (measure) in choosing what to love. Both excess and absence are removed from the good, which is the balance required for perfecting mental love.

In Canto 18, the pilgrim Dante asks Virgil about the type of love that can be the source of both virtue and its opposite, to which Virgil replies in his second *ragionamento* that the love of man is drawn to that which is pleasing:

L'animo, ch'è creato ad amar presto,
ad ogne cosa è mobile che piace,
tosto che dal piacere in atto è desto,
Vostra apprensiva da esser verace
tragge intenzione, e dentro a voi la spiega,
sì che l'animo ad essa volger face;
e se, rivolto, inver' di lei si piega,
quel piegare è amor, quell' è natura
che per piacer di novo in voi si lega. (*Purg.* 18.19–27)

[The mind, which is created quick to love, is responsive to everything that pleases, as soon as by pleasure it is roused to action. Your faculty of apprehension draws an image from a real existence and displays it within you, so that it makes the mind turn to it; and if, thus turned, the mind inclines toward it, that inclination is love, that inclination is nature which is bound in you anew by pleasure.]

Dante still sees a problem with this mental love: if love motivates man and is put in man by God, how can man be to blame for any of his actions? To this, Virgil can only reply with "ragion" [reason]; the part of the answer that involves "fede" [faith] is necessarily absent and must await Beatrice's wisdom (*Purg.* 18.46–8). Thus, even the intertext that informs Novella VIII.4 is marked by an absence. Indeed, the absence of a discussion of faith characterizes both the plot of Novella VIII.4 and the *brigata*'s response to it, but the provost himself is rather guilty of having too much faith in the widow's promise to meet him at her house – his is a misplaced faith. Ciutazza may also have too much faith in her mistress because she is willing to sacrifice her honour when the widow asks, although there is little indication that it is a sacrifice for her. The reply Virgil eventually gives, however, begins with an explanation of man's imperfect love, that not every love is worthy of praise, and then he explains the role of free will in making judgments and controlling one's desires: "Onde, poniam che di necessitate / surga ogne amor che dentro a voi s'accende, / di ritenerlo è in voi la podestate" [Wherefore, suppose that every love which is kindled in you arises of necessity, the power to arrest it is in you (*Purg.* 18.70–2)]. The question of exercising judgment has been central to the *novelle* of the *Decameron* since the first story of Ser Cepparello/Ciappelletto, a masterpiece of storytelling for its harmonious and economic narration. Novella VIII.4 certainly fits in this tradition of exercising judgment, for the provost who receives an earthly punishment for his transgression has failed to exercise his reason, and more importantly, moderation in showing his love for the widow. The widow, on the other hand, has demonstrated her reason admirably.

Reason is a mental exercise, as is mental love. According to Virgil, that which is pleasing is loved, but a mental image of the desired object that causes pleasure must be created before the soul can turn to it in love. Although implied, that which is beautiful is also pleasing, and in this way Virgil's speech hints at a theory of beauty, on which his previous speech about too much and too little vigour in love only touched. Aquinas supplies the connection among the good, the beautiful, and the physical or sensorial when he addresses the cause of love:

> The beautiful is the same as the good, and they differ in aspect only. For since good is what all seek, the notion of good is that which calms the desire; while the notion of the beautiful is that which calms the desire, by being seen or known. Consequently those senses chiefly regard the beautiful, which are the most cognitive, viz. sight and hearing, as ministering to reason; for we speak of beautiful sights and beautiful

> sounds. But in reference to the other objects of the other senses, we do not use the expression "beautiful," for we do not speak of beautiful tastes, and beautiful odors. Thus it is evident that beauty adds to goodness a relation to the cognitive faculty: so that "good" means that which simply pleases the appetite; while the "beautiful" is something pleasant to apprehend.[20]

Although love is conjured in the mind, the beautiful is apprehended through the senses, particularly sight and sound – the very senses of which the provost is deprived during his nocturnal tryst with Ciutazza. Emilia's introduction to the novella highlights the mental aspect of clerics' entreaties to women, "sollecitatori delle menti nostre" [[who] stop at nothing to force themselves on our attention (VIII.4.3)], even though her tale traffics primarily in the physical. Not only is the emphasis on the mental contrary to most of the tales in the *Decameron* narrated in an anticlerical vein, with their focus on the physical sins of the clergy, but the provost of VIII.4 is decidedly sexually ambitious. The implication for the provost is that he enjoys his evening with Ciutazza – he is found holding her in his arms in spite of the warm weather – until he sees her, because he carries the mental image of the widow and mistakenly applies it to the ugly servant. The act itself, however, seems to have pleased him.

The final part of Virgil's speech on love follows Dante's dream about the "femmina balba," the hideous, stuttering woman who is transformed into a beautiful siren. The woman is described in similar terms and with similar deformities to Ciutazza:

> mi venne in sogno una femmina balba,
> ne li occhi guercia, e sovra i piè distorta,
> con le man monche, e di colore scialba.
> …

20 "Ad tertium dicendum quod pulchrum est idem bono, sola ratione differens. Cum enim bonum sit quod omnia appetunt, de ratione boni est quod in eo quietetur appetitus: sed ad rationem pulchri pertinet quod in eius aspectu seu cognitione quietetur appetitus. Unde et illi sensus praecipue respiciunt pulchrum, qui maxime cognoscitivi sunt, scilicet visus et auditus rationi deservientes: dicimus enim pulchra visibilia et pulchros sonos. In sensibilibus autem aliorum sensuum, non utimur nomine pulchritudinis: non enim dicimus pulchros sapores aut odores. Et sic patet quod pulchrum addit supra bonum, quendam ordinem ad vim cognoscitivam: ita quod bonum dicatur id quod simpliciter complacet appetitui; pulchrum autem dicatur id cuius ipsa apprehensio placet" (Thomas Aquinas, *Opera omnia*, *ST* I.II. Q.27 A.1 *ad* 3). Translations from the *Summa Theologica* come from the translation of the Dominican Fathers.

così lo sguardo mio le facea scorta
la lingua, e poscia tutta la drizzava
in poco d'ora, e lo smarrito volto,
com' amor vuol, così le colorava. (*Purg*. 19.7–9, 12–15)

[There came to me in a dream a woman, stammering, with eyes asquint and crooked on her feet, with maimed hands, and of sallow hue ... so my look made ready her tongue, and then in but little time set her full straight, and colored her pallid face even as love requires.]

Whereas the pilgrim Dante's loving gaze changes the ugly woman into an enchantress, the situation is reversed for the provost, whose mind allowed him to believe that the ugly Ciutazza was in fact the beautiful widow, but whose gaze ultimately reveals the woman's ugliness. The *femmina balba* is an allegory for an "antica strega" [ancient witch (*Purg*. 19.58)], as Virgil calls it, the sins of avarice, gluttony, and lust for which sinners above them in Purgatory must atone. Notably, only the sin of lust applies to the provost, but the woman's transformation does not lead him to repentance but rather serves as his punishment, since the images in his mind of the woman and of himself are altered for the worse. Even though he is punished, it is not clear that the provost is repentant and actually atones for his lust. His changed mental state at the end of the tale – that he is sad, indignant, and nearly driven crazy – suggests that he may be incapable of atonement. That he is on the verge of insanity, the edge of reason, signals that he has not acquired an ability to use reason and restraint to measure his responses.

Unlike the provost, the widow limits herself to the work of her mind and a little speech, but avoids the physical, which is evident by her not being present during the revelation of the trick. While the provost has a mental image of beauty and love in the form of the widow, his attempt to derive pleasure from the physical is thwarted *ex post facto* by the revelation that he is with Ciutazza, whereas the widow devises the ruse but fails to take, or rather restrains herself from taking, pleasure in the sight of the trick, the result of her mental work. Her absence, which has been connected to moral behaviour throughout the novella, suggests that seeing the trick and taking pleasure in it are incongruous with virtue.

Conclusion

The tale barely engages the *brigata* on a day during which laughter tends to dominate the collective responses to the tales: "Fatto aveva Emilia fine al suo ragionamento, essendo stata la vedova donna commendata da tutti, quando la reina a Filostrato guardando disse … " [when Emilia had brought her story to an end, and the widow had been commended by all those present, the queen looked towards Filostrato, and said … (VIII.5.2)].[21] The passive construction in praise of the widow distances the *brigata* from the novella, as it also neglects the roles of the provost and Ciutazza in the intrigue. Although arguably enjoyable, the satisfaction derived from seeing the provost justly punished or from hearing the grotesque description of Ciutazza does not merit the attention of the *brigata*. For the *brigata* to maintain the appearance of virtue, they must behave like the widow and exercise restraint by not taking active pleasure in that which is not good in itself. Even though the ten young men and women have apprehended the ruse by hearing it narrated, they may only respond in praise of the widow if they desire to seem virtuous.

According to Virgil, free will must be shown through actions (*Purg.* 18.49–54). The pleasure of man is concerned with the senses in the *Decameron*, and it is this principle that informs Novella VIII.4 and the *brigata*'s response to it. Their collective action of praising the widow shows their choice to abstain from indulging in that which is not beautiful in itself. As the Dantean intertext suggests, the exercise of judgment is essential to this novella, made evident when the widow recuses herself and the *brigata* remains silent about the provost and Ciutazza. The implication of enjoying the tale, then, is misplacing one's pleasure in that which is not good. Ciutazza is the very embodiment of this concept, for there is a pleasure to be had in the exaggerated detail of her ugliness; the description of Ciutazza being the most in-depth of the novella. Her name is the only one used throughout the tale, assigning her a distinct identity in contradistinction to the widow – whose name is mentioned only once at the beginning – and the provost, who are known by their positions in society. The pleasure one derives from Ciutazza's ugliness is a mental pleasure, related to the nearly perfect inversion of a topical description of female beauty in medieval texts and the aptness of this perversion in setting up the provost for humiliation. Yet if the *brigata*'s response is to be a guide, demonstrating active delight in Ciutazza's ugliness and the provost's humiliation seems tantamount to an unmeasured, unreasonable response. The only appropriate response in order to show virtue is to abstain from showing that one has enjoyed the tale. In this respect,

21 Laughter is the response to VIII.2, VIII.5, VIII.6, and VIII.9, whereas VIII.3 is said to have pleased the ladies.

Emilia's novella catches her audience in an impossible situation, but designating the tale a *ragionamento* rather than a *novella* offers an escape from a morally charged and aesthetic response; one can respond with reason and logic, as the *brigata* do when they commend the widow, and one can take internal, mental pleasure that remains hidden while displaying a measured response. Indeed, the ladies of the *Proemio* who suffer from melancholy, a mental state for which they have no means of external manifestation, are advised to take solace internally through the aesthetic pleasures offered in Boccaccio's book.

Is Emilia's *ragionamento* intended as a condemnation of the other tricks recounted on Day Eight and of allowing oneself to enjoy the absence of good and beauty? The tales of Day Eight become increasingly violent and even sadistic, but they are also highly amusing. Moreover, in VIII.4 the responses of the provost and Ciutazza to their night together, and Ciutazza to her *camiscia*, are both aesthetic, but then neither character is a model of reason or moral rectitude. The absence of condemnation of either character by the *brigata* undermines a moralistic approach. The implication of VIII.4 is that the absence of beauty can be pleasurable without being morally improper. In this respect, VIII.4 subverts the comic and escapist cast of the other tales narrated on Day Eight by bringing to the fore questions of morality and aesthetics as mental activities. Ultimately, Novella VIII.4 seems to suggest that balance is required between absence and presence, between the mental pleasure and the physical execution of that pleasure, in order to achieve that which is good.

The Jokesters and the Judge (VIII.5)

WILLIAM ROBINS AND LEAH FAIBISOFF

Decameron VIII.5 tells how three Florentine jokesters – Maso del Saggio and his friends Ribi and Matteuzzo – pull down the breeches of a foreign judge, publicly humiliating Niccola da San Lepidio in his own courtroom.[1] At first blush this is a simple novella: the prank is one of the more puerile *beffe* reported in the *Decameron*, and the short narrative presents no significant complications of plot or character. Yet it enjoyed local appeal – it is the only one of Boccaccio's tales explicitly mentioned by his fellow *novelliere* Franco Sacchetti – and it encodes significant social and literary concerns, as has been revealed by recent scholarship, which notes how its tension between Florentines and non-Florentines plays into Day Eight's pitting of insiders against outsiders, and how the courtroom scene displays an incipient theatricality.[2] Building upon those insights, this essay demonstrates that *Decameron* VIII.5 registers some particularly Florentine concerns about the nature of the public sphere. We argue that Boccaccio transposes into the narrative structure of a *beffa* procedures through which Florentines, even the disenfranchised, were able to participate in juridical structures of communal governance and thereby create a sense of common knowledge and shared purpose.

---

1 The *Decameron* is cited from the text edited by Maurizio Fiorilla in Boccaccio, *Decameron*, ed. Quondam, Fiorilla, and Alfano; translations are from Boccaccio, *Decameron*, trans. McWilliam.

2 *Decameron* VIII.5 has received minimal critical attention. We have found helpful insights in Baratto, *Realtà e stile*, 260–4; Mazzotta, *The World at Play*, 185–8; Grimaldi, *Il privilegio di Dioneo*, 290–3; Savelli, "Riso"; Holmes, "Trial by *Beffa*"; Zunino, "*Florentini, trufatores*"; and Brown, "Splitting Pants and Pigs." A good summary of critical concerns is provided in Alfano's "Scheda introduttiva" to the novella in Boccaccio, *Decameron*, ed. Quondam, Fiorilla, and Alfano, 1179. Sacchetti cites Boccaccio's tale in *Il Trecentonovelle* 49.15, ed. Puccini, p. 173.

Decameron VIII.5 as a *Novella di Beffa*

The narratological schema of *Decameron* VIII.5 corresponds well to that proposed by Claude Cazalé Bérard, according to which the core pattern for a *novella di beffa* entails five steps: an initial problematic state; an opportunity; the performance of a trick; the resulting derision; and a final situation of advantage (*Stratégie*, 109–11). Here, the *initial problematic state* is the presence in Florence of foreign judges whose dress and demeanour are unworthy of their profession, with Niccola da San Lepidio singled out as especially slovenly. At stake here is a violation of the rules of judiciary decorum, for Niccola's appearance falls far short of the dignity expected of a man of his status. The *opportunity for a beffa* arises when Maso del Saggio, a local merry-maker, notices Niccola and measures him up as an easy target:

> guardato là dove questo messer Niccola sedeva, parendogli che fosse un nuovo uccellone, tutto il venne considerando. E come che egli gli vedesse il vaio tutto affummicato in capo e un pennaiuolo a cintola e più lunga la gonnella che la guarnacca e assai altre cose tutte strane da ordinato e costumato uomo, tra queste una, ch'è più notabile che alcuna dell'altre al parer suo, ne gli vide, e ciò fu un paio di brache, le quali, sedendo egli e i panni per istrettezza standogli aperti dinanzi, vide che il fondo loro infino a mezza gamba gli agiugnea. (VIII.5.6–7)

> [His gaze being attracted to the place where this Messer Niccola was sitting, he was struck by the man's curious and witless appearance, and began to scrutinize him carefully. And amongst the many strange features that he noted, unbecoming in any person of tidy habits and gentle breeding, he saw that the fur of his judge's cap was thick with grime, that he had a quill-case dangling from his waist, and that his gown was longer than his robe. But the most remarkable thing of all, to Maso's way of thinking, was a pair of breeches, the crotch of which, when the judge was sitting down and his clothes gaped open in front owing to their skimpiness, appeared to come halfway down his legs.]

Maso brings his friends Ribi and Matteuzzo to gaze upon the judge and they make plans to humiliate him the next day, as the opportunity is too good to pass up.

The *performance of the beffa* ensues the next morning. In the crowded courtroom, Ribi and Maso dupe the judge into listening to a bogus legal dispute. Haranguing the judge in a rush of local dialect and parodic courtroom language, they wheedle him into standing up, enabling

Matteuzzo, who has crawled under the judge's bench, to pull down the judge's breeches. Through its careful staging, the scene presents the classic mechanism of a *beffa*, where practical jokers employ ingenuity, bodily actions, surprise, and a dose of cruelty to turn a gullible dupe into a public laughingstock. The *resulting derision* is signalled by the embarrassment of Niccola, intensified by the continued mockery of the jokesters, and amplified by the fact that there is a large audience of onlookers:

> Il quale, questo fatto sentendo e non sappiendo che ciò si fosse, volendosi tirare i panni dinanzi e ricoprirsi e porsi a sedere, Maso dall'un lato e Ribi dall'altro pur tenendolo e gridando forte ... e tanto in queste parole il tennero per li panni, che quanti nella corte n'erano s'accorsero essergli state tratte le brache. (VIII.5.15–16)

> [Being at a loss to understand how this had come about, the judge tried to cover himself up by drawing his clothes across the front of his body and sitting down, but Maso and Ribi were still holding on to them at either side and shouting their heads off ... they held on to his clothes sufficiently long for everyone in court to perceive that he had lost his breeches.]

The in-group thus extends beyond the three pranksters to the whole courtroom audience of Florentines. The *final situation of the beffa* entails the discomfiture of the judge, leaving Niccola da San Lepidio alone, exposed, and degraded in his own courtroom. The *beffa* gives the upper hand to the Florentines, who mock the inadequacy of judge Niccola's pretensions to his exalted role and revel in his indignant bewilderment.

Following as it does "the classic pattern of the *beffa*" (Mazzotta, *World at Play*, 186), the tale has struck most readers as presenting a straightforward mechanism of low comedy. Emma Grimaldi, for example, holds that "the immediate thunder-clap of the action consummates and exhausts the distinctive trick played by Maso del Saggio on the judge from the Marche."[3] Savelli likewise maintains that "the principal of comeuppance which motivates the jokesters is not going to clash with any problematic subject; the laughter has no particular rhetorical purpose; and correspondingly this novella, with its local flavour, remains

3 "L'istantanea fulmineità del gesto assomma ed esaurisce in sé la peculiarità del tiro giocato da Maso del Saggio al giudice marchigiano" (Grimaldi, *Il privilegio di Dioneo*, 292).

marginal within the textual system of the *Decameron*."[4] Boccaccio indeed comes as close here as he ever does to a degree-zero expression of the *novella di beffa* genre; however, as we argue below, through such a pared-down schema Boccaccio evokes serious social and political issues faced by Florence's citizens.

Decameron VIII.5 signals its larger significance in its opening and closing paragraphs, which are not necessary for the narrative of the *beffa* at all, and which serve instead to evoke the socio-cultural context of Florentine governance within which the practical joke is to be understood. The first person described in the novella is not judge Niccola but rather his boss, a Podestà from the region of the Marche:

> Come voi tutte potete avere udito, nella nostra città vegnono molto spesso rettori marchigiani, li quali generalmente sono uomini di povero cuore e di vita tanto strema e tanto misera, che altro non pare ogni lor fatto che una pidocchieria: e per questa loro innata miseria e avarizia menan seco e giudici e notari che paiono uomini levati più tosto dall'aratro o tratti dalla calzoleria, che delle scuole delle leggi. Ora, essendovene venuto uno per podestà, tra gli altri molti giudici che seco menò, ne menò uno il quale si facea chiamare messer Niccola da San Lepidio, il quale pareva più tosto un magnano che altro a vedere. (VIII.5.4–5)

> [As all of you will doubtless have heard, the chief magistrates of our city very often come from the Marches, and tend as a rule to be mean-hearted men, who lead such a frugal and beggarly sort of life that anyone would think they hadn't a penny to bless themselves with. And because of their inborn miserliness and avarice, they bring with them judges and notaries who seem to have been brought up behind a plough or recruited from a cobbler's shop rather than from any of the schools of law. Now, one of these March-men came here once to take up his appointment as *podestà*, and among the numerous judges he brought with him, there was one called Messer Niccola da San Lepidio, who looked more like a coppersmith than anything else.]

This opening is a first clue that the tale will register concerns about Florentine governance and the public sphere. The judge's slovenliness

4 "Il principio di adeguatezza, virtù dei beffatori, non va a collidere con alcuna area problematica; il riso non ha alcun particolare impiego retorico; la novella, di sapore comunale, risulta, analogamente, marginale nel sistema del testo" (Savelli, "Riso," 355).

derives from the Podestà's tight-fistedness, which, in turn, is characterized as typical of the foreign officials who come to Florence from the Marche.

The Florentine public still expected a Podestà to have the charisma of a prestigious noble, as in days past: throughout the Trecento, as Richard Trexler has argued, the Podestà stood "at the center of sovereign representation" in the public rituals asserting the legitimacy and authority of the Commune (*Public Life*, 260). Nevertheless, as Jean-Claude Maire Vigueur has recently shown, the social background of foreign officials was changing over the course of the century. The job itself had largely been transformed into that of a high-level administrative functionary, increasingly requiring narrow technical and managerial competencies. The change opened the doors to members of the lesser nobility as well as men of non-elite status, especially those from small towns and remote regions trying to escape impoverishment. They entered into the legal profession in the hope of bettering their fortunes with a career as an itinerant judge or even a *rettore forestiere* (Maire Vigueur, "Nello Stato della Chiesa," 808–14; Maire Vigueur, "Flussi, circuiti e profili," 1097–9; see also Zorzi, "I rettori di Firenze"). To serve this aspirational group, law schools sprang up in numerous small centres, most notably in the region of the Marche, a geographical concentration noted by Boccaccio's own law teacher, Cino da Pistoia: "Plus dicunt quidam Moderni, ut Richardus Malumbra, quod possint hec iura hodie doceri in qualibet civitate vel castro, ut Mutine, Rhegi, Parme, Versellis, et in castris, ut vidimus maxime in provincia Marchie Anconitane" [Moreover some moderns, such as Riccardo Malombra, say that these laws today can be taught in any city or small town, for example in Modena, Reggio, Parma, Vercelli, as well as in small towns such as we see especially in the region of the Marche near Ancona (cited in Maire Vigueur, "Nello Stato della Chiesa," 813n124)].

In Boccaccio's tale, both the stingy Podestà and the dishevelled judge barely educated in "scuole delle leggi" [schools of law] have come from the Marche. For Maire-Vigueur, *Decameron* VIII.5 illustrates the scorn in which Florentine elites like Boccaccio held these rustic judges who were making inroads into positions traditionally reserved for men of noble dignity ("Nello Stato della Chiesa," 809–10). In the novella itself, however, Boccaccio imputes that scorn not to elites like himself but to lower-class Florentines such as Maso and his friends.

The judge's failure to meet traditional expectations of a decorous bearing is epitomized by his slovenly dress. Florentines expected their judges to look the part. For example, in 1366 the city's Guild of Judges and Notaries determined,

> ut dicta ars honorifica reddatur ut consuevit antiquis temporibus, et maxime circa honorificum statum et de lationem honorificarum vestium iudicum dicti collegii, quod quilibet iudex dicte artis teneatur et debeat vestes honorificas deferre quolibet tempore, et maxime fulcitas maspillis argenteis deauratis et cum cappuceo fulto vario seu sciamito vel sericino seu alio panno et cum ermellino in extremitate ipsius cappucei, sub pena librarum quinque f. p. per qualibet vice.[5]
>
> [so that the Guild might be regarded as honourable, as it was in times past, specifically with respect to honourable demeanour and the wearing of honourable clothes by the judges of this Guild, the Guild Council decrees that each judge of the Guild is expected to and must don honourable vestments on every occasion, specifically clothes adorned with gilded silver buttons, and with a hood adorned in a variegated fashion with samite or with silk or some other cloth, and with ermine around the edge of the hood, under penalty of five *lire* for every lapse.]

Amidst such expectations, judge Niccola's poor appearance, a consequence of the Podestà's stingy vulgarity, demeans his office and is an affront to all Florentines.

A socio-political context is also indicated at the novella's conclusion, which extends beyond the final situation of the *beffa* – the humiliation of the judge – to describe the reaction of the Podestà:

> Il podestà d'altra parte, sentitolo, fece un grande schiamazzio: poi per suoi amici mostratogli che questo non gli era fatto se non per mostrargli che i fiorentin conoscevano che, dove egli doveva aver menati giudici, egli aveva menati becconi per averne miglior mercato, per lo migliore si tacque, né più avanti andò la cosa per quella volta. (VIII.5.20)
>
> [When the *podestà*, for his part, was told what had happened, he practically threw a fit. But when it was pointed out by his friends that this had only been done in order to show him that the Florentines knew he had brought fools with him instead of judges so as to save money, he thought it best to hold his tongue, and nothing more was said about the matter.]

5 Florence, Archivio di Stato di Firenze, Arte dei Giudici e Notai 748, fol. 12v.

The novella's denouement stages a question about how the preceding *beffa* should be interpreted. This shift is a crucial part of the tale, as has been recently noted by Estelle Zunino. She writes that "the Podestà and his friends are extradiegetic characters who understand and decode the socio-political resonance as well as the message contained in the affront."[6] The Podestà's friends (*amici*) reveal the joke's political message, spelling out for the Podestà that the jokesters have acted to defend Florence's dignity on behalf of the civic community at large.

The narrative tension of the novella is finally resolved only when the perspectives of Florentines of very different social status, the jokesters and the Podestà's friends, are brought into alignment. A crucial feature of *Decameron* VIII.5 is that a defence of the honour and dignity of the Commune of Florence is mounted by Florentines of humble status. Maso del Saggio and Ribi, and presumably also Matteuzzo, seem to be based upon historical figures who belonged to a subaltern class of local *buffoni* (merry-makers). According to Boccaccio's acquaintance Franco Sacchetti, Maso was a Florentine *sensale* (*Trecentonovelle* 93.2, 275). *Sensali* were small-scale brokers of goods: peddlers, servants acting as stewards, handlers working for cloth merchants, etc.; not being enfranchised within any of the guilds, they belonged to the *popolo minuto*.[7] Sacchetti describes Ribi as a well-known but down-and-out *buffone* and travelling entertainer (*Trecentonovelle* 49.2–4, 170–1; Bruscagli, "Ribi buffone"). In the *Decameron*, while the occupations of the three jokesters are not specified, they evidently belong to Florence's *popolo minuto* and, more generally, are representative of the city's population as a whole. Seemingly having ample time on their hands, these men of the streets take an active interest in the public life of the city, and take it upon themselves to stand up for the dignity of the Commune.[8]

6 "personnages extradiégétiques à la beffa qui comprennent et décodent la résonance sociale et politique ainsi que le message contenu dans la sanction" (Zunino, "*Florentini, trufatores maximi*," 105).

7 See the *Opera del Vocabolario Italiano* database, under *sensal.**.

8 Our interpretation of the sociological differences staged in the novella differs significantly from Holmes, "Trial by *Beffa*." Holmes argues that the shabby dress of the judge marks him out as lower class, in comparison with the jokesters, each of whom aims to be an "ordinato e costumato uomo." To our eye the indications of social distinction read differently: Niccola da San Lepidio is a highly trained member of a professional cadre of experts, even if he is relatively impoverished compared to other judges; the three jokesters are, as Sacchetti indicates, subaltern inhabitants of the city; and the phrase "ordinato e costumato uomo" does not refer to the jokesters, but to the norm against which Niccola is measured.

As for the *amici* who check the Podestà's anger, there are two possible interpretations. Amongst the *familia* of the Podestà numbered a few aristocratic knights who kept him company, so Boccaccio could be referring to this coterie. At the same time, however, there was an important local institution, the office of the *sapientes communis*, staffed by Florentine lawyers, who routinely furnished the Podestà and his judges with advice on matters of law; the legal *consilia* they adduced were explicitly binding on judges (Guidi, *Il governo della città-repubblica*, 2:37; Kirshner, "A Critical Appreciation," 16). These experts, almost always members of the Florentine elite, served as a mediating body, providing normative interpretations of the city's *ius comune* and guarding against wrongful judgments by the foreign rectors. Considering that the *amici* in *Decameron* VIII.5 advise the Podestà on how to interpret an occurrence in one of his courtrooms, it seems appropriate to equate them with the Florentine *sapientes*, who as insiders would have understood the implications of the jest perpetrated by their fellow Florentines. The tale's conclusion, then, seems to show elite, expert Florentines aligning with their non-elite, non-expert fellow citizens, as they interpret for the sake of the Podestà the message contained in the *beffa*.

Common Knowledge

In communal Florence, institutions of governance were designed so that the authority to make politically important decisions would be distributed across a wide range of citizens. This is most powerfully exemplified in the way the highest offices were shared. The chief executive office, the *Signoria*, consisted of eight Priors plus one Standard-Bearer who held office for two months before quickly making way for a new *Signoria* with different perspectives, interests, and alliances. As for the deliberative Councils which represented the sovereignty of the city-state and whose approval was required for any legislation proposed by the *Signoria*, the three hundred members of the *Consiglio del Popolo* as well as the four hundred (after the Black Death, two hundred) of the *Consiglio del Comune* held terms of six months. Theoretically, these and other magistracies provided thousands of Florentines, elite and non-elite, with direct experience in participatory government.

Nevertheless, there were strict limits on which Florentines were eligible for high office. Women were entirely excluded. Aristocratic magnates were permitted into some, but not all, roles. Most importantly for the politics of the period, the highest offices were for the most part open only to members of the seven major guilds, and even then only for men approved as reliable by special commissions charged with the "scrutiny" (*squitinio*) of citizens eligible for major political offices. In general, the same persons who made it through the scrutinies to hold political office would subsequently become members of the scrutiny commissions, resulting in a tightly restricted political class. Demands to extend eligibility to the members of the minor guilds and include their names in the scrutinies were met with resistance by the oligarchic leaders of the guild-based *popolo* and became flashpoints in the political history of the Commune. Florentine "democracy" is thus riven by a constitutive tension: on the one hand, there was a communal, corporatist ideology which held that wide participation of citizens in political structures was desirable, while on the other hand there was a still highly hierarchical social system in which the elite *grandi* combined with sympathetic members of the guild community to limit or exclude the artisan and lower classes from having a direct say in governance (Najemy, *Corporatism and Consensus*).

"Deeply ingrained in the Florentine political mentality," Gene Brucker has noted, "was a fundamental precept of republicanism: the formulation of policy through group consultation" (*Florentine Politics and Society*, 75). Through deliberaton and debate, the social diversity of the Florentine *popolo* (guild members) became a source of strength, and the ability to participate directly in the debates about the future of the city was a matter of great pride to enfranchised Florentines (Maire Viguer and Faini, *Il sistema politico*, 95). The Commune could, at least theoretically, arrive at decisions backed by the consent of large portions of the population, and could simultaneously hold in check any overconcentration of power in specific individuals, factions, or groups. Deliberative structures and institutions that allowed for competing interests to be negotiated were the hallmark of Florentine governance at multiple levels, appearing throughout communal government and administration as well as in guild councils, confraternities, and neighbourhood organizations.

As this dynamic of participation permeated public life, "the masses of politically aware but disenfranchised workers and artisans" (Najemy, *Corporatism and Consensus*, 37), while ineligible for the *Signoria* and Councils, participated in civic life in many other ways: joining confraternities, paying taxes, launching lawsuits, and, when all else failed, taking to the streets. They desired and struggled to be included in the political system. In the absence of full enfranchisement, they had to take advantage of other available avenues to make their perspectives known on important civic issues.

In 1342, in the midst of Florence's war with Pisa, a lowly bell-ringer wondered how to make his opinions known: "Signor, pognàm ch'i' sia di vil nascenza, / I' pur nacqui nel corpo di Firenza, / Come qual c'è di più sofficienza / ... Ma perchè 'l no' m'è licito parlare / Dovr'avre' luogo quel ch'i' vo' contare / Dirò per rima che mi par da fare / A questo tratto" [My lords, even if I am of humble birth, nevertheless I was born in the bosom of Florence, just as much as someone of greater wealth ... But because I'm not allowed to speak in the proper place for the topic I want to discuss, I'll recite in verse what I think should be done at this juncture (Pucci, *Poesia popolare*, 264).] The proper place for discussion would be the Councils, where this member of the city's servant class, lacking enrolment in a guild, is not allowed to speak. Instead, he harnesses his poetic skills in order to add his voice to civic debates about the right course of action for the city to take. An expectation of widespread participation in public life underpinned the ideology of guild republicanism: concretely realized in republican institutions of governance, this expectation also created the parameters for a shared social imaginary among Florentines of diverse status, including artisans and labourers who were excluded from office-holding.

This, then, is the social dynamic that we see registered in *Decameron* VIII.5: the structural possibility that non-elite, non-expert Florentines would become engaged in the public sphere on matters of civic interest, making tactical use of available means of discourse within the wider public sphere. Such engagement harnesses what Josiah Ober in his study of pre-modern democratic regimes calls "common knowledge." Ober shows that, compared to royal or aristocratic regimes, democratic city-states could more directly tap into non-expert knowledge dispersed across a variety of social classes. Successful democracies prize this dispersed knowledge (even if, as was usually the case, they do so within defined limits), and develop institutions that allow for the idiosyncratic experiences of ordinary citizens to enhance and become integrated with overarching shared values. The alignment of so many perspectives and interests requires that knowledge dispersed among myriad individuals enters into the sphere of "common knowledge." Common knowledge needs to be built up with respect to various sorts of information: a basic repertoire of procedural rules; a grasp of the salient power distinctions within the community; an understanding of the reasons proffered for and against certain courses of action; an assessment of how credible are the commitments of different parties to follow through with a decision; and so on. A central concern for a democratic state is to develop institutions where multiple perspectives can be voiced without social disruption, where the local knowledge of ordinary citizens can challenge the views of detached experts, and where the perspectives, commitments, and intentions of various social groups can become well known to the wider public (Ober, *Democracy and Knowledge*, passim)

The *beffa* at the end of *Decameron* VIII.5, according to Zunino, functions as a mechanism of communal reprisal, with the city delegating to the jokesters the power to sanction those who have transgressed the community's code of behaviour ("*Florentini, trufatores maximi,*" 106). Ober's study of early democratic regimes brings us to an alternative reading of this scene. Rather than the community delegating a role to the jokesters, the jokesters exploit a discursive possibility so that their views about judge Niccola become common knowledge. Rather than reprimanding the Podestà themselves, they convey through their prank a message of disapproval, well understood by the Podestà's *amici*, which ultimately helps align expert and non-expert perspectives: the *beffatori* and the *amici* find common cause. Painlessly aligning diverse social groups, the seemingly straightforward novella embodies the ideology of democratic republicanism, showing that mechanisms for sharing diverse perspectives could overcome internal divisions of class and interest for the sake of the *bene commune*, the common good.

Judging the Judges

The survival of Florence's republican system of government depended to a large extent upon having a reliable, impartial system of justice. Because it was assumed that local magistrates, inevitably caught up in ties of faction, family, and patronage, would execute the law in so partisan a fashion that the common good would be entirely undermined, Florence, like other Italian communes, entrusted the administration of the judiciary to *rettori forestieri* (foreign magistrates). It was hoped that these eminent foreigners, recruited along with their accompanying judges and notaries from other cities, would provide the citizens of Florence with impartial justice. The preeminent foreign magistrate was the Podestà, represented in *Decameron* VIII.5 as a key figure of governance. Responsible for overseeing the administration of justice and public order, for guarding the city's Treasury, and for ensuring the enforcement of legislation, the Podestà also presided over the *Consiglio del Comune* and could be called upon to lead the army into the field. During his six-month term, he and his entourage of judges, notaries, policemen, and servants lived and worked in the Palazzo del Podestà. In the second half of the fourteenth century, the Podestà typically brought to Florence two supporting judges (*giudici collaterali*), two judges to preside over civil courts, and two other judges, like Niccola da San Lepidio, to preside over criminal courts (Davidsohn, *Storia di*

Firenze, 4.1:134–50; Guidi, *Il governo della città-repubblica*, 2:169–73; Stern, *Criminal Law System*, 74–114; Zorzi, "I rettori di Firenze," 456–70; Gualtieri, *Comune di Firenze*, 222–8).

The Podestà's status as an outsider was crucial to his ability to administer the city's judiciary system, but it posed serious problems. His staff might be ignorant of local law and procedure, a concern voiced by Maso and Ribi when they shout at Niccola, "di così piccola cosa, come questa è, non si dà libello in questa terra" [In this country you don't need written evidence to decide a trifling matter of this sort (VIII.5.16)].[9] The Podestà might try to enrich himself and his friends at the expense of the common good, or, worse, actively plot against Florence on behalf of foreign powers. The foreign officials were, at once, privileged insiders and dangerous outsiders. Their dual status is represented in *Decameron* VIII.5 by judge Niccola, an outsider who at the same time has a role within the city. He is easily scapegoated, for he is present within the system but at the same time can be symbolically cast out in order to assert a distinction between Florence's friends and enemies. By emphasizing a boundary line already in play in Florentine civic life, where the *rettori forestieri* were conceived of as simultaneously insiders and outsiders, the jokesters' *beffa* projects a meaningful boundary between citizens and strangers, between Florentine ingenuity and foreign boorishness.

Like the other *rettori forestieri*, the Podestà was subject to a process of review at the end of his term called the *sindacato* (syndication). It was understood that the properly impartial functioning of the position of Podestà depended upon a robust process of syndication, a crucial feature of which was that it accepted grievances from citizens of all classes, who could bring complaints in their own interest or in the name of the Commune as a whole. A syndication committee was appointed especially for the occasion by the *Signoria*, who drew the names of eight men (two from each quarter) by lot. The eight Syndics were aided by a notary, who acted as general secretary, and several jurists, who acted as their legal aides. In a process that lasted about a week, the Syndics conducted hearings on complaints about the conduct of the Podestà and his retinue, including his judges. The Syndics were obliged to consider all petitions received, their sentences could not be appealed, and conviction in a *sindacato* could disqualify a Podestà from serving in any other city (Masi, "Il sindicato"; Martines, *Lawyers and Statecraft*, 143–5; Guidi, *Il governo della città-repubblica*, 338; Maire Vigeur, *I Podestà*, 585–6; and Isenmann, "From Rule of Law to Emergency Rule").

9 McWilliam's translation has been slightly modified.

The seriousness with which Florentines approached the *sindacato* process is attested by Giovanni Villani, whose account of an uprising in July of 1337 resonates strikingly with aspects of *Decameron* VIII.5. When the outgoing Podestà, Niccola de la Serra from Gubbio, was found by the Syndics to have been culpable of malfeasance during his term, the *sindacato* process was abruptly halted by the city's other foreign rectors, including the Conservator of Peace, Accorimbono from Tolentino.

> non lasciando a' sindachi in ciò fare loro officio, gente minuta si commosse, e fue in parte la città a romore in su le piazze de le segnorie, perché non si facea iustizia de la podestà e di sua famiglia; e co' sassi cacciati fuoro e fediti, e alquanti morti delle famiglie delle dette segnorie a lloro gran difetto, spezialmente quella del detto meser Accorrimbono, onde tutta la città si comosse. (Villani, *Nuova Cronica* 12.39, 3:89)

> [When they refused to let the Syndics perform their office, the lower-class people [*gente minuta*] rose up, and a part of the city's population was in uproar in the piazzas in front of the palaces of the foreign rectors because justice was not being done against the Podestà and his retinue. And they were chased out and injured by stones, and some men from the retinues of the foreign rectors were killed, reducing their numbers considerably, especially for the retinue of Accorimbono. Then the entire population of the city was in an uproar.]

At first Accorimbono wanted to execute some of the ringleaders, but fearful of the the artisan and working classes, and unable to act because of the anger of the guildsmen, he instead issued fines to both the outgoing Podestà and the rebellion's leaders. The event was so traumatic that the Commune of Florence abolished the position of Conservator of Peace inaugurated only the year before, and decreed that the city would never again have a foreign rector from Gubbio. For Villani, the story sounds a warning against the dangers of tyranny (*Nuova Cronica* 12.39, 3:87–91).

Like the Podestà and the judge in *Decameron* VIII.5, the Conservator of Peace and the Podestà in Villani's account hail from in and around the Marche, the former coming from Tolentino, a town in the Marche, the latter from nearby Gubbio. Just as tantalizingly, in both narratives the subordinate official bears the name Niccola. More significantly, the uprising reported by Villani and the *beffa* narrated by Boccaccio reveal a dynamic of political participation in which lower-class citizens defend the polity of Florence against malfeasance by foreign officials. In both narratives, Florentine commoners assemble in public to show their outrage after a top-ranking foreign rector from the Marche turns a blind eye to the misbehaviour of a subordinate foreign official; at first the foreign rector wishes to avenge the aggression against his retinue, but when he realizes that other classes support the position of the *popolo minuto*, he settles on a more tempered reaction. Both stories exemplify Florentine citizens being vigilant against the greed and misconduct of foreign rectors.

Florentine citizens used the syndication process to turn the tables and judge their judges. As Villani's account of 1337 shows, the entire population, not just the elites, took an interest in the *sindacato*. Citizens felt it within their rights to evaluate each Podestà according to how well the chief magistrate and his retinue had served the Commune. It was understood, then, that the foreign judges would eventually be judged by Florentines, both individually and in the name of the Commune. Boccaccio explicitly relates the jokesters' *beffa* to the *sindacato* process. Ribi tauntingly tells the judge that his negligence will be an issue during the *sindacato*: "Io fo boto a Dio d'aiutarmene al sindacato!" [I swear to God I'll appeal to the Syndics! (VIII.5.17)].[10] Here Boccaccio signals how the prank of the jokesters does the work of the *sindacato* by parodic means, the narrative logic of the *novella di beffa* reproducing the juridical logic of syndication.[11]

A fine example of Florentines passing judgment on the Podestà and his judges comes from an unedited Trecento *sirventese*, slightly later than the *Decameron*, in which each stanza evaluates a Podestà, including these summary judgments upon two Podestàs from the Marche:

Messer Balighan poi viene da Iesi,
che ttra gli offenditor e ttra gli ofesi
fè moltte pace, e 'nfine enpien d'arnesi
le valigi ...
[M]esser tTomaso d'Anchona [rettore]
fu dopo lui de la città [del fiore];
questi fu monttanaro, e ['l suo cuore]
non valse un fungho.[12]

10 McWilliam's translation has been slightly modified.

11 For other novelle that evoke the Florentine *sindacato* process, see Sacchetti, *Trecentonovelle* 139.2 and 196.18–20, ed. Puccini, pp. 370 and 563.

12 Florence, Biblioteca Nazionale Centrale, MS Nuovi Acquisti 333, fols 60r–61r.

> [Sir Baligan next came from Iesi: he arranged many peaceful settlements between offenders and victims, and at the end he packed his bags full of trappings … After him, Sir Tomaso of Ancona was chief magistrate of Florence; he was a hillbilly, and his judgment wasn't worth a mushroom.]

Baligan of Iesi (Podestà from June to December 1362) is here praised for peacefully settling disputes between litigants, for which he passes through the *sindacato* process with no fines or levies, leaving with a full purse.[13] By contrast, Tomaso d'Ancona (Podestà from July to December 1364) receives scorn for his lack of dignity and his incompetence: he is just a hillbilly from the mountains. Corroborating Boccaccio's scorn for boorish rectors from the Marche, the *sirventese* shows that judging the competence and comportment of Podestàs and their retinue, anchored by the *sindacato* process, was a collective sport that helped forge Florence's republican identity.

Spectacle

In *Decameron* VIII.5 Boccaccio transposes into the form of a *novella di beffa* features of Florentine public life, some involving general tendencies within the democratic communal ideology, others involving specific institutions by which those tendencies were actualized. As we have seen, various elements of guild republicanism inform the basic narrative components of character (the humble jokesters, the unworthy foreign officials, the elite *amici*) and action (the *beffa* as a mechanism, like the *sindacato*, of judging the judges). Resonances between this *novella di beffa* and Florentine governance also inform the choice of the tale's setting at the Palazzo del Podestà, referred to simply as *il Palagio*. The Palazzo del Podestà was constructed in the 1250s to house

13 Compare the account of syndication in the Trecento translation of Brunetto Latini's *Tresor*: "Quando tu sei a ciò venuto, che convien che tu stia a sindacato, e renda ragione di tutto il tuo ufficio e di tuoi; se nullo vi fosse che si lamentasse di te, tu déi far dare le petizioni di sua dimanda, ed aver consiglio de' tuoi savi, e rispondere come ti consiglieranno … Allora, se a Dio piace, tu sarai assoluto onorevolmente, e prenderai commiato dal comune, e dal consiglio della città, e anderai con gloria, e con onore, e con buona ventura" [Because you will have to stand before the *sindacato* and render an account of your office and your officers, in order for you to have no cause to lament, from the start of your term you must follow up with all petitions you receive, take advice from your counsellors, and respond as they advise … Then, God willing, you will be honourably absolved, and you'll take your leave of the Commune and the Councils and depart with glory, honour, and good fortune (Latini, *Il tesoro* 9.34, 4:383)].

the city's new popular government, and throughout the fourteenth century it was continually enlarged and renovated, remaining the city's most important forum for conducting civic business, even after the new Palazzo della Signoria (now the Palazzo Vecchio) eclipsed it as a site of executive power. The city's judiciary system was based here, as were numerous communal offices with which citizens interacted regularly, from the city treasury to the police, the tax collectors, and the town criers. The *Consiglio del Comune*, over which the Podestà presided, debated legislation in the great Council Hall, while the Podestà and his entourage lived in apartments in the building's southern block (Davidsohn, *Storia di Firenze*, 5:569–76; Yun, *The Bargello Palace*, 123–78; see also Atkinson, *Noisy Renaissance*, 122–36).

The action of *Decameron* VIII.5 begins when Maso passes through the *Palagio*: "E come spesso avviene che, bene che i cittadini non abbiano a fare cosa del mondo a palagio, pur talvolta vi vanno, avvenne che Maso del Saggio una mattina, cercando d'un suo amico, v'andò" [Now it frequently happens that people go to the Palazzo who have no business to be there at all, and this was the case with Maso del Saggio, who had gone there one morning to look for a friend (VIII.5.6)].[14] As Maso's movements show, the *Palagio* was the nerve centre of public life, a hub like the ancient Roman forum or Athenian agora where citizens met each other and stayed abreast of news. Its space enabled all sorts of transactions among citizens of all classes, including those between non-expert citizens and civic administrators, and between the local population and the foreign Podestà and his judges. The public architecture of the Palazzo, like the open expanse of Piazza della Signoria, existed as a "shared space ... a site of civic tension where the anxieties concerning the intentions and integrity of different groupings could be expressed" (Milner, "Florentine Piazza della Signoria," 95–6). Boccaccio captures the sense of civic energy by presenting the space dynamically: we see the Palazzo not through static description, but through a rapidity of movement characteristic of *novelle di beffa*. The narrative traces Maso and his friends as they saunter in and out of the building, following them through passageways between rooms and into the urban fabric outside. Through this movement, the rather minimal story-space of *Decameron* VIII.5 expands, on the basis of the imagination and the real-world experience of the readers, into a symbolically charged narrative world.

Where the Palazzo is a place for movement, the courtroom of Niccola di San Lepidio is a place for sight. The description of the courtroom

---

14 McWilliam's translation has been slightly modified.

and the judge is focalized through the perspective of the characters, so that we see the scene first through their eyes and follow their lines of sight. The visual qualities of the courtroom (designed so that the judge's tribunal would be easily visible) are crucial to the jokesters' plan to humiliate the judge. The Florentine audience takes in the sight of Niccola on his raised bench with his breeches at his ankles: "quanti nella corte n'erano s'accorsero essergli state tratte le brache" [everyone in the court perceived that he had lost his breeches (VIII.5.16)].[15] At the courtrooms in the Palazzo del Podestà, citizens of all classes could gather together, watch cases unfold, and achieve a high degree of "common knowledge" about legal procedures and civic norms, as Maso and Ribi manifest when they mimic the language of judicial tribunals in the midst of their *beffa*.

As Josiah Ober reminds us, pre-modern democracies require an architecture where citizens can see and be seen by each other, listen to each other and learn about others' motives and interests, and make sure their own interest are also known by others (*Democracy and Knowledge*, 199–205; for communal Italy, see Tanzini, *A consiglio*, 127–36). An architecture of intervisibility is crucial because it enables both the production of common knowledge and wide participation in decision making. Florence's large interior spaces, which made possible the intervisible participation, debate, and deliberation upon which the communal structure of government depended, such as the Council Hall on the *primo piano* of the Palazzo del Podestà, are echoed in Boccaccio's portrayal of Niccola's courtroom in the same building, where an ample audience, symbolically representing the audience of Florence itself, witnesses the comeuppance of a foreign judge. By contrast, the concluding episode of the novella, involving the Podestà and his *amici*, occurs in a separate part of the Palazzo ("d'altra parte," presumably the Podestà's own apartments), supplementing the open visibility of the public court with the confidentiality of a backroom conclave.

The various narrative elements of the novella considered here – character, action, and setting – fuse together seamlessly when the jokesters stage their fictional ruse. They appear as if they were litigants, at first arguing against each other, but finally ganging up to shout at the judge in full view of the courtroom audience. Here Boccaccio juxtaposes two practices of public spectacle with which every Florentine was familiar: the sombre pomp of legal tribunals, and the popular, jester-like entertainments of *giullari*, *buffoni*, and *istrioni*. The three jokesters seem

15 McWilliam's translation has been slightly modified.

to have been identifiable as well-known local wits who earned or supplemented their livelihood by performing for gratuities at weddings and other feasts, busking in the piazzas, and clowning around. Ribi especially was famous as a *buffone* (entertainer), described by Franco Sacchetti as an entertainer who performed at aristocratic courts of northern Italy and wedding celebrations in Florence.[16] Maso and Matteuzzo are similarly dedicated to providing recreation and diversion.

Medieval entertainers, unlike modern actors, did not enjoy specific spaces set apart for their antics. They performed in streets, halls, and courtyards, adapting situationally and improvisationally, temporarily transforming public spaces into performance venues wherever they spread a cloth or set up a bench. Their diffuse theatricality was both itinerant and ubiquitous: "The medieval audience did not enter the world of the theatre, the theatre entered the world of the audience" (Cohen, *Drama of a Nation*, 35).[17] The theatricality of the jokesters in *Decameron* VIII.5 transforms the judge's courtroom: "Maso's trick on the judge seems to originate spontaneously and erupt unpremeditated into the ordinary business of life, transforming its texture into a playground, a theatrical space where Maso impersonates both the role of the defendant and the lawyer's cavils" (Mazzotta, *World at Play*, 188). Maso "appropriates the spectacle" already in play in medieval courtrooms (ibid.). The bench in Niccola's courtroom evokes the raised bench onto which medieval performers, the *saltimbanchi* and *cantimbanchi*, raised themselves to be visible to the crowd (Baratto, *Realtà e stile*, 263). The courtroom thereby takes on some of the attributes of a public piazza or an aristocratic hall where *buffoni* would crack jokes, stage pantomimes, and occasionally take it upon themselves to scold their betters.

Bringing together two traditions of visible display – the spectacle of *buffoni*, the pomp of a courtroom – Boccaccio casts judicial tribunals

16 "Questo Ribi fu piacevolissimo e fiorentino, e molto si ridusse, come fanno li suoi pari, nelle Corte de' signori lombardi e romagnuoli, perché con loro facea bene i fatti suoi, ché dava parole e ricevea robe e vestimenti; e quando venìa in Firenze, non guadagnando, ricorrea alcuna volta alle nozze, dove pur alcuna cosa leccava" [This Ribi was very quick-witted and a Florentine. Like his peers, he often visited the courts of the lords of Lombardy and Romagna, because among them he prospered well, for he bestowed upon them his words and he received from them robes and clothing. When he returned to Florence, no longer earning in that way, he sometimes attended wedding celebrations, where he at least picked up some crumbs (Sacchetti, *Trecentonovelle* 49.3, ed. Puccini, p. 171)].

17 On medieval performance traditions in Italy, see especially Allegri, *Teatro e spettacolo*; Pietrini, *Spettacoli e immaginario teatrale*; Mosetti Casaretto, *La scena assente*; and Pietrini, *I giullari*.

as performative spectacles, with judges akin to performers, while also painting the prank as a quasi-judicial mechanism of remediation and civic action. This imaginative exploration of analogies between legal proceedings and performative entertainment underpins Boccaccio's more particular strategy of transposing the juridical logic of the *sindacato* into the narrative logic of a *novella di beffa*.

Boccaccio, Florence, and the Palazzo del Podestà

Was Boccaccio's experimentation with the genre of the *novella di beffa* shaped by his own experiences holding communal office during the time when the *Decameron* was written? The date of the *Decameron*'s composition is not precisely known, but we take the traditional hypothesis of ca 1348–53 as plausible.[18] These are the same years in which Boccaccio first entered into communal employment. Between 1348 and 1354 Boccaccio represented Florence on a number of embassies, and he also performed four stints as an administrative official for the Commune of Florence. The four administrative positions were all performed in the Palazzo del Podestà, the very building that features so prominently in *Decameron* VIII.5.

As *Signore delle Gabelle* (September 1348–January 1348/9), as *Governatore della Gabella del Pane* (August 1352–February 1352/3), and as *Ufficiale della Torre* (January–April 1354), Boccaccio worked out of the *Ufficio della Torre* at the base of the tower of the Palazzo, where the ticket office of the Museo del Bargello stands today.[19] As *Camarlingo della Camera* (January–February 1350/1) he worked in the Treasury (*Camera*), now the museum hall known as the *Sala di Michelangelo*;[20] while fulfilling the role of *Camarlingo* he also appeared regularly at the meetings of the Councils in the great Council Hall on the floor immediately above, now the *Sala di Donatello*.[21] The offices of the Tower (*Torre*) and of the Treasury

---

18 Tradition assigns the completion of the *Decameron* to 1353, Branca retrodates it to 1351, while Lucia Battaglia Ricci and Cursi prudently remind us there is no evidence of circulation that definitely predates 1360 (Branca, *Tradizione*, 2:147–8; Battaglia Ricci, *Boccaccio*, 122; Cursi, *Il Decameron*, 19).

19 See Tanturli and Zamponi, "Biografia"; Regnicoli, "Documenti su Giovanni Boccaccio"; and Regnicoli, "Codice diplomatico di Giovanni Boccaccio."

20 Yun, *The Bargello Palace*, 181–2. The *Ufficio della Torre* was responsible for accounting for all communal property, recording it in the so-called *Libro dello Specchio*. Tower officials rented and administered communal properties, the tenants of which were protected by the Podestà, the Capitano del Popolo, and/or the Executor of the Ordinances of Justice.

21 While Camarlingo, Boccaccio may even have lodged and dined in the Palazzo; see Caferro, *Petrarch's War*, 141.

(*Camera*) were immediately adjacent to each other on the ground floor of the western block of the Palazzo, with doors opening both onto the busy thoroughfare of the Via del Proconsolo and into the central *cortile* of the Palazzo. Across the courtyard, on the other sides of the Palazzo, were the offices and the private chambers of the Podestà and his retinue. Off the courtyard itself is where some of the city's criminal courts, like the one over which Niccola da Lepidio presided, may have been located.[22] Boccaccio had a deep understanding of the proceedings of these criminal courts, having himself brought and lost two cases there in 1352.[23]

Boccaccio's first communal positions in Florence were thus performed at the very heart of the city's administrative and judicial apparatus. He worked in offices humming with the busy activities of notaries, judges, accountants, tax collectors, public works personnel, and members of the Podestà's retinue. On a daily basis the Palazzo was filled by Florentines of all ranks who had routine or special business to conduct. And as Boccaccio tells us in *Decameron* VIII.5, it was also a meeting place for Florentines with time on their hands: "E come spesso avviene che, bene che i cittadini non abbiano a fare cosa del mondo a palagio, pur talvolta vi vanno" [Now it frequently happens that people go to the Palagio who have no business there at all (VIII.5.6)].[24]

It is not inconsequential that Boccaccio set one of his novellas in the building where he himself worked. Boccaccio was not only a subject of institutional authority, he was also an expert agent of it. His experience in these offices gave him a deep, practical understanding of how institutional processes functioned on an everyday basis and how they reflected the values of the republican Commune.[25] Boccaccio's spells of working for the Commune in the Palazzo would have taught him first-hand how to negotiate the tricky dynamics of communal governance and strengthened his background appreciation for the city-state's

22 This is how Yun (*The Bargello Palace*, 150) understands Giovanni Villani's comment about the flood of 1333: "E al palagio del Comune dove sta il podestà salì nella corte di sotto dove si tiene la ragione braccia VI" (*Nuova cronica* 12.1, 3:6).

23 The records of these lawsuits are reported in Florence, Archivio di Stato di Firenze, Podestà 826, fols 28r–v and 78v, and edited in Dorini, "Contributi alla biografia," and Regnicoli, "Documenti su Giovanni Boccaccio," 402.

24 McWilliam's translation has been slightly modified.

25 For instance, the Camarlinghi della Camera del Comune (including Boccaccio during his tenure in January–February 1350/1) were expected to call upon the advice of established Florentine judges (*savi*) in performing their duties and were subject to a process of review and syndication at the end of their term, not unlike the Podestà in *Decameron* VIII.5; see Caferro, *Petrarch's War*, 154.

structures and values. In *Decameron* VIII.5, such knowledge and commitment are translated into a narrative of jest.

The *Decameron* is often seen as Boccaccio's response to the cultural energies that he found in Florence in the years after he returned from Naples in 1340–1. Comparison with his previous immersion in the aristocratic world of Naples allowed him to comprehend what made the social mores and the customary modes of expression in republican Florence both similar to and different from courtly forms. The *Decameron* explores ways to register, in forms of *narratio brevis*, the distinctiveness of this mercantile, municipal, republican culture. Such an estimation of the *Decameron*'s *fiorentinità* in light of Boccaccio's biographical coordinates is commonplace, yet very few studies have attempted to pinpoint more precisely the particular biographical experiences in Florence which might have spurred Boccaccio into adapting specific aesthetic forms in response to the city-state's social realities.

With *Decameron* VIII.5, set in the Palazzo del Podestà with which he was so familiar, Boccaccio boils down the genre of the *novella di beffa* into its essential components, developing resemblances between the narrative logic of the *beffa* genre and central aspects of Florence's participatory democracy. The core analogy lies between the *sindacato* and the *beffa*: the first a mechanism for unmasking wrongdoing by foreign magistrates and preserving the viability of the republican Commune, the second a means for unmasking inflated pretensions and forming an in-group around the shaming of an outsider. The *sindacato* and the *beffa* enable even disenfranchised members of the *popolo minuto* to make known their views on civic matters, and thus help build up common knowledge across the city. In *Decameron* VIII.5 as in the *sindacato*, an ideology of the common good sees the views of the elite and the non-elite, of the experts and non-experts, eventually coming into a beneficial alignment. Such resemblances between the logic of a *beffa* and the dynamics of civic participation are reinforced by casting law and popular entertainment as analogous forms of public spectacle. In these respects, it is not just the content of *Decameron* VIII.5 which is deeply Florentine, but also the form of the *novella di beffa* itself. In this tale, Boccaccio's experimentation – which boils the genre of the *novella di beffa* down to its core structure, and effects a convergence between that narrative structure and mechanisms of political participation in Florence's public sphere – channels the civic energies of Florence into the very forms of storytelling.

The Tale of Calandrino and the Stolen Pig (VIII.6)

RHIANNON DANIELS

The tale of Calandrino and the stolen pig is the second of four *novelle* known as the Calandrino cycle: a micro-collection of stories within the macro-structure of the *Decameron* featuring the Florentine painter Calandrino and his two companions, Bruno and Buffalmacco.[1] In this instalment of their escapades, narrated by Filomena, Calandrino is once again the victim of a cruel joke. Bruno and Buffalmacco manage not only to steal the pig which he has carefully nurtured throughout the year, claiming that Calandrino is in fact the thief and has sold the pig to avoid sharing the proceeds, but they also blackmail him into handing over two pairs of capons.

The Calandrino tales are part of the comic *beffa* tradition, in which the relationship between the *beffatori* and the *beffato* is founded on the nexus between ingenuity and gullibility.[2] The *ingegno* exemplified by Bruno and Buffalmacco, to which Calandrino's archetypal foolishness and credulity is the ultimate foil, is interpreted as a typically Florentine quality.[3] Florentineness is also emphasized because the four

1 The other three *novelle* in the cycle are VIII.3, IX.3, and IX.5. The cycle could be extended to five *novelle* if the main characters are counted as Bruno and Buffalmacco, who appear without Calandrino in VIII.9. On the "'ciclo' di Bruno," see Surdich, "La 'varietà delle cose.'" On the definitions of macrotext and the Calandrino cycle, see Forni, *Forme complesse*, 21, and cf. William Robins's Introduction to the present volume, 12–17.

2 On the *beffa*, see Fontes-Baratto, "La thème de la *beffa*"; Di Maria, "Structure of the Early Form of the *Beffa*"; and Ferroni, "Sulla struttura della beffa." On the comic mode in the *Decameron*, see Mazzotta, "Games of Laughter"; Forno, "L'amaro riso"; and Savelli, "Riso."

3 See, for example, Baratto: "Perché a Firenze si può non solo accertare un profondo impegno intellettuale, ma anche avvertire nella battuta, nel gusto mordace, nella beffa ingegnosa, l'espressione, talvolta del tutto disinteressata, di un'attività dell'intelligenza, l'abitudine insomma ad esercitare quotidianamente l'ingegno"

stories which make up the micro-cycle are set in and around the city, often in named and recognizable locations. Thus, for example, the first Calandrino tale of the heliotrope moves between the Baptistery and the banks of the Mugnone river outside the city gates, while our tale of Calandrino and the stolen pig is set in the *contado*, on a smallholding not far from the city.

The main characters are members of the artisanal and middle classes: Calandrino, Bruno, and Buffalmacco are all introduced as painters (VIII.3.4); other characters featured in VIII.6 include the local priest and a crowd of locals from neighbouring farms called in to witness the *beffa*.[4] This focus on the ordinary working people of Florence and their movements between familiar locations has encouraged a reading of the Calandrino tales which sees them as emblematic of the mimetic tradition.[5] Indeed, the strength of Boccaccio's narrative realism – buttressed by large sections of dialogue, as we shall see – has been such that many scholars have embraced the idea that the tales must be derived from localized collective memory.[6]

It is only comparatively recently that scholars have begun to reveal and explore likely sources, ranging from vernacular and classical literary traditions to biblical and patristic texts, emphasizing the complexity of the intertextual resonances which are at play in these apparently simple comic tales of trickery and counter-trickery.[7] Michelangelo

---

(*Realtà e stile*, 31). Calandrino is thus the "anti-Florentine" (Nissen, *Ethics of Retribution*, 71).

4 Martinez notes that there is an increased focus on Florence in the Days in which the Calandrino tales are narrated, as well as a shift toward the "lesser popolani and *artigiani*, working people one might say" ("Calandrino and the Powers of the Stone," 2).

5 In this context, Marcus's comments in relation to VIII.3 stand for the whole micro-cycle: "the tale has been firmly grounded in the real – a recognizable Florence in a recognizable time in her history, populated by characters whose historicity is a matter of public record" (*An Allegory of Form*, 84).

6 This interpretation persists even in the most recent critical edition of the text, where, in the context of VIII.3, Alfano writes: "Il fatto che questa novella non abbia precedenti nelle fonti antiche ha giustamente fatto pensare a un anedotto fissatosi nella memoria colletiva cittadina. Ciò non vuol dire che si tratti necessariamente di un evento reale … piuttosto, come già s'è visto in precedenza, andrà intesa come un episodio della memoria fiorentina e in particolare della considerazione che si aveva in città per l'ingegno artistico" (Alfano, "Giornata VIII: Scheda introduttiva," 1184). Picone traces the claim for lack of sources back to Vittore Branca's opening note to VIII.3, and to Cesare Segre's judgment that the whole of Day Eight was lacking in known source material (Picone, "L'arte della beffa," 211n26).

7 See, for example, Watson, "The Cement of Fiction"; Kirkham, "Painters at Play"; and Marchesi, *Stratigrafie decameroniane*, 105–36.

Picone has identified a possible source for our tale of the stolen pig in the French fabliau *Barat et Haimet*, in which a side of bacon is stolen by two of the owner's companions. In this new critical context, the previously evoked "memoria municipale" is recalibrated as "memoria letteraria," and the "spirito fiorentino" reworked instead as "tradizionale comicità romanza" (Picone, "L'arte della beffa," 211–13).

Taking my cue from this return to the literary qualities of Calandrino, I argue that the literariness of VIII.6 should be read in the context of the heterogeneous culture in which Boccaccio was operating, wherein both oral performance and textual cultures collided and coalesced.[8] We are used to thinking about the hybridity of the *Decameron* in terms of the mixing of different genres and influences, and the compilatory nature of the work is suggested by the primary narrator himself in his reference to "novelle, o favole, o parabole or istorie" [stories or fables or parables or histories (Proem.13; McWilliam 3)] in the Proem.[9] The concept of hybridity in this case, I argue, encompasses a combination of different modes of production (which itself reflects mobilities in Boccaccio's social, geographical, and literary cultures).[10] The *Decameron* models what John Ahern has called the "dynamics of performance" on an unprecedented scale (Ahern, "Dioneo's Repertory," 56). Indeed, one of Boccaccio's main innovations is the juxtaposition between the inherently oral world of the *brigata*, who not only tell each other stories drawn from their own memorial repertories but also sing a wide range of different types of texts, and the primary narrator, who self-presents as a scribe, transmuting the oral world of the *brigata* into the written word.[11] It is this bringing together of performance mechanisms

8 Here I also acknowledge my debt to Ahern's highly stimulating article "Dioneo's Repertory," in which he opens with this comment on the *Decameron* as a whole: "The very ease with which the text lent itself to performance blinded readers to its literariness" (41).

9 All quotations from the *Decameron* are from Quondam, Fiorilla, and Alfano's 2013 edition. Translations marked with page numbers are from *The Decameron*, translated by McWilliam; all others are my own. Battaglia Ricci argues that the Proem's presentation of the contents excludes "novelle di beffa e di motto" ("Il *Decameron*," 163). On Boccaccio's use of sources and the influence of the fabliaux tradition in particular, see Brown, *Boccaccio's Fabliaux*.

10 On this mobility, see Armstrong, Daniels, and Milner, "Boccaccio as a Cultural Mediator," 3–19.

11 The *Decameron* merits a brief mention by Ong in his seminal work *Orality and Literacy*, thanks to the way in which Boccaccio retains attention to the oral within his written text: "Boccaccio and Chaucer will provide the reader with fictional groups of men and women telling stories to one another ... so that the reader can pretend to be one of the listening company" (103).

which distinguishes the *Decameron* from previous unframed collections of *novelle*, and which left such an important mark on the subsequent development of the novella tradition.[12]

Ahern argues that Boccaccio uses one of the intradiegetic storytellers, Dioneo, to move the text from the oral mode to the written mode, in the process shifting the audience from the group of listening storytellers to the private reading experience of the individual. This reminds us of the importance of thinking about performance not only from the perspective of those who are producing oral or written texts but also in relation to modes of reception. However, in contrast to Ahern's model, which privileges development from one mode to another, I will use my focus on an individual novella in order to explore the ways in which the dynamic between oral and written cultures is not always accompanied by a sense of progression. The movement between oral culture and written culture is figured across the multiple narrative layers which make up the *Decameron* – composed of the world of the primary narrator, the world of the *brigata*, and the *novelle* themselves. Rather than simply shift from the oral to the written, I argue that Boccaccio appears to privilege a mode which fluctuates between the two poles, and/or incorporates elements of both simultaneously.

The tale of Calandrino and the stolen pig can be divided into four sections. The first section (VIII.6.1–15) incorporates both Filomena's introduction and the opening mechanics of the *beffa* where we see Bruno and Buffalmacco developing their plan to steal the pig, and then plying Calandrino with drink and removing the pig while he is in a drunken stupor; the second section (VIII.6.16–29) concerns Calandrino's response to the discovery of the theft and consists largely of dialogue between Calandrino and Bruno; in the third section (VIII.6.30–50) Calandrino is put on public trial and found guilty when he is unable to swallow the ginger sweets which have been doctored with bitter aloe by Bruno and Buffalmacco; the final short section (VIII.6.51–6) consists of additional cruelty when Calandrino is threatened with further retribution and forced to part with two braces of capons. In what follows, my aim is to demonstrate how the humour developed in the core of the tale (sections two and three) is created through a meditation on the clash of oral and written cultures, mixed in with social and cultural stereotyping. Calandrino represents an oral culture associated predominantly

12 See also Brown on the ways in which fabliaux manuscripts "modeled the bringing together of Eastern frames and Western compilations for the *Decameron*" (*Boccaccio's Fabliaux*, 102).

with rural communities, and Bruno and Buffalmacco are more sophisticated and literate urbanites. Within the novella itself, therefore, modes of orality and literacy are connected to a broader cultural conception of character types. This core is then framed by the opening and concluding sections, which are heavily shaped by the *brigata*'s approach to performance and reception, located in oral culture. In turn, these are framed by the culture of the primary narrator, whose first concern is his textual, scribal function of committing the world of the *brigata* to paper (or parchment), and yet who continues to engage with and operate in oral modes.

Orality, Textuality, and Intratextual Reading in the Frame

With the exception of the first and ninth days of storytelling, the one hundred *novelle* in the *Decameron* are linked via a shared theme established by the queen or king for the day. At a more informal level, another network of connections comes into play as the narrators cross-reference each other and use characters, settings, and other details as the source or stimulation for the beginning of a new tale. The persistent use of these self-referencing strategies, which cut through and across the *Decameron*, means that the entire work might be described as fundamentally "intratextual."[13] However, the process is arguably at its most visible within the Calandrino tales, which form an explicit intratextual sequence. In this context the second tale in the series is crucial, as it is the first to establish that Calandrino and his comrades will constitute a narrative cycle of their own. Filomena's opening introduction is concise and appears at first reading to lead almost straight into the plot, and yet the brief reference that she makes to the source of her inspiration is in fact key to understanding the whole novella and Filomena's own performance and reading strategies.

As she explains (VIII.6.3), Filomena is inspired by Elissa in VIII.3 to offer another tale about the exploits of Calandrino and his companions in the same way that Filostrato, in VIII.5, was inspired by the name of Maso del Saggio in VIII.3 to tell another story with Maso as

13 In this context I am using the term *intratextuality* to signal the way in which a text (in this case, the *Decameron*) refers to itself; it is commonly accepted that the *Decameron* is a single text, even while it contains within itself multiple *novelle* which – in a different context – might be extracted and work as stand-alone texts. *Intertextuality* is usually understood to explore the relationship between at least two texts, i.e., in this case between the *Decameron* and a different work, by either Boccaccio or a different author.

the protagonist.[14] The two strands of these individual chain reactions are thus rooted in the common source of VIII.3, creating a particularly dense web of intratextual references. Here, Filomena not only reveals the source of her inspiration, but – by offering an analogy with Filostrato's inspiration – she brings to the surface the compositional process and highlights the importance of an intratextual reading for her tale. The link to VIII.3 is not simply a superficial pretext for beginning her tale, but a key for understanding fully what is to come.[15] As Filomena herself reminds us, the audience is already familiar with the protagonists and therefore has no need of the usual direct characterization: "Chi Calandrino, Bruno e Buffalmacco fossero non bisogna che io vi mostri, ché assai l'avete di sopra udito" [It is unnecessary for me to explain to you who Calandrino, Bruno and Buffalmacco were, for you have heard enough on that score in the earlier tale (VIII.6.4; McWilliam 579)]. With this incitement to recall actively the recently heard (read) novella of the heliotrope, the audience is appropriately predisposed to begin to supplement their reading of this tale with pre-knowledge from the first Calandrino tale.

Filomena's gesture to the previous tale thus recovers memories of how easily Calandrino was tricked and encourages her audience to anticipate what the trick will be in this instance. On the surface it is Calandrino who apparently initiates the first direct contact with Bruno and Buffalmacco, boastfully inviting them to come and observe his excellent husbandry of the pig (VIII.6.6). The earlier representation of the painters in VIII.3, however, suggests that their decision to follow Calandrino to his farm means that they have some tricksy behaviour in mind. This anticipation that they will conform with audience expectations is indeed confirmed by Bruno's opening exclamation: "Deh! come tu sè grosso!" [My goodness, how stupid you are! (VIII.6.7)], which synthesizes Calandrino's role as the simple-minded idiot who will be the butt of the joke devised and perpetrated by Bruno and Buffalmacco, and thereby acts as a neat substitute for the direct characterization which

14 Maso is also mentioned by Fra Cipolla in *Decameron* VI.10.43.

15 It has been common in the critical literature to look at isolated incidences of intratextuality (see, for example, Del Popolo, "Un'espressione di Calandrino"), or to consider connections between *novelle* in terms of the way in which the characterization of Calandrino has developed (see, for example, perhaps the first piece of sustained criticism centred on Calandrino, Trabalza, "La coerenza estestica"). I am arguing here that an intratextual reading does not concern the character Calandrino alone but is a mode of reading which affects the whole of VIII.6.

Filomena deemed unnecessary. Bruno's suggestion that Calandrino should then sell the pig, enjoy the proceeds, and pretend to his wife that the pig has been stolen lays the foundation for the *beffa*, both in terms of the events that will take place – or be deemed to take place – and in terms of the linguistic play on words in which lies the particular ironic cruelty of the trick: Bruno's injunction to "di' che ti sia stato imbolato" [say that it's been stolen (VIII.6.7)] will continue to echo through the tale and the *beffa*, as we shall see. Without knowledge of the previous Calandrino tale it would not be entirely clear at this stage whether Bruno has yet planned to doublecross Calandrino: indeed, had Calandrino agreed to the suggestion and shared the proceeds with Bruno and Buffalmacco, he could have joined his companions as a *beffatore* and made his wife, Monna Tessa, the object of the *beffa*. It is here, however, that the irony begins. Calandrino's refusal to act dishonestly is what ultimately leads to his companions framing him as a thief.

With this brief introduction, Filomena sets up an ideal, intratextual, mode of reading for the novella which depends on a linear chronology: in other words, her presentation of the tale presumes, and commands, that the audience for this tale listens (or reads) in a fixed order, which begins from the third tale of Day Eight and moves forwards through the fifth tale before arriving at the sixth one. As we shall see, the real force of this mode of reading is brought to bear on the final section of the tale. Filomena's oral performance celebrates the storyteller's ability to delve into a personal repertory and select a tale which is appropriate for context and audience. The connections she draws with previously told *novelle* demonstrate the expert way in which she moulds the source material to her own interests and those of her audience, bound by a particular time and place. Rather than repeat internalized chunks of information in the mode of oral-formulaic composition, which an oral performer might do to recall previous incarnations of the same character, Filomena chooses instead to build her narrative through omission, deeming it unnecessary to repeat information which has already been "performed," such as the direct characterization of Calandrino and his companions.

The primary narrator's act of writing down the *novelle* commits Filomena's ephemeral oral performance to a fixed and repeatable position within the larger narrative. The specifics of an individual performance and reception "moment" are now locked into place, cemented by the additional material authored by the primary narrator: rubrics, proem and final conclusion, introductions and conclusions to each day. Writing enforces Filomena's particular choice of order in which VIII.6 depends on VIII.3. At the same time, however, the relative fixity of the written page encourages the primary narrator to propose a reading strategy that undermines Filomena's personal intratextual performance. The defence of the contents presented in the final Conclusion plays with the notion of passing responsibility for the selection and delectation of material to the reader, whilst simultaneously retaining authorial control by "authorizing" this strategy through the narrator's exhortation to do so. The reader of the written text is instructed to be guided to his or her tale of choice by the visual mnemonic embodied in the rubric attached to each novella: "Tuttavia che va tra queste leggendo, lasci star quelle che pungono e quelle che dilettano legga: elle, per non ingannare alcuna persona, tutte nella fronte portan segnato quello che esse dentro dal loro seno nascoso tengono" [And the fact remains that anyone perusing these tales is free to ignore the ones that give offence, and read only those that are pleasing. For in order that none of you may be misled, each of the stories bears on its brow the gist of that which it hides in its bosom (Concl.Aut.19; McWilliam 801)]. This might be read as an attempt on the part of the primary narrator to talk back to the "deadness" of written speech, bringing it back to life by encouraging an individually defined non-linear reading experience. The reader, who is unable to petition the oral narrator to rehearse a particular detail or theme in real time, is instead able to reread at will, recreating a dynamic reception scenario in a different mode.[16] Thus, the written culture of the primary narrator both enforces and subverts Filomena's linear strategy, and uses the visual tools of writing to recall the oral source material.

Reading within the Novella

Moving from the frame to the novella, we see how a number of additional binary relationships are layered on to the nexus of oral-written culture: rural-urban; foolishness-wit; words-deeds. While I am not suggesting that the reality of late medieval Florentine culture falls into these neat categories, in this literary context of short stories, the juxtaposition of binaries is used for concise characterization and as a key tool for setting characters against each other within the art of the *beffa*. At the simplest level, Calandrino is characterized as a rustic who is too easily fooled by the oral power of the word, in contrast with his

16 Early studies of orality and literacy were keen to emphasize radical differences between oral and written cultures and the effects of writing and print culture on thought; see in particular Ong, *Orality and Literacy*. More recent studies emphasize the ways in which orality continues to permeate and affect literacy; see Degl'Innocenti, Richardson, and Sbordoni, *Interactions between Orality and Writing*.

urban associates, who are able to "read" social situations and decipher the meaning of words with a higher degree of literacy. However, as we shall also see, the social and geographical mobility of the protagonists in this novella allows Boccaccio to explore the city-country divide in a more nuanced way than the binary initially suggests.

As David Wallace has noted, in each of the Calandrino tales, Calandrino leaves the city and heads for the countryside: "This gravitational pull away from the city suggests that there is something of the countryman about Calandrino: he embodies an enduring rustic simplicity and credulity against which Florentine urbanity defines and exercises itself. Business-minded urbanites always triumph over ingenuous rustics in the *Decameron*."[17] We can see here how the social class of the main protagonists is intimately connected to their geographical location, and each of these elements is in turn overlaid with differing degrees of *ingegno*. At a narratological level, the city-countryside dialectic has also been explored separately from a connection with social class: Marga Cottino-Jones's work shows how geographical setting can be used to create a framework in which pairs of *novelle* are thematically counterbalanced through opposition. Thus, within the structure of the eighth day, the two Calandrino tales form one of these pairs such that "Calandrino's foolishness *in city* vs Bruno and Buffalmacco's wit" balances "Calandrino's foolishness *in country* vs Bruno and Buffalmacco's wit" (Cottino-Jones, *Order from Chaos*, 153). This shows more clearly how it is Calandrino's personal character which is fixed as the archetypal fool, while his social and cultural status is, in contrast, defined by a lack of stability, moving between the two poles of city and countryside in different contexts.

The complexity and fluidity of the social geography explored in the Calandrino cycle is emphasized in the first tale of Calandrino and the heliotrope (VIII.3), when Elissa links both protagonist and city through the adjective *nuovo*: "Nella nostra città, la qual sempre di varie maniere e di *nuove* genti è stata abondevole, fu, ancora non è gran tempo, un dipintore chiamato Calandrino, uom semplice e di *nuovi* costumi" [Not long ago, there lived in our city, where there has never been any lack of unusual customs and *new* people, a painter called Calandrino, a simple fellow of *new* habits (VIII.3.4, emphasis added; McWilliam 561,

17 Wallace, *Giovanni Boccaccio: Decameron*, 95. Wallace's comment is emblematic of many critical perspectives which connect Calandrino and his (lack of) intelligence to geographical location; see also Baratto, *Realtà e stile*, 309; Boccaccio, *Novelle scelte dal Decamerone*, ed. Russo, 311–14; and Grimaldi, *Il privilegio di Dioneo*, 282–3, 290.

adapted)]. Calandrino is thus an individual representative of an urban population, and yet the structure of the city is itself hybrid and in flux, newly augmented by the recent arrival of "new" people from the *contado*.[18] Calandrino's main home is in Florence, but as we have already seen, the action shifts between city and countryside in a manner which suggests that he has not yet become fully urbanized, and even his name hints at his peasant origins.[19] The rigidity of medieval social hierarchies mapped on to geographical divisions stretching between the city and the spaces beyond it (ranging from the *città* with *cittadini* to the *villa* with *villani* and the *contado* occupied by *contadini* and *lavoratori*), which have been revealed through lexical analysis of the *Decameron*, illuminates the framework against which the threat from social mobility is explored in this novella (Quondam, "Le cose (e le parole) del mondo," 1729–33). The social politics at play do not operate on a grand scale between the upper reaches of society and the lowest realms, or even in terms of a clear-cut opposition between city and countryside, but explore tensions on a more reduced scale within the community of painters represented by Calandrino, Bruno, and Buffalmacco, now also figured as representatives of different shades of oral and written culture within the same milieu.

The *beffa* of the stolen pig hinges on the disjunction between word and deed; the same disjunction which is at the heart of the first tale in the Calandrino cycle,[20] and therefore, according to Filomena's instructions to have present the tale of the heliotrope as we read about the stolen pig, we are predisposed to understand that Calandrino will represent a culture which retains a strong attachment to the performative power of the oral word. The almost exclusively rural setting for VIII.6 suggests that this attachment will be stronger than ever.[21] As we have learned from the heliotrope, for Calandrino there is no "gap" between a word and the thing that the word describes: the act of giving something a name calls that thing into being. Thus in VIII.3 Calandrino swallows

---

18 On the use of this adjective, see also Marcus, *An Allegory of Form*, 82–4.

19 For example, Grimaldi comments: "il sapore di contado implicito nel soprannome Calandrino ... è certo tutt'uno con la sua primaria accezione ornitologica, essendo appunto, quello di 'calandra', il nome indicante una particolare specie di allodola" (*Il privilegio di Dioneo*, 282).

20 See, for example, Marchesi's comments: "Tanto VIII. 3 quanto IX. 3 hanno come centro motore un problema di interpretazione: in entrambi i casi la credulità di Calandrino è la diretta conseguenza della sua incapacità di andare oltre la superficie delle parole che gli vengono rivolte" (*Stratigrafie decameroniane*, 108).

21 In other words, rural types are more likely to be less literate (less able to decipher the written word), and therefore more strongly attached to oral culture.

without question the tale of the land where magic stones can be found, which is spun so artfully by Maso del Saggio, and continued by Bruno and Buffalmacco, who use their superior "reading" ability to understand the difference between sign and signified to enact the *beffa*.[22]

Calandrino's is an act of profound misreading, indeed, a type of illiteracy, which is condemned by the primary narrator. Part of the narrator's defence for his text is based precisely on the argument that, in order to understand appropriately, the audience for the *Decameron* should not take words at face value without considering carefully the context in which they are used; in other words, should not behave like Calandrino:

> E se forse pure alcuna particella è in quelle, alcuna paroletta più liberale che forse a spigolistra donna non si conviene, le quali più le parole pesan che' fatti e più d'apparer s'ingegnan che d'esser buone, dico che più non si dee a me esser disdetto d'averle scritte che generalmente si disdica agli uomini e alle donne di dir tutto dì "foro" e "caviglia" e "mortaio" e "pestello" e "salsiccia" e "mortadello," e tutto pien di simiglianti cose. (Concl.Aut.5)

> [And even if the stories do, perhaps, contain one or two trifling expressions that are too unbridled for the liking of those prudish ladies who attach more weight to words than to deeds, and are more anxious to seem virtuous than to be virtuous, I assert that it was no more improper for me to have written them than for men and women at large, in their everyday speech, to use such words as *hole*, and *rod*, and *mortar*, and *pestle*, and *crumpet*, and *stuffing*, and any number of others. (798–9)]

Of course, the whole of the narrator's concluding defence is built on a strategy of bluff and double bluff, designed to appeal to the most sophisticated audience of all, since he deftly builds in an extra layer of irreverent sexual subtext whilst defending himself from that very charge. An extra layer of combined connection (and disassociation)

---

22 See Martinez, "Calandrino and the Powers of the Stone." Calandrino's continuous habit of taking what he is told at face value leads him into further trouble in the following tales on Day Nine, when he believes he is pregnant and that a magic scroll will induce a young woman to sleep with him. See also Mazzotta: "As a fool and madman, he lives in a world of pure exchange in the sense that everything can be mistaken for everything else, and a word, literally nothing, can give access to the whole world. By mistaking what are only words for reality, Calandrino ultimately obliterates the value of words" (*The World at Play*, 198).

between the narrator and Calandrino is brought to bear in the next paragraph, in which it is argued that both writers and painters should share the same freedom to create illusory surfaces as the vehicles for underlying truths.[23] It is no coincidence, therefore, that the Calandrino cycle, whose main protagonists are painters, should deal with the fundamental relationship between illusion and reality, figured here as words (which are only arbitrary connections of letters and therefore illusory) and deeds (which concern the material reality of objects and actions).

In the tale of the heliotrope, Calandrino's foolishness is displayed because of the way in which he takes Maso – and later Bruno and Buffalmacco – at their word. In the tale of the pig, the situation is ironically reversed, so that it is Calandrino who expects to be taken at his (truthful) word when he says he has not stolen his own pig. Calandrino is in fact innocent of any wrongdoing, beyond the fact that he allowed himself to get drunk. The story is comic (although it is difficult for a modern audience to get beyond the cruelty of the injustice) in large measure because we have the perception that Calandrino is foolish from our knowledge of VIII.3. However, the more Calandrino repeats the truth that he has not stolen the pig, the deeper he falls into the trap set by Bruno and Buffalmacco, and the more idiotic he appears.

Calandrino's belief in the inherent ability for words to reflect the truth is played out through his repeated insistence that someone else has stolen the pig, captured in the simple phrase "il porco mio m'è stato imbolato" [my pig has been stolen (VIII.6.17)]. His naïvety in believing that repeatedly telling the truth will cause others to believe him and the culprit to be located elsewhere is ironically emphasized and implicitly held up to ridicule through the interplay between Calandrino's increasingly desperate assertions and Bruno's conciliatory responses. The echo

---

23 The text of the Conclusion continues: "Sanza che alla mia penna non dee essere meno d'auttorità conceduta che sia al pennello del dipintore, il quale senza alcuna riprensione, o almen giusta, lasciamo stare che egli faccia a san Michele ferire il serpente con la spada o con la lancia e a san Giorgio il dragone dove gli piace, ma egli fa Cristo maschio e Eva femina, e a Lui medesimo, che volle per la salute della umana generazione sopra la croce morire, quando con un chiovo e quando con due i piè gli conficca in quella" [Besides, no less latitude should be granted to my pen than to the brush of the painter, who without incurring censure, of a justified kind at least, depicts Saint Michael striking the serpent with his sword or his lance, and Saint George transfixing the dragon wherever he pleases; but that is not all, for he makes Christ male and Eve female, and fixes to the Cross, sometimes with a single nail, sometimes with two, the feet of Him who resolved to die thereon for the salvation of mankind (Concl.Aut.6; McWilliam 799)].

resounds in a gathering crescendo from Bruno's initial suggestion that Calandrino should sell the pig and tell his wife that it was stolen – "di' che ti sia stato imbolato" [say that it's been stolen (VIII.6.7)] – through the indirect description of Calandrino's actions when he finds that it is gone – "incominciò a fare il romor grande: oisé! dolente sé, che il porco gli era stato imbolato" [he began to make a great outcry: alas! he was grieved that the pig had been stolen from him (VIII.6.16)] – to the first words which Calandrino cries to Bruno and Buffalmacco when he gets up in the morning and finds his pig missing: "Oimè, compagni miei, che il porco mio m'è stato imbolato!" [Woe is me, my friends, my pig has been stolen! (VIII.6.17)]. The crescendo is constructed not only in the repetition of the phrase, but also in the increasingly desperate imprecations with which Calandrino embellishes the core phrase: "Al corpo di Dio, che io dico da dovero che egli m'è stato imbolato" [God's body, man, I tell you it's been stolen, it really has (VIII.6.21; McWilliam 581)]; "Tu mi faresti dar l'anima al nemico: io dico che tu non mi credi, se io non sia impiccato per la gola, che egli m'è stato imbolato!" [You'll drive me to perdition in a minute … Do I have to hang myself by the neck before I can convince you that it really has been stolen? (VIII.6.23; McWilliam 581)]; finally Calandrino resorts to shouting his innocence: "Calandrino incominciò a gridare e a dire: 'Deh perché mi farete disperare? e bestemmiare Idio e' santi e ciò che v'è? Io vi dico che il porco m'è stato stanotte imbolato'" [Calandrino began to shout and to say "Why are you so intent on driving me to despair and provoking me to curse God and all the Saints in Heaven? I tell you the pig was stolen from me during the night" (VIII.6.29; McWilliam 582)].[24] From Calandrino's perspective there is a single reading of the truth – he himself did not steal the pig, but the pig is missing, and therefore someone else must have taken it – and all he can do is continue to repeat the accusation, which simultaneously claims his own innocence.

While Bruno compliments Calandrino for speaking well, his own remarks highlight the superior ability of the *beffatore* to manipulate words, and recognize that words and the things they represent are not always in alignment: "E Bruno diceva: 'Ben di', ben di': e' si vuol ben dir così, grida forte, fatti ben sentire, *sì che egli paia vero*'" [And Bruno said, "Well said, well said: you want to carry on like that, shout loudly, make yourself heard, *so that it will seem true*" (VIII.6.22, emphasis

24 See also Russo's comments on this linguistic refrain in his chapter "Calandrino e il porco imbolato" in *Letture critiche del Decameron*, 310–11. On the use of interjections designed to draw the audience into the subject of the text, see Alazard, "Ahimé, ahi, o deh."

added)]. Bruno's next response counters Calandrino's insistence on repeating the same words with some physical evidence for his own position: "Io il vidi pure ieri costì" [I saw it there myself only yesterday (VIII.6.24; McWilliam 581)]. Bruno's provocative and playful follow-up question "credimi tu far credere che egli sia volato?" [Are you trying to make me believe it's flown away? (VIII.6.24; McWilliam 581)] advertises his linguistic dexterity with a humorous repetition of the verb *credere* and interchange of *imbolare* for *volare*, creating the amusing image of a flying pig, whose subtleties and significance are entirely missed by Calandrino. Calandrino's reply underlines his limited ability to "read" Bruno's speech, or even to learn from it by offering his own physical evidence, and reveals instead the limits of his self-absorbed and stubborn adherence to the literal sense: "Disse Calandrino: 'Egli è come io ti dico'" [Calandrino said: "It is as I am telling you" (VIII.6.25]. Bruno's counter-question, in contrast, signals an open-ended dialogue and implicit interest in the varying levels of interpretation which might be applied to words which are read symbolically: "'Deh!' disse Bruno 'può egli essere?'" ["No!" said Bruno, "can it really be?" (VIII.6.26)]. Thus, the two modes of understanding represented by Calandrino and Bruno, or *beffato* and *beffatore*, are encapsulated and condensed into this exchange, which marks the culmination of the second part of the novella.

The success of the *beffatore* at the expense of the *beffato* suggests that what is important is not *what* one says (even if one is innocent), but rather *how* one speaks. The mechanics of effective speech cannot be separated from the skill with which one engages and manipulates an audience. Calandrino is the key audience member whom Bruno seeks to persuade. The verbal exchange between them when Calandrino discovers that the pig is missing is the nucleus of the second part of the four-part structure of the novella. Despite the sophistication of Bruno's technique, however, Calandrino is doggedly immune to Bruno's repeated insinuations that he is lying. In the rural world in which the novella is staged, there is little room for verbal sophistication. When Calandrino's protestations reach shouting pitch (VIII.6.29), and it is clear that any form of verbal reasoning is no longer possible, the *beffatori* abruptly change tactics and move from verbal persuasion to persuasion through the production of physical proof.

At this juncture Buffalmacco re-enters the dialogue and offers to help Calandrino find the culprit with the bread and cheese test – a medieval form of lie detector which, he says, will instantly reveal which of

Calandrino's neighbours is the guilty party (VIII.6.32).[25] Bruno retains his role as the mastermind of the *beffa* by transmuting ordinary bread and cheese into the more exotic ginger sweets and vernaccia wine in order – he claims – to disguise it as a trick and encourage more people to take part.[26] The decision to change the foodstuffs in order to conceal until the last minute that this is a lie detector test is presented as a practical solution to the possibility that the thief would avoid appearing if she or he knew what was at stake. In practice, however, it is an entirely unnecessary precaution, since Bruno and Buffalmacco know that none of Calandrino's neighbours is guilty.[27] Indeed, when the community has gathered and Bruno explains the reason for the "test," they are all eager to join in and prove their innocence: "Ciascun che v'era disse che ne voleva volentier mangiare" [All of them were only too eager to eat one of the sweets (VIII.6.44; McWilliam 584)]. Therefore, "upgrading" from bread and cheese to ginger sweets and vernaccia is simply another example of the flashy sleight of hand and mystification that Bruno and Buffalmacco specialize in, and which now draws in not only Calandrino but also the wider community, allowing Boccaccio to poke fun not only at the individual simpleton but also at the superstitious beliefs of simple rural folk.

Bruno and Buffalmacco distinguish themselves from the inhabitants of the *contado* and cement their links with the urban community of Florence, and thus their role as the more sophisticated masterminds, when they return to the city to procure the necessary ingredients to carry out the test (VIII.6.39). The wider *contado* community for whom Calandrino is the figurehead, consisting of a mix of full-time peasants and partially integrated city dwellers like himself – "giovani fiorentini

25 On the origins of the bread and cheese test, see Bottari, "Lezione sopra la novella sesta della giornata ottava."

26 The use of ginger to make the sweets was for a long time a source of misunderstanding among critics, who misinterpreted the reference to "quelle del cane" (VIII.6.39) as the addition of dog feces. The identification of "dog ginger" as a water plant was made by Pastore Stocchi in his article "Altre annotazioni." This type of "false ginger" was much cheaper because it had none of the culinary or medicinal qualities of ginger. The text tells us that it was mixed with an incredibly bitter type of aloe, which Pastore Stocchi notes was considered to be so strong that it would restore consciousness and speech to patients on the point of death.

27 Pastore Stocchi presents the substitution as an opportunity for Bruno and Buffalmacco to doctor the ginger sweets more easily, since they are rolled in sugar which would cover any visual differences between those doctored with bitter aloes and those that were not ("Altre annotazioni," 200–1).

che per villa erano e di lavoratori" [some were farmworkers and others were young Florentines who happened to be staying in the country (VIII.6.41; McWilliam 583)] – makes up the audience gathered to witness his humiliation. At the level of the novella, Calandrino is the butt of the joke when his "guilt" confirms the community's corresponding "innocence." At the level of the frame tale and above, the *brigata*, the audience of idle ladies, and the historical audience can laugh at the way in which the rural community is taken in by belief in the reliability of this test. The novella parodies the use of these tests by revealing the mechanics to be simple cause and effect. In the "original" bread and cheese tests it is supernatural forces which cause the guilty party to be detected; here there is a direct correlation between the bitter aloe selectively added by Bruno and Buffalmacco and Calandrino's natural physical reaction.

Ingestion of the sweets is key to identifying the thief. The main purpose of the wine seems to lie in its appeal as a reward for the crowd. In his initial set-up, Bruno clearly implies that the best way of gathering a good crowd will be by offering them a drink ("Vorrebbesi fare con belle galle di gengiovo e con bella vernaccia, *e invitargli a bere*" [What we ought to do ... is to use the best ginger sweets we can get hold of, along with some fine Vernaccia wine, *and invite them round for a drink* (VIII.6.35, emphasis added; McWilliam 582)]. This suggestion is repeated once the ingredients have been procured and Bruno instructs Calandrino to invite his neighbours to join him for a drink: "[Bruno] se ne tornò in villa a Calandrino e dissegli: 'Farai che tu inviti domattina a ber con teco tutti coloro di cui tu hai sospetto: egli è festa, ciascun verrà volentieri'" [He returned to Calandrino's place in the country, and said to him: "See to it that you invite all the people you suspect to come and drink with you tomorrow morning. It's a holiday, so they'll all come readily enough" (VIII.6.40; McWilliam 583)]. At this stage in the proceedings they do not know the ulterior motive for the invitation, and the added implication is that, since it is a holiday, they will be even more eager than usual to have a drink. The promise of a free drink is thus used as a lure for the rural community in the same way that Bruno and Buffalmacco set in train the whole *beffa* thanks to Calandrino's enjoyment of a drink (or three) at someone else's expense.

The bread and cheese test is a ritual which has been traced back to antiquity, and which combined both pagan and religious ritual.[28]

28 See Bottari's study, in which he notes: "E quantunque questi sortilegj in tutte le lor parti avessero sì rei, e malvagj principj, pure erano tanto divenuti familiari,

The same elements of superstition mixed with religious blessings are retained in Bruno's new version. He explicitly reassures both Buffalmacco and Calandrino that the sweets and wine can be blessed in the same way as the bread and cheese – "così si possono benedicer le galle del gengiovo come il pane e 'l cascio" [it's just as easy to bless ginger sweets as it is to bless bread and cheese (VIII.6.35; McWilliam 582)] – but then refers to his own version as an "'ncantagione" [a spell (VIII.6.40)], and gives a description of how he will perform the necessary rites. This is both playful and patently sends up the process: Bruno's explanation maintains the comic tension between the *beffatori* and an audience who collude with them in understanding that the ritual is meaningless, and Calandrino, who takes them at their word in all seriousness: "io stesso le darò e farò e dirò ciò che fia da dire e da fare" [I myself shall give out [the sweets] and do and say everything that needs to be said and done (VIII.6.40)]. Nevertheless, if some of the religious ritual is thereby dissipated in Bruno's own version of the incantation, the test still takes place in the churchyard, with the people gathered around an elm tree.

After the community witness the test, their role of making public Calandrino's stupidity and also being victims of the *beffa* themselves is over, and the focus returns, with full force, to the gullibility of Calandrino. Even though he knows that he isn't guilty, he nevertheless does not think to question the test itself – he is caught in mute stasis: after the failure of words to claim his innocence, and now the demonstration of his guilt by deeds, all he can do is cry. Even though Bruno asks him what is the matter, he can't answer (VIII.6.46). The community exits the plot as quickly as they were assembled, without pausing even to show their disapproval with much vehemence.[29] As soon as Bruno and Buffalmacco are left on their own again with Calandrino, they resume their insistent bullying, but Calandrino's spirit seems to be

che avendo perduta la faccia di colpe enormi, com'elle erano in verità, non si tenevano più per tali dal più degli uomini, il che divenir tuttora, aveva già osservato l'acutissimo ingegno di S. Agostino, e come si vede eziandio ne' nostri tempi, che molti gravi delitti hanno perduto fin al denominazione di peccato; conciosiachè sieno in una regione, o anche in una Città divenuti comuni. Con questo goffo, e strano divisamento sembrava loro d'avere schifata ogni ombra di delitto, e di peccato, e d'avere un sortilegio trasformato in un sagramentale, e d'una cosa demoniaca fattone una divina, e sagra" ("Lezioni sopra la novella sesta della giornata ottava," 184–5).

29 "Tutti dissero che per certo Calandrino se l'aveva imbolato egli stesso; e furonvene di quegli che aspramente il ripresero" [everyone declared that Calandrino had obviously stolen the pig himself, and there were one or two who gave him a severe scolding about it (VIII.6.49; McWilliam 584)].

so broken now that he isn't given any more direct speech in the rest of the novella.

The *beffa* could finish here, since Bruno and Buffalmacco have apparently achieved what they set out to do: to steal the pig and blame its theft on Calandrino. The final section, in which Calandrino is forced to hand over two pairs of capons, therefore seems particularly cruel, but this final exchange between *beffatori* and *beffato* is essential for the structure of the narrative.[30] Bruno opens his final verbal assault on Calandrino with the claim that, during the ginger sweets and wine test, he heard from one of Calandrino's neighbours that Calandrino had sent his pig to a lover (VIII.6.53). It isn't relevant to the substance of the *beffa* whether this information really has been suggested to Bruno, or whether it is simply another untruth added by Bruno himself; its function is to pave the way for the climax of the tricksters' cruelty – Bruno's claim that Calandrino is in fact the trickster: "Tu sì hai apparato a esser beffardo!" [You have learned to become the trickster, haven't you? (VIII.6.54)]. The statement derives its rhetorical force from its ironic reversal of the truth, and thus also from the metafictional allusion to Bruno's own status as a trickster. The theme of the trickster who is tricked is a classic trope, which in this context is used ironically to underscore the exact opposite: the person who has been tricked is doubly tricked, if you like, by being innocent of the crime he is accused of, and yet "proved" to be guilty by both the tricksters (Bruno and Buffalmacco) and the community.

As the ginger sweets and wine were used as physical evidence for Calandrino's guilt, so now Bruno offers incontrovertible evidence for his statement that Calandrino has become the trickster with a pivotal, intratextual, reference back to the episode of the heliotrope related in VIII.3:

> Tu ci menasti una volta giù per lo Mugnone raccogliendo pietre nere: e quando tu ci avesti messi in galea senza biscotto, e tu te ne venisti e poscia ci volevi far credere che tu l'avessi trovata! e ora similmente ti credi co' tuoi giuramenti far credere altressì che il porco, che tu hai donato o ver venduto, ti sia stato imbolato. (VIII.6.54)

---

30 Even the listening *brigata* deem this final insult to be unnecessarily cruel: "Molto avevan le donne riso del cattivello di Calandrino, e più n'avrebbono ancora, se stato non fosse che loro increbbe di vedergli torre ancora i capponi a coloro che tolto gli avevano il porco" [Though the ladies shook with laughter over the hapless Calandrino, they would have laughed even more if the people who had stolen his pig had not relieved him also of his capons, which made them feel sorry for him (VIII.7.2; McWilliam 585–6)]. The cruelty demonstrated here could be read as an important precursor to the novella of the scholar and the widow, which follows on immediately, and which contains examples of even more extreme and sustained cruelty.

> [Remember the time you took us along the Mugnone? There we were, collecting those black stones, and as soon as you'd got us stranded up the creek without a paddle, you cleared off home, and then tried to make us believe that you'd found the thing. And now that you've given away the pig, or sold it rather, you think you can persuade us, by uttering a few oaths, that it's been stolen. (McWilliam 585)]

For Calandrino this is presumably as confusing as being unable to swallow the ginger sweets, since he appears to continue to believe that he did in fact find the heliotrope, and therefore leave Bruno and Buffalmacco in the lurch still looking for stones by the Mugnone. For the novella's audience it is a reminder of Filomena's opening instruction to read intraxtextually, and thus also a bringing together of two narrative layers: the novella and the frame tale concerning the *brigata*. Thus, the climax of the novella contains multiple elements of symmetry which bring us thematically and structurally full circle, not only back to the first novella in the cycle but also back to the figure of Calandrino's wife, Tessa, who figured at the opening of the tale as the reason for which Calandrino was not prepared to steal the pig, and who is named for the first time in the story as Bruno invokes her as a final and effective threat: "noi intendiamo che tu ci doni due paia di capponi, se non che noi diremo a Monna Tessa ogni cosa" [unless you give us two brace of capons, we intend to tell Monna Tessa the whole story (VIII.6.55; McWilliam 585, adapted)]. The invocation of Tessa is not only a way of tying up this tale but also a prefiguration of the neatness of the circularity of the whole Calandrino cycle of four tales, since the severity of the beating which Tessa receives at Calandrino's hands at the end of the first tale (VIII.3) is reversed and vindicated when she gives him a good thrashing at the end of the final tale (IX.5). We are left, then, with a strong message about the importance of an intratextual reading strategy which seems to be at odds with the primary narrator's instruction to read at will. As the rigidity of the medieval social hierarchy forms a framework against which the nuances of social mobility can be explored and commented upon, so an apparently robust narrative structure enables a metaliterary commentary to be performed. Thus the clash of communication cultures enacted by Calandrino and his companions is framed by the clash of performance and reception strategies proposed and enacted by the *brigata* and the primary narrator, while characters and narrators take turns to transgress their bounds and bleed into the narrative layers above and below them, refiguring the tale of the stolen pig as another potent meditation on the art of telling tales.

The Scholar and the Widow: Corrupt Appetite and Moral Failure in Society's Intellectual Elite (VIII.7)

TEODOLINDA BAROLINI

Social Templates: The Mixed-Gender *Brigata* and the Intellectual Lover

In a 2008 speech, the feminist legal scholar Mary Anne Case voices her concern about the fragility of an integrationist view of the sexes, noting to her listeners that their current experience of "a group of males and females, unrelated to one another, promiscuously intermingled" might well be a "fragile and endangered" practice.[1] Case comes back to the fragility of an integrationist vision of the sexes in a subsequent essay, where she cites Ruth Bader Ginsberg citing Thomas Jefferson on the moral need to prevent women from "mix[ing] promiscuously in the public meetings of men," despite that mixture being the expression of "a pure democracy": "Thomas Jefferson stated the view prevailing when the Constitution was new: 'Were our State a pure democracy ... there would yet be excluded from their deliberations ... women, who, to prevent depravation of morals and ambiguity of issue, could not mix promiscuously in the public meetings of men.'"[2]

Case's view resonates with the argument that I have made in recent years regarding Boccaccio's radical thought-experiment of a mixed-gender *brigata*, in which he defies both contemporary usage of the word *brigata* and contemporary views on the public mixing of the sexes.[3] Read in isolation, the *Decameron* reaffirms the patriarchy as that to which the mixed-gender *brigata* returns when it returns to Santa Maria Novella at the end of Day Ten. Read in historical context, however, the text's failure to emancipate the mixed-gender *brigata* from reality does

1 Case, "Feminist Fundamentalism," 2008 (citation ends at minute 7:42).

2 See Case, "Feminist Fundamentalism as an Individual and Constitutional Commitment," 565, and, for Thomas Jefferson, 567.

3 For the argument and contemporary context, see Barolini, "Sociology of the *Brigata*."

not diminish the liberating power of its imaginative licence, whereby Boccaccio effectively imagines a different social order from that which he can predict or endorse. He uses imaginative licence to model a social template in his possible world – that of a mixed-gender *brigata* of seven women and three men – that is transgressive with respect to his real world.

The transgressive social template of the mixed-gender *brigata* is the baseline that the *Decameron* establishes before taking us on a journey that disrupts that idyll. *Decameron* VIII.7 plays a huge role in the disruptive narrative of the latter half of the *Decameron*. But the baseline exists for a reason. We must attend to Boccaccio's conjuring, to the Boccaccian invention that we take quite for granted: the mixed-gender *brigata* of seven women between the ages of eighteen and twenty-eight (all of noble blood, as specified in I.Intro.49), and three men over the age of twenty-five. None is married, although the women are old to be unmarried: the historian Christiane Klapisch-Zuber discusses the suspicions that accrue to unmarried women and notes that "among the 'best people,' therefore, families did not include females over twenty years of age who were not married" (Klapisch-Zuber, *Women, Family, and Ritual in Renaissance Italy*, 119). The narrator states both that the men are in search of their lady-loves and that each finds her in the group of ladies and also that some of the ladies are kinswomen of some of the men (I.Intro.79). Yet never in the course of the frame tale do any of the men seek to sequester or restrict any of the ladies.

Boccaccio has a long history of fascination with the social templates that in the *Decameron* he brings to vivid, circumstantial, life. The *Decameron*'s structure, its ten storytellers telling one hundred stories over ten days, captures the dialectic of infinite variety (the *novelle*) constructed on lasts that are abstract and enduring (the themes of the days). A fascination with social templates is already evident in the youthful narrative *Filocolo*, where Boccaccio stages the episode in which thirteen young people propose thirteen "questions of love" and a fourteenth is the ruler who resolves each case: "ordiniamo uno di noi qui in luogo di nostro re, al quale ciascuno una quistione d'amore proponga, e da esso a quella debita risposta prenda" [let us ordain, among ourselves, one in particular to be our king. And then to him, each of us shall propound a Question of Love so that in return we may receive an apt and suitable resolution to such a question submitted (*Filocolo* 4.17.5, p. 382; trans., p. 12)].[4] Each "quistione d'amore" is a debate on a social issue, drawing

4 The *Filocolo* is cited in the edition of Quaglio in *Tutte le opere di Giovanni Boccaccio*. The translation is from Boccaccio, *Thirteen Most Pleasant and Delectable Questions of Love*.

from the rich tradition of amatory debates that were a staple of both Latin and vernacular medieval literature.[5]

The *Filocolo*'s episode of the "Questioni d'amore" already boasts the mixed-gender *brigata* that will be the hallmark of the *Decameron*'s frame tale, albeit with less radical gender proportions, and has long been considered an early model of the *Decameron* frame.[6] I argue here that the third of the *Filocolo*'s thirteen "Questioni d'amore," which features the type of the intellectual lover – in other words, a type of Boccaccio himself, as he presents himself in the Introduction to Day Four of the *Decameron* – anticipates the novella of the scholar and the widow. The "Questioni d'amore," which also feature widows, are thus the birthplace of the Boccaccian social templates that interest us with respect to *Decameron* VIII.7. The type of the wise lover, constructed by imbricating the category of lover with the category of scholar-philosopher-poet-intellectual-clerk, in an amalgam that carries significant personal associations for our author, is one that Boccaccio explores throughout his life, from the early *Filocolo* to the late *Corbaccio*.

I have posited the mixed-gender *brigata* as the undergirding social template of the *Decameron*, and as such its hermeneutic baseline for interpretation on issues of gender. At the same time, the *Decameron* is a text in which location inflects meaning. One of its prime hermeneutic levers is the issue of where we find ourselves in a possible world that includes representations of patriarchal reality as well as transgressive thought-experiments. Constraint and repression of the socially marginalized, notably women who are presented as enclosed in their rooms and cut off from society in the *Proemio*, build in the latter half of the *Decameron*. Measured by the yardstick of *consolazione*, the opportunities for women diminish as the *brigata* moves back toward Florence and the patriarchal social order after their sojourn outside the city. Moving from Fiammetta's prologue of VII.5 to Emilia's counter-prologue

5 Quaglio glosses "quistione d'amore" thus: "Assai care al costume di vita medievale: basti ricordare il *De amore* di Andrea Cappellano (III 7) e i poemetti d'oltralpe, come *La cour d'Amour* di Peire Guillem, o il *fablel* di *Hueline et Aiglantine*, e quelli composti in latino, o la trattatistica scolastica come il *De arte honeste amandi* di Andrea Cappellano, ove (II 7) si riferiscono giudizi di dame su questioni amorose" (*Filocolo*, p. 853).

6 The *brigata* of the *Filocolo* is composed of nine men and five women. One of the five young women is unnamed. The group originally elects a king, Ascaleon, not a queen; Ascaleon proposes that Fiammetta be queen. Not only the gender ratio but the governance model is less progressive than that of the *Decameron*'s *brigata*. On the sources of the *Filocolo*, see Rajna, "L'episodio delle questioni d'amore nel *Filocolo*," esp. 35.

of IX.9, a repressive ideology clearly emerges.[7] In the prologue of VII.5, Fiammetta notes that women are constrained to remain all the week "rinchiuse," a word that echoes the *Proemio*'s programmatic mission statement on the enclosed ("racchiuse") and marginalized status of women.[8] She argues that a day of rest should be allowed to shuttered domestic workers as to all other workers, and she invokes both canon and civil law to support the idea that "some consolation, some peace" (VII.5.4) should be available to female as to male workers. But Emilia in the counter-prologue of IX.9 invokes nature, custom, and law to remind the ladies that they are subservient to men; a woman should practise humility, patience, and obedience in order to make sure that she achieves *consolazione* and *quiete* with "the man to whom she belongs" [a' quali s'appartiene (IX.9.3)]. Where Fiammetta in VII.5 views *consolazione* as a good that a woman may attempt to procure for herself, Emilia in IX.9 posits that *consolazione* is a good that a woman is obliged to produce for a man. We are heading toward the reality that Gualtieri, the Marquis of Saluzzo and husband/owner of Griselda, is the *Decameron*'s most "consoled" character.[9]

The yardstick of consolation takes us to our story, the longest in the *Decameron*, for it happens that the *Decameron*'s most textually disconsolate heroine, a woman whose own actions rather than bad fortune have made "sconsolata," is Elena, the widow who is one of the two actors of VIII.7. Elena is three times "sconsolata," a characterization that is deployed while she is undergoing the extreme "vengeance" that the narrator, Pampinea, introduces as a novelty of this tale. Pampinea claims that this novella is the first among the stories of *beffe* to feature a counter-*beffa*, a "vendetta" exacted in payment for the original misdeed: "Noi abbiamo per piú novellette dette riso molto delle beffe state fatte, delle quali niuna vendetta esserne stata fatta s'è raccontato" [Many of the stories already narrated have caused us to laugh a great deal over tricks that people have played on each other, but in no case have we heard of the victim avenging himself (VIII.7.3)]. Although there are tales outside of the days devoted to *beffe* that feature the tricked trickster

7 See Sherberg, *The Governance of Friendship*.

8 See Barolini, "'Le parole son donne e i fatti son maschi.'" The *Decameron* is cited in the 1976 edition of Vittore Branca, in *Tutte le opere*. The translation is that of G.H. McWilliam; I occasionally substitute my own translation for McWilliam's when a more literal rendering is required.

9 For the findings on Gualtieri, see Barolini, "The Marquis of Saluzzo, or the Griselda Story Before It Was Hijacked." For the implications of these findings in a wider context, see Barolini, "A Philosophy of Consolation."

(for instance II.9), *vendetta*, of immense topical relevance to Boccaccio's audience, is highlighted in VIII.7: of twenty-four uses of the noun *vendetta* in the *Decameron*, eighteen occur in VIII.7 and its companion tale VIII.8 (*vendetta* appears ten times in VIII.7 and four times in VIII.8). Given the function of *vendetta* as a mechanism for achieving justice, VIII.7 and VIII.8 constitute an idiosyncratic meditation on what justice is and when one can say it has been achieved.[10] Boccaccio's meditation on *vendetta* in VIII.7 is further complicated by Pampinea's recourse to a Dantean retributive frame and to Dantean intertextuality.

In VIII.7 a *vendetta* is exacted by the scholar Rinieri on the widow Elena for the *beffa* that she inflicted on him: he causes her to be marooned naked on a roof-top in summer and severely burned, in payment for having been locked in her courtyard on a snowy winter's night and severely frozen. The triple "sconsolata" of VIII.7 (§109, 131, 144) is a textual signifier that underscores the message: Elena pays dearly for thinking that she can make social sport of the scholar while taking sexual sport with her lover. The tactical error that propels the widow into the scholar's vengeance-trap is her naïve request for a favour; she asks him to use necromancy to help her win back her straying lover. Her desperate love makes her foolish (she is not innately foolish)[11] and she overlooks both the scholar's jealous resentment toward her lover and his failure to have used necromantic skills to save himself when imprisoned in her courtyard. But, as I said, these are tactical errors; her larger strategic error is the social one of not assessing carefully the target of her *beffa*. This is the lesson, "non senza utilità" [not without utility], that Pampinea begins to impart in the prologue to her tale: "E questo udire non sarà senza utilità di voi, per ciò che meglio di beffare altrui vi guarderete, e farete gran senno" [Nor will it be unprofitable for you to hear this tale, for it will teach you to think twice before playing tricks on people, which is always a sensible precaution (VIII.7.3)]. She drives home this message in her final words: "E per ciò guardatevi, donne, dal beffare, e gli scolari spezialmente" [I advise you therefore to think

10 On *vendetta*, see Dean, "Marriage and Mutilation," and Scionti, *Capitalisti di faida*. For a discussion of the judicial function of vengeance in modern jurisprudential literature, see Olivia Holmes in this volume.

11 I agree with Guido Almansi's assessment that the widow "mai non perde la sua intelligenza e il suo spirito" ("Alcune osservazioni sulla novella dello scolaro e della vedova," 139). The dismissals of the widow that pervade the critical literature suggest an identification with the scholar, marked in Robert M. Durling's "A Long Day in the Sun."

twice, ladies, before you play such tricks, especially when you have a scholar to deal with (VIII.7.149)].

This very lesson, that of correctly gauging one's target, was underscored by Pampinea in her first tale, I.10, which is also the *Decameron*'s first novella featuring a widow. In I.10 Pampinea stresses the importance of taking all circumstances into consideration (the time, the place, and the person to whom one is speaking) in order to accurately assess one's likelihood of success:

> È il vero che, cosí come nell'altre cose, è in questa da riguardare e il tempo e il luogo e con cui si favella, per ciò che talvolta avviene che, credendo alcuna donna o uomo con alcuna paroletta leggiadra fare altrui arrossare, non avendo ben le sue forze con quelle di quel cotal misurate, quello rossore che in altrui ha creduto gittare sopra sé l'ha sentito tornare. (I.10.7)
>
> [In this as in other things one must, it is true, take account of the time and the place and the person with whom one is speaking. For it sometimes happens that men or women, thinking to make a person blush through uttering some little pleasantry, and having underestimated the other person's powers, find the blush intended for their opponent recoiling upon themselves.]

At the end of I.10 Pampinea extends this lesson to the listening ladies, noting that if they are "wise" ("savie"), they will be careful: "di che voi, se savie sarete, ottimamente vi guarderete" [And if you ladies are wise, you will guard against following her example (I.10.20)]. Pampinea's language here is similar to her admonishment at the end of VIII.7. The conclusions of both I.10 and VIII.7 tell women to be on their guard in a perilous world ("vi guarderete" in I.10 and "guardatevi, donne" in VIII.7). The last words of VIII.7 add a caveat regarding a precise social cohort, specifying the higher level of caution required when dealing with "scholars especially" [e gli scolari spezialmente (VIII.7.149)]. She thus seals the novella with an emphasis on the caste – *gli scolari*, clerks, intellectuals – that is Boccaccio's true target.

Pampinea has a track record of being hard on women in what she claims is their own best interest, their *utilità*, as she does in VIII.7. Thus she introduces her first story, I.10, with a long meditation on the foolishness and vanity of the women of today, fated to lose in social intercourse because of their lack of wit and speaking ability. Pampinea's prologue to I.10 is a historical analysis of the education of women, in which she claims that women of the past ("passate" [I.10.5]) were once much better able to speak up for themselves in society, to conduct themselves as intellectually endowed creatures, whereas now "le moderne" [modern women (I.10.50)] have turned to bodily ornamentation at the expense of their minds: they cannot properly speak if spoken to.[12] This state of affairs is not caused by nature, asserts Pampinea; rather, society has failed to educate women. She therefore emphasizes the need for women to become "instructed" ("ammaestrate"), so that they can engage in social jousts with learned men on a more equal footing. It is her goal to teach women ("voglio ve ne renda ammaestrate") as a form of social protection:

> Per che, acciò che voi vi sappiate guardare, e oltre a questo acciò che per voi non si possa quello proverbio intendere che comunemente si dice per tutto, cioè che le femine in ogni cosa sempre pigliano il peggio, questa ultima novella di quelle d'oggi, la quale a me tocca di dover dire, voglio ve ne renda ammaestrate, acciò che, come per nobiltà d'animo dall'altre divise siete, cosí ancora per eccellenzia di costumi separate dall'altre vi dimostriate. (I.10.8)

> [Wherefore, in order that you may learn to be on your guard, and also in order that people should not associate you with the proverb commonly heard on everyone's lips, namely that women are always worsted in any argument, I desire that the tale which it falls to me to relate, and which completes our storytelling for today, should be one which will make you conversant with these matters. Thus you will be able to show that you are different from other women, not only for the noble qualities of your minds, but also for the excellence of your manners.]

Here Pampinea is eloquent about the need for women to be socially dexterous, lest they always be social losers. And, although Pampinea does not say that widows are in particular need of such coaching, we might surmise as much from her choice of a widow as her first protagonist. Perhaps a widow's need of instruction is in proportion to her greater social liberty.

The common denominators between Pampinea's tales VIII.7 and I.10 include the social positions of the protagonists, for in both *novelle* the

12 The virtue of past women in Pampinea's account is fully historical and does not belong to a "Golden Age return, a recuperation of lost innocence" as per the reading of Millicent Marcus, "The Tale of Maestro Alberto" (citation from 226). Thus, Pampinea's critique of bodily ornamentation that takes the place of wit is not a "a rejection of corporeality" but part of an indictment of contemporary society's failure to educate women.

women are widows and the men are learned. I.10 introduces the precise social dynamic of VIII.7: the social presumptuousness of a lovely widow (she presumes that old men cannot court beautiful young women) is checked by an erudite man, the great medical doctor Maestro Alberto, "un grandissimo medico e di chiara fama quasi a tutto il mondo" [a brilliant physician of almost universal renown (I.10.9)]. I.10 features the same tit-for-tat model that will be full-blown in VIII.7, with the same gendered alignment whereby the man gets the better of a woman who has not sufficiently considered her target. Malgherida dei Ghisolieri, the widow of I.10, is shamed by the learned doctor whom she had thought to shame, as per the story's rubric: "Maestro Alberto da Bologna onestamente fa vergognare una donna, la quale lui d'esser di lei innamorato voleva far vergognare" [Maestro Alberto of Bologna honourably shames a lady who had wanted to shame him for being in love with her (I.10.1; translation mine)]. She is defeated by the man whom she expected to defeat, as per the story's last sentence: "Così la donna, non guardando cui motteggiasse, credendo vincer fu vinta" [Thus the lady, thinking she would score a victory, underestimated the object of her raillery and was herself defeated (I.10.20)]. But Maestro Alberto shames Malgherida "onestamente" – honourably, that is appropriately, not excessively, not cruelly. Maestro Alberto does not provoke the censure or concern of the *brigata*'s ladies, as does the scholar of VIII.7, whom the ladies in their discussion call excessively severe and relentless, not to say downright cruel: "rigido e constante fieramente, anzi crudele" (VIII.8.2). It is here, in the issue of modality and proportion, that the difference between Pampinea's two stories comes into focus. Not present in I.10 is the issue of disproportionate retribution that will become the thematic and ethical focus of VIII.7.

The widow of VIII.7 enters the novella with high social standing. Like the widowed princess Ghismunda, who possesses "animo altiero" (IV.1.30), Elena too is "d'anima altiera": "una giovane del corpo bella e d'animo altiera e di legnaggio assai gentile, de' beni della fortuna convenevolmente abondante" [fair of body, proud of spirit, very gently bred, and reasonably well endowed with Fortune's blessings (VIII.7.4)]. Like the widow Monna Giovanna of V.9, Elena does not wish to remarry, but – unlike Monna Giovanna and like Ghismunda – this is because she has fallen in love with a man of her own choosing: "La quale rimasa del suo marito vedova, mai piú maritar non si volle, essendosi ella d'un giovinetto bello e leggiadro a sua scelta innamorato" [When her husband died prematurely, leaving her a widow, she made up her mind that she would never remarry, having fallen in love with a handsome and charming young man of her own choosing (VIII.7.4)]. Elena thus has a will of her own and the financial means with which to pursue it. Albeit in a less tragic vein, our story will reinforce the logic of Ghismunda's tale with respect to female choice: despite her very real social advantages of lineage and wealth, Elena does not possess sufficient social capital to underwrite the pursuit of *consolazione* fully on her own terms and fully through the deployment of her own agency. (The same logic holds, in differing circumstances, for Monna Giovanna of V.9.) In this way VIII.7 further distances us from the fantasy of the English princess who chooses her Florentine moneylender husband in II.3 and conforms to its place on the declining arc of "the wheel of the *Decameron*":[13] repression builds as the *brigata*'s return to patriarchal Florence nears. The ladies listening to VIII.7 learn that, while female agency may be applauded in theory (to wit, in the Valle delle Donne, if a woman has the good fortune to find that gendered *locus amoenus*),[14] in practice social context can never be safely overlooked: men are in general more powerful than women, and a man who feels threatened in his importance by a woman, even if he is only an apparently impotent scholar, may yet find the means to exact a great, even a disproportionate, revenge.

Boccaccio artfully designs intertwined axes of gender and of social position in VIII.7. Moreover, he brings together two social categories – the *savio amante* and the widow – that had already captured his interest in the *Filocolo*'s "Questioni d'amore," where, however, they did not overlap: Rinieri reflects the intellectual lover of the *Filocolo*'s third question and Elena reflects the widows who are featured in questions 9 and 10. (These same two social categories will be intertwined again in the *Corbaccio*.) The widow of VIII.7 is not just of noble lineage but also in the particular social position created by financially well-endowed widowhood. Rinieri is not just from the nobility but also a scholar, or "clerk" (deriving from *clericus*), one whose prickly masculine pride might compensate for the diminished masculinity accruing to that social position (again, we think of the *Corbaccio*). From this perspective it is fascinating that Boccaccio's own illustration of Rinieri in his autograph copy of the *Decameron* depicts him as a cleric, tonsured and dressed in what Branca calls "solenni vesti dottorali" [solemn doctoral robes].[15] The defensiveness

13 For the movement of the *brigata* out of Florence and then back, see Barolini, "The Wheel of the *Decameron*."

14 For a counter-view of the Valle delle Donne, see Gittes, "Boccaccio's 'Valley of Women.'"

15 The illustration in Boccaccio's autograph manuscript (Berlin, Staatsbibliothek Preussischer Kulturbesitz, MS Hamilton 90) may be seen, with Branca's quotation, in Branca, *Boccaccio visualizzato*, 1:18.

inherent to the status of scholar or cleric, as compared to being a hyper-masculine knight, is exemplified in medieval debates such as the *Carmina Burana*'s "Altercatio Phyllidis et Florae," which poses the question as to whether the *miles* or the *clericus* is the better lover. Normally, in these debates the verdict favours the cleric, indicating that the clerical authors are engaged in buttressing their own social status.[16]

The third of the *Filocolo*'s "Questioni d'amore" poses essentially the question of the "Altercatio Phyllidis et Florae" about the relative amatory merits of the knight versus the cleric: "To which of three aspirants should a lady give her preference? To him who excels in valor, or to him who is most courteous and liberal, or to him who is the wisest?"[17] While in the earlier material the *miles* is poor,[18] Boccaccio has adjusted the itinerant knight-for-hire of feudal France to suit the Italian Trecento landscape in which valour and liberality are both hallmarks of the knight. Thus, for Dante, the Malaspina family possesses both "the glory of the purse and of the sword" [pregio de la borsa e de la spada (*Purg*. 8.129)]. Moreover, while the "Altercatio Phyllidis et Florae" assigns not only wealth but also liberality to the *clericus*, noting that he "bestows gifts in

---

16 Charles Oulmont, in *Les débats du clerc et du chevalier*, collects all the debates, both Latin and vernacular. He writes: "Les poètes de nos débats d'amour s'ingénuent à enlaidir les chevaliers pour grandir le prestige des clercs, ils font des premiers une caricature plutôt qu'un portrait (seule exception le *Florence* anglo-normand, où les chevaliers triomphent)" (21).

17 This is the summary heading provided for the third Question of Love by the sixteenth-century English translator "H.G." (Boccaccio, *Thirteen Most Pleasant and Delectable Questions of Love*, 33).

18 Oulmont's description of the poor knights who travel to support themselves, leaving their women behind for the clerics to prey on, is reminiscent of Boccaccio's merchants who must also travel for work and risk the fidelity of their wives. While II.9 features travelling merchants, many tales focus on the other side of the equation: the willingness of clerics to take advantage of marital instability, however caused. On the poverty of the knights featured in the debates, Oulmont writes: "Quels sont donc les chevaliers dépeints dans nos poèmes? Ce ne sont pas les grands seigneurs ni les riches suzerains: sans fortune, ils sont toujours partis pour guerroyer ou tournoyer; guerres et tournois leur donnent l'argent avec la gloire, s'ils s'y comportent bien. Il sont bien nés, comme on dira quelques siècles plus tard; mais parce qu'ils sont pauvres, ils vont offrir leur épée à un prince, ils sont à la merci des aventures. Leur métier est fatigant et plein d'incertitudes. Aussi ne peuvent-ils résister un long temps à cette vie errante et pénible. Leurs dames regrettent à la fois leurs absences prolongées et leur lassitude au retour. En revanche ces absences sont toujours agréables aux clercs, rivaux des chevaliers" (*Les débats du clerc et du chevalier*, 20).

abundance,"[19] the motif of clerical avarice is a favourite in the *Decameron*; unlike the authors of the debates, Boccaccio does not associate *liberalitas* with clerics. Hence, although the *Filocolo*'s third question poses a choice among three possible lovers – one exceptional in "corporale fortezza" [bodily force], one in "la cortesia e la liberalità" [courtesy and liberality], and one in "sapienza" [wisdom (*Filocolo* 4.27.5, p. 393; trans. p. 35)] – the question resolves itself into the standard binary between knight and cleric, since physical valour and liberality are for Boccaccio both hallmarks of the knight. Book-learning that takes the form of *sapienza*, on the other hand, belongs to the cleric, and the intellectual lover (to whom in the *Filocolo* Fiammetta awards the victory, just as the cleric wins in the "Altercatio") has wisdom such that it surpasses all others: "il terzo è di sapienza piena tanto, che gli altri savi avanza oltra misura" [the third is full of wisdom, so that he surpasses all other wise men beyond measure (*Filocolo* 4.27.5, p. 393; trans. p. 35)].

As the historical context of amatory debates helps us to see, in VIII.7 Boccaccio has deftly created an ambiguous social category. He makes his protagonist a scholar-clerk – as mentioned above, in Boccaccio's illustration Rinieri is tonsured, as was the custom for all university students at Paris and Oxford[20] – but also aligns him with the nobility and immunizes him from the venal aspects of clerkly status, stipulating that Rinieri is financially independent and therefore is not one of those who sets out to attain knowledge in order to make money. Boccaccio had good reason to know that he was doing something novel, in the Italian context of his day, in creating a clerical gentleman: Dante in the canzone *Poscia ch'Amor* specifically indicates that the virtues proper to a *cavaliere* are different from the virtues proper to a scholar or philosopher.[21]

---

19 In strophe 38 we find that the cleric "et largitur dona" [bestows gifts in abundance]. The "Altercatio Phyllidis et Florae" is found in *Les débats du clerc et du chevalier*, 107–21; I take text and translation from "The Debate of Phyllis and Flora," translated by Douglas Caverly, where the text is from the edition of the *Carmina Burana* edited by Hilka and Schumann, 94–103.

20 "An essential difference between Bologna and its two great northern sisters lies in the fact that, at Paris and Oxford, masters and scholars alike were all clerks, possessing the tonsure and wearing the clerical garb, though not necessarily even in minor orders. They could thus claim the privileges of ecclesiastical jurisdiction" (Rait, *Life in the Medieval University*, 46). My thanks to Alex Cuadrado for this reference.

21 Writing of the virtue *leggiadria*, proper to a knight, Dante explicitly notes that this virtue is excluded by clerics and philosophers: "Non è pura virtù la disvïata, / poich'è blasmata, / negata là ov'è più vertù richesta, / cioè in gente onesta / di vita spiritale / o in abito che di scïenza tene" [This errant quality is not a pure virtue,

In this way Boccaccio sets the stage for the moral drama of VIII.7, posing the implicit questions: what is the wisdom searched for and attained by those who have the liberty to pursue wisdom without need of financial gain, and how does it manifest itself in society? The implicit reply, that the uncontaminated philosophical wisdom pursued by Rinieri is surely one of society's greatest resources, if not squandered by a corrupt appetite, provides the frame for my reading, wherein I propose a Boccaccio who is more critical of the scholar than of the widow.

Rinieri arrogates to himself more than the superiority of gender and caste that the story allows him; he ultimately construes himself as a Godlike arbiter of life and death, losing all contact with the ethical guidelines that his deep philosophical learning should have imparted. Moreover, learning should ultimately constitute virtue, and Rinieri does not behave virtuously. The unfolding of the character of Rinieri allows Boccaccio to construct VIII.7 as an *in malo* exploration of the basic tenets of the *Decameron*. Rinieri exemplifies what it means to repress *compassione*, the very *compassione* that Pampinea says she is eliciting at the story's outset and that was established as the fundamental requirement for humanity in the *Decameron*'s famous opening salvo: "Umana cosa è aver compassione degli afflitti" [To take pity on people in distress is a human quality (Proem.2)].

VIII.7 investigates and exposes for its vanity and shallowness the social caste of scholar, intellectual, philosopher, poet – "clerk" in the capacious sense with which Chaucer denotes Petrarch a "worthy clerk" and "lauriat poete" (*Clerk's Tale*, 4.27 and 31; *Riverside Chaucer*, ed. Benson, p. 137). It is the scholar's desire for the lovely widow that sets off the plot and gives the scholar primary position in the story's *rubrica*: "Uno scolare ama una donna vedova" [A scholar loves a widow]. It is the scholar's desire that modulates from desire for carnal satisfaction in the form of sexual intercourse to desire for carnal satisfaction in the form of brutal corporeal vengeance. Though Rinieri has studied "la ragion delle cose e la cagion d'esse" [the reasons and causes of things

since it is blamed, even excluded, there where virtue is especially called for – that is, in people of dignity in the spiritual life or whose bent and disposition is learning (*Poscia ch'Amor*, 77–82)]. Similarly, Jacopo Passavanti stipulates that the confessor priest not be "leggiadro" (see *Specchio della vera penitenza* 5.4, pp. 124–5). My thanks to William Robins, whose sociological lens on Boccaccio is evident in his essay "The Case of the Court Entertainer," for sharing Passavanti's passage with me. The text of Dante's lyrics *Poscia ch'Amor* and *Le dolci rime* is from *Rime*, edited by Domenico De Robertis. The translations are from *Dante's Lyric Poetry*, translated by Kenelm Foster and Patrick Boyde, with some emendations.

(VIII.7.5)], he gives the lie to Virgil's maxim from the *Georgics* that "felix qui potuit rerum cognoscere causas" [happy is the man who knows the causes of things (*Georgics* 2.490, p. 217; my translation)];[22] his insecurity and need to prove himself superior to the widow do not bespeak happiness. Finally, he fails in the all-important philosopher's quest to know and understand himself. He has no understanding of his own true motivations and true desires, and comes out of the events of the novella without having employed or deepened in wisdom. Elena learns more from the experience than does Rinieri and is endowed by Boccaccio with more capacity for ethical insight.

The long tradition of interpreting VIII.7 through an autobiographical lens is relevant to my reading, not in the literal sense of information to be gleaned about Boccaccio's own love life but because in our novella Boccaccio is considering the social group to which he himself belongs.[23] Boccaccio demonstrates ever less confidence in his own tribe, moving from the *Filocolo*'s affirmation of the *savio* as the best lover in the third "Questione d'amore" to the dyspectic characterization of the scholar-husband who is the protagonist of the *Corbaccio*. And, while there are worthy intellectuals in the *Decameron*, including the great poets with whom Boccaccio aligns himself in the Introduction to Day Four, we have not given enough critical attention to the cohort of scholars-philosophers-clerks whom Boccaccio skewers for their allegiance to self-serving sophistry rather than to true philosophy.[24] Into this cohort, further confirming the structural relevance of VIII.7 to the deep logic of the *Decameron*, we must place the envious and pedantic critics of Boccaccio himself, those unnamed clerks whose sophistic attacks are set forth and then deconstructed in the Introduction to Day Four, Boccaccio's authorial touchstone and manifesto.

The *Decameron* boasts a large and varied set of twisted philosophers whose learning serves only solipsistic ends: this set plausibly begins in earnest with Ambruogiuolo in II.9 (to whom Bernabò says defensively

22 For this trope and the importance of the *Georgics*, see Papio, "'Merus phylosophie succus.'" The trope seems to be associated with clerics for it is also present in the "Altercatio Phyllidis et Florae," where we learn that the cleric "celi vias dividit et rerum naturas" [divides the ways of heaven and the natures of things (*Altercatio* 39.4; "The Debate of Phyllis and Flora," pp. 64–5)].

23 For a discussion of the autobiographical impulse in VIII.7 and a metaliterary reading of the novella, see Marcus, "Misogyny as Misreading."

24 While the behaviour of Bergamino, the intellectual of I.7, is exemplary, I disagree with the conclusion reached by Michelangelo Picone in his reading of I.7, whereby "the new intellectual class" is one "that the *Decameron* consistently exalts" ("The Tale of Bergamino," 171).

that he, unlike his sophistical opponent, is not a "fisofolo" [II.9.18]),[25] although the notary Cepperello of I.1 is already a card-carrying member of the guild. Some sophists are friars, like Frate Rinaldo in VII.3, whom Boccaccio associates with Guido da Montefeltro, the sophist of *Inferno* 27: while Guido is bested by a devil who boasts "Forse / tu non pensavi ch'io löico fossi!" [Perhaps you did not think that I was a logician (*Inf.* 27.122–3)], Rinaldo is able to seduce Madonna Agnesa because "loica non sapeva" [she did not know logic (VII.3.22)]. Boccaccio returns to Rinaldo's self-serving use of *silogizzare* at the end of Day Seven: "Le quali cose se frate Rinaldo avesse sapute, non gli sarebbe stato bisogno d'andar silogizzando quando convertì a' suoi piaceri la sua buona comare" [And if only Friar Rinaldo had known as much as Meuccio, there would have been no need for him to make up syllogisms when persuading Madonna Agnesa to minister to his pleasures (VII.10.30)].

Other sophistic reasoners, like Tedaldo in III.7, are not friars. The *Decameron*'s set of corrupt syllogizers culminates with Titus of X.8, the Athenian trained in philosophy whose education provides the sophistical arguments with which to persuade his best friend, Gisippus, to surrender his betrothed, Sophronia, without her consent or even her knowledge. Although this story is usually read as the account of a perfect friendship, Titus's arguments are self-serving and override Sophronia's very personhood; they also coerce Gisippus in a manner that is not compatible with the high standards of true *amicitia*.[26] The member of this syllogizing coterie whom Boccaccio most exposes is the one closest to himself in cultural terms: Rinieri is a Florentine, who was educated in Paris, hence enjoying the excellent philosophical training that Boccaccio himself (trained in the law) might well have desired.

In the *Decameron* Boccaccio explores a new social group composed by imbricating the first and second estates of the traditional European template, according to which society's three estates are nobility, clergy, and commoners. While money-earning lawyers and notaries and scholars for hire are offshoots of clerics, the new social group is one that combines the independent income of the nobility with the learning of the clergy. By mixing the status of gentility, for Rinieri is a "gentile uomo" (VIII.7.5), with the erudition of clergy, a new kind of male citizen

25 For Ambruogiuolo's arguments, see my "'Le parole son donne e i fatti son maschi,'" 286–7; for Dioneo's salutary appropriation and recasting of Ambruogiuolo's arguments, see 287–9.

26 For this reading of X.8, see Barolini, "A Philosophy of Consolation," 102.

arguably emerges: the urbane "clerical" gentleman. Thus, Rinieri lives in Florence "cittadinescamente" (VIII.7.5), an urban gentleman (one imagines that he no longer sports a tonsure, depite Boccaccio's illustration): not a feudal lord in his castle and not a cleric in orders, yet possessed of an independent income and thereby distinguished from lawyers and other urban dwellers whose erudition serves to earn them money. He is perhaps the perfect foil for that other relatively new social construct: the widow whose money and agency are also connected to an urban rather than feudal setting (the two will eventually meet and hatch the plan that enables the scholar's revenge in the still existing church of Santa Lucia dal Prato [VIII.7.50]). Elena too is independently wealthy, and although her independence is not that of the great feudal lady in the courts of Provence, her gentility is such that she possesses land outside of the city. It is in fact her isolated country property in "Valdarno di sopra" [the upper reaches of the Arno valley (VIII.7.60)] that provides Rinieri with the ideal location to carry out his *vendetta*.

Boccaccio's *homo philosophicus*, an urban citizen whose learning does not relegate him to the social margins but who is socially more than acceptable, finds its apex in the portrayal of Guido Cavalcanti in VI.9. We recall that Guido, a nobleman and philosopher who is not at all clerical, is strenuously pursued by Betto Brunelleschi as an ideal recruit for his male social club.[27] Rinieri similarly is a gentleman and a scholar, whose study is labelled a perfect pursuit for a "gentile uomo" (VIII.7.5). As a "gentile uomo" he goes to Paris to learn, not to earn:

> Avvenne in questi tempi che un giovane chiamato Rinieri, nobile uomo della nostra città, avendo lungamente studiato a Parigi, non per vender poi la sua scienza a minuto, come molti fanno, ma per sapere la ragion delle cose e la cagion d'esse, il che ottimamente sta in gentile uomo, tornò da Parigi a Firenze; e quivi onorato molto sì per la sua nobiltà e sì per la scienza cittadinescamente viveasi. (VIII.7.5)

> [Now it happened that around that time, a young nobleman of our city called Rinieri, having spent some years studying in Paris with the purpose, not of selling his knowledge for gain as many people do, but of learning the reasons and causes of things (a most fitting pursuit for any gentleman), returned from Paris to Florence. There he was held in high esteem for his nobility and his learning, and he led the life of a gentleman.]

27 For the social context of the attempt to recruit Guido, see Barolini, "Sociology of the *Brigata*," 14–15.

Not being obliged to study in order to "sell his knowledge for gain as many people do," Rinieri has the luxury of studying in order to learn "the reasons and causes of things," and as a result he reaps double social benefits. Boccaccio tells us that Rinieri was honoured by his fellow citizens both for his nobility and for his knowledge, and that this double honour is the hallmark of his civic and urban lifestyle: "sí per la sua nobiltà e sí per la sua scienzia cittadinescamente viveasi" (VIII.7.5). His *nobiltà* and his *scienza* combine to allow him to live *cittadinescamente*: his widom is situated within the social order, not outside of it, and enhances his social prestige.

But the scholar shows little nobility and less wisdom in his reaction to the widow. His behaviour does nothing to raise the consciousness of the social order that has honoured him for his wisdom. Instead, he sinks to a level that is revealed to be low by any standard, a level that will immediately be surpassed by the Sienese *popolani* of the next story, who are not noble or learned but rather "due giovani assai agiati e di buone famiglie popolane" [two prosperous young men of good plebeian families (VIII.8.4)]. As discussed by Olivia Holmes in her treatment of VIII.8 in this volume, the two Sienese achieve a "balanced retribution." The retribution of VIII.7, in contrast, bespeaks lack of balance. Despite the apparent symmetries on which many readings of VIII.7 focus, the story is, as I will make clear, deeply asymmetrical.

Rinieri does not achieve balance or Aristotelian *misura*, the philosophical framework that connects specifically to his training. Aristotelian ethics is founded in the idea of *misura*, of virtue as moderation. This idea from *Nicomachean Ethics* – "est igitur habitus electivus in medietate existens quoad nos" (II.6.1107a.1) – was explicitly translated by Dante in his canzone *Le dolci rime*, a canzone that Boccacio transcribed on numerous occasions.[28] In *Le dolci rime* Dante defines virtue as a habit of choosing that keeps to the "mezzo" or mean, in a literal translation of Aristotle's "Etica":

> Quest'è, secondo che l'Etica dice,
> un abito eligente
> lo qual dimora in mezzo solamente,
> e tai parole pone. (*Le dolci rime*, 85–8)

---

28 Aquinas's Latin version of the *Nicomachean Ethics* is cited by Foster and Boyde in their commentary to *Le dolci rime* (*Dante's Lyric Poetry*, 221). For Boccaccio as transcriber of Dante's canzoni, see the Introduction to my commentary on Dante's youthful lyrics, in Dante Alighieri, *Dante's Lyric Poetry: Poems of Youth and of the Vita Nuova*.

[This is, as the Ethics states, a "habit of choosing which keeps steadily to the mean" – those are the very words.][29]

In their discussion of VIII.7, the *brigata* explicitly raises the idea that the scholar's revenge was disproportionately harsh, was lacking in moderation and *misura*, and that he himself was unbending and cruel: "rigido e constante fieramente, anzi crudele" [excessively severe and relentless, not to say downright cruel (VIII.8.2)]. Fiammetta announces VIII.8 as an antidote to VIII.7, telling her comrades that she intends to recount a "novelletta," a diminutive novella, as relief from the excess of VIII.7; the correlation of novella length and excess is a point to which I shall return. Fiammetta defines the protagonist of VIII.8 in contrast to Rinieri and uses the precise Aristotelian terminology of moderation: he is a young man "il quale con piú mansueto animo una ingiuria ricevette e quella con piú moderata operazion vendicò" [who took a more charitable view of an injury he received, and devised a more moderate way of avenging himself (VIII.8.3)]. He thus differs from his predecessor in exacting "moderate" vengeance ("con piú moderata operazion"), and his behaviour allows Fiammetta to promote moderation as an ethical principle, as noted by Forni.[30]

From the protagonist of VIII.8 the *brigata* can understand the principle of sufficiency. It "must be enough" [dee bastare] to pay back in vengeance the amount that one received, without "going beyond the appropriate measure" [soprabondando oltre la convenevolezza]:

per la quale potrete comprendere che assai dee bastare a ciascuno se quale asino dà in parete tal riceve, senza volere, soprabondando oltre la convenevolezza della vendetta, ingiuriare, dove l'uomo si mette alla ricevuta ingiuria vendicare. (VIII.8.3)

[You will thereby be enabled to apprehend, that when a man seeks to avenge an injury, it should be quite sufficient for him to pay back exactly what he has received, like an ass does, without wanting to inflict a punishment out of all proportion to the original offence.][31]

In other words, the plebeian protagonist of VIII.8 possesses the Aristotelian *misura* that the scholar, trained in philosophy in Paris, lacks. There

29 On the Aristotelian principle of the mean in Dante, see Barolini, "Aristotle's *Mezzo*, Courtly *Misura*, and Dante's Canzone *Le dolci rime*."

30 See Forni, *Adventures in Speech*, 19–20.

31 McWilliam's translation has been slightly modified, here and above.

is great irony in Boccaccio's deployment of *popolani* who behave more virtuously than the *gentile uomo* who is also a trained philosopher.[32]

Rinieri behaves in a way that demonstrates no special connection to philosophical wisdom. His motivations for vengeance are concern for his own social standing and a deep-seated fear of having been bested by a woman. His fear and panic at having been tricked by the widow and consequently unmanned, turned by her into a "mounted Aristotle," cause him to fail a philosopher's test: the scholar fails a test in Aristotelian ethics. I turn now to a more detailed analysis of Rinieri's failure and of Boccaccio's endorsement in VIII.7 of the Aristotelian values that his scholar fails to embody.

Rinieri Becomes a Mounted Aristotle and Fails a Test in Aristotelian Ethics

The motif of the "mounted Aristotle," widely disseminated in the course of the thirteenth century,[33] communicates an offensively misogynyist view of sexual infatuation: sexual infatuation can reduce a superior man to the inferior of a woman. The point of the motif is that even the wisest of philosophers can be stripped by sexual infatuation of his agency and reason: as is graphically visualized in the many surviving images, "Aristotle" is literally lowered from superior to inferior, reduced to being utterly subjected to the will of the young woman who, frequently brandishing a whip, rides him like a horse. The image of the lover being "ridden by Love," common in the lyric tradition (see, for instance, the opening verses of Guido delle Colonne's canzone *Amor, che lungiamente m'hai menato*) as a way of expressing the lover's loss of reason and agency, is thereby imbued with misogyny: the rider is not a sexually ambiguous Amor but a young woman who makes a fool of an old man. And, to drive the lesson home, she makes a fool of not just any old man, but of one who should truly "know better," namely a philosopher.

32 Even the *asini* of Boccaccio's proverb "quale asino dà in parete tal riceve" behave better than our scholar; even asses engage in tit for tat – equalized – justice. On "Tit-for-Tat" as used by game theorists and political scientists, see Olivia Holmes's essay on VIII.8 in this volume. On the proverb, see the *Vocabolario degli accademici della Crusca*: "In proverb. Quale Asino dà in parete, tal riceve; e si dice quando Alcuno riceve la pariglia dell'ingiuria, ch'egli ha fatta. Lat. par pari referre" (s.v. "parete e pariete").

33 See Marilynn Desmond's discussion of the "mounted Aristotle" motif in *Ovid's Art and the Wife of Bath*, 13–27.

Rinieri becomes a mounted Aristotle and subsequently becomes unhinged. In Boccaccio's unusual and (in my view) progressive treatment of the mounted Aristotle motif, Rinieri is unhinged not because of sexual infatuation, but because of his reaction to being sexually and socially rejected. Rinieri's turn toward becoming a mounted Aristotle is spelled out in a sentence that links those who have greatest "awareness of life's profundities" to their vulnerability in love: "Ma come spesso avviene coloro ne' quali è piú l'avvedimento delle cose profonde piú tosto da amore essere incapestrati, avvenne a questo Rinieri" [But it frequently happens that the more keen a man's awareness of life's profundities, the more vulnerable he is to the forces of Love, and so it was in the case of this Rinieri (VIII.7.6)]. Specifically, Boccaccio states that those who have most awareness "delle cose profonde" – in other words the philosophical, the wise, the "Aristotles" – can more easily be "da amore incapestrati," where *incapestrati* signifies *presi al capestro*, or "taken by the halter," like a horse.

Elena, who takes pleasure in the scholar's vulnerability to her manipulations, applies a market logic to her actions, believing that "quanti più n'adescasse e prendesse col suo piacere, tanto di maggior pregio fosse la sua bellezza e massimamente a colui al quale ella insieme col suo amore l'aveva data" [the more men she could entice and conquer with her charms, the more highly would her beauty be prized, especially by the young man on whom, along with her love, she had bestowed it (VIII.7.9)]. From her perspective (perhaps socially accurate), she has good reason to entice Rinieri, and we notice that Boccaccio uses a verb that, like *incapestrati*, signals Elena's predatory actions: the phrase "quanti più n'adescasse e prendesse col suo piacere" casts Elena's beauty as able to hook (*adescare*) and catch its prey. Rinieri is a willing victim, who fulfils the mounted Aristotle paradigm by losing the wits ("perdere il senno") that he brought home from Paris, as Elena duly notes: "Hai veduto dove costui è venuto a perdere il senno che egli ci ha da Parigi recato?" [I wonder where he's left all that wisdom that he brought back with him from Paris? (VIII.7.12)]. Rinieri does not succeed in actualizing the state of intellectual lover; rather, Elena torments her scholarly suitor to kindle sexual pleasure in the lover she had already chosen. And she makes fun of Rinieri as an intellectual, pointing out that his great wisdom does not translate into the intelligence to understand and therefore withstand her manipulations.

The narrator, Pampinea, also refers pointedly to Rinieri's identity as a scholar, interrupting her story in order to point to the danger of challenging a man from this social cadre: "Ahi cattivella, cattivella! ella non sapeva ben, donne mie, che cosa è il mettere in aia con gli scolari" [Ah, what a poor, misguided wretch she must have been, dear ladies, to suppose that she could get the better of a scholar! (VIII.7.13)]. The same adjective used for Elena in Pampinea's apostrophe, "Ahi cattivella, cattivella!," reappears to modify Rinieri, "lo scolare cattivello," in the moment of his conversion experience, when – realizing that he has been tricked – his love turns to hate:

> Lo scolar cattivello, quasi cicogna divenuto sì forte batteva i denti, accorgendosi d'esser beffato più volte tentò l'uscio se aprir lo potesse e riguardò se altronde ne potesse uscire; né vedendo il come, faccendo le volte del leone, maladiceva la qualità del tempo, la malvagità della donna e la lunghezza della notte insieme con la sua semplicità, e sdegnato forte verso di lei, il lungo e fervente amor portatole subitamente in crudo e acerbo odio trasmutò, seco gran cose e varie volgendo a trovar modo alla vendetta, la quale ora molto piú disiderava che prima d'esser con la donna non avea disiato. (VIII.7.39–40)

> [Perceiving that he had been duped, the scholar, whose teeth were chattering so vigorously that he seemed to have been turned into a stork, tried the door several times to see whether it would open, and searched all round the courtyard for some other way out. But finding none, he paced to and fro like a lion in a cage, cursing the severity of the weather, the perfidy of the lady, the inordinate length of the night, and his own stupidity. So indignant did he feel about the way he had been treated by the lady that his fervent and longstanding love was transformed into savage and bitter hatred, and his mind dwelt on various elaborate schemes for securing his revenge, which he now desired far more ardently than he had formerly yearned to hold her in his arms.]

This pivotal scene begins with a simile comparing the freezing scholar to a chattering stork ("cicogna"), in a deliberate recall of the chattering teeth of Rinaldo d'Asti of II.2 (Rinaldo is also exposed to snow but then rescued by a lovely widow and ministered to in every way, including sexually).[34] The scene offers first recognition, the moment when Rinieri realizes he has been duped ("accorgendosi d'esser beffato"), followed by conversion: his "lungo e fervente amor" is suddenly transformed into savage hatred, "crudo e acerbo odio." His radical change of heart

---

34 The word *cicogna* occurs only twice in the *Decameron*, in VIII.7 and in II.2, where we find "sentì il pianto e 'l triemito che Rinaldo faceva, il quale pareva diventato una cicogna" [Rinaldo, who sounded from the way his teeth were chattering as if he had been turned into a stork (II.2.22)].

is preceded by an inner cursing of these key elements: the weather (his torment of her will involve reversing cold to heat), her "malvagità" or perfidy (even more *malvagio* than she, he will twice be compared by Pampinea to the devil), the length of the night (an excess that he will strive to exceed), and, most important to him, his own stupidity. Rinieri's focus on this last element, the "simplicità" or stupidity that allowed him to be duped by the widow, signals the moment in which the scholar, under the pressure of Elena's *beffa*, redefines his life's pursuit. No longer committed to the pursuit of knowledge for its own sake, and no longer defined as one who seeks to understand the causes of things, whose motivation is "sapere la ragion delle cose e la cagion d'esse" (VIII.7.5), Rinieri has come to a new definition of his identity as an intellectual, one that coincides with the implicit characterization that Pampinea has been offering all along: a scholar is someone who is not *beffabile*.

When Rinieri turns his attention to becoming not *beffabile*, a self-construction to which he will cleave rigidly for the rest of the novella, he ceases to strive to understand *la ragion delle cose*, including *la ragion* of his own behaviour, of his own desires. This point is signalled in the key passage cited above, a passage situated one-quarter of the way through this excessive story (VIII.7.40 ends at 2179 words, out of a total of 8712 words). In other words, three-quarters of the novella will be devoted to Rinieri's behaviour *after* he converts from love to hate. I stress the word count bcause it is essential to the novella's message. This is not a story with two halves, a story of balance, as is frequently stated.[35] It is a story about excess that thematizes and performs excess. That excess is first signalled here, by Rinieri's conversion to hatred at only the one-quarter mark of the novella. Nor is it overstated to claim that this story depicts a conversion *in malo*: the narrative length affords the scholar repeated opportunities to relent, to renounce his hatred and desire for vengeance, which he repeatedly resists. Textual continuity *after* conversion is required to show conclusively that conversion has occurred, as we know from Augustine's *Confessions*. The same narrative principle applies to the conversion *in malo* of VIII.7. After renouncing multiple opportunities to return to a self that behaves more like the courtly gentleman he was at the beginning of VIII.7, the scholar's character has fundamentally altered by the novella's end.[36]

35 For instance, Robert Hollander views the story as "perfectly balanced" and treats the protagonists as morally balanced as well, as "two victims of uncontrolled appetites, one for sexual pleasure, another for a displaced form of the same, sexual revenge" (*Boccaccio's Last Fiction*, 21).

36 Hollander's statement that Rinieri "has temporarily become a maddened old man" (*Boccaccio's Last Fiction*, 21) is astute with respect to what Rinieri has become, and indeed the last section of this essay treats the "old man" syndrome. I dispute

Immediately after describing the scholar's conversion from love to hate, the narrator introduces Rinieri's desire for *vendetta* and stipulates that his desire for *vendetta* is now greater than his original erotic desire to possess the widow carnally: "seco gran cose e varie volgendo a trovar modo alla vendetta, la quale ora molto piú disiderava che prima d'esser con la donna non avea disiato" [his mind dwelt on various elaborate schemes for securing his revenge, which he now desired far more ardently than he had formerly yearned to hold her in his arms (VIII.7.40)]. Rinieri's desire is the issue: he now desires vengeance, as first he desired Elena.[37] But, for all his philosophical training, he does not recognize this desire as desire and he does not treat it like any other form of desire: an impulse that must be moderated and regulated, controlled and tempered if the desirer is to remain virtuous. Failing to grasp this key point, Rinieri will not deepen in understanding, only in malice. And, in fact, he will be far more dextrous in consummating his desire to injure Elena than he was in consummating his desire to have sex with her.

The analysis of desire that Boccaccio executes in VIII.7 goes to the Aristotelian heart of the matter, keyed to the ideas of *misura* and its counterpart, *dismisura* or excess. These ideas are also essential to Dante, who mediates Boccaccio's Aristotelian inheritance with respect to sin and virtue, an inheritance that does not carry with it only the concept of *contrapasso* (as many readings of this novella suggest) but also Aristotle.[38] Boccaccio at this point in the story refers to Rinieri as *savio* and temperate, in a deeply ironic move, for Rinieri here tempers his desire for vengeance only so that he can keep it disguised and execute it more effectively later on. This "temperance" is therefore not virtuous, for it is in the service of his cunning. Not wanting to put Elena on guard, he is clever enough to suppress that which a "non temperata volontà" [not temperate will] would have revealed:

> Lo scolare isdegnoso, sì come savio il qual sapeva niuna altra cosa le minacce essere che arme del minacciato, serrò dentro al petto suo ciò che la non temperata volontà s'ingegnava di mandar fuori. (VIII.7.42)

> [Though seething with indignation, the scholar was wise enough to know that menaces simply forearm the person who is threatened, and so, he

"temporarily": Rinieri could of course go on to repent, but within the parameters of the novella as it exists there is no indication that his transformation is temporary.

37 As Marcus notes, "the lustful and punitive desires are not so far apart" ("Misogyny as Misreading," 35).

38 See Barolini, "Aristotle's *Mezzo*, Courtly *Misura*, and Dante's Canzone *Le dolci rime*."

repressed within himself that which a not temperate will was striving to unleash.][39]

Here Rinieri behaves *come savio* ("as a sage"), using his *senno* ("wisdom") to control his passion, in a passage in which Boccaccio has marvellously realigned all the markers of ethical wisdom: here Rinieri moderates his passion only so that ultimately he can give more effective vent to it.

Boccaccio further illuminates the incremental pathologizing of Rinieri's lust to achieve dominance over Elena through the arc of the adjective *lieto* (happy). What starts out as a designator of Rinieri's naïvely happy pursuit of love (VII.7.14 and 17) curdles into a sick joy after he has come to hate Elena. He is "tutto lieto" at learning that God has given him the opportunity to hurt the "malvagia femina" who hurt him:

> La fante fece l'ambasciata bene e diligentemente; la quale udendo lo scolare, tutto lieto seco medesimo disse: "Idio, lodato sie tu: venuto è il tempo che io farò col tuo aiuto portar pena alla malvagia femina della ingiuria fattami in premio del grande amore che io le portava." (VIII.7.49)

> [The maid scrupulously delivered the message, on hearing which the scholar was overjoyed, and said to himself: "Praise be to God, for with His assistance, the time has come for me to punish the wicked hussy for the wrong she did me in exchange for all the love I bore her."]

The happiness that Rinieri experiences here is a moral hazard; it is reminiscent of Sapìa's joy, the "letizia … a tutte altre dispari" [joy without equal (*Purg.* 13.120)] that Sapìa feels when she witnesses the defeat of her fellow Sienese, whom she hates, at the hands of the Florentines in the battle of Colle di Val d'Elsa. As VIII.7 unfolds, Rinieri's happiness becomes ever more pathological, ever more a moral hazard. It surfaces again in VIII.7.64, where Rinieri is happy that his plan for *vendetta* is materializing: "Lo scolar, lieto di ciò che il suo avviso pareva dovere avere effetto" [Delighted at the prospect of what was about to happen]. The arc of the word *lieto* to modify Rinieri culminates in VIII.7.91, where the scholar's vengeance-inspired happiness fully blossoms into vicious – and blasphemous (hence the allusion to Capaneo) – excess.[40]

39 I have altered the translation of the latter part of the sentence in order to render "la non temperata volontà," absent from McWilliam's translation.

40 The scholar echoes the blasphemer Capaneo's "allegra vendetta" from *Inferno* 14.60 in his wish that God will make him "allegro" in his "vendetta" (VIII.7.100).

Rinieri tells Elena that, if she should jump from the top of the tower where he has stranded her and, with God's help, break her neck, she will make him "il piú lieto uom del mondo" [the happiest man in the world]: "E a un'ora con l'aiuto di Dio, fiaccandoti tu il collo, uscirai della pena nella quale esser ti pare e me farai il piú lieto uom del mondo" [With God's help, you would break your neck, and so release yourself from the pain you seem to be suffering, at the same time making me the happiest man in the world (VIII.7.91)].

Rinieri, in the above passage, has become the victim of his own sophistry and has crafted for himself an encounter of extreme moral hazard. How did Rinieri get to this point from his point of departure? The length of VIII.7 – its excessive length – is correlated to the vice, in the Aristotelian form of excess, that takes root and blossoms within him. His vice is that he allows himself to be dominated by passion: his passion for revenge. This vice, nurtured in the soil of lack of introspection and lack of self-knowledge – hence the irony of Rinieri's claim to Elena, to which we will arrive, that she has allowed him finally to know himself – takes over Rinieri, compelling and corrupting him from within. He does not have the moral or psychological ballast, despite his years of philosophical training, to withstand his lust for vengeance and its corrupting effects. Vice can burrow into and corrupt the soul even of an educated person; similarly, Boccaccio's critics in the Introduction to Day Four were not able to withstand the corrupting effects of their envy. In Rinieri's case, his philosophical training actually serves to enable the compulsion, by providing him the sophistical reasoning with which the scholar persuades himself that he is on the right path.

There are several key moments that mark Rinieri's long slide into vice and ultimately his loss of self, as that self was originally constituted at the beginning of the novella. They are the moment in which his love converts to hate (VIII.7.39–40, analysed above), the moment that constitutes his first moral crossroads, when he desires Elena as she passes in the night and nonetheless lets her go (VIII.7.66–8), and then a second moral crossroads, a second opportunity to choose moderation and virtue, which consitutes a moral tipping point (VIII.7.80–5). The first moral crossroads serves as an opportunity for Boccaccio to create a stark contrast between the ethical choice made by Rinieri and the ethical vision of the *Decameron*, in which it is more virtuous to succumb to carnal desire that is linked to compassion than to suppress that carnal desire and with it compassion. This linking of "compassione" to "lo stimolo della carne" is a hallmark of Boccaccio's personal and quite anomalous ethical credo, put forth in the Introduction to Day Four of the *Decameron*, and underlined in VIII.7 through the scholar's rejection of it. After a lyrical prelude in which the narrator conjures the whiteness of Elena's naked body glimmering in the dark, we learn that her beauty causes him "to feel some compassion for her": "sentì di lei alcuna compassione" (VIII.7.66). At the same time the stimulus of the flesh ("lo stimolo della carne") assaults him and causes him to consider a sexual resolution to his craving for revenge:

> E d'altra parte lo stimolo della carne l'assalì subitamente e fece tale in piè levare che si giaceva e confortavalo che egli da guato uscisse e lei andasse a prendere e il suo piacer ne facesse: e vicin fu ad essere tra dall'uno e dall'altro vinto. (VIII.7.67)
>
> [Moreover, being suddenly assailed by the desires of the flesh, which caused a recumbent part of his person to stand, he was strongly tempted to sally forth from his hiding-place, seize her in his arms, and take his pleasure of her. So that, what with his pity on the one hand and his lust on the other, he was very nearly conquered.][41]

Rinieri is almost conquered ("vinto") by his combined feelings of compassion and lust. But instead – here is his moral crossroads – he overcomes those feelings and recommits himself to *vendetta*. He does so by remembering "who he is" and the injury he received and from what source: "chi egli era e qual fosse la 'ngiuria ricevuta e perché e da cui" (VIII.7.68). The issue of his identity thus comes to the fore, and the identity that the scholar chooses is not that of someone who understands the causes of things. He chooses his social identity; he chooses to essentialize both himself and his antagonist in terms of their positions in the social hierarchy. In this way he is able to reignite anger in himself ("nel lo sdegno raccesosi"), simultaneously dispelling both "compassione" and "carnale appetito": "nello sdegno raccesosi e la compassione e il carnale appetito cacciati" [his indignation was rekindled, dispelling all his pity and fleshly desires (VIII.7.68)]. Here Boccaccio brilliantly recasts the traditional language of carnal appetite that needs to be suppressed so that the hero can remain "firm in his resolve": "stette nel suo proponimento fermo, e lasciolla andare" [he remained firm in his resolve, and he let her go (VIII.7.68; translation mine)]. At this novel moral crossroads engineered by Boccaccio, the hero remains "firm" in what for Boccaccio is the wrong resolve, letting her go rather than

41 I have modified the last part of this translation, where McWilliam has "he very nearly gave himself away."

engaging her sexually. What needs to be suppressed at the moral crossroads engineered by Boccaccio is not an immoderate carnal appetite, but an immoderate desire for vengeance. Indeed, in Boccaccio's ethical vision, the pursuit of carnal desire would in this moment be preferable, because at this moment within him "lo stimolo della carne" and "compassione" are aligned.[42]

The scholar rejects the *Decameron*'s ethical vision. He does not use the situation available to him to master his appetite for vengeance.[43] Rather, by reminding himself of "who he was, the wrong he had suffered, the reason for it, and the person who had inflicted it upon him," he stokes his wounded vanity, nurturing his feelings of indignation at having become a mounted Aristotle: he of all people should not have been outsmarted by a female! Rinieri deliberately cultivates the feelings that will keep him in the state of mind that the *brigata* will ultimately define as "rigido e constante fieramente, anzi crudele" [excessively severe and relentless, not to say downright cruel (VIII.8.2)]. We note that the *brigata* qualifies the adjective "constante" with the adverb "fieramente" in order to turn a virtue – constancy – into a vice (literally, he is "fiercely unbending and constant"). They follow precisely the inverted moral alignment of the crossroads scene we have just discussed, in which Rinieri's fixity, his remaining "firm in his resolve," is viewed not positively, but negatively. As a result of deliberately driving out of himself both compassion and carnal desire – "e la compassione e il carnale appetito cacciati" – the scholar induces the state of mind that will eventually be condemned by the *brigata*.

Importantly, this is already the scholar's state of mind as we reach the mid-point of this long novella. The scholar will prove inflexible in the face of all appeals to bend and to show compassion. The widow's appeals and Rinieri's rejoinders will be substantively worthy of analysis, as we shall see in the next section of this reading. But they also exist for a simple dramatic and structural reason: they offer Rinieri the opportunity to experience compassion and nonetheless repeatedly to reject it. None of the subsequent lengthy pleas, which require as long again to narrate as the events that we have discussed thus far, are able

42 As Michael Papio writes of this passage, "physical attraction and compassion are treated as nearly synonymous terms" ("'Non meno di compassion piena che dilettevole,'" 117).

43 While to us the pursuit of non-consensual sex is just as problematic as the pursuit of corporal *vendetta*, Boccaccio here suggests otherwise. Moreover, we do not know that sex with Elena at this point, had Rinieri pursued it, would have been non-consensual. Elena later offers herself to Rinieri (VIII.7.94) and is rejected.

to cause him to relent. Instead he remains fixed in his resolve, "fiercely unbending and constant." Which is to say, the scholar remains constant in his vice. The length of VIII.7 is a textual dramatization that performs the scholar's unbending fixity in the wrong *proponimento*, as he shows himself to be unable or unwilling to discern the better path.

The mid-point of VIII.7 occurs when the scholar, having successfully lured the widow naked to the tower and having shaken off the compassion and carnal desire that would have spared her as she made her way in the darkness to the site of her punishment, wakes up refreshed at dawn. He then approaches the widow on the tower with the sarcastic quip that exposes her stupid credulity. We recall that she originally made herself vulnerable to his trap by seeking magical aids to win back her straying lover, and that the aids he offers include incantations that summon *damigelle* (ladies in waiting) to do her bidding. As a result the scholar is now able to reap the satisfaction of addressing the widow thus: "Buon dí, madonna; sono ancor venute le damigelle?" ["Good morning, madam," he said. "Have the young ladies arrived yet?" (VIII.7.75)]. With this quip, which comes at the precise mid-point of the tale (at the end of his query we are at 4338 words, of a total of 8712 words), the scholar turns the scales between himself and the widow back to what he considers their normative position, in which he is smart and she is stupid. After imparting his lesson about his superior intelligence and making fun of her stupidity, he could, if he wanted, accept her apology, which is the next plot element. He could let her down from the tower, and this all too long story could end. But instead it is only at the mid-way point. The length of VIII.7 is an index of how far the scholar veers off the path of wisdom and righteousness: the length of VIII.7 *is* his excess. And, in an Aristotelian context, excess is vice.

Excess and Sophistry

The second half of VIII.7 dramatizes excess as vice with language in two ways: with its inordinate length and also with its display of virtuosic sophistry. The scholar will now be granted much rope, in the form of sophistic language, with which to hang himself. He shows his willingness to abuse the tools of philosophical reasoning and to employ them to self-serving and lower than philosophical ends. In the arguments that he enthusiastically employs to bludgeon Elena, Rinieri lowers himself to the level of an Ambruogiuolo, the sophistic misogynist of II.9. But whereas Zinevra learns and prevails and Ambruogiuolo is punished by death (the ultimate social cost meted out to him by Zinevra's protector, the sultan), Elena learns and survives and Rinieri pays no social price (there is no sultan to function as *deus ex machina* in the more sober and realistic world of Day Eight). As discussed previously, location drives messaging in this text. At this point on the wheel of the *Decameron*, the patriarchal system is reaffirmed and men are indemnified simply by virtue of the fact that they are men. But, although society lets the scholar off the hook, Boccaccio does not.

While the first part of VIII.7 might seem to suggest that the widow has as much latitude for sadistic pranks as the scholar, the social costs meted out to the novella's two protagonists diverge markedly in the second half. When Elena finds that she cannot descend from the tower, the first thought that comes to her is the irremediable social cost in the form of her (gendered and sexual) *onore*:

> La tua onestà, stata cotanta, sarà conosciuta essere stata falsa; e se tu volessi a queste cose trovare scuse bugiarde, che pur ce ne avrebbe, il maladetto scolare, che tutti i fatti tuoi sa, non ti lascerà mentire. Ahi misera te, che a un'ora avrai perduto il male amato giovane e il tuo onore! (VIII.7.74)
>
> [Your fair repute will be seen as merely an empty façade; and if you try to brazen it out by giving some spurious explanation or other, you will be exposed by this accursed scholar, who knows all about your private affairs. Ah, poor wretch, that at one and the same moment you should have lost not only the young man you were foolish enough to love, but your good name into the bargain!]

The qualifier *gentile* is used for both protagonists, but *onestà* is exclusively Elena's to lose; we now begin to see the gendered divergence in the cost of misbehaviour. She will beg Rinieri, whom she now addresses by name for the first time (VIII.7.77), to be conscious of his own inner sense of honour (VIII.7.79), an appeal that he can (and does) choose to ignore without paying a penalty. She, however, fears losing her outer good name, her good name in society, a good that she cannot choose to ignore.

In her apology, which begins immediately after the scholar's quip about the *damigelle*, Elena is naïve about the form of Rinieri's vengeance, thinking his punishment consisted only of the night she has just spent naked on the tower. Translated into the language used to classify afterlife punishments, we could say that the widow does not realize that the scholar's retribution will be exacted first through analogy to her "sin" (a nocturnal exposure weakly analogous to the one she inflicted on him) and then – additionally, excessively – through opposition to it (the opposite of what she did to him is a day of scorching heat).

The model of Dantean *contrapasso* by analogy or by opposition is thus a means to highlight Rinieri's excessive response, since he has already exacted a punishment through analogy and yet proceeds to add a punishment through opposition.

Elena is intelligent enough to frame the issue as one of excess immediately, arguing that Rinieri must accept what he has already done to her as sufficient retribution. She clarifies that there are two divergent (because gendered) types of honour at stake. She begs him not to take away her honour, very tangible because sexually based, which once taken cannot be restored. And she begs him to love himself enough to consider his own honour, an intangible good that is entirely within his own power to maintain, and that is tied to the issue of sufficiency. He must love himself enough, she says, to maintain an equilibrium, to see what is enough: "E per ciò io ti priego, non per amor di me, la quale tu amar non dei, ma per amor di te, che se' gentile uomo, che ti basti per vendetta della ingiuria la quale io ti feci quello che infino a questo punto fatto hai" [I therefore implore you, not for love of me, whom you have no reason to love, but for your own sake, as a gentleman, to let this suffice by way of revenge for the injury I did you (VIII.7.78)].

Elena continues to hammer on the ethics of sufficiency, forcefully deploying the verb *bastare*: "Bastiti adunque questo" [Let it suffice you (VIII.7.79)]. She astutely plays the gender card, calling herself "una femina" and thereby offering him a way out of the moral dilemma he has crafted for himself. It is beneath him to exact further revenge on a lowly female; what he has already done should be enough, and to go further is to risk his own honour ("per onor di te"):

> Bastiti adunque questo: e, come a valente uomo, sieti assai l'esserti potuto vendicare e l'averlomi fatto conoscere. Non voler le tue forze contro a una femina essercitare: niuna gloria è a una aquila l'aver vinta una colomba; dunque, per l'amor di Dio e per onor di te, t'incresca di me. (VIII.7.79)
>
> [Let it suffice you, as a gentleman, to have succeeded in avenging yourself and making me aware of the fact. Don't apply your strength against a mere woman: the eagle that conquers a dove has nothing to boast about. For the love of God and the sake of your honour, do have mercy on me.]

Elena's repetition of "basti" and "bastiti" shows that she, an uneducated "femina," has a firmer grasp of Aristotelian ethics with respect to the regulation of human passion than does the scholar: virtue requires moderation. Stipulating the superior virtue of her humble Sienese protagonist in the next story, Fiammetta will use the same verb used by

Elena, *bastare*, noting that a proportionate vengeance "dee bastare" [must be sufficient" (VIII.8.3)]. Elena's repetition in the above passages of "per amor di te" and "per onor di te" shows moreover that she intuits the moral cost of Rinieri's failure to abide by the ethics of sufficiency: the implication is that if he values *himself* he will not take the desire for vengeance too far. She is warning him not to allow his desire for vengeance to deform and corrupt his self. She is warning him of moral hazard.

The rest of VIII.7 depicts Rinieri's failure to heed Elena's warning and chronicles his *soprabondare*, his excess, "soprabondando oltre la convenevolezza della vendetta" [exceeding an appropriate measure of vengeance (VIII.8.3)]. The remaining 4110 words – half the novella – is devoted to marking the way stations of self-deformation and self-corruption wrought by the scholar's unrestrained appetite. This is a man, after all, whom the narrator links to the devil.[44] Again Boccaccio designs a moral crossroads, as he had earlier, again pitting the scholar's humanity, his compassion, against the pleasure he feels at punishing the presumptuous widow. The scholar's natural human compassion is a source of irritation to him, causing him "noia," while inflicting punishment satisfies his sadistic desire. In the following passage, Rinieri feels his humanity moving him to compassion (the phrase "movendolo la umanità sua a compassion" aligns *umanità* with *compassione*, as per the *Decameron*'s first sentence):

> Lo scolare, con fiero animo seco la ricevuta ingiuria rivolgendo e veggendo piagnere e pregare, a un'ora aveva piacere e noia nell'animo: piacere della vendetta la quale piú che altra cosa disiderata avea, e noia sentiva movendolo la umanità sua a compassion della misera. (VIII.7.80)

---

44 There are multiple comparisons of the characters in VIII.7 to the devil and to figures in *Inferno*. The narrator, Pampinea, compares the scholar to the devil twice, in §56 and §149. The scholar compares the widow to the devil in §87 and §126. In §98, Rinieri allusively aligns himself with Ciampolo, the barrater who escapes the devils in *Inferno* 22; like Ciampolo, he boasts of his many wiles ("Io n'aveva mille altre, e mille lacciuoli"). In §100 he aligns himself with Capaneo, the blasphemer of *Inferno* 14. In §146, Pampinea practically cites verbatim *Inferno* 22.109, the same verse about Ciampolo's cleverness in evading the devils previously adopted by the scholar in §98: "Ond' ei, ch'avea lacciuoli a gran divizia" (*Inf.* 22.109) has become "la donna, che aveva a gran divizia lacciuoli" (VIII.7.146). Only now, in Pampinea's usage, it is Elena whose cleverness allows her to fabricate a story for her relatives that will salvage her reputation, thus evading the scholar-devil's trap, and confirming her as his intellectual equal.

[The scholar, indignantly reflecting on the injury she had done him, and perceiving her tears and her entreaties, was filled with pleasure and irritation at one and the same time: the pleasure of that revenge which he had desired above all else, and the irritation engendered by his compassionate nature at the sight of her distress.][45]

And yet Rinieri's humanity does not win out. Unlike the uneducated Zeppa of VIII.8, who is perceived by his comrade Spinelloccio as behaving "umanamente" (a Decameronian hapax) in adjudicating his revenge (VIII.8.29), Rinieri's "humanity is unable to conquer the fierceness of his appetite" [non potendo la umanità vincere la fierezza dello appetito (VIII.7.80)].[46] I substitute my translation for McWilliam's in order to highlight Boccaccio's technical precision here. As in Dante's paradigmatic "la ragion sommettono al talento" [they [the lustful] put reason under desire (*Inf.* 5.39)], Boccaccio makes clear which faculty is above and which faculty is below. Replacing Dante's "talento" with the more technical "appetito" and Dante's "ragion" with the less technical "umanità," Boccaccio signals his personal value-system based on *compassione*. The scholar puts humanity under appetite; or rather, he puts appetite above humanity. Which is to say, Rinieri *is* a mounted Aristotle indeed, for he has allowed appetite – in his case, appetite for vengeance – to govern him.

Rinieri hides his inability to conquer his appetite in language that is frequently sophistic: his sophistry attempts to masquerade the ethical and intellectual bankruptcy of his arguments. While he is a passionate spokesman for misogyny, his argumentation is not particularly effective (Ambruogiuolo's misogynistic rhetoric is sharper), and he does not vanquish Elena rhetorically.[47] He deploys the intellectually meagre categories "stupid" – "stolta che tu se'" [you stupid woman (VIII.7.83)] – versus "smart," and from these categories he spins fallacious moral precepts. He assigns to Elena a lesser and gendered quality of intelligence, cunning ("astuzia" VIII.7.85), with which she is now

45 I translate "noia" as "irritation" in this passage, in place of McWilliam's "sorrow."

46 Two of four uses of *umanità* in the *Decameron* belong to our story (the other two are in II.2 and X.7); the only use of *umanamente* is this citation in VIII.8.

47 The more common view is that of Marcus, who views Rinieri as "a forceful and articulate spokesman" of misogyny ("Misogyny as Misreading," 24). And see Papio: "The lengthy debate, which is almost as painful to read as the descriptions of the widow's broken flesh, is not as much about sadistic torture as it is the showcasing of the scholar's ability to break down each of the widow's arguments" ("'Non meno di compassion piena che dilettevole,'" 117).

trying to dissuade him from his legitimate right to punish her. Because in her appeal she called him *gentile* and *valente*, he rejects *gentilezza*, thinking in this way to outsmart her, showing himself to be immune to her flattery ("le tue lusinghe" VIII.7.85). Instead the scholar now outsmarts himself, showing that he is not smart enough to recognize that the person who wronged him can also be right. He is not wise enough to realize that his lust for vengeance is corrupting his essence – or is revealing an essence that is not worthy of the categories that he used in the past to construct his self: *gentile, nobile, valente, savio*. In opposition to the widow, he remakes himself as *non-beffabile*, proof to her wiles. He rejects her pleas that he behave with nobility and "come magnanimo" (VIII.7.85), and commits to building an *in malo* version of his self constructed in opposition to her. What happened to all those years of learning before he ever met Elena? Are they worth so little? He allows her to define him and then says that he learned more about himself in one night of being maltreated by her than in all his years in Paris:

> E ancora, la tua astuzia usando nel favellare, t'ingegni col commendarmi la mia benivolenzia acquistare e chiamimi gentile uomo e valente, e tacitamente che io come magnanimo mi ritragga dal punirti della tua malvagità t'ingegni di fare; ma le tue lusinghe non m'adombreranno ora gli occhi dello 'ntelletto, come già fecero le tue disleali promessioni; io mi conosco, né tanto di me stesso apparai mentre dimorai a Parigi, quanto tu in una sola notte delle tue mi facesti conoscere. (VIII.7.85)

> [What is more, by cunningly mincing your words, you attempt through flattery to soften my heart towards you, calling me a gentleman, and quietly trying to dissuade me from punishing you for your wickedness, by appealing to my better nature. But the eyes of my mind will not be clouded now by your blandishments, as once they were by your perfidious promises. I know myself better now than I did earlier, for you taught me more about my own character in a single night than I ever learned during the whole of my stay in Paris.]

What then did Rinieri learn from his night in the snow? That he is not *gentile, valente*, or *magnanimo*? Rinieri says he "knows himself" – "io mi conosco" – in the very moment when he fails to know himself and to understand his own motivations, in the moment when he loses a self worth knowing. He says "io mi conosco," but he does not seem to know what he is becoming. His need to have his superior intelligence vindicated is cancelling out his virtue, his nobility, his humanity – and even his intelligence, since he now demonstrates only cunning. The very *astuzia* that he throws at the widow to degrade her has become an apt descriptor of his own malicious cunning, as Pampinea will state explicitly at the novella's end, noting that scholars, most of them anyway, "sanno dove il diavolo tien la coda" [know where the devil keeps his tail (VIII.7.149)].[48] The scholar claims he has learned not to be blinded by passion; he claims that the eyes of his mind that before were "clouded by your blandishments" are now wide open. And yet precisely now the scholar is blinded by passion. He thus utters "io mi conosco" as he fails the basic test of the sage as passed down from antiquity: *nosce te ipsum*, know thyself.[49]

Elena's appeal to Rinieri to behave "come magnanimo" leads him to a flourish of legalistic rhetoric as he declares that, even supposing he were he a magnanimous man – "Ma presupposto che io pur magnanimo fossi" (VIII.7.86) – there would be no need to be magnanimous toward her, for she is to be treated as a wild animal, not as a human:

> Ma presupposto che io pur magnanimo fossi, non se' tu di quelle in cui la magnanimità debba i suoi effetti mostrare: la fine della penitenzia nelle salvatiche fiere come tu se', e similmente della vendetta, vuole esser la morte, dove negli uomini quel dee bastare che tu dicesti. (VIII.7.86)
>
> [But even supposing I were a charitable man, you are not the sort of woman who deserves to be treated with charity. For a savage beast of your sort, death is the only fit punishment, the only just revenge, though admittedly, had I been dealing with a human being, I should already have done enough.]

Again we watch Rinieri outsmart himself, for his labours to reclassify Elena as not human also result in reclassifying himself as not *magnanimo*, not like the great-souled sages of old. He uses sophistic argumentation

---

48 See the comment of Fanfani: "Modo famigliare per accennare un furbo trincato, un uomo astutissimo e da non potersi o doversi beffare" [A proverbial way of indicating a man of ultimate craftiness, extraordinarily astute and whom one cannot or should not try to trick], cited by Branca in Boccaccio, *Decameron*, ed. Branca 1976, p. 1442 (737n3). Pampinea's two uses of proverbial language regarding the devil's tail underline scholarly familiarity with diabolical trickery. Maybe Elena was not completely wrong when she judged Rinieri as one who might be versed in *nigromantia*.

49 See Courcelle, "Connais-toi toi-même". My thanks to Michael Papio for sharing his erudition on the transmission of *nosce te ipsum* through Cicero and Seneca and to Grace Delmolino for finding the following *nosce te ipsum* citation in Boccaccio's *De casibus*: "Se ipsum noscere virtutis exitus et initium est" [Knowing oneself is the beginning and ending of virtue (5.18.10)].

to contend that she is not human, floating assertions based on grossly simplistic misogynist categories of superiority and inferiority. He is attempting to give himself a legitimate basis for resisting the claims of her humanity. She is right, he says, that the punishment meted out so far would be sufficient for a human – "negli uomini quel dee bastare che tu dicesti" (VIII.7.86) – but Elena is not a human; she is a wild beast for whom death is the only fit punishment. The reclassification of the widow as less than human is picked up linguistically by the narrator, who describes her body after her ordeal as "non corpo umano ma più tosto un cepperello innarsicciato parere" [not a human body but looking more like a burnt log (VIII.7.140; translation mine)]. The triple presence of *umano* in VIII.7 (two uses of *umanità* and one of the adjective *umano*) is a unique concentration within the *Decameron*, again testifying to the *mise-en-abîme* status of this novella within the macrotext. The scholar has cancelled out his own humanity and tried to reduce the widow to less than human, both with his sophistic argumentation and with the actual violence done to her body, "non corpo umano" by the time it is discovered by her maid.

And yet the above passage, in which the scholar "wins" by arguing that the first stage of his vengeance would have been sufficient if she were human but is not sufficient because she is not human, marks the moment in which the scholar is bested in argument by the widow. He now becomes a new kind of mounted Aristotle, surpassed in logical disputation by a woman. For all that he flaunts logical-sounding terminology like "presupposto che" [presupposing that], the scholar loses the argument once he concedes that the punishment exacted thus far would be sufficient were she human. This concession validates the law of sufficiency as the widow has stipulated it and features the very phrase "dee bastare" that will be used by Fiammetta in her harsh assessment of the scholar at the beginning of the next novella. If we fast forward 2133 words from VIII.7.86, cited above, to VIII.7.122, which is still 1490 words from the end, we reach the point at which this story is finally (slowly) drawing to its conclusion. Here the widow, still on the roof of the tower where she has cooked all day, issues an indictment of excess. This is her summation. She calls out the scholar for having indulged in a vengeance that is "oltre misura" [beyond measure] and she repeats the adverb of excess, *oltre*, charging him with having added hunger and thirst on top of ("oltre a") the roasting that she has received:

> Rinieri, ben ti se' oltre misura vendico, ché, se io feci te nella mia corte di notte agghiacciare, tu hai me di giorno sopra questa torre fatta arrostire, anzi ardere, e oltre a ciò di fame e di sete morire. (VIII.7.122)

[Surely your revenge has exceeded all the bounds of reason, Rinieri. For whereas I made you freeze by night in my courtyard, you have roasted me on this tower by day, or rather burnt me to a cinder, and on top of that caused me to die of hunger and thirst in the process.][50]

The key technical phrase, "oltre misura," appears also in a previous passage in which the narrator refers to Elena as "oltre misura dolente" [suffering beyond measure (VIII.7.112)]. Taken together, these two usages amount to a clear condemnation of Rinieri, whose intemperate and excessive vengeance results in his victim's intemperate and excessive suffering.

Long before the widow's culminating indictment above, in the denunciation that follows her initial apology and plea for an ethics of sufficiency (VIII.7.79), the scholar had acknowledged the power of the argument of sufficient and proportionate vengeance. His acknowledgment that her argument is compelling takes the form of an attempt to defuse it, which he does by mounting a sophistic defence based on two distinctions: the first between vengeance and punishment and the second between the value of her life and his. The scholar's frivolous distinction between vengeance and punishment revises the ethics of sufficiency by substituting *trapassare* for *bastare* and claiming that "la vendetta dee trapassar l'offesa" [revenge must exceed the offence (VIII.7.87)]. In other words, his treatment of her up to this point does not exceed the offence and and therefore does not properly constitute vengeance, but only punishment. His further argument rests on the morally spurious and un-Christian distinction he posits regarding the relative worth of their lives. Her life is worth so little, given that she is nothing but "una vile e cattiva e rea feminetta" [a vile and bad and wicked little female (VIII.7.88)], that taking her life would be insufficient vengeance: "la tua vita non mi basterebbe togliendolati, né cento altre alla tua simiglianti, per ciò che io ucciderei una vile e cattiva e rea feminetta" [it would not suffice for me to take your life by way of revenge, nor a hundred others like it, since I should only be killing a foul and wicked strumpet (VIII.7.88)].

Here we see the scholar use the key verb *bastare* used by Elena and Fiammetta, thus reversing his previous rejection of sufficiency, in order to make the case that "taking her life would not be enough" because his value as a human being is so much greater than hers. Rinieri reaches

50 I have added "on top of that" to McWilliam's translation in order to render "oltre a ciò."

this claim of literally existential superiority by engaging in the lowest form of argumentation, name-calling; he reclassifies and essentializes Elena, using various hoary misogynistic tropes, such as linking her to the devil.[51] While she is worth so little, he is a "valente uomo ... la cui vita ancora potrà più in un dì essere utile al mondo che centomilia tue pari non potranno mentre il mondo durar dee" [gentleman ... who can bring more benefit to humanity in a single day than a hundred thousand women of your sort can bring to it for as long as the world shall last (VIII.7.89)].

Despite his grandiose claim, our scholar has not contributed to the world (as far as we know) anything more substantive than did George Eliot's Casaubon. His superiority to the widow is not based on his having penned a great work of scholarship or philosophy. Rather, even his education and his ability to wield the pen are seen by him through the lens of vengeance. He turns to the pen as the medium of revenge that he could have used if all other means had failed (in the terms of Boccaccio's own oeuvre, the scholar is saying that he could have written the *Corbaccio*):

> non mi fuggiva la penna, con la quale tante e sì fatte cose di te scritte avrei e in sì fatta maniera, che, avendole tu risapute, ché l'avresti, avresti il dì mille volte disiderato di mai non esser nata. (VIII.7.99)
>
> [I should still have had my pen, with which I should have lampooned you so mercilessly, and with so much eloquence, that when my writings came to your notice (as they certainly would), you would have wished, a thousand times a day, that you had never been born.]

The last words above, in which the scholar imagines Elena's wish that she had never been born, reveal the scholar's lust for Elena's existential inferiority, to the point of cancelling her existence. Boccaccio links this lust to the scholar's ability to write; the scholar's ability to wield the pen affords him the opportunity to annihilate the widow, so that she will wish that she had never been born. This encomium to "the powers of the pen" [Le forze della penna" (VIII.7.99)] constitutes

51 See, for instance, Cecco d'Ascoli: "Femena, che fe' meno a che fera / radice e ramo e fructo d'onne male: / superba, avara, sciocca, matta, austera, / veneno che venena el cor del corpo, / via iniqua e porta infernale" [Woman has less faith than a wild beast; root and branch and fruit of all evil, she is proud, miserly, foolish, mad, severe, the poison that poisons the heart of the body, the path of iniquity and the gate of hell (*Acerba* 4.9.4403–7, p. 389; my translation)].

Boccaccio's explicit inscribing of the scholar of VIII.7 into the guild of clerks: writers, wordsmiths, intellectuals, scholars, philosophers, and sophists, users and abusers of words. And it constitutes Boccaccio's challenge to his guild: without a moral foundation based on a principle of *misura*, an educated man can still be prey to the lowest of instincts and impulses, leading him to deploy his talents in an abusive manner.

The lengthy dialogue between the scholar on the ground and the widow on the tower spins variations on the topoi that we have already examined. For instance, as late as VIII.7.124 the scholar again feels "a little compassion" for the widow ("un poco di compassione gli venne di lei") and again represses it, showing us once more that the pathological pleasure he derives from her suffering and self-abasement is too great for him to resist. Appetite controls him – he is a new kind of mounted Aristotle, mounted by his fierce appetite for existential dominance. Rinieri can resist compassion, and he can also resist eros, as we saw earlier. The theme of Rinieri's rigid resistance to the power of eros is revisited in the part of their dialogue in which Elena implores him to act according to his youth. The widow pleads with the scholar to diminish his severity, using the noun, "rigidezza" (VIII.7.93), whose adjectival analogue "rigido" will be picked up by Fiammetta in her prologue to VIII.8 (VIII.8.2). Elena attempts in vain to redirect Rinieri's lust toward her beauty, reminding him that female "beauty should be prized, if for no other reason than because it brings sweetness, joy, and solace to a man's youth," and, she adds pointedly, "you are not an old man" [la quale [bellezza] … se per altro non fosse da aver cara, sì è per ciò che vaghezza e trastullo e diletto è della giovanezza degli uomini: e tu non se' vecchio (VIII.7.94)]. To this Rinieri replies by presenting himself as an old lover, a move that brings us back to the social templates with which we began.

Young Old Men and Old Young Men

The scholar enters VIII.7 "a young man called Rinieri" [un giovane chiamato Rinieri (VIII.7.5)], and yet he later presents himself as an old savant who critiques the young seducers to whom the widow is drawn. This counterfactual self-construction suggests a resentment toward more successful lovers that the courtly tradition views as endemic to his intellectual caste. All the more interesting, then, that Rinieri casts himself as an old man in a passage that reads like a compendium of the *Decameron*'s erotics. The scholar allies himself with experienced older lovers by using two of the *Decameron*'s signature sexual metaphors.[52] Women consider younger men to be better riders, while in fact a smoother ride can get you to the inn in better shape. And, while younger men are sexually more forceful – "con maggior forza scuotono i pilliccioni" [will shake your skin-coat with greater vigour] – older men bring expertise to the task: they, "sì come esperti, sanno meglio i luoghi dove stanno le pulci" [being more experienced, have a better idea of where the fleas are lurking (VIII.7.103)]. Here the scholar uses a metaphor that will ultimately be used by Dioneo in X.10.69 to advocate female resistance against abusive husbands like the Marquis of Saluzzo, but which Rinieri turns into a strange form of self-advocacy:[53] he aligns himself with the older experienced lover in order to vindicate his sexual prowess in the eyes of a woman who has rejected him. A lady may not at first be attracted to him, preferring the harder trot of the younger man, but, after all, he has experience and he knows how to get the job done.

After his foray into the sexual metaphors that suture this passage to the *Decameron*'s signature textual DNA, Rinieri proceeds to an explicit list of the benefits of having an older lover. While a young man desires many women, an older lover will be satisfied with one woman and will provide her a stable experience; while a young man boasts of his conquests, a older man will be secretive and will protect her good name. In this jaded version of a courtly manual, secrecy is a key point, as in all courtly contexts. The palm of victory is given to the wise lover in the third "Question of Love" in the *Filocolo* because he knows how to be secretive – but the *savio amante* of the "Questioni d'amore," like the cleric in the amatory debates, is not old. Moreover, while the wise lover of the *Filocolo*'s "Questioni d'amore" is chosen as the most useful kind of lover precisely because he can control his emotions, and as a result is more likely to be able to keep a secret and to protect his lady's reputation, the scholar of VIII.7 loses control of his emotions and does his best to destroy the widow's reputation.[54]

52 On the sexual metaphors of the *Decameron* as carriers of the text's signatture DNA, see Barolini, "'Le parole son donne e i fatti son maschi,'" 300–2.

53 Dioneo's sexual metaphor at the end of X.10 is not a "pornographic gloss" that "sabotages Griselda's exemplum of superhuman steadfastness" (Marcus, "The Tale of Maestro Alberto," 231), but rather a form of advocacy for female empowerment in the high-stakes matrimonial power game that is Boccaccio's X.10. See Barolini, "The Marquis of Saluzzo, or the Griselda Story Before It Was Hijacked," 27.

54 Elena thwarts the scholar's desire to destroy her reputation by using her wits. Her ability to narrate brilliantly and fictitiously in order to save her reputation is reminiscent of Alatiel (see II.7.146).

In another link to the *Decameron*'s erotic playbook, Rinieri notes that women resort to the sexual ministrations of friars because friars keep silent: the propensity of young (secular) lovers to boast drives many a woman "sotto a' frati, che nol ridicono" [under the friars, who do not tell tales (VIII.7.105)]. Finally, there is the important issue of financial largesse. While young men steal from women, older men are generous with their gifts: "Essi ancora vi rubano, dove dagli attempati v'è donato" (VIII.7.105). Liberality with money is also one of the hallmarks of the superiority of the *clericus* over the *miles* in the "Altercatio Phyllidis et Florae," as we saw. But the cleric's liberality in the "Altercatio" inheres in his clerical wealth, not in his age, for – again – that clerk is not an old man.

In this passage Rinieri voluntarily strips himself of youth and *cortesia*, completing the transformation wrought over the course of VIII.7 by his surrender to a corrupting appetite. He is no longer the jaunty young nobleman and philosopher about town whom we meet at the novella's beginning. As a *gentile uomo* he was less akin to the clerics and more akin to the *cavalieri* of yore (thus constituting an amalgam impossible in the social analysis of Dante's canzone *Poscia ch'Amor*), *cavalieri* celebrated in Tuscany as aspirational models by recent poets like Folgore da San Gimignano as well as by Dante. Rinieri now voluntarily positions himself as a cynically experienced lover whose virtues are those of the friars, the wily cynics whose sexual prowess populates the *Decameron* and who are far from constituting the text's most respected social cadre. His view of love has curdled, and, while his appetite still exists, it is corrupt. It is not the "naturale affezione" [natural affection (IV.Intro.32)] that drives Filippo Balducci's son in the Introduction to Day Four, a "naturale affezione" that also drives great poets to love in old age.[55]

In the Introduction to Day Four, Boccaccio responds to the critics who harp on the unsuitability of his love of women in two steps. He first allusively defends the sexuality of the old by faulting those who do not understand that "although the leek's head is white, it has a green tail" [perché il porro abbia il capo bianco, che la coda sia verde (IV.Intro.33)]. He then identifies himself with the great poets Guido Cavalcanti and Dante Alighieri, who loved "già vecchi" (already old), and in the case of Cino da Pistoia "vecchissimo" (very old):

> rispondo che io mai a me vergogna non reputerò infino nello stremo della mia vita di dover compiacere a quelle cose alle quali Guido Cavalcanti e

55 I do not agree that Boccaccio joins the company of Guido, Dante, and Cino "as one more dirty old man unable to renounce a lifetime propensity for womanizing" (Marcus, "The Tale of Maestro Alberto," 237).

> Dante Alighieri già vecchi e messer Cino da Pistoia vecchissimo onor si tennero, e fu lor caro il piacer loro. (IV.Intro.33)

> [I shall never feel any compunction in striving to please the ones who were so greatly honoured, and whose beauty was so much admired, by Guido Cavalcanti and Dante Alighieri in their old age, and by Cino da Pistoia in his dotage.]

In using the allusive language of the leek in his self-defence, Boccaccio identifies himself with the initiator of leek metaphorics in the *Decameron*: Maestro Alberto, our learned doctor of I.10, who defends old lovers by pointing out that the tasty part of the leek is the head, although ladies for some reason prefer the leaves (I.10.17).

Despite his years, learning, and great fame, Maestro Alberto at the age of almost seventy remains young at heart because he is infused with the youth-enhancing values of *cortesia*: "Il quale, essendo già vecchio di presso a settanta anni, tanta fu la nobiltà del suo spirito, che, essendo già del corpo quasi ogni natural caldo partito, in sé non schifò di ricevere l'amorose fiamme" [Although he was an old man approaching seventy, and the natural warmth had almost entirely departed from his body, his heart was so noble that he was not averse to welcoming the flames of love (I.10.10)]. Maestro Alberto is reminiscent of the youthful *savio* of the *Filocolo*'s third "Questione d'amore," while Rinieri over the course of VIII.7 takes on the worst crabbed features of his intellectual tribe – resentful, defensive, insecure with respect to his social and sexual appeal, old in spirit if not in the flesh.[56]

The widow of this novella is a love object who is moneyed and socially mobile and endowed with a social freedom that is exasperating to the scholar. She enables the contrast between the man who feels *naturale affezione* even when physically old (a category that includes Maestro Alberto, Guido Cavalcanti, Dante Alighieri, Cino da Pistoia, and Giovanni Boccaccio) and the man who does not feel *naturale affezione* even when physically young, because his appetite has been corrupted. In this latter category belong the learned and sophistic trolls of the Introduction to Day Four, for whom Boccaccio uses ethical terminology that precisely anticipates the language later used for Rinieri. They are men whose "pleasures" are distinct from the author's in that they are "corrupt appetites": "e ne' lor diletti, anzi appetiti corrotti standosi" [let

56 By the end of his transformation in VIII.7, Rinieri has become very similar to the protagonist of the *Corbaccio*, suggesting that the protagonist of the later text may have a similar back-story.

them remain in their pleasures, or rather in their corrupt appetites (IV. Intro.42)].

In the *Filocolo*'s third "Questione d'amore," the narrator does not deny that wise men can know evil, and can even do evil. But, says the narrator, the *savi* do not therefore lose their wisdom ("non perdono il senno"). Armed with *senno*, the wise are able to stave off bad behaviour and its consequences. At whatever point they desire ("qualora essi vorranno"), the *savi* will use *ragione* to rein in the will (the verb *raffrenare* in "la volontà raffrenare" evokes the image of the sage who is riding the horse and using the *freno*, rather than being ridden):

> Ma noi non negheremo però che i savi non conoscano il male, e pur lo fanno; ma diremo che essi per quello non perdono il senno, con ciò sia cosa che, qualora essi vorranno, con la ragione ch'elli hanno, la volontà raffrenare, elli nell'usato senno si rimarranno, guidando i loro movimenti con debito e diritto stile. (*Filocolo* 4.30.2)
>
> [And yet we will not deny that the wise know the evil and do it. But for all that, we will say that they do not thereby lose their wit. For, as long as it pleases them, with the reason they have to bridle their wills, they will remain in their accustomed wit, guiding their emotions in a due and straight order.][57]

The scholar of VIII.7 is not endowed with the strength of character of the *savio* described in the *Filolcolo*'s third "Questione d'amore." He *does* lose his wisdom, even before he is pathologized by rejection: the widow's witticism on the scholar's having lost his *senno*, leaving it behind in Paris (VIII.7.12), becomes a reality with precise ethical implications. The scholar loses his *senno* and with it his reason and the ability to rein in his will. In *Decameron* VIII.7, Boccaccio depicts a life devoted to philosophical learning in which the acquired wisdom nonetheless fails to provide a bulwark against moral collapse. The philosopher becomes a novel mounted Aristotle, in a much more profound sense than the traditional misogynist trope of a man who is governed by a woman. The sage of *Decameron* VIII.7 is unable to govern his will, thus proving himself to be not sage.

In the years between the *Filocolo* and the *Decameron* Boccaccio's view shifted. He no longer sees learning and wisdom as a guaranteed prophylaxis against an appetite corrupted by the darkest impulses of our

57 I have slightly modified the translation here.

nature. The story of the scholar and the widow is a referendum on some of the deepest issues of the *Decameron,* a novella in which Boccaccio returns to his fundamental manifesto for human intercourse, the Introduction to Day Four, and embodies in Rinieri the learned but corrupt pedants who enviously and maliciously attacked him and his text: Rinieri in this sense is the anti-Boccaccio. In order to be shielded from the "appetiti corrotti" [corrupt appetites (IV.Intro.42)] of the critics of the Introduction to Day Four, the "appetiti corrotti" that do indeed overcome Rinieri, learning is not enough: like Boccaccio himself, and like the great poets with whom Boccaccio identifies in the Introduction to Day Four, a learned man must remain in touch with *umanità* and *compassione*. A better protection than an elite Parisian education is our non-elite *umanità* and *compassione,* sometimes more accessible to the uneducated *popolano* (see VIII.8) than to the most learned of scholars.

Doing unto Others, or Sienese Polyamory (VIII.8)

OLIVIA HOLMES

In the eighth novella of the *Decameron*'s eighth day, a young man nicknamed "il Zeppa" (the wedge) avenges his wife's seduction by his best friend Spinelloccio (a diminutive of *spina*, or "thorn") by having sex with Spinelloccio's wife on top of a chest that the friend is locked inside. The tale concludes: "Il Zeppa fu contento, e nella miglior pace del mondo tutti e quatro desinarono insieme; e da indi innanzi ciascuna di quelle donne ebbe due mariti e ciascun di loro ebbe due mogli, senza alcuna quistione o zuffa mai per quello insieme averne" [Zeppa was satisfied, and the four of them dined together in the most perfect concord; and from then on, each of the women had two husbands and each of the men two wives, without ever having a quarrel or coming to blows over the matter (VIII.8.35)].[1] That is, after the events of the story, its protagonists live happily ever after in polygamous bliss, without any further need for retaliation or revenge. I will argue that this story can be read as a meditation on the nature of corrective justice and that its comically happy ending both attempts to provide a serious model for symmetrical retribution as a means for resolving disputes, and at the same time parodies and undermines the very notions of ethical and narrative closure.

Let us set the story in its larger context. The theme of Day Eight is, of course, *beffe* (tricks or practical jokes), and not just those of one kind, as on Day Seven, dedicated to the tricks that women play on their husbands, but those *beffe* that "tutto il giorno o donna a uomo o uomo a donna o l'uno uomo all'altro si fanno" [women play on men, or men

1 The *Decameron* is cited from the 2013 edition of Quondam, Fiorilla, and Alfano. Translations of the *Decameron* are my own.

on women, or men on men, all the time (VII.Concl.4)].[2] A number of the day's tales are explicitly organized around reciprocal *beffe*, thus adhering to the recognizable narrative pattern of "l'arte ... dall'arte schernita" [cunning mocked by cunning (VIII.7.3)] or, as we might put it, the "trickster tricked" or "beguiler beguiled."[3] In both the seventh and tenth stories of the day, for instance, a woman tricks a man, and then the man inflicts on the woman either the trick's specular inverse or an even worse version of the same ruse. In Novella VIII.8, however, the two *beffe* are almost identical and are clearly of the type that "l'uno uomo all'altro si fanno." Indeed, the phrase "l'uno ... all'altro," from the definition of day's topic, is echoed in the rubric preceding this story, which outlines the plot as a pair of symmetrical actions in which "due usano insieme" [two men are close companions], but "l'uno con la moglie dell'altro si giace" [one sleeps with the other's wife] and then, "l'altro ... con la moglie dell'un si giace" [the other sleeps with the first one's wife] (VIII.8.1). Neither of the two protagonists is named yet, thus emphasizing their equivalency and interchangeability.[4]

---

2 It should be noted that this list does not include tricks played by women on women, which category may have been excluded as unworthy of attention. Mary Anne Case remarks on the topic of Day Eight, "*Uomo* here, when paired with *donna*, means *man* as male; however, unless we are to think women playing tricks on other women either never occurs or is not to be discussed by the *brigata*, *uomo* in the latter half of the topic description does indeed refer to 'people in general, men and women alike'" ("What Turns on Whether Women Are Human for Boccaccio and Christine de Pizan?" 192–3). The days' *novelle* do not actually relate any instances of women tricking other women, however.

3 See the proverb cited by the Reeve at the end of the Chaucer's *Reeve's Tale*: "A gylour shal himself bigyled be" (*Reeve's Tale* 1.4321; *Riverside Chaucer*, ed. Benson, p. 84). D.P. Rotunda's *Motif-Index of the Italian Novella* includes two related categories, "The cheater cheated" (J1510) and "Deceiver falls into own trap" (K1600). Boccaccio's tales adhering to the trickster-tricked pattern are not confined to Day Eight. See Novella II.1, which is introduced as teaching the lesson that "chi altrui s'è di beffare ingegnato ... s'è con le beffe e talvolta col danno a sé solo ritrovato" [those who try to trick others ... wind up not only being tricked themselves, but sometimes injured as well (II.1.2)], and also II.9, which is said to impart the proverb that "lo 'ngannatore rimane a piè dello 'ngannato" [the deceiver ends under the feet of the dupe (II.9.3)]. On this story-type, see Rebhorn, "Redefining the *Beffa*," esp. 214–17.

4 On this story, see Marilyn Migiel, "The Untidy Business of Gender Studies," according to whom "the rubric, by suppressing Spinelloccio's and Zeppa's names so that they appear only as *l'uno* and *l'altro*, reinforces our sense that they are practically interchangeable" (226); also Grimaldi, *Il privilegio di Dioneo*, 309–10; and Sherberg, *The Governance of Friendship*, 187–9.

Boccaccio begins this story by describing the storytellers' response to the previous one, as is his usual practice. Indeed, he opens with a general consideration on the nature of audience engagement with narrative, remarking: "Gravi e noiosi erano stati i casi d'Elena a ascoltare alle donne, ma per ciò che in parte giustamente avvenutigli gli estimavano, con piú moderata compassione gli avean trapassati" [Elena's misfortunes were grievous and painful for the ladies to hear, but they felt only a moderate degree of compassion for her because of them, inasmuch as they thought she had partly deserved them (VIII.8.2)]. He suggests here that audience empathy is generally regulated or qualified by our sense of justice, since – as philosophers since Aristotle have recognized – we do not feel as much compassion if we believe that a person's predicament is chosen or self-inflicted.[5] One is reminded of Dante's struggles in the *Inferno* to reconcile the pity that the pilgrim feels for its inhabitants with the sinners' liability for their own actions.[6] Boccaccio explicitly invites his readers to feel compassion, however, famously beginning the *Decameron*'s Preface: "Umana cosa è aver compassione degli afflitti" [Having compassion for those who suffer is a human quality (Proem.2)]. The ladies' compassion for the misfortunes of the widow Elena in VIII.7 recalls this opening dictum, but their pity for her is tempered by their sense that she brought her sufferings on herself. They deem Elena's punishment only *partly* merited, however, and judge the scholar Rinieri to be "rigido e constante fieramente, anzi crudele" [severe and harshly uncompromising, indeed cruel (VIII.8.2)], thus implicitly raising the issue of how justice might be administered more benevolently.

I have argued elsewhere that in Day Eight's recurrent depictions of the retaliation occasioned by tricks, Boccaccio reflects on the social consequences of feuds and on society's need for effective judicial

5 See Nussbaum, *Political Emotions*, 143. Aristotle makes this point indirectly when he says that tragic plots should not depict "a thoroughly villainous person falling from good fortune into misfortune: such a structure can contain moral satisfaction, but not pity or terror, for the former is [felt] for a person underserving of his misfortune, and the latter for a person like [ourselves]" (*Poetics* 4.1.1, p. 16). On compassion in the *Decameron*, see Barolini, *Dante and the Origins of Italian Literary Culture*, 224–44; Giusti, *Dall'amore cortese alla comprensione*; Papio, "'Non meno di compassion piena che dilettevole'"; and Surdich, "Tra Dante e Boccaccio."

6 Dante's struggle to suppress his sympathy for the sinners in Hell is played out especially in *Inferno* 5. See also Canto 20, in the *bolgia* of the diviners, where Dante sheds empathetic tears and Virgil criticizes him for doing so, declaring: "Qui vive la pietà quand' è ben morta" (*Inf.* 20.28).

mechanisms.[7] The nineteenth-century jurist Oliver Wendell Holmes argued that early legal codes grew out of the victim's desire to avenge intentional wrongs, and that vengeance has never ceased to be one of the objectives of jurisprudence (*The Common Law*, 62ff). In cases such as murder, for example, in which indemnity or compensation is out of the question because the injured party can never be restored to their former situation, punishment is inflicted on the wrongdoer for the very purpose of causing pain and thus making the criminal "pay" for the crime. Anthropologists have observed that among the first cultural institutions to appear when human societies increase in scale above hunter-gatherer groups are conflict resolution devices such as vengeance systems, which regulate and coordinate human behaviour; as David Sloan Wilson argues, feuding "is properly understood as part of an intensely moral system that keeps the peace much more than breaking it" (*Darwin's Cathedral*, 202).

The contemporary legal scholar Richard Posner points out the inadequacies of revenge practices as a legal system, however, since no matter how much harm is done to the aggressor in return, the original harm suffered is never annulled (*Law and Literature*, 49–50). Posner observes that "Justice as vengeance is crude from a moral standpoint once one steps outside the moral framework of the vengeance system itself" because "its sanctions bear no systematic relation to the gravity of the harms inflicted" and "are imposed regardless of fault" (54). Therefore the principle of retribution, or exact retaliation for a wrong (an eye for eye, a tooth for a tooth, etc.), evolved to alleviate some of the problems of revenge practices and to reduce "the likelihood of overreactions (your life for my eye) that are likely to engender feuds" (56). That is, balanced retribution is a moderating principle, a device for establishing the natural end to a dispute.

Dante's elaborately precise system of corrective justice, embodied in the *Inferno*'s law of the *contrapasso* (counter-suffering), was also – at least in part – a specific response to the injustices fomented by the political chaos and consequent disintegration of the social fabric in northern

7 See my "Trial by *Beffa*"; and on the logic of *beffe*, also Ferme, "*Ingegno* and Morality in the New Social Order"; Fontes-Baratto, "Le thème de la *beffa* dans le *Decameron*"; Forno, "L'amaro riso"; Ferroni, "Sulla struttura della beffa"; and Picone, "L'arte della beffa." For the *Decameron* as revenge literature, see Sherberg, *The Governance of Friendship*, esp. 17–18 and 55; Nissen, *The Ethics of Retribution in the Decameron*. On political feuding in late medieval and Renaissance Italy, see Coleman, "Cities and Communes"; Martines, *Violence and Civil Disorder in Italian Cities*; Muir, *Mad Blood Stirring*; Peters, "*Pars, Parte*."

Italy during his time, when political factions divided the northern Italian cities and Roman law was largely supplanted by local control and the logic of feuds and vendettas.[8] The *Decameron*'s comical representations and reconsiderations of the nature of crime and punishment on Day Eight respond, in turn, to Dante's depiction of a Christian system of impartial justice, transcending time and place, and thus to Boccaccio's moment in both political and literary history.[9] As Victoria Kirkham reminds us, since the number 8 was connected in medieval tradition with Sunday, the day that Christ arose from the tomb, it was generally associated with the Second Coming and with the theme of justice; Saint Augustine explains that the phrase "pro octava" [for the octave] in the first verse of Psalm 6, for instance, was taken as alluding to the Last Judgment at the end of worldly time, which revolves through seven periods of a thousand years, referred to as seven days.[10] The fact that Boccaccio's Day Eight also occurs on a Sunday reinforces the suggestion that it can be read as a burlesque Day of Judgment, and we may expect the theme of justice to be especially relevant to this particular story, with the double set of eights in its designation.

8 Dante uses the word "contrapasso" in *Inf.* 28.142 to indicate the principle of justice in Hell and Purgatory according to which the particular sin committed by a soul determines the precise form of punishment; see Pertile, "Contrapasso"; cf. Steinberg, "Dante's Justice?," who argues that the term is not meant to refer to the *Commedia*'s system of punishment as a whole, but to denote a limited and overly mechanistic concept of justice that the poem warns against. On the legal ambiguities arising from the jurisdictional struggles between Church and Empire, see Steinberg's *Dante and the Limits of the Law*, which, by emphasizing the *Commedia's* incongruities and showing how it explores a series of limit cases and exceptions to the general rule, also problematizes the notion that Dante presents a perfect, transcendent judicial system.

9 Day Eight's representations of justice may also be seen as responding to Boccaccio's moment in economic history, and to the burgeoning of trade in the previous century, which was especially spearheaded by Italian merchants; see Branca, *Boccaccio medievale*, 134–64. According to Giuseppe Mazzotta (*The World at Play*, 190), fundamental to the day's *beffe* is a paradigm of equal exchange that mimics the laws of the market; see also Migiel, who describes Day Eight as "dedicated to showing how the forces of economic exchange and accountability (*ragione*) work to exclude women" (*A Rhetoric of the Decameron*, 57).

10 Augustine, *Enarrationes in Psalmos*, 36:91; see Kirkham, *The Sign of Reason in Boccaccio's Fiction*, esp. 233–4. See also the final chapter of Augustine's *City of God*, where he writes that we should "count the ages as 'days' according to the periods of time which we see expressed in Scripture; for that Sabbath will then be found to be the seventh of those ages," the end of which "will not be an evening, but the Lord's Day, as an eighth and eternal day, consecrated by the resurrection of Christ, and prefiguring the eternal rest not only of the Spirit, but of the body also" (1182).

The novella's narrator Fiammetta – whom Janet Smarr interprets as the mouthpiece for reason and temperance among the *Decameron*'s narrators[11] – introduces this tale of reciprocal tricks as a specific corrective to the excessive nature of Rinieri's revenge against Elena in VIII.7. She recognizes that the previous tale's inflationary spiral of *beffa* and counter-*beffa* exacerbated audience tension, but she says that she intends to "ramorbidare gl'innacerbiti spiriti" [calm embittered spirits] by showing that a man can give as good as he gets, "senza volere, soprabondando oltre la convenevolezza della vendetta, ingiuriare" [without meaning to provoke injury beyond what is appropriate for revenge (VIII.8.3)]. She responds to the ladies' dismay at the scholar's exaggerated cruelty – and perhaps to Novella VIII.7's immoderate length as well – by proposing to tell "una novelletta d'un giovane, il quale con piú mansueta animo una ingiuria ricevette e quella con piú moderata operazion vendicò" [a short story about a young man who suffered a wrong in a calmer spirit, and took revenge for it in a more harmless way (VIII.8.3)]. Pier Massimo Forni points out that although the narrative vector of this novella is comic and the characters' behaviour is objectionable in conventional terms, Fiammetta "has a genuine ethical principle to promote, that of moderation in retribution" (*Adventures in Speech*, 20). A peaceable equilibrium can only be arrived at, she says, if we restrain our vengeance, so that the harm done is equal to and no greater than the original offence. It should be sufficient, that is, if "quale asino dà in parete tal riceve" [that which an ass gives to the wall he gets back (VIII.8.3)] – or as Dioneo paraphrases the same proverb in conclusion to another novella, "chi te la fa, fagliele" [do to others what they do to you (V.10.64)].

Rinieri himself was also careful in Novella VIII.7 to defend his actions as adhering to the principle of balanced retribution, rather than enacting the crude justice of revenge, "in quanto la vendetta dee trapassar l'offesa" [inasmuch as revenge has to exceed the offence (VIII.7.87)]. His punishment of Elena falls short of her offence against him, he contends, because her life is worth less than his, since she is merely "una vile e cattiva e rea feminetta" [a base, wicked, evil little woman (VIII.7.88)], whereas he is a man of learning. Rather than agreeing with Rinieri's estimation of the relative values of women and men (or of women and scholars), however, Boccaccio seems to caricature here a certain kind of academic and legalistic reasoning. The trick that Rinieri plays on

11 Smarr, *Boccaccio and Fiammetta*, 181–92; on Fiammetta, see also Migiel, *A Rhetoric of the Decameron*, 29–63.

Elena can only be characterized as punishment, rather than revenge, by means of his sophistry, which does not fool the ladies of the *brigata*, who rightly deem that tale's outcome to be unbalanced and unjust.

Unlike Rinieri and Elena, however, the two male protagonists of Novella VIII.8 are presented as extremely similar, and thus in a better position to play tricks that are precisely equivalent. They are from the same neighbourhood, love each other like brothers, and both have beautiful wives (who are not given any other distinguishing traits, not even names). When Zeppa discovers his friend and his wife making love, he doesn't say anything, "ma conoscendo che per far romore né per altro la sua ingiuria non ne diveniva minore, anzi ne crescea la vergogna, si diede a pensar che vendetta di questa cosa dovesse fare, che, senza sapersi da torno, l'animo suo rimanesse contento" [but realizing that by creating any kind of uproar the injury to him would not thereby diminish, but rather his shame would increase, he got to thinking what revenge he ought to take for this affair, so that, without making it public knowledge, his feelings would be appeased (VIII.8.9)]. Like modern legal theorists, he recognizes that taking public revenge would not annul the original harm suffered, but on the contrary, would increase the cost to him of the initial aggression, thus metaphorically throwing good money after bad (see Posner, *Law and Literature*, 50; Sherberg, *The Governance of Friendship*, 188). So Zeppa elects not to harm his companion in any substantial way. When he reveals to his wife what he knows, he tells her "tu hai fatto male" [you have done wrong (VIII.8.13)], and that if she wants his forgiveness, she must do exactly as he says, and no injury will come to Spinelloccio: "io non gli farò male" (VIII.8.14). This promise recalls Fiammetta's admonition at the beginning that in taking revenge for a wrong, one should try not to inflict harm that exceeds the appropriate measure. Indeed, the penalty that Zeppa devises is strictly analogous to the offence against him: having furtively and silently witnessed his wife's infidelity, he contrives to have her hide Spinelloccio (the metaphoric "thorn" in his side) in a chest, and then induces Spinelloccio's wife to have sex with him on top of it. He assures his friend's wife as well that because of the friendship, he does not mean to take more revenge on her husband than the occasion merits. The uneven power dynamics between Zeppa and the woman and the level of coercion here are revealed in the language that he uses to compel her to submit to him willy-nilly: "egli ha la mia donna avuta, e io intendo d'aver te" [he has had my wife, and I intend to have you (VIII.8.24)].

The two men's situations are not exactly or entirely identical either: when Spinelloccio originally made love to Zeppa's wife, Zeppa was not directly below them, locked in a chest, for example. Another extraneous element that needs somehow to be managed to make the account perfectly balanced is the fact that Zeppa goes on to promise Spinelloccio's wife a "caro e bel gioiello" [costly and beautiful jewel (VIII.8.27)] in exchange for sex with him; Spinelloccio did not use any such inducements. When Spinelloccio's wife later asks for the promised jewel, Zeppa calls his own wife into the room, and she proclaims, laughing, "'Madonna, voi m'avete renduto pan per focaccia'" ["Madam, you have traded me bread for focaccia" (VIII.8.30)] – in other words, they have exchanged not two identical items, but similar ones of equal value: one kind of bread for another, a thorn (Spinelloccio) for a wedge (Zeppa). Zeppa then opens the chest and reveals Spinelloccio inside it, explaining to his friend's wife that her husband was the jewel that he intended.[12] Spinelloccio, recalling that he was the one who first gave offence, concludes that Zeppa "aveva ragione" [was right] and had behaved "umanamente" [humanely] toward him (VIII.8.29). He then climbs out of the chest and tells Zeppa, "noi siam pari pari" [we're even (VIII.8.34)]. Everyone remains on good terms and they dine together in the end "nella miglior pace del mondo" [in the greatest peace in the world (VIII.8.35)]. The mention of Zeppa's humane behaviour recalls again the opening statement in the *Proemio* that having compassion for others is a distinctively human trait. By not giving way to the passion for revenge, but responding to an affront in a calculated, rational way, Zeppa avoids either falling out with his friend or committing violence – surely a positive outcome.

We might think about this story in terms of the puzzle known as the "prisoners' dilemma," which is used by evolutionary biologists and others for modelling the complications of social cooperation. Peter Singer (*A Darwinian Left*, 47–8) describes his version of this dilemma as follows: two prisoners are confined to separate cells in police headquarters, and the interrogator offers each of them a deal: if he confesses,

12 Zeppa's offering to Spinelloccio's wife a jewel that turns out to be her husband recalls a hagiographic topos in which the Church's hidden treasures are revealed to be spiritual ones. See, for instance, *Legenda Aurea* 113 on Saint Lawrence, Martyr (Jacobus de Voragine, *Legenda Aurea*, 2:758) and *Legenda* 176 on Saints Barlaam and Josaphat, in which Barlaam gains access to the king's son Josaphat by saying that he has a precious stone to give him, which turns out to be his faith (2:1242ff). See also the vernacular life of "Macario prete d'Alexandria," who tells a rich but uncharitable virgin that he has come into a number of jewels that he will give her for a small sum; she pays him the money, which he distributes to the needy, and when she later asks for the jewels, he shows her rooms full of male and female invalids, saying "Questi sono li iacinti … Questi sono li smaraldi" (Cavalca, *Vite dei santi padri*, 1:781).

implicating the other in his crime, he will be freed and the other will be locked away for twenty years. If, however, he refuses to confess and the other does, he will be the one to get twenty years and the other will go free. If both of them confess, they will each get ten years. If neither confesses, they can only be held for another six months. Singer uses the term "cooperate" to describe remaining silent, and the term "defect" as a label for confessing. As he points out, "even though in each choice the participants can do better by not cooperating, over time cooperation may be the better strategy."[13] Thus the best approach to the problem depends on the relationship between the two prisoners: if dealing with an untrustworthy stranger, the rational solution is probably to defect, but if faced with repeated choices of this sort, the prisoners may come to recognize the long-term advantages of cooperation over the pursuit of immediate self-interest.

The political scientist Robert Axelrod invited a number of professional game theorists and academics in other fields to send him suggestions for how to produce the best outcome for repeated prisoners'-dilemma-type situations, and he designed a computer program to test which one was the most successful by pitting them against each other in a kind of round-robin tournament (*The Evolution of Cooperation*, 27–54). The winner of the tournament was the simplest strategy, dubbed "Tit-for-Tat" (TFT), which opens every new encounter with another "prisoner" by cooperating, but after that simply does whatever the other player did the previous time: if the partner cooperated, it cooperates; if the partner defected, it defects. According to Axelrod, important components of the success of this method in the tournament were "its property of never being the first to defect ('niceness') and its propensity to cooperate after the other player defected ('forgiveness') with the exception of a single punishment" (42). Variations of this basic strategy, including a variant called "Contrite Tit-for-Tat" (CTFT), which accepts two selfish acts from its partner before retaliating, and another variant called "Generous Tit-for-Tat" (GTFT), which forgives selfish acts without retaliating with a frequency proportional to that of the partner's defections, were later shown sometimes to fare even better (Wilson, *Darwin's Cathedral*, 192). Without meaning to overstate the analogy here, *Decameron* VIII.8 can be read as an enactment of these latter sorts of solutions to the prisoner's dilemma. Let us use the term "cooperation" as a label for Zeppa and Spinelloccio's friendship, and "defection" to describe their seducing

13 Singer, *A Darwinian Left*, 49–50; see also Axelrod, *The Evolution of Cooperation*, 7–19; and Boyd, *On the Origin of Stories*, 51–66.

each other's wives. The two partners start by cooperating, but when one defects, the other defects, too. Spinelloccio engages a version of the CTFT strategy by admitting that Zeppa was in the right and had behaved humanely toward him, and then refraining from retaliating. Zeppa engages a version of GTFT by forgiving his friend's initial selfish act and agreeing to further collaboration, whereby they are both rewarded with increased sexual opportunities.

Even if Novella VIII.8 seems to offer a serious model for non-lethal conflict resolution, the reader is left to wonder how one is supposed to take all this. Is the story really meant to advocate open marriages and the community of women? And what about the two unnamed women in the novella: is the reader to understand that they, too, are happy with the final arrangement? The outcome of the trick that one friend devises to punish the other's betrayal may be equable, but in the Christian medieval context, in which marriage was conceived of as strictly monogamous, it is absurd![14] Although the *beffa* is a representation of corrective justice, it is a comic one. Marilyn Migiel points out the gendered asymmetry of the novella's exchange: "the wives of Spinelloccio and Zeppa remain nameless, mere objects of exchange in the eroticized dealings of their husbands" ("Untidy Business," 227). I would argue that among the objects of Boccaccio's parody is the very idea that things can be tied up so neatly, without something – the subjective desires or resentments of the two women, for instance – inevitably escaping and unsettling the narrative conclusion. That is, equivalency is not identity; a perfect balance, or perfect justice, can never be achieved. At the story's conclusion, Boccaccio once more uses the members of the fictional audience embedded in the frame story to direct our attention toward problematic aspects of the tale. Before the narration of the next story, we are told that the women of the *brigata* "alquanto ebber cianciato dello accomunar le mogli fatto da' due sanesi" [had chatted for a while about the community of wives put into place by the two Sienese

---

14 For the western medieval Church, as for the ancient Romans, marriage was restricted to only one spouse at a time, but the Church went even further than Roman law, also prohibiting divorce and remarriage, and denying the promise of salvation to those who rejected the exclusive constraints of a conjugal sexuality; see Duby, *Love and Marriage in the Middle Ages*, esp. 10–12. The ethos of courtly love also insisted on erotic monogamy; as Marie de France says, for example, "li vilain curteis, / Ki [j]olivent par tut le mund … N'est pas amur, einz est folie / E mauveisté e lecherie" [those vile courtly people / who amuse themselves with everyone … That is not love; rather, it's folly / and wickedness and lechery" (*Guigemar* vv. 488–92, in *The Lais of Marie de France*, 78–9)].

men (VIII.9.2)]. The ladies recognize that such an arrangement is not a conventionally acceptable one, although the tone here suggests that they are more amused than angry or shocked. Novella VIII.8's patently ridiculous and ethically objectionable outcome (at least for Boccaccio's time and place) suggests not only the impossibility of exact retribution, but also the inanity of this sort of pat ending.

In parodying the principles of retributive justice, the novella also interrogates the satisfactions to be found in literary depictions of justice being served, and thus also the very principle of narrative closure. Let us expand our perspective on this story to the wider one of why humans enjoy the sort of narrative that concludes with conflicts being resolved and malefactors punished. William Flesch argues that fictional narratives tend to contain versions of three basic figures: "an innocent, someone who exploits that innocent, and someone else who seeks to punish the exploiter" (*Comeuppance*, ix), and that an underlying psychic motivation for our interest in them is the evolutionary advantage of social cooperation and our instinctual desire to see non-cooperators punished. As a species whose specific environmental niche involves social and intellectual collaboration, one of the characteristics for which we have been selected at a group level is altruism, the tendency to increase the fitness of others even at the expense of our own fitness (Sober and Wilson, *Unto Others*, 6). We have also evolved to track the cooperation of others, and our intense emotional interest in the non-actual reflects this: people enjoy stories, at least in part, because they learn from them just who the innocent and the guilty are, and because they like seeing the guilty get their comeuppance (see Flesch, *Comeuppance*, 21–74). Clearly, this is a somewhat reductive explanation for the pleasures of literature, and does not apply to all kinds of fiction. It is nonetheless a useful scheme for analysing the tales of Day Eight, which build on and imitate legal and narratological principles of balance and reciprocity, with a counter-trick frequently putting things back into place after an original trick that either involved the exploitation of innocence or upset an implied hierarchy of value (such as when someone tries to outwit a Florentine).[15] Novella VIII.7 implicitly raises the question of how to contain a situation in which, however, the punishment that is meted out is greater than the original "crime" and might seem to call once more for reciprocation, in a widening circle of revenge. Boccaccio answers this

---

15 Christopher Nissen shows how the persistent narrative motif of retribution in the *Decameron* responds to certain kinds of offensive behaviour, including lack of virtue or intelligence, hypocrisy, jealousy, and unjustified *beffe* (*The Ethics of Retribution*, 34).

question with VIII.8, a tale that, in the perfect symmetry of its retaliation, appears to enact – but also to mock – the Dantean doctrine of the *contrapasso*, as well as the normative conventions of pedagogical and exemplary literature, in which people are generally shown to get what they deserve.[16]

The story's status as parody is also signalled by the fact that it is set in Siena, Florence's historic rival.[17] At this point let us give a sidelong glance at two of the *Decameron*'s other Sienese *novelle*. The tenth tale of Day Seven also takes place in Florence's sister-city and also deals with a relationship between two inseparable friends ("non usavano se non l'un con l'altro" [VII.10.8]) – in this case, Tingoccio Mini and Meuccio di Tura – who desire the same woman. The reversal of initials in their two names (T.M. and M.T.) suggests, once more, the men's near interchangeability. Tingoccio has more access to the desired woman, however, because he is her child's godfather, and thus manages to have his way with her, whereupon he over-exerts himself sexually and promptly drops dead. After death, he returns to Meuccio to tell him about the afterlife, as each promised the other he would, and reveals that "di qua non si tiene ragione alcuna delle comari" [up here nobody is concerned with the mothers of godchildren (VII.10.28)] – i.e., God does not consider sex with them especially sinful. Although the tale's Florentine narrator Dioneo introduces the story as exemplifying "la bessaggine de' sanesi" [the stupidity of the Sienese (VII.10.7)], the two companions seem almost to exemplify shrewdness; Meuccio makes valuable use of the information that Tingoccio gives him about the punishments accorded for each sin – a patent allusion to Dante – by no longer abstaining from prohibited behaviours that have no eternal consequences. Their friendship and the reciprocal promise that they made have a generally positive outcome.[18]

16 On medieval literary exemplarity and its relation to mendicant preaching in the vernacular, which used exemplary anecdotes as concrete illustrations of moral generalizations or injunctions, see esp. Delcorno, *Exemplum e letteratura*; Scanlon, *Narrative, Authority, and Power*.

17 During the thirteenth and fourteenth centuries, both Florence and Siena grew in economic and military power, and both tried to enlarge their territories, causing inevitable friction between them. The two cities fought many battles (the most famous of which is probably that of Montaperti in 1260, won by the Sienese), but eventually Florence gained the upper hand and Siena was incorporated into its Duchy in 1557. See Waley, *Siena and the Sienese*, esp. 114–19 and 205–7, and his *The Italian City-Republics*, 207.

18 Boccaccio's only other novella that is actually set in Siena is *Decameron* VII.3, in which Frate Rinaldo sleeps with his godchild's mother, and then convinces her

The other Sienese story that I'd like briefly to examine, Novella IX.4, is not set in the city, but among Sienese characters outside of Siena, and their friendship is depicted in a much less favourable light. The two friends who "ispesso n'usavano insieme" [often spent time together] are named here Cecco di messere Angiulieri (i.e., the comic poet Cecco Angiolieri) and Cecco di messer Fortarrigo, both of whom are historical figures. The fact that they have the same first name would seem to emphasize, yet again, their equivalency. The plot does not involve any sort of benevolent interchange, however. On the contrary, while Angiulieri sleeps, Fortarrigo gambles away not only everything that he himself possesses, but all of Angiulieri's money as well. Later, when Angiulieri tries to get away from him, Fortarrigo runs after the other Cecco dressed in only his shirt and accuses his friend of having robbed him, which incites some peasants to seize Angiulieri. Fortarrigo then puts on Angiulieri's clothing and rides away. As this brief outline makes evident, the tale does not depict balanced, reciprocal *beffe*, but two outrageously unjust tricks, both played by the same person on the same other. The tale ends, however, with its narrator Neifile saying that "la malizia del Fortarrigo … non fosse a luogo e a tempo lasciata impunita" [Fortarrigo's malicious trick didn't go unpunished in its time and place (IX.4.25)]. That is, Angiulieri does eventually take revenge, although outside of the confines of this particular novella.

All three of these Sienese stories (VII.10, VIII.8, and IX.4) deal in different ways with male friendship, as well as with questions of reciprocity and retribution. Other *novelle* also related to VIII.8, but not set in Siena, are IV.9, the tale of Guiglielmo Rossiglione, who slays his wife's lover Guiglielmo Guardastagno (another set of friends who have the same name) and gives her his heart to eat; and X.8, the tale of Roman Tito, who falls in love with the fiancée of his Greek friend Gisippo. Gisippo demonstrates his true friendship for Tito by tricking his betrothed into marrying his friend. Tito later saves Gisippo from being put to death for a murder that he did not commit by claiming to have committed the crime himself, thus returning the favour. Like VIII.8, both IV.9

husband that he has been treating the child for illness. This story is clearly related to both VII.10 and VIII.8, as it also deals with issues of literal or figurative incest, that is, of who is permitted to have sex with whom, and how to deal with broken sexual taboos. The *bessaggine* exemplified in VII.3 is that of the husband, who is depicted as gullible and overly devout. Other Sienese characters in the *Decameron* are the bandit Gino di Tacco "di Siena cacciato" [exiled from Siena (X.2.5)] and the "dicitore in rima" [vernacular rhymester (X.7.18)] Mico da Siena.

and X.8 address the issue of what happens when desire for a woman comes between two male friends, with varying outcomes. The echoes and interrelations among all these stories are examples of Boccaccio's recombinatory method – what Guido Almansi calls his "ars combinatoria" – whereby alternative versions of the same tale can contain different elements and impart different lessons.[19] The basic outlines of *novelle* IV.9, VIII.8, and X.8 are in fact very similar: in all three, a man covets his neighbour's wife (or the neighbour's intended). But the outcome of IV.9 is tragic, whereas X.8 idealizes friendship and ends happily, after a prolonged narrative. Novella VIII.8 arguably ends even more happily, by addressing the problem quickly and appropriately, but its resolution is a comic and impracticable one.

Boccaccio's method of splitting and recombining stories points to the instability of narrative meanings, as well as to that of moral standards and social practices. I do not wish to over-emphasize the defamiliarizing or destructive nature of the *Decameron*'s methodology, however. Boccaccio's procedure of repeatedly creating and dissolving patterns, echoing past plots and anticipating future ones, while constantly reconfiguring how the different parts fit together, may also be identified with the kind of playful hypothesis-testing that neuroscientists recognize as among the primary techniques of harmonious art and literature.[20] Novella VIII.8 adopts and parodies an established narrative pattern, the trickster-tricked tale, making the two tricks perfectly balanced to the point of absurdity, but the story also makes a serious point about the need for effective judicial mechanisms with suitable (that is, not overly harsh) punishments. As Lauretta points out at the beginning of the following novella, there is no reason to reprimand "chi fa beffa alcuna a colui che la va cercando o che la si guadagna" [anyone who plays a trick on someone who is asking for it or has it coming], and Spinelloccio "la si guadagnò" [had it coming (VIII.9.3)]. In making fun of this sort of symmetrical retribution, Boccaccio acknowledges the impossibility of ever achieving perfect closure, either in literature or in life.

The notion of perfect closure alludes to the logic of Christianity as well. The economic paradigm of *quid pro quo* also underlies the basic

19 Almansi, *The Writer as Liar*, 63–107. See also Velli, *Petrarca e Boccaccio*, 112–21, and Cazalé Bérard, "Filoginia/misoginia," 124 (who refers to Boccaccio's "gioco combinatorio ed emulativo," or repetition with variation).

20 See esp. Boyd, *On the Origin of Stories*, 80–112; Armstrong, *How Literature Plays with the Brain*, 48–53.

Christian doctrine that Christ died to atone for humanity's sins and that he thereby put an end to God's need to inflict any further punishment or revenge upon humanity.[21] While the tale's attitude toward the possibility of perfect justice is mostly satirical, at the same time its genial outcome may seem strangely – even comfortingly – hopeful.[22]

21 In Christian theology this is the theory of atonement, whereby Christ was punished in place of sinners, thus satisfying the demands of justice so that humans could be forgiven for their sins; see the Vulgate Bible, 1 John 2:2, "et ipse est propitiatio pro peccatis nostris / non pro nostris autem tantum sed etiam pro totius mundi"; also Romans 5:8–11; 2 Corinthians 5:21.

22 Teodolinda Barolini points out that the word *conforto* appears in the first sentence of the *Decameron*'s Preface in close relation to the word *consolazione*, which Boccaccio uses there and elsewhere to describe his goal as author ("A Philosophy of Consolation," 89).

The Three Faults of Master Simone (VIII.9)

ELISA BRILLI

An Unsparingly Comedic Tale

Judging from the reaction of the women of the *brigata*, the *beffa* devised by the two companions Bruno and Buffalmacco against the physician Simone makes for one of the most amusing tales of the eighth day: "niuna ve ne era a cui per soperchio riso non fossero dodici volte le lagrime venute in su gli occhi" [they laughed so much that the tears ran down their cheeks a dozen times at the very least (VIII.10.2)].[1] Indeed, of the thirty-six novellas of the *Decameron* openly presented as comical, this one stands out as an especially ingenious compendium of comical devices (Segre, "La beffa e il comico," 15), for the practical joke, the chosen theme for Day Eight, is here strikingly combined with a range of hilarious gimmicks.

The usual ridiculing of the victim in a *beffa* is amplified throughout the narrative thanks to Master Simone's vaingloriously inflated sense of self-worth. The rhetoric by which Bruno persuades him to take part in a rite of necromancy in order to enjoy the world's most delightful luxuries adopts a half-serious, half-comical register, filled with sarcastic allusions, nonsense, neologisms, and distorted references to Florentine

1 Sergio Knipe translated a first draft of this essay into English from Italian; the English text also benefited greatly from William Robins's suggestions and those of Jeff Espie. The author would like to thank them as well as many colleagues and friends – namely Carla Casagrande, Anna Fontes Baratto, Johannes Bartuschat, Renzo Bragantini, Giuseppe Mazzotta, and Antonio Montefusco – for listening to her thoughts, sharing their expertise, and encouraging her in this exploration of, to her, relatively uncharted territories. Sergio Knipe also translated extracts from primary and secondary sources not available in English translation. The *Decameron* is cited from the 2013 edition of Quondam, Fiorilla, and Alfano; English translations, unless otherwise indicated, come from McWilliam's translation.

topography. Bruno and Buffalmacco's playing for time fuels the physician's desires, even as it multiplies the favours the two painters enjoy at his expense. As their art passes from linguistic and pictorial to theatrical means, the audience of the tale can relish the comical effect that comes from recognizing the rupture between the terrible initiation rite experienced by Master Simone and Bruno and Buffalmacco's behind-the-scenes stage-management: while Simone sees a "bestia nera e cornuta non molto grande" [black creature with horns … though not very large (VIII.9.82)], the jester Buffalmacco, "messosi indosso un pillicion nero a rovescio, in quello s'acconciò in guisa che pareva pure un orso, se non che la maschera aveva viso di diavolo e era cornuta" [having donned a coat of black fur, got himself up to look exactly like a bear, except that his mask had the face of the devil and was furnished with horns (VIII.9.92)]. A similar mismatch between Simone's expectations and what actually transpires occurs when his hoped-for intercourse with the Countess Civillari entails being dumped in the sewers near San Iacopo di Ripoli, "turning," as Holmes puts it, "his promised necromantic orgy into a coprophiliac one" ("Trial by *Beffa*," 374). The narrative coda features not just reproaches from Simone's wife but also fabricated reproaches from Bruno and Buffalmacco, who, covered in painted bruises, accuse Simone of having brought the demons' wrath down upon them. When the narrative ends, Master Simone, the only character not to recognize the events for what they are, remains trapped in the fiction, as he continues to provide Bruno and Buffalmacco with free meals out of fear that they might publicly mock him.

It is hardly surprising, therefore, that the women of the *brigata* laugh to the point of tears, and that some modern readers have viewed this novella as a perfect illustration of the comical aims of the eighth day, or even as "the carnivalesque apex of the *Decameron*."[2] More surprising, however, is the complete absence of any sympathy toward Simone on the part of the *brigata*. Even if for any *beffa* the audience is led to sympathize with those who perform the practical joke, and not with the dupe, in this case the lack of pity for the victim is total, especially in comparison with the *brigata*'s reactions to the *beffe* orchestrated by Bruno and Buffalmacco against Calandrino (see VIII.7.2). In Simone's case the

2 "vertice carnevalesco del Decameron" (Surdich, *Boccaccio*, 177). See also Bettinzoli, "Sul comico e sulla 'metamorfosi,'" 178–80; Mazzotta, *The World at Play*, 201; and Lupo, "Elementi carnevaleschi," 794. According to Blow, the laughter here is hysterical because of the memory of the plague (*Doctors, Ambassadors, Secretaries*, 59). For a general appraisal of the functioning of this theme and genre, see Ferroni, "Sulla struttura della beffa."

brigata's behaviour confirms and amplifies the perspective of Lauretta, the narrator of the novella and queen of Day Eight. She introduces the story as illustrating a particular kind of justice, a prank meted out to someone who is asking for it:[3] "e io intendo di dirvi d'uno che se l'andò cercando, estimando che quegli che gliele fecero non da biasimare ma da commendar sieno" [and now I propose to tell you of a man who went around asking for it, for I consider that those who played the trick upon him are worthy rather of praise than of blame (VIII.9.3)].[4] In the same fashion the narrative voice never lets up on Simone, as it adopts his tormentors' perspective throughout. If Simone "se l'andò cercando" [asked to be made a fool of], then his grotesque nocturnal escapades must be regarded as a rightful act of retribution.[5] But where exactly does the physician's fault lie? Where does he go wrong?

Of course, typical of any *beffa* is an opposition between cleverness and foolishness, and such an opposition is at work in the encounter between Bruno and Buffalmacco on the one hand, and Master Simone on the other. But there are also other tensions that enrich this tale. There is a geographical, which is to say socio-cultural, dialectic between Florence, represented by Bruno and Buffalmacco, and Bologna, where Master Simone was born and raised.[6] The painters' rambling speeches are a triumph of parochialism, a Florentine linguistic *pastiche* peppered with so many regional place names as to prove unintelligible to Simone. As Lauretta points out: "Il medico, che a Bologna nato e cresciuto era, non intendeva i vocaboli di costoro" [Having been born and bred in Bologna, the physician was unable to grasp the meaning of their words (VIII.9.78)].[7] Furthermore, there is also a social and professional tension between the "poveri uomini e dipintori" [painters, who hadn't a

3 For this reason Bettinzoli speaks of a "giudizio aprioristico e senza possibilità d'appello" ("Sul comico e sulla 'metamorfosi,'" 174). On the normative character of Lauretta, see Bragantini, "Dialogo," 108.

4 McWilliam's translation has been slightly modified.

5 Forno counts this beffa among the "esempi di una programmatica 'utilità,' quasi di una segreta eticità" ("L'amaro riso," 133–4). Kirkham, "Painters at Play," and Holmes, "Trial by *Beffa*," identify the main theme of the *beffa* as that of judgment.

6 The tension here is further complicated by the opposition between the city and the countryside: Simone's father is a country nobleman, whereas his mother's family is from Vallecchio, a village in the Florentine countryside (VIII.9.50). On the category of *rusticitas*, the traditional antonym of *urbanitas* in municipal Tuscan culture and literature, see Mazzoni, "Tematiche politiche," 361.

7 This also holds, at least to some extent, for critics, who have long debated the origins and exact meanings of some of Bruno and Buffalmacco's linguistic coinages. For an analysis of this aspect of the tale, see Bruni, *Boccaccio*, 395–400.

penny to bless themselves with (VIII.9.8)] and the "dottor di medicine, secondo che egli medesimo dicea" [man calling himself a doctor of medicine (VIII.9.5)], who is also the scion of a wealthy family. Simone's social pretensions are in play when Buffalmacco describes the procedure he must follow to receive the title of "cavalier bagnato" [knight of the Bath (VIII.9.81 and 88)]. Throughout the tale, these geographical and professional tensions are closely intertwined with each other. For instance, together they underpin the small masterpieces of *ekphrasis* in Bruno and Buffalmacco's speeches to Simone. When describing the land of Cockayne, for instance, and necromantic rituals, their discourse created seductive overlaps between visual and linguistic mediums.[8] In short, in addition to the foolishness which is the hallmark of all victims of mockery, Simone would appear to have another set of faults: he is doubly foreign to the world of Florentine painters. As other critics have remarked, the *beffa* played against him functions as a ritual for ostracizing the foreigner from the city (Fontes-Baratto, "Le thème de la *beffa*," 30; Holmes, "Trial by *Beffa*," 374).[9]

At the same time, the very reasons that keep Simone from gaining any sympathy suggest that the profiles of the artists Bruno and Buffalmacco as shrewd and successful can be seen as a mask for the author himself. Combined with Boccaccio's well-known fondness for the visual arts, this similarity between the ingenuity of these two pranksters and Boccaccio's own artistry has helped bring into relief the metaliterary quality of this novella and of the eighth day more generally.[10]

This essay aims to enrich and add a new degree of complexity to the traditional interpretative framework of this novella. My analysis will offer a new identification of Boccaccio's potential sources of inspiration, as well as the first comprehensive appraisal of the points of contact between this *beffa* and Petrarch's polemic against physicians. Thanks to these new intertextual and contextual findings, we can re-evaluate both the exemplary nature of Master Simone's faults and the metaliterary significance of Boccaccio's invention.

8 On this important aspect of Boccaccio's writing, see Bartuschat, "Appunti sull'ecfrasi."

9 See also Grimaldi with respect to *Decameron* VIII.5 (*Il privilegio di Dioneo*, 291).

10 See Marcus, *An Allegory of Form*, 79–92, and Bettinzoli, "Sul comico e sulla 'metamorfosi,'" 172. This metaliterary aspect is extensively investigated by Ciccuto ("Il novelliere *en artiste*," 118–30), and highlighted by Picone with reference to the "alone artistico" of the eighth day ("L'arte della beffa," 205–6). See also Watson, "The Cement of Fiction"; Gilbert, "Boccaccio's Devotion to Artists and Art"; and Guerin, "De l'image au texte."

Master Simone's First Fault: Pseudo-Royal Pretensions and Materialism

Lauretta presents this tale as a recent anecdote, and her opening line lends it a realistic touch: "Sì come noi veggiamo tutto il dì … " [We are constantly seeing … (VIII.9.4)].[11] This veneer of realism, along with the local, Florentine quality of the story, may explain why studies of the novella so rarely focus on its sources and intertextual contexts.[12] A close reading of *Decameron* VIII.9, however, reveals that some of its key elements are also found in two well-known narrative sequences from the medieval repertoire of exempla, a repertoire which has long been acknowledged as one of the major sources of inspiration for Boccaccio.[13]

The encounter between Simone and the painters occurs at his initiative, not theirs. Having arrived in Florence, Simone looks at all the people passing down the street and asks about each one, duly making note of what he is told about them.

> E intra gli altri, li quali con più efficacia gli vennero gli occhi addosso posti, furono due dipintori de' quali s'è oggi qui due volte ragionato, Bruno e Buffalmacco, la compagnia de' quali era continua, e eran suoi vicini. E parendogli che costoro meno che alcuni altri del mondo curassero e più lieti vivessono, sì come essi facevano, più persone domandò di lor condizione. (VIII.9.7–8)

> [Among the people who aroused his greatest curiosity were the two painters already mentioned twice here today, Bruno and Buffalmacco,

11 See the reflections on these formulas in Forni, "Realtà/verità," 316.

12 This novella is not among those studied by Lee, *The Decameron: Its Sources and Analogues*. Although Simone da Villa is usually described as a real-life character, he has never been identified; see, most recently, Quondam's commentary in Boccaccio, *Decameron*, ed. Quondam, Fiorilla, and Alfano, 1306n5. Of all the various studies devoted to this novella, only Kirkham, "Painters at Play," has attempted to go beyond the received view of it as an anecdote in order to explore its possible intertextual references, particularly to Dante; see also Mazzotta, *The World at Play*, 202–4. For a reflection on an analogous link between Florentinism and realism in Dante, see Brilli, *Firenze e il profeta*, 21–9.

13 For a discussion of the definition and genre of the exempla, see Berlioz and Polo de Beaulieu, *Les exempla médiévaux*; and Bremond, Le Goff, and Schmitt, *L'exemplum*. Within the vast literature on Boccaccio and exempla, see Battaglia, "Dall'esempio alla novella"; Delcorno, *La predicazione*; Branca, "Studi sugli *exempla*"; Degani, "Riflessi"; Delcorno, "Studi sugli *exempla*"; Delcorno, *Exemplum e letteratura*; Baldi, "La retorica"; Battaglia Ricci, "'Una novella per esempio'"; and Battaglia Ricci, "*Exemplum* e novella." A useful overview is provided by Fonio, "Dalla legenda alla novella."

who were neighbours of his and never out of one another's company. Since they seemed to him the jolliest and most carefree fellows in the world, as was indeed the case, he made various inquiries about their social condition].

Simone's excessive curiosity and his rude practice of staring at passers-by have a close parallel in a tale from the medieval narrative repertoire, one later incorporated in the collections of exempla used by preachers. In this exemplary tale, a king is visiting a city at night in the company of a counsellor when he comes across a very poor couple and starts spying on them. Even though they live in an underground hovel and wear nothing but rags, the husband and wife conduct themselves so merrily that the ruler is amazed. When the counsellor observes that even the sovereign's sumptuous life seems wretched to the elect few who enjoy eternal life, this wise observation earns the king's applause. The rather banal point of the exemplum is to challenge the assumption that material wealth corresponds with spiritual well-being.

This brief summary is based on the version of the tale from the well-known Latin *Life of Barlaam and Josaphat*, which circulated as part of the *Vitae Patrum.*[14] A similar yet more concise version features in Jacques de Vitry's *Sermones vulgares* from the first half of the thirteenth century, as well as in a related anonymous collection of exempla.[15] An even more abridged version set the seal on the tale by including it within the most monumental medieval collection of exempla, the *Alphabetum narrationum*. Compiled by Arnold of Liège between the late thirteenth and early fourteenth centuries, the *Alphabetum* circulated throughout the Christian West, mainly via the libraries and *studia* of the Dominican order. Arnold's version records the tale under the rubric "Paupertas" (poverty) and informs the reader that it is also relevant to the theme of "contemptus mundi" (contempt of the world).[16]

---

14 *Vita Sanctorum Barlaam eremitae et Josaphat Indiae regis*, cols. 503–5.

15 Jacques de Vitry, *Exempla*, no. 78, pp. 35–6; see also pp. xlviii and 168 for information about the inclusion of the tale in one of the witnesses of an anonymous collection (London, British Library, MS Harley 463, fol. 16). On the redaction by Jacques de Vitry, see also Hinnebusch, "Extant Manuscripts," 162–3; and Louis, *L'exemplum en pratiques*, 141–2.

16 Arnold of Liège's version is brief enough to quote here in full: "PAVPERTAS. Paupertas leta multum est commendabilis. Iacobus de Vitriaco. Rex quidam cum quodam milite sibi secreto, quadam nocte, per ciuitatem suam iuit ut uideret que in ea fiebant. Venientes ergo ad quemdam locum, uiderunt lumen per foramen in quodam subterraneo in quo sedebat homo cum uxore et liberis, cum uestibus sordidis et laceratis, qui cantabant et magnum festum faciebant. Tunc rex ait militi:

This exemplary narrative and the opening scene of *Decameron* VIII.9 share an urban setting, while their primary characters, the sovereign and Simone, display a similar interest in the life of local inhabitants and a similar amazement at the mirth of the pair of paupers whom they behold. The portraits of the paupers are of much the same stamp, combining abject wretchedness with the greatest cheerfulness. Also striking, in light of the filthy end met by Simone, is the advisor's acknowledgment, found in most medieval versions, that magnificent garments, buildings, and other pleasures seem to the elect to be "stercoribus … fetidiores" [fouler than excrement].[17]

Despite these similarities, two crucial deviations from the exemplum stand out. The first has to do with the protagonists' rank. The interest shown by the sovereign and his desire to spy upon the lives of the poor couple apparently fall within his royal prerogatives, constituting an expression of his sovereignty. By contrast, the adoption of the same attitude by a physician, and a foreign one at that, is wholly unjustified. Simone is under the illusion that the professional title he has earned from the University of Bologna allows him to take extraordinary liberties toward the inhabitants of Florence: "e quasi degli atti degli uomini dovesse le medicine che dar doveva a' suoi infermi comporre, a tutti poneva mente e raccoglievagli" [and he duly noted and remembered everything he was told about them, as though this information was essential in prescribing the right medicine for his patients (VIII.9.6)]. Comparison with the tradition of the exemplum underscores the awkward presumptuousness of Simone, who in this respect – as much as in his choice of clothing, "scarlatto e con un gran batalo" [in scarlet robes

'Valde mirabile est quod nec mihi nec tibi umquam tantum placuit uita nostra qua tantis affuit diuitiis et gloria, quantum istis paupertas sua.' Cui miles: 'Multo amplius reputant uitam nostram stultam uere uite amatores.' Hoc etiam ualet ad contemptum mundi. Ad hoc etiam facit quod dicitur supra de diuitiis I et II" (Arnoldus, *Alphabetum*, no. 622, p. 346; for the redaction and circulation of the collection, see pp. xiii–xliv). The tale is also recorded by Tubach, *Index exemplorum*, no. 4390. The possibility that Boccaccio could have known this exemplum hardly needs to be discussed, given the oral as well as written circulation of this narrative. It is nonetheless worth noting that the *Alphabetum narrationum* features many of the exempla used by Boccaccio: see Arnoldus, *Alphabetum*, no. 170 (for *Dec.* IV.Intro.); no. 411 (*Dec.* IV.2, on which see Toldo, "Dall'*Alphabetum*," 293–7); no. 417 (*Dec.* X.1); no. 547 (*Dec.* VII.4); no. 629 (*Dec.* V.8, on which see Perrus, "La nouvelle V, 8"); and no. 636 (*Dec.* X.9).

17 "Atque auro rutilantes aedes, ac praeclara haec indumenta, caeteraeque vitae delicia … stercoribus et coeno fetidores videntur" (*Vita Sanctorum Barlaam eremitae et Josaphat Indiae regis*, col. 504). Similarly, in Jacques de Vitry: "qui splendida palatia nostra et vestes et divitias tanquam stercora reputant" (*Exempla*, p. 36).

with a fine-looking hood (VIII.9.5)] – mistakes his own prerogatives for those of a king.

Second, unlike the king in the exemplum, Simone draws no moral lesson from the sight of two poor yet happy people. On the contrary, paying no attention to the fact that others have confirmed that these two men are in fact poor, he figures that they must have a secret source of wealth:

> e udendo da tutti costoro essere poveri uomini e dipintori, gli entrò nel capo non dover poter essere che essi dovessero così lietamente vivere della lor povertà, ma s'avvisò, per ciò che udito aveva che astuti uomini erano, che d'alcuna altra parte non saputa dagli uomini dovesser trarre profetti grandissimi. (VIII.9.8)
>
> [and everyone told him that these two men were painters, who hadn't a penny to bless themselves with. But as he was unable to conceive how they could possibly lead such merry lives without visible means of support, he came to the conclusion, having heard that they were very clever, that they must be drawing huge profits from a source that other people had no knowledge of.]

Not only is Simone wholly mistaken about Bruno and Buffalmacco, his assumption also conflicts with a longstanding, authoritative tradition in the exemplary repertoire that taught Christians to draw the opposite conclusion from the same premises. In this light, it is easier to understand why, according to Lauretta, the physician only has himself to blame for the prank played upon him. Indeed, this is the real "kernel of the *beffa*."[18] The exemplary intertext clarifies that the physician's first fault lies less in his conviction that there are secret reasons for Bruno and Buffalmacco's wealth, and more in his belief that happiness always has a material foundation. While this confirms Simone's "tendency to commodify knowledge" (Holmes, "Trial by *Beffa*," 372), it also reveals his remarkable ignorance of the principles of Christian morality laid out in traditional exemplary literature.

Master Simone's Second Fault: Necromancy between the Exempla and the Arts

By ignoring Christian morality, Master Simone finds himself involved in a necromantic ritual. Buffalmacco provides a detailed description of

18 "germe della beffa" (Picone, "L'arte della beffa," 218).

it for Simone's instruction. The ritual requires considerable courage. It will take place at night "su uno di quegli avelli rilevati che poco tempo ha si fecero di fuori a Santa Maria Novella" [on one of the raised tombs that were erected just recently outside Santa Maria Novella (VIII.9.81)]. There a diabolical beast will appear: Simone will have to mount and ride it, he is told, in order to join the devotees of a secret society and take part in their orgiastic banquets.

The *Alphabetum*, under the rubric devoted to necromancy, lists two exempla: "Nigromantica arte uti est ualde periculosum" [Performing the art of necromancy is very dangerous (Arnoldus, *Alphabetum* no. 572, pp. 319–20)] and "Nigromantie discipulus a demone rapitur et deportatur" [A student of necromancy is kidnapped and carried off by a demon (no. 573, p. 320)]. Both tales come from Caesarius of Heisterbach's *Dialogus miraculorum*, one of the most important sources for the *Alphabetum* (Brilli, "The Making of a New *Auctoritas*"). The first story describes a knight who, sceptical about the existence of demons, asks a master named Philip to show him some. Philip accepts and "in quodam biuio" [at a certain crossroads] traces a circle on the ground with his sword, warning the knight never to cross that boundary with any part of his body, lest he be snatched away by the demons. A huge, pitch-black man then appears who attempts to carry the knight off but, as soon as Philip comes to his rescue, the monstrous creature vanishes.[19] The second story tells of a group of necromancy students who ask their master to put what they have learned into practice. The master agrees: he leads them "in campum" [into a field], traces the usual circle, and gives the neophytes words of advice not unlike those in the previous exemplum. The demons now manifest themselves in the semblance of knights and dancing women. A student accepts a golden ring from one of the most beautiful women and as soon as he touches it, she kidnaps him. Upon hearing his pupils' screams, the master comes to the rescue and summons the demon: the demon argues that the student ignored the warnings, but finally brings him back, pale and bruised. Horrified by the experience, the student forswears necromancy and joins the Cistercian order.[20]

The *Clavicula Salomonis* (*Key of Solomon*), one of the most famous medieval treatises on the magical arts, already known to Pietro d'Abano

19 Caesarius, *Dialogus miraculorum* 5.2, 1:276–8; Arnoldus, *Alphabetum narrationum*, no. 572, p. 319. The tale is mentioned by Cohn, *Europe's Inner Demons*, 103–4 and is recorded in Tubach, *Index exemplorum*, no. 1070.

20 Caesarius, Dialogus miraculorum 5.4, 1:279–81; Arnoldus, *Alphabetum narrationum*, no. 573, p. 320. The tale is recorded in Tubach, *Index exemplorum*, no. 1071a.

(1256–1310), also attests to the importance of the magic circle. This treatise distinguishes between rituals which require a circle and less challenging ones which can be performed without it; detailed instructions are also provided on how to trace it.[21] In the posthumous trial of Boniface VIII (ca 1230–1304, born Benedetto Caetani), one of the witnesses claimed that one night he had seen Caetani – who at the time was secretary to Nicholas III – make his way out of the palace in Viterbo, trace a circle with a sword in the garden, stand at the centre of it, and perform a necromantic ritual. When a mysterious voice told him, "Give us a part," Caetani seized a rooster he had just killed and flung it outside the circle, saying "Here is your part" (Cohn, *Europe's Inner Demons*, 122). As Cohn explains, the magic circle "marked out a field of concentrated divine power, a barrier which no demon could cross" (ibid., 110).[22]

In short, a Christian in the thirteenth and fourteenth centuries would have had at least two pieces of general knowledge about necromantic rituals: first, they usually occur in non-urban areas, and never on consecrated land (such as that of the cemetery of Santa Maria Novella); and second, their participants must trace a magic circle and never cross it or touch the demons either directly or through an object. In light of these protective measures, Buffalmacco's advice to Simone appears absurd. It overturns the basic rules governing necromancy found both in ordinary beliefs (as in Caesarius and the *Alphabetum*) and in more technical accounts (as in the *Clavicula Salomonis* and the process against Boniface VIII).

Does Boccaccio's scene consciously caricature necromantic rituals and narrative tales about them? In the *Decameron* VIII.8, Bruno claims that Michael Scot (ca 1175–ca 1236) is the founder of the occult sect in Florence (VIII.8.17). In addition to Oxford, Paris, Rome, Salerno, and Bologna, Scot's name was universally linked to Toledo, where he lived for roughly ten years (1210–20) and translated various Arab scientific works, including a series of astronomical treatises by Alpetragius.[23] Caesarius sets the tale about the kidnapped student who later became a Cistercian monk in Toledo, a city which frequently figures in exempla about necromancy owing to its fame as a crossroads between Arab, Jewish, and Latin culture and hence as a centre of diffusion for occult

21 *The Key of Solomon*, 14–17 and 89–90. On the *Clavicula Salomonis*, see Boudet, *Entre science et nigromance*, 353–9 and 559–61. Pietro d'Abano mentions the *Clavicula* in his *Lucidator dubitabilium astronomiae* (Pietro d'Abano, *Trattati di Astronomia*, 117).

22 For other examples, see Véronèse, "La magie divinatoire."

23 For Scot's biography, see Burnett, "Michael Scot," and Morpurgo, "Michele Scoto."

science and lore.[24] It may have been through his acquaintance with exempla set in Toledo that Boccaccio came up with the idea of bringing Michael Scot into play, a figure notoriously associated not only with necromancy[25] but also with that city.

However, Boccaccio's caricature is even more biting. As we have seen, Master Simone is deceived because he knows nothing about the necromantic art of his day. If there is little surprise in his lack of familiarity with exemplary literature, such a lack of knowledge about necromancy is a striking failing for a physician graduated from Bologna. The boundaries between medicine, astrology, natural philosophy, alchemy, and what was regarded as secret and occult lore, including magic, were blurry and still in the process of being defined in Boccaccio's times. Hence the frequent occurrence, on the one hand, of scholars mastering these various disciplines and, on the other, of attempts to distinguish these fields by acts of normalization, punishment, and condemnation.[26] This historical remark holds particularly true in contexts such as Bologna. Here the study of medicine was associated with that of the arts and conceived as the crowning glory of this curriculum. This academic arrangement accounts for certain peculiarities, such as the subordination of the *artes* to medicine; the primacy assigned to natural philosophy among the various branches of philosophy; and the particular status of astrology as a discipline bridging natural philosophy and medicine.[27] Over the course of the fourteenth century and well beyond, Bologna was home to scholars of medicine and astrology who had just as much expertise in the divinatory and necromantic arts. These scholars include famous, and often controversial, figures such as Pietro d'Abano (although he was distant from the group of university physicians in Bologna), as well as Cecco d'Ascoli (1269–1327), Taddeo da Parma (active between 1318 and 1321), Biagio Pelacani da Parma

---

24 For an example, see the tale about a magister of Toledo recorded by Etienne de Bourbon (Berlioz, " Maître Melchita," 301–2).

25 Scot is featured among the soothsayers in Dante's *Commedia* (*Inf.* 20.115–17). The possibility that Dante may have influenced Boccaccio's tale has been argued by Mazzotta, *The World at Play*, 202–4; Kirkham, "Painters at Play," 220–1; and Holmes, "Trial by *Beffa*," 374.

26 See Boudet, *Entre science et nigromance*; and Federici Vescovini, *Medioevo magico*. On the connection with alchemical lore, see Crisciani and Paravicini Bagliani, *Alchimia e medicina*. On the emergence of demonology within Scholastic thought, see Boureau, *Satan hérétique*.

27 See Bianchi, "Conclusione," 543–4. On the specific context of Bologna, see Casagrande and Fioravanti, *La filosofia in Italia*; and especially Tabarroni, "La nascita dello Studio," and Tabarroni, "Notizie biografiche."

(1357–1416), and Antonio da Montolmo (active as a teacher of grammar from 1369, and of astrology and medicine from 1387).

From a historical standpoint, then, it is incongruous for someone who had studied medicine in Bologna, like Simone, to have to wait until he returns to Florence to be (poorly) instructed in necromancy. One feels inclined to agree with Buffalmacco's remark here: "voi non apparaste miga l'abicì in su la mela, come molti sciocconi voglion fare, anzi l'apparaste bene in sul mellone, ch'e così lungo" [you didn't learn your ABCs by writing them on an apple, the way many fools try to do it, but instead you used that great big, long melon of yours (VIII.9.64; Rebhorn translation)]. Simone will further confirm his incompetence as a physician in the epilogue, where he is once again duped by Bruno and Buffalmacco, this time for not being able to distinguish painted bruises from real ones.

Master Simone's Third Fault: Medicine according to Boccaccio and Petrarch

The elements I have highlighted above suggest that the *beffa* against Master Simone not only condemns foreigners, misers, and graduates, but also mocks medicine – or, at least the kind of medicine endorsed by certain practitioners. Such a send-up raises the possibility that the novella is also to be understood in relation to another interdiscursive context.

In her intertextual analysis of the novella, Kirkham refers to Petrarch's *Invective contra medicum* as an example of the association between medicine and excrement which similarly marks the ending of *Decameron* VIII.9.[28] Indeed, this topic occurs often in the *Invective*, four letters which Petrarch wrote against an anonymous physician working at the pontifical court in Avignon – the first from March/April 1352, the others from the early months of 1353 – and then brought together into a single collection.[29] The similarities between Petrarch's opponent and

28 Kirkham, "Painters at Play," 218–19, and note 10. I cite Petrarch's Latin *Invective* from Bausi's 2005 edition; English translations come from the translation by Marsh in Petrarch, *Invectives*.

29 In the first invective, latrines are presented as the place to which physicians naturally belong, by contrast to the *loci amoeni* familiar to the poet (Petrarca, *Invective* 1.29, pp. 28–9), and the medical profession is said to revolve around the observation of urine and other things that Petrarch is too ashamed to mention (1.135, pp. 42–3). The second letter states that physicians write "inter latrinas" and "inter urinas" and, in the closing tirade, that the pallor of which doctors make a

Master Simone go far beyond their association with the more bodily aspects of human life.

Both characters are not only vainglorious and greedy but also representatives of a venal and foolishly materialistic way of thinking. (This is Master Simone's first fault, as discussed above, a fault which leads him to fall for, or even to invite, the *beffa*.) In the second invective, Petrarch depicts the physician as the fool who, according to the Psalmist, denies God; he also simulates the physician's inner conversation as he broods over poorly understood *auctoritates*; and he accuses him of Averroism, that is to say, of unbelief (*Invective* 2.234–43, pp. 76–8). Greed and ignorance lead Petrarch's physician to worship the devil: "Et quoniam blasphemare quem mundus adorat publice non audetis, hostem eius sacrilegum ac blasphemum paulominus adoratis" [Since you do not dare to blaspheme publicly the one whom the world worships, you practically worship his sacrilegious and blasphemous enemy (*Invective* 2.244, p. 78; trans. *Invectives* 2.85, p. 69)].[30] This detail resonates with *Decameron* VIII.9, considering Simone's readiness to embark on necromantic rituals as soon as he is given the chance to do so.

Beyond the charges of materialism and devil worshipping, Petrarch's physician and Boccaccio's Simone are also both accused of lying and of cheating their patients.[31] In the first of Petrarch's *Invective*, this accusation

---

boast, as though it were a sign of wisdom, is merely a consequence of the days they spend examining chamber pots and sewers – until they acquire the colour, smell, and even taste of what they are inspecting (2.30–2, pp. 54–5, and 2.325–30, pp. 86–9). Finally, the metaphorically "low" place in which Petrarch's opponent exercises his profession is taken as evidence of the fact that he himself is scum (3.140, p. 109, and see also 3.222, pp. 120–1).

30 The same theme later crops up in Petrarch's *Seniles* 5.3 (10 December 1365), again criticizing medicine. Here Petrarch recounts the failed attempt to cure Galeazzo Visconti's gout made by a famous physician who, having run out of treatments, requested certain books on magic, which he referred to as sacred: "libros nescio quos magicos – sacros vocat ipse." The doctor thus tarnished his Hippocratic fame ("ypocratica illa fama") by indulging in eccentricities and magic ("in iocos atque in magia") (*Res seniles* 5.3.107–9, 2:72).

31 On this point it is worth recalling Buffalmacco's sarcastic remark, which immediately earns Simone's applause: "E come m'abbia detto che voi studiaste a la in medicine, a me pare che voi studiaste in apparare a pigliare gli uomini: il che voi, meglio che altro uomo che io vidi mai, sapete fare con vostro senno e con vostre novelle" [Bruno tells me you were studying medicine up there in Bologna, but it seems to me that you studied how to capture men's minds, for what with your wisdom and your singular ways, you're a better exponent of that particular art than any other man I ever saw (VIII.9.65)]. However, owing to his limited intelligence, Simone is not very successful in this, except with poor Calandrino (in *Decameron* IX.3).

is tied to the different relation between truth and falsehood to be found in medicine and poetry. Whereas Petrarch accuses the former of producing harmful lies, he claims that it is proper to the latter to adorn the truth with useful *velamina* (veils) which make the learning process harder yet sweeter (Petrarch, *Invective* 1.162–4, p. 46). What is original here is neither the topos of poetic veils protecting hidden knowledge nor that of the proportionality of difficulty and pleasure, but the epistemological and ethical opposition drawn between medicine and poetry in view of the different reasons why they seek to sugar-coat the truth. Petrarch's invectives against doctors provide an opportunity for him to comment on the nature of poetry, suggesting a further affinity with Boccaccio's *beffa* in VIII.9, given the metaliterary implications that arise from Bruno and Buffalmacco's machinations.

Finally, all of these points inform Petrarch's criticism of how physicians distort rhetoric. This is shown not just by the fact that doctors regard rhetoric as the handmaid of medicine, but also by their common use of a mystifying jargon and their attempts to pass themselves off as "authors":

> O ridiculum animal – volebam dicere – librum scribis; rectius dixerim quod tue professionis est proprium: aromatum lenta fedas involucra; et ubi periculosis ambagibus dictare soles miserorum mortes, utque vilia magno costent, fallasque licentius, radicibus nostri orbis imponere peregrina vocabula, ibi nunc, ut tibi videtur, philosophicos locos, ut ego sentio, tabificos iocos scribis. Sed ut libri formam habeant, versutus opifex, distinguis in partes; et forsitan victor eris: apothecarii scripsisse te librum dicent. (*Invective* 2.13–14, p. 53)
>
> [O ridiculous animal, I was going to say: You are writing a book. But let me speak more correctly, using the term of your profession. You are befouling the sticky wrappers for your spices. In your work you often use dangerous hocus-pocus to prescribe the deaths of your wretched patients. And you often graft foreign names on roots from our soil, so that you can charge a high price for such rubbish and cheat your patients more easily. Just so, now you are writing what you think are metaphysical notions, but what I consider mephitical nothings. To give them the shape of a book, O wily craftsman, you divide them in various sections. Perhaps you will succeed, and the shopkeepers will say you have written a book. (*Invectives* 2.44, pp. 35–7)][32]

32 In the third invective, Petrarch calls his opponent an ignoramus in the very use of his native language, which is why he is "semper scolastice literator, numquam literatus aut magister" (*Invective* 3.252 and 254, pp. 122–4). As noted by Berté and

Such a distortion of rhetoric and language is not much different from that carried out by Simone and, *mutatis mutandis*, Bruno and Buffalmacco. To dupe the physician, the two mocking pranksters invent a special language. Intentionally abstruse, it both ennobles and twists all aspects of reality, from the simplest and most humble things, which are made unrecognizable, to the *auctoritates* established as the foundation of the medical science in the Middle Ages, namely Hippocrates and Avicenna, whose names metamorphose into "Porcograsso e Vannacenna" (VIII.9.38). This process of linguistic reshuffling also encompasses various "pseudoscientific inflections,"[33] such as the inappropriate use of the technical scholastic term "qualitativo" [qualitative (VIII.9.15)]. Read alongside the *Invective*, then, the unbridled linguistic experimentalism of Boccaccio's jokers appears to be not just a means to carry out the *beffa*, but part of the *beffa* itself: a parody of the mystifications of medical jargon. This claim is supported by a comment that Bruno himself makes when, in response to Simone's question of whether he is saying "Ippocrasso" (Hippocrates) and "Avicena" (Ibn-Sīnā), he taunts: "Gnaffé! io non so: io m'intendo così male de' vostri nomi come voi de' miei" [You may well be right ... for these names of yours mean about as much to me as mine do to you (VIII.9.39)].

Petrarch's *Invective* cannot be reduced to any simplistic formula and his attack on the *ars mecanica* of medicine has been subject to contrasting interpretations. It has been understood as "an archetypal Renaissance confrontation of rhetoric and medicine, as well as a primitive encounter of Humanism and science, or at least pseudo-science" (Struever, "Petrarch's *Invective contra medicum*," 659),[34] or as a representation of the dispute between the arts typical of a Parisian context and brought up to date to suit a fourteenth-century climate (Boulnois, "Scolastique et humanisme"). Other scholars have recognized in the *Invective* a crucial piece of evidence to understand Petrarch's "rearguard" cultural battle (Bausi, *Petrarca antimoderno*), and an attempt to defend what was considered to be the loftiest form of philosophy at the time, a philosophy both Socratic and Christian, which is to say Augustinian (Trottmann, "Philosophie, médecine et rhétorique"). Regardless of these interpretative differences, it is easy to understand why, as medicine was gaining increasing socio-cultural prestige and starting to subordinate other disciplines as lower stages in the study curriculum, Petrarch might have

Rizzo, "Le *Senili* mediche," 265, this theme is later amplified in *Seniles* 5.3, which mocks physicians' predilection for words of Greek as opposed to Latin, origin (*Res seniles* 5.3.114–15, 2:74).

33 "inflessioni pseudoscientifiche" (Branca, "Il paesaggio nel Boccaccio," 44).

34 Streuver's work is very useful for its analysis of the issue of language.

selected physicians as opponents to contrast with his own intellectual and moral model.

Petrarch's scathing portrayal of physicians presents several affinities with Boccaccio's depiction of Master Simone. This comes as no surprise, considering the ongoing dialogue between the two of them about medicine. It was to Boccaccio that Petrarch addressed his *Invective* from Milan in 1355 or 1357, once he had chosen to publish them, and Boccaccio was one of the first people to read them.[35] Over the following years, Boccaccio remained a privileged recipient of Petrarch's polemics against the medical profession: seven of Petrarch's *Epistolae seniles* on this topic were addressed to him, more than to any other correspondent.[36] While it is difficult to establish when their exchange about medicine began, this topic was deeply intertwined with other interests that they shared, and presumably also took place in spoken conversations which are utterly lost to us. Moreover, Pliny's *Natural History* (29.1–8) is one of the main sources for Petrarch's polemic against physicians: Petrarch was able to obtain a copy of this work for his own private use in July 1350, and this codex was perused by Boccaccio during one of their meetings.[37]

Notwithstanding the fact that we cannot establish a clear chronology, I would like to draw attention to one last, possibly crucial, piece of the puzzle. This is the short account we find in Petrarch's first invective of how Socrates praised a painter's choice to become a physician by saying that, whereas artists' faults are visible to all, those of physicians are buried in the ground (along, that is, with their victims' bodies): "Iure igitur Socrates, cum factum de pictore medicum audisset, 'Caute,' inquit: 'artem enim deseruit que defectus suos habet in aperto, eamque amplexus est cuius error terra tegitur'" (*Invective* 1.64, p. 32). Petrarch also jotted down this anecdote, of unknown origin, in his aforementioned copy of Pliny,[38] and Boccaccio will recall it in his defence of poetry in Book 14 of his *Genealogie*, where he observes that "Medici

35 The accompanying letter (in Petrarca, *Lettere disperse* 40, pp. 314–21) does not give any year but is only dated "IV Idus Iunii"; therefore, it may have been written either in 1355 or in 1357. For the *status quaestionis*, see Bausi, *Petrarca antimoderno*, 20, and Billanovich, "Il più grande discepolo," 208–9.

36 These are *Seniles* 2.1, 3.1, 3.5, 5.1, 5.3, 15.8, and 17.2. See Berté and Rizzo, "Le *Senili* mediche," 265.

37 On the importance of Pliny as a model for Petrarch, see Berté and Rizzo, "Le *Senili* mediche," 280–1. The long-established hypothesis that Boccaccio borrowed Petrarch's copy of Pliny and that his notes depend on that copy has been refuted by Petoletti, "Boccaccio e Plinio il Vecchio."

38 Paris, Bibliothèque nationale de France, MS Latin 6802, fol. 195r. See Bausi's note to Petrarca, *Invective* 1.64, 32–3.

errores suos terra tegunt, hi prohibitionibus atque flammis suas conantur ignorantias occultare" [Doctors bury their mistakes in the ground. These charlatans try to hide their ignorance in prohibitions and flames (14.18)], thereby setting them in contrast to poets.[39] For Socrates, then, physicians stand in opposition to painters, just as Master Simone does to Bruno and Buffalmacco. And for both Petrarch and Boccaccio, who knew Socrates's maxim well, physicians stand in opposition to poets, just as Master Simone implicitly stands in contrast to the author of the *Decameron* who is reflected through the comic mask of Bruno and Buffalmacco. Perhaps the women of the *brigata* laugh so heartily, and readers to this day, faithful to Lauretta, consider this *beffa* so fitting, because for once it is not the patient, but the doctor, who ends up being buried along with all his faults?

Conclusion

Decameron VIII.9 is certainly one of the highlights of Boccaccio's comical writing. Building on the interpretations of the novella provided by other scholars, I have advanced some additional considerations based on the tale's parallels with the exemplary tradition and cultural context. These findings corroborate Delcorno's assessment of Boccaccio's creative method: "like a true demiurge of medieval literature, Boccaccio works up these exemplary materials, these fossils of collective memory, changing their meaning with light strokes, certain that the reader will detect a familiar pattern in the tale, but also, with a liberating sense of surprise, a different message."[40] Yet what is the purpose of this rewriting and what is its message?

The reworking of exempla is an integral part of the comical device that Boccaccio has set up, for the reader who is able to recall these exemplary tales and detect their reversal will laugh with even more

---

39 Shortly afterwards, Boccaccio confirms the attribution of the maxim to Socrates: "O sententia Socratis felices medici, quorum terra teguntur errores, cum scriptorum sepissime etiam bene dicta, quoniam in propatulo sint, caninis lacerentur dentibus, aut saltem infestentur latratibus" [Think of Socrates' saying – "O happy physicians, whose blunders are hidden underground!" But with authors how different! For their choice utterances are exposed to the fangs of hounds, or at least harassed by their yelps (Boccaccio, *Genealogie deorum gentilium*, ed. Zaccaria, 14.18, p. 756; translation from Osgood, in Boccaccio, *Boccaccio on Poetry*, 107)]. Cochin (*Boccace*, 138) and Osgood (*Boccaccio on Poetry*, 187) have stressed the proximity of Boccaccio's phrasing to that of Petrarch's passage.

40 "Da vero demiurgo della narrativa medievale, egli lavora questi materiali, questi fossili della memoria collectiva, mutandone con lievi tocchi il senso, sicuro che il lettore riconoscerà nella novella uno schema già noto, ma anche, con un moto di sorpresa liberante, un diverso messaggio" (Delcorno, "Studi sugli exempla," 294).

gusto. Such rewriting also lends the *beffa* an exemplary quality, as the innovations introduced all tend to stigmatize Master Simone as a venial and ignorant physician. Finally, such reworking constitutes an essential feature of the metaliterary mechanics of the novella: just as Bruno and Buffalmacco mock the doctor by parodying his jargon and the learning he ought to have mastered, Boccaccio plays with the tradition of exempla. Unlike many other cases in the *Decameron*, however, this rewriting does not seem designed to attack either the exemplary tradition or the cultural policies of mendicant orders who were closely associated with the dissemination of exempla.[41] Yet this is not to say that Boccaccio's send-up in VIII.9 is utterly malice-free. Of all the possible places in which he might have set this necromantic ritual, Boccaccio chose the cemetery of Santa Maria Novella: the library of the Dominican monastery preserved numerous volumes of exemplary literature, which, if Simone had read them, would have prevented him from becoming the victim of a story that had partially already been written.

While Boccaccio does not openly engage here in any polemic against the mendicant orders, the novella attacks certain aspects of the medical profession, which is here set in opposition to the poor yet joyful mode of life of Bruno and Buffalmacco. In stressing this opposition, *Decameron* VIII.9 reveals a remarkable proximity to Petrarch's *Invective* and his reflection on the artistic skills and ethical qualities proper to literary work. As Savelli notes, laughing is first and foremost a social and political phenomenon: "two or more persons … laugh at a third person who is outside of the group, delivering a message that has the double effect of controlling that person's pretensions of superiority and of integrating him into the group at a lower level in the hierarchy."[42] In the stigmatizing of Master Simone we see such in-group formation at work at several levels: not only within the fictional community of Bruno and Buffalmacco and, at the level of the frame tale, within the community of the *brigata*, but also, at a third level, within the historical community of Boccaccio and Petrarch.

41 The satirical criticism of friars loses some of its prominence over the course of the *Decameron*, becoming, if not less scathing, at least less apparent. On Boccaccio's polemic against mendicant orders and on its models, see Montefusco, "Dall'Università di Parigi."

42 "La relazione sociale propria del riso ha forma triadica: due o più soggetti … ridono di un terzo, estraneo al gruppo, con un messaggio che ha il duplice effetto di controllarne le pretese di rango e di integrarlo nel gruppo al livello gerarchico più basso" (Savelli, "Riso," 345).

However, Petrarch's and Boccaccio's projects and strategies should not be conflated. Petrarch's satirical streak is as distant from Boccaccio's comic one as the hills where the former was fond of retiring are from Florence, the latter's natural milieu. Equally distant is the way in which each author seeks to oppose the claims made by fourteenth-century medicine as a discipline straddling practical know-how and theoretical doctrines.[43] Petrarch carries out a "high-profile" operation, pitting a new Christian philosophy against the physicians' scholastic philosophy. That of Boccaccio is, at least apparently, a "low-profile" operation which emphasizes the industriousness and talent of minor artists. Yet Boccaccio's approach comes across as being more nuanced and complex than that of his admired friend. Boccaccio's recurrent shots at exposing the inadequacy of *ars medica* (consider the failure of physicians to treat the plague, lovesickness, and common illnesses, which in the *Decameron* are always treated more effectively by non-professional healers than by graduates)[44] go hand in hand with an ambition to recover medicine's therapeutic function, as is manifested both in the ubiquitous theme of the healing power of literature and in the way Boccaccio rewrites prescriptions of late medieval medical *regimina* to suit the *brigata*'s lifestyle.[45]

---

43 The affirmation of this twofold nature, both theoretical and practical, is the chief strategy adopted in fourteenth-century texts from Bologna in the attempt to legitimize medicine. See Crisciani, "Medici e filosofia."

44 See, respectively, (on the plague) the description in the Introduction (I.Intro.13) and the physicians' mistaken verdict of Catellina's death (X.4); (on lovesickness) the young physician who discovers the real cause of the sickness experienced by the man in love with Giannotta, and whose wisdom lies precisely in admitting his inability to provide any cure for it (II.8), as well as those doctors who try in vain to treat Lisa (X.7); (on ordinary illnesses) Gilletta's success in treating the King of France's fistula, where many court physicians had failed (III.9), and the brigand Ghino di Tacco, who treats the Abbot of Cluny's stomach ache (X.2). The few physicians who successfully exercise their art pay the consequence: the doctor of Salerno, whose skill is turned against him by his cheating wife's cunning (IV.10), and the one serving the necromancer in Torello's novella (X.9). The only physician who receives a positive portrayal in the *Decameron* is Master Alberto (I.10), but his professional qualification is chiefly intended to support Boccaccio's defence of the naturalness of love in old age.

45 On literature as a remedium, see Olson, *Literature as Recreation*; Ciavolella, "La tradizione della *aegritudo amoris*"; and Tonelli, *Fisiologia*, esp. 206–21. For an analysis of the *brigata*'s lifestyle in the light of medical-hygienic handbooks of the period, see Robin, "Una modalità di conservazione della vita." Boccaccio's views of medicine may also have been influenced by the milieu of Naples, where the institutional organization of the *studia*, having established the subordination of this discipline to theology, also upheld its moral function; see Robert, "Médicine et théologie."

As both a rewriting of several medieval narrative topoi and as a pamphlet which plays a part in a broad cultural debate about medicine and poetry, a debate that lies at the very heart of the intellectual exchange between Boccaccio and Petrarch, *Decameron* VIII.9 reminds us of something we should not forget: in literary terms, writing *beffe* is serious business.

The Tale of Salabaetto and Iancofiore (VIII.10)

ROBERTA MOROSINI

Set in the port cities of Palermo and Naples, mentioning as well the ports of Salerno, Messina, Pisa, Constantinople, and Monaco, and referring to goods from Cyprus and the Western Mediterranean, the story of Salabaetto and Iancofiore told in *Decameron* VIII.10 is structured around the connectivity of the commercial circuits of the Mediterranean Sea.[1] As the story reveals, such connectivity is not simply a matter of geography and maritime routes; it also is manifest in the material, social, and cultural relations regulating the activities of inhabitants and visitors in Mediterranean port cities. Where many other tales in the *Decameron* depict characters in the act of boarding ships, crossing water, and encountering storms and shipwrecks, *Decameron* VIII.10 never actually shows its characters on the sea. Instead, the Mediterranean shapes the novella's form and content. The sea links distant places together and enables the personal interactions upon which the exchanges of commerce, and also the plot of the novella, rely. The sea structures the narrative space of *Decameron* VIII.10: the doubled pattern of the novella, with its *beffa* and counter-*beffa*, maps onto a back-and-forth rhythm of the protagonist's two arrivals and departures at the port of Palermo, invoking the rhythmic movements of the Mediterranean's tides and trading seasons. Furthermore, in *Decameron* VIII.10, many things, events, and people traditionally associated with the sea now appear as characteristics of life in the city, effecting a literary transposition of features of the

1 Many of the arguments in this essay, especially those concerning the "connectivity" of the Mediterranean and the comparison of *Decameron* VIII.10 to its analogues, are explored further in Morosini, "The Merchant and the Siren." I would like to thank William Robins and Jeff Espie for proposing some of the lines of argumentation that I have followed in both pieces, and for allowing me to use some of their felicitous phrasing.

sea into features of the land. Throughout the novella, the sea governs the tale's plot, setting, and characters as a powerful absent-presence.

The Opening *Beffa*: The Dogana, the Baths, and the House of Iancofiore

The plot of *Decameron* VIII.10 opens with the arrival in Palermo of Niccolò da Cignano, a young Florentine merchant known colloquially as Salabaetto. He has been sent there by the Compagnia Scali with a consignment of fabric, worth about five hundred florins, left over from the fair at Salerno.The Florentine family of the Scali existed historically, and enjoyed special trading privileges in Angevin territories in Naples and Sicily until they went bankrupt in 1326 (Borsari, *Una compagnia di Calimala*; Fryde, "The Bankruptcy of the Scali"; Petralia, "Sicilia e Mediterraneo nel Trecento"). Salabaetto is directed to Palermo because the Sicilian city had a major *dogana*, a bonded warehouse where the foreign merchants brought their merchandise.

Dioneo, who narrates VIII.10, begins his tale by first describing the activities taking place at these warehouses in *terre marine*: "Soleva essere, e forse che ancora oggi è, una usanza in tutte le terre marine che hanno porto così fatta, che tutti i mercatanti che in quelle con mercatantie capitano, faccendole scaricare, tutte in un fondaco, il quale in molti luoghi è chiamato dogana, tenuta per lo comune o per lo signor della terra, le portano" [In all the maritime cities that have ports, it used to be the custom – and perhaps it still is today – for any merchant arriving there with his goods to unload them and have them transported to a warehouse, which in many places is called the customs house [*dogana*] and is maintained either by the commune or by the local ruler (VIII.10.4)].[2] The following description of the handling of goods is our earliest recorded account, based no doubt upon Boccaccio's personal experience, of the workings of a bonded warehouse (Rea, "Boccaccio a Napoli," 261). *Dogana*s tended to be vast complexes comprising hostelries and warehouse facilities for merchants arriving from many different economic regions (Constable, *Housing the Stranger*). A feature of the city on terra firma, the *dogana* of Palermo was a crucial hub in the Mediterranean network of trading and exchange, a node, on land, of the connections and movements that extended far away in all directions across the sea.

2 The text of the *Decameron* is cited from the 2013 edition by Quondam, Fiorilla, and Alfano. English translations are from Rebhorn's translation.

Cicero had characterized port cities as possessing "a certain corruption and degeneration of morals; for they receive a mixture of strange languages and customs, and import foreign ways as well as foreign merchandise."[3] For Boccaccio, such a mixture of languages and customs is signified in part by reminders of the presence of the Orient. The Italian word *dogana* is Arabic in origin, as is the name *Salabaetto* (Franceschini, "'Salabaetto'"). While these and other Arabic-derived words are "elements that lend an exotic flavor to the narrative" (Boccaccio, *Decameron*, trans. McWilliam, 857n1), they also add to the apparent realism of Boccacio's detailed description of the *dogana*. Similarly realistic is the attention to the role played by written records in mercantile transactions at the warehouse: when he arrives in Palermo, Salabaetto hands over an invoice, a written description of the cargo, to the customs officers, and after he puts the goods in the storeroom, the officers record in their accounting books all the details of his merchandise – proof, Boccaccio notes, that the goods belong to that merchant.

Medieval seaports were sites of inevitable tension between local inhabitants and foreign merchants, and the *dogana* was a forum where that tension could be formalized, contained, and negotiated. The *dogana*, as Boccaccio notes, is maintained by the commune or by the ruler of the state. Its rules, while based on shared mercantile customs, are ultimately local, communal rules. The local brokers were part of a restricted network of insiders; indeed, it is such customs-house accomplices who inform Iancofiore of the arrival of Salabaetto's goods and later of their successful sale. Both Salabaetto and Iancofiore belong to a world of exchanges across the Mediterranean Sea. Salabaetto is a "mercatante forestiere" [a foreign merchant (VIII.10.8)], connected to other ports. The perpetrators of deception upon him, Iancofiore and the brokers, exhibit the survival modality distinctive of the local inhabitants of a maritime city who live off their encounters with foreign traders.

Iancofiore, the young Sicilian lady who tricks Salabaetto, is described as belonging to a class of women who hang around the *dogana*, making a living by tricking foreign merchants. She bears many similarities to Fiordaliso, the Neapolitan prostitute of *Decameron* II.5; however, Iancofiore has a deep sense of commercial knowledge and guile: she even loans money at usurious rates of interest. Since the merchants arriving in Palermo are generally greedy, she can easily trick them, especially

3 "Est autem maritimis urbibus etiam quaedam corruptela ac demutatio morum; admiscentur enim novis sermonibus ac disciplinis et inportantur non merces solum adventiciae, sed etiam mores" (Cicero, *On the Republic* 2.1.4, p. 117).

by enticing them with amorous favours. As soon as Salabaetto hands his bill of lading to the officers of the *dogana*, puts his goods in storage, and, without showing any eagerness to dispose of them, heads out to see what amusements the city can offer, Iancofiore receives the brokers' insider information and directs her attention toward seducing this foreign merchant and exploiting him.

The novella here emphasizes the importance of the gaze. Salabaetto, described as "bianco, biondo e leggiadro molto e standogli ben la vita" [a good-looking man, with a fair complexion, blond hair, and an elegant figure (VIII.10.10)], looks at himself narcissistically. Noticing that he cares more about his own self-image than about the goods entrusted to him, Iancofiore sees that this man's self-regard is his weak spot, the key to tricking him. She casts sensual glances at him, and Salabaetto's reaction is exactly what she had expected:

> di che egli accorgendosi, estimando che ella fosse una gran donna, s'avvisò che per la sua bellezza le piacesse e pensossi di volere molto cautamente menar questo amore; e senza dirne cosa alcuna a persona incominciò a far le passate dinanzi alla casa di costei. La quale accortasene, poi che alquanti dì l'ebbe bene con gli occhi acceso, mostrando ella di consumarsi per lui, segretamente gli mandò una sua femina. (VIII.10.10–11)
>
> [He noticed what she was doing, and assuming her to be some great lady who was taken with his good looks, he thought that if he had an affair with her, he would have to be extremely cautious in managing it. Consequently, without uttering a word on the subject to anyone, he began walking back and forth in front of her house, where she soon spotted him, and after she had spent several days inflaming his passion by casting glances in his direction and making it seem as though she were languishing away for him, she secretly sent one of her maidservants to him.]

Looking at objects to gauge their worth is an important skill for merchants, and in this set of exchanges Iancofiore shows her scheming powers of observation and display: she will set out objects for Salabaetto to gaze upon, treating him like a potential customer. Salabaetto's amorous gaze, by contrast, remains on the surface of things.

Iancofiore instructs him to meet her at the *bagno* (public baths along the lines of an Arabic *hammam*), which Iancofiore has reserved for her own use. There she entices Salabaetto with a rich display of sensory objects, trapping him through sights, tastes, and smells. His first sight there is of two slave girls carrying a luxurious cotton mattress ("un materasso di bambagia bello e grande in capo") and baskets of accoutrements into one of the rooms of the bathhouse, where they lay out a bed equipped with silk-edged sheets, sumptuous pillows, and "una coltre di bucherame cipriana bianchissima" [a coverlet of the whitest Cyprian linen (VIII.10.14)]. As the girls bathe, Iancofiore arrives with two more slave girls. Soon Iancofiore and Salabaetto enter into the bath, where Iancofiore washes Salabaetto with perfumed soap and in turn is washed by her servants. Wrapped in scented sheets, the two lovers are carried to the bed, sprinkled with fragrant waters, and served refreshments until they are left alone to enjoy the fruits of love.

> E tratti del paniere oricanni d'ariento bellissimi e pieni qual d'acqua rosa, qual d'acqua di fior d'aranci, qual d'acqua di fiori di gelsomino e qual d'acqua nanfa, tutti costoro di queste acque spruzzarono; e appresso tirate fuori scatole di confetti e preziosissimi vini alquanto si confortarono. A Salabaetto pareva essere in Paradiso. (VIII.10.18–19)

> [Beautiful little vials of silver were then taken from the basket, some filled with rose water, others with waters of orange blossoms and jasmine flowers, and yet others with oil of oranges, which the slave-girls sprinkled all over them. Finally, boxes of sweets and the most precious wines were produced, with which the couple refreshed themselves. Salabaetto was convinced he was in Paradise.]

Iancofiore's naked slave girls, the precious bedding, the scented sheets, the perfumed waters, create a perfect stage to deceive Salabaetto. At the same time, these exotic, orientalist elements underscore the tension between Iancofiore's Palermitan customs and the Tuscan upbringing of Salabaetto: "toscano acanino" [my darling Tuscan (VIII.10.15)], she calls him.[4]

This bath is a privileged space in *Decameron* VIII.10, and it is worth considering how it constitutes a condensation and transmutation of the Mediterranean setting of the tale. The Mediterranean Sea has brought Salabaetto and Iancofiore together, and now in this refuge of the bathhouse very different manifestations of water bring them even closer. The risky expanse of the sea has been transposed into, and replaced by, the tranquil *bagno* where the lovers wash, and by the waters with

4 This bath scene represents an orientalist scene of temptation, one that medieval writers themselves could not resist. Akin to the descriptions of paradise by Marco Polo and in the *Book of the Ladder of Muhammad*, Boccaccio's detailed portrayal of the bath offers a distortion of the Islamic conception of paradise.

which they are sprinkled: the phials of "acque odoriere" [sweet-scented waters (VIII.10.21)] contrast decidedly with the casks "piene di acqua marina" [filled with sea water (VIII.10.66)] which figure at the end of the tale. Even the Cyprian linen, like the Cyprian birds (a kind of decorative incense) soon to be seen in Iancofiore's house, invoke at one and the same time the maritime networks for exchanging luxury goods across the Mediterranean, and the oceanic origins of the goddess of love, Cyprian Venus, born in the sea off the coast of Cyprus.[5]

As Salabaetto and Iancofiore move from the public bath to her private house, the setting continues to present an accumulation of desirable objects enrapturing all senses: rich clothes, splendid decorations, and magnificent food. In her bedroom, "sentì quivi maraviglioso odore di legno aloè e d'uccelletti cipriani, vide il letto ricchissimo e molte belle robe su per le stanghe. Le quali cose, tutte insieme e ciascuna per sé, gli fecero stimare costei dovere essere una grande e ricca donna" [He smelled the wonderful fragrance of aloeswood and Cyprian birds, and looking around, observed the luxurious bed she had as well as the multitude of beautiful gowns that were hanging on pegs. All of these things, both taken together and considered individually, convinced him that she had to be a great lady with a substantial fortune (VIII.10.24)]. With this accumulation of sensuous objects, Iancofiore's house becomes a productive space: she displays herself and her goods here in order to turn a profit as merchants do, conjuring credit and trust with the ultimate aim of obtaining Salabaetto's wealth (Morosini, "From the Garden to the Liquid City"). Meanwhile, in these highly adorned spaces, Salabaetto falls into idleness, which seems to represent his professional failure as an astute merchant.

Over the next few days, as Salabaetto goes back and forth between the entrepôt of the *dogana* and the comfort of Iancofiore's house, he becomes more ensnared in her wiles, even as he manages to dispose of his merchandise: "E usando una volta e altra con costei senza costargli cosa del mondo e ognora più invescandosi, avenne che egli vendé i panni suoi a contanti e guadagnonne bene. Il che la buona donna non da lui ma da altrui sentì incontanente" [And as he continued to spend time with her on a regular basis, all at no cost whatsoever to himself, he became increasingly caught up in her snares. Eventually, he happened to sell his cloth for ready cash, making a tidy profit on the deal, and the good lady was immediately informed about it, though by someone

5 On this origin story for Venus, see Boccaccio, *Genealogie deorum gentilium* 3.23.1–3, ed. Zaccaria, pp. 350–3.

else, not by Salabaetto himself (VIII.10.26–7)]. The apparently money-free zone of amorous pleasure seems to him to have nothing to do with the profit-driven world of trade. But now that he has sold his woollens for a profit, Iancofiore is ready to reap a return on her investment of display. Having enkindled his passion and gained his trust, she can now execute her trick.

Iancofiore's culminating act of deception, also performed at her house, relies less on the display of objects than on the fictions of speech. In tears, she tells Salabaetto the news that her brother, in serious trouble in Messina, needs a thousand florins to be sent within a week or his head will be cut off. There isn't enough time, she says, to collect a large debt owed to her or to arrange the sale of any family estates. Moved by her story, Salabaetto offers to help: as luck would have it, he has sold his woollens the previous day, and is able to lend her five hundred florins. Eager to help, he takes her spoken promise to pay him back as a sufficient bond, and brings her the money the next day: "per mostrarsi bene liberalissimo suo servidore, senza alcuna richesta di lei aspettare, le portò cinquecento be' fiorin d'oro, li quali ella ridendo col cuore e piagnendo con gli occhi prese, attenendosene Salabaetto alla sua semplice promessione" [in order to prove how generous and devoted he was, he brought her five hundred fine gold florins without waiting to be asked for them. She accepted his money with tears in her eyes – and laughter in her heart – while he contented himself with nothing more than the simple promise she made to repay it (VIII.10.37)].

Time passes, and Iancofiore begins to invent excuses not to see him. As more time passes and he is not repaid, Salabaetto realizes that he is the victim of a confidence trick. He realizes that he has no claim on the loan, as nothing about it was ever written. He blames both the "arte della malvagia femina" [the wicked woman's cleverness] and his own "poco senno" [lack of good sense] and "bestialità" [stupidity]:

> Laonde, avvedendosi Salabaetto dell'arte della malvagia femina e del suo poco senno e conoscendo che di lei niuna cosa più che le si piacesse di questo poteva dire, sì come colui che di ciò non aveva né scritta né testimonio, e vergognandosi di ramaricarsene con alcuno, sì perché n'era stato fatto avveduto dinanzi e sì per le beffe le quali meritamente della sua bestialità n'aspettava, dolente oltre modo seco medesimo la sua sciocchezza piagnea. (VIII.10.40)

> [Having finally come to see the wicked woman's cleverness as well as his own lack of good sense, Salabaetto was exceedingly distressed and wept inwardly over his folly. There was nothing he could say against

> her, however, unless she were willing to confirm it, for he had no written evidence of their arrangement, nor had there been any witnesses to it. Moreover, he was ashamed to go and complain about her to anyone, not just because he had been warned about her beforehand, but because of the well-deserved ridicule he expected to be exposed to because of his stupidity [*bestialità*].]

When his principals send letters asking him to change the money and forward it to them, Salabaetto, fearing that his lapse will become known if he remains longer in Palermo, decides to leave for Naples.

Analogues and Intertexts

This moment when Salabaetto leaves Palermo for Naples concludes the first half of *Decameron* VIII.10, during which the *beffa* played by Iancofiore upon Salabaetto has been recounted. At this point the novella switches gears to begin its second half, the story of the counter-*beffa* that Salabaetto will play at the expense of Iancofiore, devised and set in motion during his brief interlude in Naples. Before discussing that latter portion of the novella, I will briefly turn aside from the action in order to comment on the main differences that set Boccaccio's handling of this narrative material apart from its closest analogues. Many of these differences, I will argue, are to be understood in light of Boccaccio's interest in the connectivity of the Mediterranean, and, as I will also show, some of Boccaccio's most notable additions are modelled upon the classical accounts of Ulysses, Circe, and the Sirens, ancient legends that highlight the Mediterranean as a mythic arena of long-distance travel and as a seascape of danger, luck, and ingenuity.

Boccaccio fashions *Decameron* VIII.10 out of a traditional plot and counter-plot that tells how a man journeying abroad deposits a sum of money with a local businessman, but the businessman does not return the deposit; then, following the advice of a local woman, the traveller fools the greedy businessman into thinking that he can obtain even more money if he returns the first sum, and as a consequence dupes the businessman. The closest analogues are the *Exemplum de decem cofris* (*The Story of Ten Chests*) found in the *Disciplina clericalis* by Petrus Alfonsi (1062–1140), and a short anecdote by Jacopo da Cessole (1288–1322) in his *Ludus schacorum* (*Book of the Game of Chess*) in a section dedicated to money-changers.[6] Their retellings or versions close to them

6 A critical edition of Jacopo da Cessole's *Ludus schacorum* is lacking; see the digitized incunable (1474) in the Koninklijke Bibliotheek, Nationale bibliotheek van Nederland (Jacopo da Cessole, *Solatium ludi schachorum*). For this study I have also consulted the

likely provided narrative "source" material that Boccaccio adapted to his purposes.

The polarization of foreign/local which is so essential to the unfolding of Boccaccio's novella is already found in these analogues. In Alfonsi's exemplum, an unnamed Muslim leaves Spain and stops in Egypt on his way to Mecca, while in da Cessole's anecdote a merchant travels abroad for business in some unspecified land. Da Cessole's retelling, in which Alfonsi's pilgrim has become a merchant, introduces a more mercantile context, and acknowledges the importance of written records for commercial transactions, for his central character makes the same mistake that Salabaetto makes in the *Decameron* by not keeping a written record of the money he had lent.

The *Decameron*'s detailed representation of space allows for geographically real places to become cultural signifiers. Boccaccio's depiction of the Palermo *dogana* is one of the greatest innovations brought about in his retelling of the plot, and is crucial to his success in writing a story of mercantile ethics and commercial trades in the Mediterranean (Barsella, "Ethics and Theology"). The representational style of the *Decameron* also allows for the characters to be presented as realistically occupying particular spaces. This is markedly different from the fixed personae and the emblematic settings found in the analogues. Boccaccio also makes significant changes to the gender of the story's characters. In Alfonsi's and da Cessole's versions, the wicked merchant who refuses to return the money is a local man of business, while Boccaccio assigns this act of deception to a woman, Iancofiore. Moreover, in both of these analogues, it is an old lady who comes up with the idea of preparing beautifully decorated coffers to fool the eyes of the greedy businessman; in the *Decameron*, the male Pietro dello Canigiano replaces the figure of the old woman.

The relocation of the setting to the port city of Palermo and the changes in gender help connect *Decameron* VIII.10 with a body of mythology set around the Mediterranean Sea and the Italian peninsula. In reworking and amplifying his inherited narrative material, Boccaccio harnesses a literary tradition descending ultimately from Homer's *Odyssey*, casting Iancofiore as a Siren and also as a modern Circe depriving men of their money, reason, and humanity.

Sirens charm sailors and merchants with illusory paradises of desirable bodies and charms. Their enticing sweetness darkens the vigilance

---

medieval Italian translation (Jacopo da Cessole, *Volgarizzamento del libro de'costumi*). A nearly identical version of this particular story appears in the *Gesta Romanorum* (Tale 118, *De fallacio et dolo*).

of human reason, as Boccaccio knew from numerous *auctoritates*. Iancofiore's sweetness, her "dolcitudine" (VIII.10.43), recalls not only the "Sirenes usque in exitium dulces" [Sirens who are sweet to the point of death] that Boethius mentions in the opening of the *Consolation of Philosophy* (1.1.39–41, pp. 134–5), but also the "dolce serena" (sweet Siren) encountered by Dante in purgatory: "cominciava a cantar sì, che con pena / da lei avrei mio intento rivolto" (she started singing in a way that would / have made it hard for me to turn aside [*Purg*. 19.17–18]).[7] As the commentary to the *Commedia* by Pietro di Dante Alighieri explains: "She is called a Siren from *syren* in Greek, which means 'to attract' [*attrahere*] ... This Siren, i.e. attraction, in the middle of the sea, i.e. in the midst of this world, with her song, i.e. with her false pleasure, causes us to become submerged in the three vices of gluttony, lust, and avarice, unless, as the poem says, an honest woman arrives, i.e. our intellectual virtue."[8]

The similarity of Iancofiore, a Sicilian woman, to the Sirens is partly geographical: the rocky islands where they lived were identified with various locations along the south Italian and Sicilian coasts. In the *Genealogie deorum gentilium*, Boccaccio locates their home off Sicily's Cape Pelorus, now Punta del Faro (7.20). Moreover, there and in his *Rime* he repeats the tradition that Naples's Greek name, Parthenope, derives from a Siren who was buried there: "dove fu Partenopè sepolta, / ov' ancor le sirene uson cantare" [where Partenopè was buried, and where the Sirens still perform their songs (*Rime*, 48.5–6)].[9] The similarity is also set up etymologically in the opening rubric to the tale: "Una ciciliana maestrevolmente toglie a un mercantante ciò che in Palermo ha portato" [A Sicilian lady masterfully relieves [*toglie*] a merchant of the goods he has brought to Palermo (VIII.10.1)]. Boccaccio uses a form of the verb *torre* (to take away), which is comparable to what *syren* is said to mean by Pietro di Dante, *attrahere*, meaning "to drag by force," "pull," or "attract," and so to take away man's awareness of himself. The *Ottimo commento* notes that the sirens "maliziosamente sodduceano

---

7 Quotations and translations from Dante's *Commedia* are from Dante Alighieri, *The Divine Comedy*, translated by Robert and Jean Hollander.

8 "Ideo dicitur Sirena a sirin graece, quod latine est *attrahere*; quae Sirena, idest attractio praefata, in medio mari, idest in medio hujus saeculi, suo cantu, idest sua fallaci delectatione, nos facit submergi in dictis tribus vitiis, nisi veniat domna honesta, de qua hic dicitur, idest, intellectualis nostra virtus" (Alighieri, *Petri Allegherii ... Commentarium, ad Purg*.19.17–18).

9 See also *Rime* 36.1–3: "Scrivon alcun Partenopè, sirena / ornata di bellezze e piena d'arte, / aver sua stanza eletta in questa parte."

li uomini, e *tolto loro l'avere*, li conduceano a morte perché erano meretrici" [would maliciously seduce the men, and once they had taken all their possessions would kill them, because they were prostitutes (*Ottimo commento*, ad *Purg*. 19.16–24, emphasis added).

When Salabaetto was charmed by Iancofiore, his amorous passions, we are told, had taken away ("tolto") his good sense: "l'amorose fiamme avevano gran parte del debito conoscimento tolto" (VIII.10.32). The erotic attractions of Iancofiore, especially when appearing with four slave girls in the bath, recall the Sirens and their allegorical significance as seducers of men.

Iancofiore is not only a siren, she is also a modern Circe, a treacherous woman living off the coast of Italy who transforms men into beasts.[10] Such a conflation of the Sirens and Circe was common. Indeed, the Siren from Dante's *Purgatorio* was often identified with Circe, as the *Ottimo commento* confirms:

> Al tempo, che Ulisses si dilettò cercare il mondo … fu riceuto per una delle sopradette Sirene, chiamata Circe, incantatrice. Sì che altro non vuole dire la detta femina, se none: io sono donna di dilettazione libidinosa circa le temporali delettazioni, la quale compiaccio sì a chi con meco s' ausa, che non sanza briga si partono da me. (*Ottimo commento*, ad *Purg*. 19.16–24)
>
> [When Ulysses took delight in touring the world … he was received by one of these Sirens, named Circe, an enchantress. Accordingly, the woman appearing here indicates nothing other than this: "I am the lady of lustful enjoyment in worldly pleasures, and I give such delight to those who indulge in me that they cannot leave me without a struggle."]

When Boccaccio describes Circe in his *De mulieribus claris*, he notes that she is famous, singularly beautiful, knowledgeable about herbs, and very prudent. Following tradition, he locates her island at Monte Circeo, a promontory about 150 kilometres north of Naples, a key landmark on the sea route between Rome and Naples. He relates how sailors arrive at her island, and she, by singing spells and offering drugged potions, deprives them of their reason.

> First of all, they say that any sailors who landed on purpose or were driven by storms onto the shore of the promontory, formerly an island, were changed into various kinds of animals through Circe's enchantments

10 On Boccaccio's Circe, see also Morosini, *Il mare salato*.

> or poisonous potions. It is reported that the companions of Ulysses during his wanderings were among those who suffered such a fate, but he himself was saved thanks to Mercury's advice.[11]

Boccaccio then expands on the underlying sense of this story:

> In some versions, this woman, who lived not far from the Campanian city of Gaeta, was forceful and eloquent but not overly concerned with keeping her chastity untarnished so long as she got something she wanted. With her wiles and charming words not only did she entice many who reached her shore to join in her wantonness: some she pushed into robbery and piracy; others she induced with her tricks to cast all honor aside and take up commerce and trading; many she made arrogant because they loved her inordinately. We would thus be right in believing that the men changed into the kinds of wild beasts appropriate to their misdeeds were those who had lost their human reason through this unfortunate woman's influence.[12]

In his allegorical interpretation of the story, he affirms that there are many Circes everywhere:

> If we consider human behavior, we see plainly enough from this instance that there are many Circes everywhere, and many more men whose lust and vice change them into beasts. Ulysses, however, equipped in advance with Mercury's counsel, obviously signifies the wise man who cannot be ensnared by fawning tricksters.[13]

---

11 "Volunt igitur ante alia quoscunque nautas, seu ex proposito, seu tempestatis inpulsu, ad dicti montis, olim insule, litora applicantes, huius artibus cantatis carminibus, seu infectis veneno poculis, in feras diversarum specierum fuisse conversos; et hos inter vagi Ulixis fuisse sotios, eo, Mercurii mediante consilio, servato" (Boccaccio, *Famous Women* 38.3, pp. 150–1).

12 "Sunt qui dicant hanc feminam haud longe a Caieta, Campanie oppido, potentissimam fuisse viribus et sermone, nec magni facientem, dummodo aliquid consequeretur optatum, a nota illesam servasse pudicitiam; et sic multos ex applicantibus litori suo blanditiis et ornatu sermonis non solum in suas illecebras traxisse, verum alios in rapinam et pyrraticam inpulisse, nonnullos, omni honestate postposita, ad exercenda negotia et mercimonia dolis incitasse, et plures ob sui singularem dilectionem in superbiam extulisse. Et sic hi, quibus infauste mulieris opera humana subtracta videbatur ratio, eos ab eadem in sui facinoris feras merito crederetur fuisse conversos" (Boccaccio, *Famous Women* 38.5, pp. 152–3). Circe is also portrayed in Boccaccio, *Genealogie deorum gentilium* 4.14.

13 "Ex quibus satis comprehendere possumus, hominum mulierumque conspectis moribus, multas ubique Cyrces esse et longe plures homines lascivia et crimine

When Boccaccio writes that "there are many Circes everywhere, and many more men whose lust and vice change them into beasts," he could just as well be describing the situation of *Decameron* VIII.10. Iancofiore's skill with words and the display of objects, including the enticing food and drink served to Salabaetto, a skill described as the "arte della malvagia femina," align her with Circe. Salabaetto is seduced to the point of lamenting that he has acted like a beast, "sua bestialità" (VIII.10.40).

Whereas the seductive voices and the sirens lured sailors at sea into shipwreck, Iancofiore carries out her deception entirely on land, like Circe, enchanting merchants with her desirable body, appealing to their desire and greed. The transformation enacts in narrative the allegorical interpretations proposed by Christian exegetes. For example, Isidore of Seville wrote that although the Greeks imagined the sirens as women whose singing decoyed sailors to shipwreck, they were really prostitutes who led travellers into poverty. They are said to have wings and claws because Love flies and wounds, and they stay in the waves because a wave created Venus (*Etymologiae* 11.3.30; see also Buti, *Commento*, ad *Purg.* 19.16–33). As Salabaetto is deprived of his reason by his own lust and superficiality, Iancofiore is a fresh take on Circe, who could transform any man into a beast.

Salabaetto, in this manner, is a modern Ulysses. He is a seafarer, putting in at ports around the Mediterranean, narrowly escaping the dangers of modern-day Sirens and Circes. His encounter with Iancofiore has left him lamenting his own *bestialità*. Like sailors who listen to the Sirens, he has been taken in by *dolcitudine* (sweetness), as his friend tells him: "troppi denari a un tratto hai spesi in dolcitudine" [You've squandered entirely too much money at one stroke in easy living (VIII.10.43)]. The moral to be drawn from the Circe and Siren episodes in the story of Ulysses, of course, is that it is proper for a wise man to free himself from such seductions. After staying with Circe for a period of time, Ulysses, thanks to the advice of Mercury, eventually succeeds in freeing himself and his men from her snares, and he leaves the island "full of wisdom" [et ab ea plenum consilii discessisse (Boccaccio, *Famous Women* 38.4, pp. 150–3)]. Salabaetto is not at first as wise as Ulysses, until he becomes aware of Iancofiore's guile and his own lack of reason. Thanks to his Mercury, Pietro dello Canigiano (a figure who shares with the

suo versos in beluas. Ulixes autem, Mercurii consilio predoctus, prudentem virum satis evidenter ostendit, quem adulantium nequeunt laqueare decipule, quin imo et documentis suis laqueatos persepe solvit a vinculo" (Boccaccio, *Famous Women* 38.6, pp. 152–3).

Roman god an expertise in the arts of commerce and finance), Salabaetto does not remain a victim, and eventually escapes triumphantly from Iancofiore's island and from the enticements of her seductions.

With Boccaccio's repurposing of the story of Ulysses and Circe and the Sirens, we see again how the sea silently governs *Decameron* VIII.10. The encounter of Salabaetto and Iancofiore is modelled to a large extent on the encounter of Ulysses and Circe, evoking archetypes of sea-wandering and marine dangers. As Francesco da Buti's commentary on Dante puts it with respect to Ulysses and the Sirens, "ogni mondano è marinaio" [every worldly human is a sailor (*Commento*, ad *Purg*. 19.16–33)]. The wandering of Ulysses is condensed into a dramatic encounter between a contemporary Florentine man and Palermitan woman, and the seascape of the Mediterranean is transposed into fixed spaces – a warehouse, a street, a bath, and a palace – within the urban fabric of Palermo.

The Counter-*Beffa*: Salabaetto's Return to Palermo

The counter-*beffa* narrated in the second half of *Decameron* VIII.10 is set in motion when Salabetto, ashamed at having been fooled, arrives in Naples and describes his experiences in Palermo to his good friend there, fellow Florentine Pietro dello Canigiano, "trasorier di madama la 'mperatrice di Constantinopoli, uomo di grande intelletto e di sottile ingegno" [a man of great intellect and supple wit, who was treasurer to Her Highness the Empress of Constantinople (VIII.10.42)]. A historical figure, Pietro Canigiani was an acquaintance of Boccaccio's, and did serve a spell as treasurer to Catherine of Valois-Courtenay (1301–46), Empress of Constantinople, the sister-in-law of King Robert of Anjou of Naples (Mallett, "Canigiani, Piero"; Budini Gattai, "La percezione del mondo greco"). Pietro, hearing of Salabaetto's mishaps, criticizes the young man's bad personal and professional conduct and his disloyalty toward his masters. However, Pietro also elaborates a plan to trick Iancofiore and recover Salabaetto's money, although readers are not informed of its details until Salabaetto puts the plan into effect.

Salabaetto returns to Palermo as a private vendor. The setting in Palermo is the same, as are the network of informants and the processes of accountability at the *dogana*. However, Salabaetto himself has changed in the time between his earlier departure from Palermo and his return there from Naples, in keeping with the rhythm of movement at sea that is so important for structuring this tale. The sequence of events that unfolds is similar to what befell during his first sojourn in Palermo. After he stores his goods in the *dogana*, Iancofiore is quickly informed of their value, said to be worth at least two thousand florins, and of merchandise worth more than three thousand that is yet to come "di Ponente" [from the West (VIII.10.48)]. She decides she can repay Salabaetto his five hundred florins as a gambit for getting hold of the much larger sum of five thousand, and asks to see him.

At this point, the narrator Dioneo notes that Salabaetto has now "divenuto malizioso" [grown cunning (VIII.10.46)]. The past participle *divenuto* (become) acknowledges the change in Salabaetto since his last visit to Palermo. Now it is Salabaetto who employs a persuasive rhetoric, peppered with references to his wonderful business prospects, saying that he is even thinking of starting his own business in Palermo. And this time it is Iancofiore who is taken in.

Having received his money back from Iancofiore, Salabaetto moves to the next stage in his trick. He tells her that pirates have captured the ship that was bringing his additional merchandise to Sicily and are demanding a thousand florins as his share of the ransom. If he does not pay, his merchandise will go straight to Monaco, a known haven of pirates. This sum is too large for him to raise, for it is a bad time to sell his goods, subject as they are to the rhythms of Mediterranean trading patterns, and as a foreigner he is not well enough known to get credit with any locals: "E se io vorrò al presente vendere la mercatantia la quale ho qui, per ciò che non è tempo, appena che io abbia delle due derrate un denaio; e io non ci sono sì ancora conosciuto che io ci trovassi chi di questo mi sovenisse" [If I were to sell the goods I have on hand at the moment, I'd hardly get half price for them because it's not the right time to put them on the market, and there's nobody around here who knows me well enough yet to help me out (VIII.10.57–8)]. With this mention of *corsari* (pirates), *Decameron* VIII.10 opens up yet another semantic field associated with sea narratives. "From the Hellenistic romance through the *Tempest*, shipwreck, along with pirate attack, is the form fortune assumes in Mediterranean literature" (Kinoshita and Jacobs, "Ports of Call," 166–7). In many stories familiar to Boccaccio's audience, the attack of rapacious pirates occurred on the Mediterranean's treacherous waters, as indeed happens in other tales of the *Decameron*.[14] Here the pirates are fictive, appearing only in Salabaetto's invention and Iancofiore's imagination.

Iancofiore decides to lend him the money, arranging a loan (seemingly from a moneylender, but in fact from her own funds) with a 30 per cent interest rate. Salabaetto secures the loan by placing the merchandise

14 Such as *Decameron* II.4, II.6, II.10, V.6, and V.7.

in the *dogana* to the credit of the moneylender. Where the earlier trick at Salabaetto's expense had succeded thanks to a network of locals, this trick is made possible by Salabaetto's understanding of how he, even as a foreigner, can use those local dynamics to his own advantage: "come il dì fu venuto, ella mandò per un sensale di cui ella si confidava molto e, ragionato con lui questo fatto, gli diè mille fiorin d'oro li quali il sensale prestò a Salabaetto e fece in suo nome scrivere alla dogana ciò che Salabaetto dentro v'avea" [And so the next morning she sent for a broker who enjoyed her complete confidence, and having explained the arrangement to him, she gave him a thousand gold florins, which he, in turn, lent to Salabaetto, after having everything that Salabaetto had stored in the customshouse put under his own name (VIII.10.63)]. Salabaetto's ruse likewise depends upon satsifying her prudent need for written documentation: "e fattesi loro scritte e contrascritte insieme e in concordia rimasi, attesero a' loro altri fatti" [once they had signed and countersigned a number of receipts for one another, and everything was concluded between them, they both went off to attend to other business (VIII.10.63)].

Now in possession of a thousand florins on top of the five hundred he has recovered, Salabaetto sails immediately back to Naples, where he celebrates his success with Pietro dello Canigiano. Finally, having pursued his livelihood on the sea, Salabaetto moves away from it, rejecting the world of ports, merchants, and Sirens: "di quindi, non volendo più mercatante essere, se ne venne a Ferrara" [he left Naples and went to Ferrara, having resolved never to be a merchant again (VIII.10.64)]. Previously making his living by moving back and forth across the water, Salabaetto finds himself at last in a landlocked home.

Back in Palermo, Iancofiore is alarmed by Salabaetto's disappearance:

> e poi che ben due mesi aspettato l'ebbe, veggendo che non veniva, fece che il sensale fece schiavare i magazzini. E primieramente tastate le botti che si credeva che piene d'olio fossero, trovò quelle esser piene d'acqua marina, avendo in ciascuna forse un baril d'olio di sopra vicino al cocchiume; poi, scogliendo le balle, tutte, fuori che due che panni erano, piene le trovò di capecchio. (VIII.10.65–6)

> [after waiting two months for him to return and still seeing no sign of him, she got the broker to force open the storerooms. First, they sounded the casks, which they thought were full of oil, and found they were filled with seawater, except for a small quantity of oil floating on top near the spouts. Then they untied the bales to discover that all except two of them, which actually contained cloth, were packed with tow.]

Tow, *capecchio*, consists of the fibres left over after combing flax or hemp, a nearly worthless off-product of textile production that was used for stuffing, including for mattresses. By being mentioned here, Salabaetto's tow serves as a *reductio ad absurdum* of the luxurious cotton mattresses of the earlier bath scene. The salt water in the oil-jars signals a similar reduction of that episode's erotic *bagno* and perfumed waters: in the oil-jars is not beautifully scented water (*acque odorifere*) but sea water (*acqua marina*). From the grand locus of commercial exchange and mercantile risk, the sea is here confined within these small containers on land. Just as the *dogana* is a feature of terra firma that functions as part of the wide connectivity of the Mediterranean Sea, so these casks of sea water in the *dogana* evoke, from a fixed spot on the land, the vast expanse of the sea upon which Salabaetto has now sailed away.

The Mediterranean as a Structuring Element of the *Beffa*

In *Decameron* VIII.10, the novella's two halves repeat the same basic pattern of events, although with inverted results (Holmes, "Trial by *Beffa*"). In both the *beffa* and the counter-*beffa*, the con game is framed by Salabaetto's arrival and departure from Palermo. The resulting *dispositio* of the novella is a back-and-forth rhythm, one that reflects the cycles of the sea, with the movement of its waves, the motion of its tides, and the seasonal rhythms of the traders, what Fernand Braudel speaks of as the "constant repetition, ever-recurring cycles" of the Mediterranean itself (*The Mediterranean*, 20).

Boccaccio has altered his sources so as to make the sea a silent presence, giving rhythmic shape to the *fabula* and defining the horizon for the tale's setting and events. The sea determines the purpose of the *dogana* as well as the charms and the dangers of Palermo as a port city, including its exotic and oriental aura. The events of the tale take place on land but evoke the sea, giving new significance to the term *terre marine* that Boccaccio uses for port cities like Palermo. At the same time, the sea governs the mythic exemplarity of the novella, which takes Ulysses's journeys across the Mediterranean, and especially his encounters with Circe and with the Sirens off the coast of southern Italy, as a narrative model.

The Mediterranean defines the cultural distance between the two major characters, one Florentine and one Sicilian, upon which the *beffa* and counter-*beffa* turn. Travelling with merchandise across the sea identifes Salabaetto as a merchant, and is the reason why he catches the eye of Iancofiore. Iancofiore herself is defined by activities only possible in a port city, as Dioneo's opening paragraphs explain. The connectivity of the sea brings Salabaetto and Iancofiore into contact, but it also separates them, with Salabaetto departing twice for Naples, first in humiliation and secondly in triumph. Salabaetto travels and crosses the sea, while Iancofiore stays in her fixed place. Her livelihood, like the existence of Circe and the Sirens, depends upon a system in which foreign merchants pass by in their sea-travels. Even the minor characters – the Florentine principals, the Palermitan brokers, the slave girls at the bath, and the pirates of Salabaetto's invention – are intrinsically related to the sea and the risks for those who cross it.[15]

The sea even becomes an instrument of the *beffa* for Salabaetto, who fills his casks with water taken from the sea. His containers are found to be filled not with stones, as is the case in the analogues, but with salt water. The opening rubric for *Decameron* VIII.10 draws attention to the rhythmic back-and-forth travel of the merchant, to the Circe-like deceitfulness of the Sicilian lady, and to this residue of water:

> Una ciciliana maestrevolmente toglie a un mercatante ciò che in Palermo ha portato; il quale, sembiante faccendo d'esservi tornato con molta più mercatantia che prima, da lei accattati denari, le lascia acqua e capecchio. (VIII.10.1)

> [A Sicilian woman masterfully relieves a merchant of the goods he has brought to Palermo, but when he later returns, pretending he has much more merchandise than before, he borrows money from her and leaves her with nothing but water and tow instead.]

The conclusion of the *beffa* and counter-*beffa* is a reminder of how deceiving the sea can be. While at one time it might bring riches, at another time it leaves just salty water.

15 See Arbel, *Intercultural Contacts in the Medieval Mediterranean*, 120–3; Heers, *Esclaves et domestiques*.

Bibliography

Manuscripts

Berlin, Staatsbibliothek Preussicher Kulturbesitz, MS Hamilton 90.
Florence, Archivio di Stato di Firenze, Arte dei Giudici e Notai 748.
Florence, Archivio di Stato di Firenze, Podestà 826.
Florence, Biblioteca Medicea Laurenziana, MS Pluteo 29.8.
Florence, Biblioteca Medicea Laurenziana, MS Pluteo 42.1.
Florence, Biblioteca Nazionale Centrale, MS Banco Rari 50.
Florence, Biblioteca Nazionale Centrale, MS Nuovi Acquisti 333.
London, British Library, MS Harley 463.
Paris, Bibliothèque nationale de France, MS Italien 482.
Paris, Bibliothèque nationale de France, MS Latin 6802.
San Marino, California, Huntington Library, MS El 26 C 9.

Primary Sources

Alfonsi, Petrus. *The Disciplina clericalis of Petrus Alphonsi*. Edited by Eberhard Hermes. Translated by P.R. Quarrie. London: Routledge & Kegan Paul, 1977.

Alighieri, Pietro. *Petri Allegherii super Dantis ipsius genitoris Comoediam Commentarium*. Edited by Vincenzo Nannucci. Florence: G. Piatti, 1845. Available online at the Dante Dartmouth Project: https://dante.dartmouth.edu.

Andreas Capellanus. *The Art of Courtly Love*. Translated by John Jay Parry. New York: Columbia University Press, 1960.

Aristotle. *Nicomachean Ethics*. Translated by Robert C. Bartlett and Susan D. Collins. Chicago: University of Chicago Press, 2011.

– *Poetics*. Translated by Richard Janko. Indianapolis: Hackett, 1987.

Arnoldus of Liège. *Alphabetum narrationum*. Edited by Elissa Brilli, from preliminary works by Colette Ribaucourt, with Jacques Berlioz and Marie Anne Polo de Beaulieu. Turnhout: Brepols, 2015.

Augustine of Hippo. *The City of God against the Pagans*. Edited and translated by R.W. Dyson. Cambridge: Cambridge University Press, 1998.

– *Enarrationes in Psalmos*. In *Patrologiae cursus completus: Series Latina*, vols 36–7.

Balbi, Giovanni. *Catholicon*. Strasbourg: Adolf Rusch, 1475.

Baldovini, Francesco. *Lamento di Cecco da Varlungo, colle note di Orazio Marrini*. Florence: Gaspero Ricci, 1817.

Boccaccio, Giovanni. *Boccaccio on Poetry*. Translated by Charles G. Osgood. 1930. Indianapolis: Bobbs-Merrill, 1956.

– *Caccia di Diana*. Edited by Vittore Branca. In *Tutte le opere opere di Giovanni Boccaccio*, vol. 1. Milan: Mondadori, 1967.

– *Corbaccio*. Edited by Giorgio Padoan. In *Tutte le opere opere di Giovanni Boccaccio*, vol. 5/2, 413–614. Milan: Mondadori, 1994.

– *Decameron*. Edited by Vittore Branca. In *Tutte le opere di Giovanni Boccaccio*, vol. 4. Milan: Mondadori, 1976.

– *Decameron*. Edited by Vittore Branca. Turin: Einaudi, 1980; 1992.

– *The Decameron*. Translated by G.H. McWilliam. 1972. 2nd ed. Harmondsworth: Penguin, 1995.

– *Decameron*. Edited by Amedeo Quondam, Maurizio Fiorilla, and Giancarlo Alfano. Milan: BUR Classici, 2013.

– *The Decameron*. Translated by Wayne A. Rebhorn. New York: Norton, 2013.

– *Decameron: Edizione critica secondo l'autografo Hamiltoniano*. Edited by Vittore Branca. Florence: Accademia della Crusca, 1976.

– *Decameron: Edizione diplomatico-interpretativa dell'autografo Hamilton 90*. Edited by Charles S. Singleton. Baltimore: Johns Hopkins University Press, 1974.

– *Decameron: Facsimile dell'autografo conservato nel Codice Hamilton 90 della Staatsbibliothek Preussischer Kulturbesitz di Berlino*. Edited by Vittore Branca. Florence: Alinari, 1975.

– *De casibus virorum illustrium*. Edited by Pier Giorgio Ricci and Vittorio Zaccaria. In *Tutte le opere opere di Giovanni Boccaccio*, vol. 9. Milan: Mondadori, 1983.

– *Famous Women*. Edited and translated by Virginia Brown. Cambridge, MA: Harvard University Press, 2001.

– *Il Filocolo*. Edited by Antonio Enzo Quaglio. In *Tutte le opere di Giovanni Boccaccio*, vol. 1. Milan: Mondadori, 1967.

– *Genealogie deorum gentilium*. Edited by Vincenzo Romano. Bari: Laterza, 1951.

– *Genealogie deorum gentilium*. Edited by Vittorio Zaccaria. In *Tutte le opere di Giovanni Boccaccio*, vols 7–8. Milan: Mondadori, 1998.

– *Ninfale Fiesolano*. Edited by Armando Balduino. In *Tutte le opere di Giovanni Boccaccio*, vol. 3, 273–421. Milan: Mondadori, 1974.

– *Novelle scelte dal Decamerone, con un'appendice delle opere minori.* Edited by Luigi Russo. Florence: Sansoni, 1954.
– *Rime.* Edited by Vittore Branca. In *Tutte le opere di Giovanni Boccaccio,* vol. 5/1. Milan: Mondadori, 1992.
– *Thirteen Most Pleasant and Delectable Questions of Love: Entitled a Disport of Diverse Noble Personnages.* Translated by H.G. 1566. Revised by Harry Carter. New York: Potter, 1974.
– *Tutte le opere di Giovanni Boccaccio.* Edited by Vittore Branca. 10 vols. Milan: Mondadori, 1964–98.
Boethius, Anicius Manlius Severinus. *The Consolation of Philosophy.* In *Theological Tractates; The Consolation of Philosophy,* edited and translated by H.F. Stewart, E.K. Rand, and S.J. Tester, 130–435. Cambridge, MA: Harvard University Press, 1973.
Buti, Franceso da. *Commento sopra la Divina Commedia di Dante Alighieri.* Edited by Crescentino Giannini. 3 vols. Pisa: Nistri, 1858–62. Available online at the Dante Dartmouth Project: https://dante.dartmouth.edu.
Caesarius of Heisterbach. *Dialogus miraculorum.* Edited by Joseph Strange. 2 vols. Cologne: Heberle, 1851–7.
Carmina Burana. Edited by Alfons Hilka and Otto Schumann. 2 vols. Heidelberg: Carl Winters, 1930–41.
Cavalca, Domenico. *Vite dei santi padri.* Edited by Carlo Delcorno. 2 vols. Florence: SISMEL, 2009.
Cecco d'Ascoli. *Acerba aetas (L'Acerba).* Edited by Marco Albertazzi. 3rd ed. Lavis: La Finestra, 2016.
Chaucer, Geoffrey. *The Riverside Chaucer.* Edited by Larry D. Benson. 3rd ed. Boston: Houghton Mifflin, 1987.
Cicero, Marcus Tullius. *De officiis.* Edited and translated by Walter Miller. Cambridge, MA: Harvard University Press, 1913.
– *De Oratore.* 2 vols. Edited and translated by Harris Rackham. Cambridge, MA: Harvard University Press, 1942.
– *On the Republic.* In *De Republica; De Legibus,* edited and translated by Clinton Walker Keyes, 1–286. Cambridge, MA: Harvard University Press, 1928.
Dante Alighieri. *Commedia: Inferno.* Edited by Giorgio Inglese. Rome: Carocci, 2007.
– *La Commedia secondo l'antica vulgata.* Edited by Giorgio Petrocchi. 4 vols. Milan: Mondadori, 1966–7. 2nd ed. Florence: Le Lettere, 1994.
– *Dante's Lyric Poetry.* Translated by Kenelm Foster and Patrick Boyde. Oxford: Oxford University Press, 1967.
– *Dante's Lyric Poetry: Poems of Youth and of the Vita Nuova.* Edited by Teodolinda Barolini. Translated by Richard Lansing. Toronto: University of Toronto Press, 2014.

– *The Divine Comedy*. Translated by Robert M. Durling. 3 vols. New York: Oxford University Press, 1996–2011.

– *The Divine Comedy*. Translated by Robert Hollander and Jean Hollander. 3 vols. New York: Doubleday, 2001–7.

– *The Divine Comedy*. Translated by Charles S. Singleton. 3 vols. Princeton: Princeton University Press, 1970.

– *Rime*. Edited by Domenico De Robertis. Florence: Edizioni del Galluzzo, 2005.

"The Debate of Phyllis and Flora." Translated by Douglas Caverly. *Allegorica* 5 (1980): 50–79.

Les débats du clerc et du chevalier dans la littérature poétique du Moyen-Age: Étude historique et littéraire suivie de l'édition critique des textes. Edited by Charles Oulmont. Paris: Champion, 1911.

Filippi, Rustico. *Sonetti satirici e giocosi*. Edited by Silvia Buzzetti Gallarati. Rome: Carocci, 2005.

Gellius, Aulus. *The Attic Nights*. Edited and translated by John C. Rolfe. 3 vols. Cambridge, MA: Harvard University Press, 1961–70.

Horace. *Ars poetica*. In *Satires, Epistles, and Ars poetica*, translated by H. Rushton Fairclough, 450–89. Cambridge, MA: Harvard University Press, 1926.

Isidore of Seville. *De differentiis verborum*. In *Patrologiae cursus completus: Series latina* 83:9–70.

– *Etymologiae*. Edited by Wallace Martin Lindsay. Oxford: Oxford University Press, 1911.

Jacobus de Voragine. *Legenda Aurea*. Edited by Giovanni Paolo Maggioni. 2 vols. 2nd ed. Florence: SISMEL, 1998.

Jacopo da Cessole. *Solatium ludi schachorum*. Utrecht: Nicolaus Ketelaer and Gerardus de Leempt, 1474. Available online at https://archive.org/details/ned-kbn-all-00001808-001.

– *Volgarizzamento del libro de'costumi e degli offizii de'nobili sopra il giuco degli scacchi*. Milan: Ferrario, 1829.

Jacques de Vitry. *The Exempla or Illustrative Stories from the Sermones vulgares of Jacques de Vitry*. Edited by Thomas Frederick Crane. 1890. New York: Franklin, 1971.

Justinian. *The Digest of Justinian*. Edited by Theodor Mommsen and Paul Kreuger. Translated by Alan Watson. Philadelphia: University of Pennsylvania Press, 1985.

– *Justinian's Institutes*. Edited by Paul Kreuger. Translated by Peter Birks and Grant McLeod. 4 vols. Ithaca: Cornell University Press, 1987.

The Key of Solomon the King (Clavicula Salomonis). Edited and translated by S. Liddell MacGregor Mathers. London: Redway, 1889.

Latini, Brunetto. *Il tesoro di Brunetto Latini volgarizzato da Bono Giamboni.* Edited by Polycarpe Chabaille. 4 vols. Bologna: Romagnoli, 1878–83.
Marie de France. *The Lais of Marie de France.* Edited and translated by Claire M. Waters. Peterborough, ON: Broadview, 2018.
Nouveau recueil complet des fabliaux. Edited by Willem Noomen and Nico van den Boogaard. 10 vols. Assen: Van Gorcum, 1983–98.
Ottimo commento della Divina Commedia. Edited by Alessandro Torri. 3 vols. Pisa: Capurro, 1827–9. Available online at the Dante Dartmouth Project: https://dante.dartmouth.edu.
Passavanti, Jacopo. *Specchio della vera penitenza.* Edited by Filippo Luigi Polidori. Florence: Le Monnier, 1863.
Patrologiae cursus completus: Series latina. Edited by Jacques-Paul Migne. 221 vols. Paris: Garnier, 1841–64. Available in electronic format, [S.l]: Chadwyck-Healey, 1996.
Petrarca, Francesco. *Invective contra medicum; Invectiva contra quendam magni status hominem sed nullius scientie aut virtutis.* Edited by Francesco Bausi. Florence: Le Lettere, 2005.
– *Invectives.* Edited by and translated by David Marsh. Cambridge, MA: Harvard University Press, 2003.
– *Lettere disperse: Varie e miscelanee.* Edited by Alessandro Pancheri. Parma: Fondazione Pietro Bembo, 1994.
– *Res seniles.* Edited and translated by Silvia Rizzo and Monica Berté. 4 vols. Florence: Le Lettere, 2006–17.
Pietro d'Abano. *Trattati di astronomia.* Edited by G. Federici Vescovini. Padua: Programma, 1992.
Pliny the Elder. *Natural History.* Edited and translated by Harris Rackham, W.H.S. Jones, and D.E. Eichholz. 10 vols. Cambridge, MA: Harvard University Press, 1938–63.
Pucci, Antonio. *La poesia popolare di Antonio Pucci.* Edited by Ferruccio Ferri. Bologna: Beltrami, 1909.
Quintilian. *Institutiones oratoriae.* Edited and translated by Donald A. Russell. 5 vols. Cambridge, MA: Harvard University Press, 2001.
Rhetorica ad Herennium. Edited and translated by Harry Caplan. Cambridge, MA: Harvard University Press, 1954.
Rimatori del Trecento. Edited by Giuseppe Corsi. Turin: UTET, 1969.
Sacchetti, Franco. *Il Trecentonovelle.* Edited by Davide Puccini. Turin: UTET, 2008.
– *Le Trecento Novelle.* Edited by Michelangelo Zaccarello. Florence: Edizioni del Galluzzo per la Fondazione Ezio Franceschini, 2014.
Sercambi, Giovanni. *Novelle.* Edited by Giovanni Sinicropi. Rev. ed. 2 vols. Florence: Le Lettere, 1995.

– *Il novelliere*. Edited by Luciano Rossi. 3 vols. Rome: Salerno, 1974.

Thomas Aquinas. *On Aristotle's Love and Friendship: Ethics, Books VIII–IX*. Translated by Pierre Conway. Providence: Providence College Press, 1951.

– *Opera omnia, iussu impensaque Leonis XIII P.M. edita*. 50 vols. Rome: Typographia Polyglotta S.C. de Propaganda Fide, 1882–1992.

– *Summa Theologica*. Translated by Fathers of the English Dominican Province. 3 vols. New York: Benzinger Brothers, 1948.

Varro, Marcus Terentius. *De lingua latina*. 2 vols. Translated by Roland G. Kent. Cambridge, MA: Harvard University Press, 1938.

Vasari, Giorgio. *Le vite: Edizioni Giuntina e Torrentiniana*. Pisa: Centro Ricerche Informatiche per i Beni Cuturali, 1994. http://vasari.sns.it/vasari/consultazione/index.html.

Villani, Giovanni. *Nuova cronica*. Edited by Giuseppe Porta. 3 vols. Parma: Guanda, 1990–1.

Virgil. *Georgics*. In *Eclogues; Georgics; Aeneid, Books 1–6*, edited and translated by H. Rushton Fairclough, revised by G.P. Goold, 97–260. Cambridge, MA: Harvard University Press, 1999.

Vita Sanctorum Barlaam eremitae et Josaphat Indiae regis, auctore sancto Joanne Damasceno, interprete Jacobo Billio Prunaeo. In *Patrologiae cursus completus: Series latina* 73:443–604.

The Vulgate Bible: Douay-Rheims Translation. 6 vols. Edited by Swift Edgar. Cambridge, MA: Harvard University Press, 2010–13.

Secondary Sources

Ahern, John. "Dioneo's Repertory: Performance and Writing in Boccaccio's *Decameron*." In *Performing Medieval Narrative*, edited by Evelyn Birge Vitz, Nancy Freeman Regalado, and Marilyn Lawrence, 41–58. Cambridge: D.S. Brewer, 2005.

Alazard, Florence. "Ahimé, ahi, o deh: Interjections and Orality in *Lamenti* during the Italian Wars." In Degl'Innocenti, Richardson, and Sbordoni, *Interactions between Orality and Writing in Early Modern Italian Culture*, 67–80.

Albanese, Gabriella. "La corrispondenza fra Petrarca e Boccaccio." In *Motivi e forme delle Familiari di Francesco Petrarca*, edited by Claudia Berra, 39–98. Bologna: Cisalpino, 2003.

Alfano, Giancarlo. "Giornata VIII: Scheda introduttiva." In Boccaccio, *Decameron*, edited by Quondam, Fiorilla, and Alfano, 1175–1204.

– *Introduzione alla lettura del Decameron di Boccaccio*. Bari: Laterza, 2014.

Allegri, Luigi. *Teatro e spettacolo nel Medioevo*. Bari: Laterza, 1988.

Almansi, Guido. "Alcune osservazioni sulla novella dello scolaro e della vedova." *Studi sul Boccaccio* 8 (1974): 137–45.

– *Il ciclo della scommessa*. Rome: Bulzoni, 1976.

– *The Writer as Liar: Narrative Technique in the Decameron*. London: Routledge & Kegan Paul, 1975.

Arbel, Benjamin, ed. *Intercultural Contacts in the Medieval Mediterranean*. Portland, OR: Cass, 1981.

Arend, Elisabeth. *Lachen und Komik in Giovanni Boccaccios Decameron*. Frankfurt: Klostermann, 2004.

Armstrong, Guyda, Rhiannon Daniels, and Stephen J. Milner. "Boccaccio as a Cultural Mediator." In Armstrong, Daniels, and Milner, *Cambridge Companion to Boccaccio*, 3–19.

Armstrong, Guyda, Rhiannon Daniels, and Stephen J. Milner, eds. *The Cambridge Companion to Boccaccio*. Cambridge: Cambridge University Press, 2015.

Armstrong, Lawrin, and Julius Kirshner, eds. *The Politics of Law in Late Medieval and Renaissance Italy: Essays in Honour of Lauro Martines*. Toronto: University of Toronto Press, 2011.

Armstrong, Paul. *How Literature Plays with the Brain*. Baltimore: Johns Hopkins University Press, 2013.

Ascoli, Albert. "The History of a Story: Manetti's 'La Novella del Grasso Legnaiuolo.'" In *Ritual and Culture in Early Modern Europe: Essays in Honour of Edward Muir*, edited by Marj Jurdjevic and Rolf Strøm-Olsen, 211–34. Toronto: Centre for Reformation and Renaissance Studies, 2016.

Asor Rosa, Alberto. "*Decameron*." In *Letteratura italiana: Le opere*, edited by Alberto Asor Rosa, 1:473–591. Turin: Einaudi, 1992.

Atkinson, Niall. *The Noisy Renaissance: Sound, Architecture, and Florentine Urban Life*. University Park: Pennsylvania State University Press, 2016.

Auerbach, Erich. *Mimesis: The Representation of Reality in Western Literature*. Translated by Willard R. Trask. Princeton: Princeton University Press, 2003.

Axelrod, Robert. *The Evolution of Cooperation*. New York: Basic Books, 1984.

Bacci, Pèleo. "Gli affreschi di Buffalmacco scoperti nella chiesa di Badia in Firenze." *Bollettino d'arte del Ministero della Pubblica Istruzione* 5 (1911): 1–27.

Bakhtin, Mikhail. "Forms of Time and Chronotope in the Novel: Notes toward a Historical Poetics." In *The Dialogic Imagination*, edited by Michael Holquist, translated by Caryl Emerson and Michael Holquist, 84–258. Austin: University of Texas Press, 1981.

Baldi, Andrea. "La retorica dell'*exemplum* nella novella di Nastagio (*Decameron*, V, 8)." *Italian Quarterly* 32 (1995): 17–28.

Barański, Zygmunt G. *Language as Sin and Salvation: A Lectura of Inferno 18*. Binghamton, NY: Center for Medieval and Renaissance Studies, 2014.

– "Scatology and Obscenity in Dante." In *Dante for the New Millennium*, edited by Teodolinda Barolini and Wayne Storey, 259–73. New York: Fordham University Press, 2003.

Barański, Zygmunt G., and Theodore J. Cachey, eds. *Petrarch and Dante: Anti-Dantism, Metaphysics, Tradition*. Notre Dame: University of Notre Dame Press, 2009.

Baratto, Mario. *Realtà e stile nel Decameron*. Rome: Editori Riuniti, 1970, 1984.

Bàrberi Squarotti, Giorgio. "Qualche dubbio sulla metafora." In *Il sogno della letteratura*, 211–34. Milan: Franco Angelio, 1988.

Barchiesi, Marino. *Un tema classico e medievale: Gnatone e Taide*. Padua: Antenore, 1963.

Barkan, Leonard. *Unearthing the Past: Archaeology and Aesthetics in the Making of Renaissance Culture*. New Haven: Yale University Press, 1999.

Barolini, Teodolinda. "Aristotle's *Mezzo*, Courtly *Misura*, and Dante's Canzone *Le dolci rime*: Humanism, Ethics, and Social Anxiety." In *Dante and the Greeks*, edited by Jan Ziolkowski, 163–79. Cambridge, MA: Harvard University Press, 2014.

– *Dante and the Origins of Italian Literary Culture*. New York: Fordham University Press, 2006.

– "The Marquis of Saluzzo, or the Griselda Story Before It Was Hijacked: Calculating Matrimonial Odds in *Decameron* 10.10." *Mediaevalia* 34 (2013): 23–55.

– "'Le parole son donne e i fatti son maschi': Toward a Sexual Poetics of the *Decameron* (*Dec.* 2.9, 2.10, 5.10)." *Studi sul Boccaccio* 21 (1993): 175–97. Reprinted and revised in Barolini, *Dante and the Origins of Italian Literary Culture*, 281–303.

– "A Philosophy of Consolation: The Place of the Other in Life's Transactions ('se Dio m'avesse dato fratello o non me lo avesse dato')." In *Boccaccio 1313–2013*, edited by Francesco Ciabattoni, Elsa Filosa, and Kristina Olson, 89–105. Ravenna: Longo Editore, 2015.

– "Sociology of the *Brigata*: Gendered Groups in Dante, Forese, Folgore, Boccaccio – From *Guido, i' vorrei* to Griselda." *Italian Studies* 67 (2012): 4–22.

– "The Wheel of the *Decameron*." *Romance Philology* 36 (1983): 521–39. Reprinted in Barolini, *Dante and the Origins of Italian Literary Culture*, 224–44.

Barsella, Susanna. "Ethics and Theology in Boccaccio's Merchants: *Decameron* II 4." *Memorie domenicane* 33 (2002): 195–212.

– "La parola icastica: Strategie figurative nelle novelle del *Decameron*." *Italianistica* 38 (2009): 91–102.

Bartuschat, Johannes. "Appunti sull'ecfrasi in Boccaccio." *Italianistica* 38 (2009): 71–90.

Battaglia, Salvatore. "Dall'esempio alla novella." 1960. In *Capitoli per una storia della novellistica italiana: Dalle Origini al Cinquecento*, edited by Vittoro Russo, 153–208. Naples: Liguori, 1993.

Battaglia, Salvatore, ed. *Grande dizionario della lingua italiana*. 21 vols. Turin: UTET, 1961–2002.

Battaglia Ricci, Lucia. *Boccaccio*. 2nd ed. Rome: Salerno, 2008.
– "Il *Decameron*: Amore, beffa, avventura nelle novelle di Boccaccio; Il problema delle 'fonti.'" In Battaglia Ricci, *Boccaccio*, 162–83.
– "*Exemplum* e novella." In *Letteratura in forma di sermone: I rapporti tra predicazione e letteratura nei secoli XIII–XVI*, edited by Ginetta Auzzas, Giuseppe Baffetti, and Carlo Delcorno, 281–93. Florence: Olschki, 2003.
– *Ragionare nel giardino: Boccaccio e i cicli pittorici del Trionfo della morte*. Rome: Salerno, 1987.
– *Scrivere un libro di novelle: Giovanni Boccaccio autore, lettore, editore*. Ravenna: Longo Editore, 2013.
– "'Una novella per esempio': Novellistica, omiletica e trattatistica nel primo Trecento." *Studi sul Boccaccio* 28 (2000): 106–24.
Bausi, Francesco. "Gli spiriti magni: Filigrane aristoteliche e tomistiche nella decima giornata del *Decameron*." *Studi sul Boccaccio* 27 (1999): 205–53.
– *Petrarca antimoderno: Studi sulle invettive e sulle polemiche petrarchesche*. Florence: Cesati, 2008.
Bec, Christian. *Cultura e società a Firenze nell'età della Rinascenza*. Rome: Salerno, 1981.
Becker, Marvin. "Changing Patterns of Violence and Justice in Fourteenth- and Fifteenth-Century Florence." *Comparative Studies in Society and History* 18 (1976): 281–96.
Bell, Rudolph M. *How to Do It: Guides to Good Living for Renaissance Italians*. Chicago: University of Chicago Press, 1999.
Bellosi, Luciano. *Buffalmacco e il Trionfo della Morte*. Turin: Einaudi, 1974.
– "Buffalmacco, pittore girovago." In Bellosi, *Buffalmacco e il Trionfo della Morte*, 68–73.
Berlioz, Jacques. "Maître Melchita, magicien de Tolède: Un *exemplum* inédit (conte type 817*) du dominicain Etienne de Bourbon." In *Formes et difformités médiévales: Hommage à Claude Lecouteux*, edited by Florence Bayard and Astrid Guillaume, 287–302. Paris: Presses universitaires de la Sorbonne, 2010.
Berlioz, Jacques, and Marie Anne Polo de Beaulieu, eds. *Les exempla médiévaux: Nouvelles perspectives*. Paris: Honoré Champion, 1998.
Berté, Monica, and Silvia Rizzo. "Le *Senili* mediche." In *Petrarca e la medicina: Atti del convegno di Capo d'Orlando, 27–28 giugno 2003*, edited by Monca Berté, Vincenzo Fera, and Tiziana Pesenti, 247–379. Messina: Centro interdipartimentale di Studi Umanistici, 2006.
Bettinzoli, Attilio. "Sul comico e sulla 'metamorfosi': Appunti in margine a una novella del *Decameron*." In *Miscellanea di studi in onore di Vittore Branca*, vol. 2, *Boccaccio e dintorni*, 169–80. Florence: Olschki, 1983.
Bevilacqua, Mirko. *Leggere per diletto: Saggi sul Decameron*. Rome: Salerno, 2008.

Bianchi, Luca. "Conclusione." In Chandelier and Robert, *Frontières des savoirs en Italie*, 541–56.

Biggs, Frederick M. *Chaucer's Decameron and the Origin of the Canterbury Tales*. Cambridge: D.S. Brewer, 2017.

Billanovich, Giuseppe. *Petrarca e il primo umanesimo*. Padua: Antenore, 1996.

– "Il più grande discepolo di Petrarca." In *Petrarca letterato: Lo scrittoio del Petrarca*, 59–294. Rome: Edizioni di Storia e letteratura, 1947; 1995.

Blow, Douglas. *Doctors, Ambassadors, Secretaries: Humanism and Professions in Renaissance Italy*. Chicago: University of Chicago Press, 2002.

Bolpagni, Marcello. *La geografia del Decameron*. Novate Milanese: Prospero, 2016.

Borsari, Silvano. *Una compagnia di Calimala: Gli Scali (secc. XIII–XIV)*. Macerata: Università degli Studi di Macerata, 1994.

Bottari, Giovanni. "Lezione sopra la novella sesta della giornata ottava: Letta nel 1762." In *Lezioni di Monsignore Giovanni Bottari sopra il Decamerone*, 2:177–90. Florence: Gasparo Ricci, 1818.

Boudet, Jean-Patrice. *Entre science et nigromance: Astrologie, divination et magie dans l'occident médiéval, XIIe–XVe siècle*. Paris: Publications de la Sorbonne, 2006.

Boulnois, Olivier. "Scolastique et humanisme: Pétrarque et la croisée des ignorances." In Francesco Petrarca, *Mon ignorance et celle de tant d'autres*, translated by Juliette Bertrand and Christophe Carraud, 5–43. Grenoble: Jérôme Millon, 2000.

Bourdieu, Pierre. *Language and Symbolic Power*. Edited by John Thompson. Cambridge, MA: Harvard University Press, 1991.

Boureau, Alain. *Satan hérétique*. Paris: Odile Jacob, 2004.

Bowsky, William M. "The Medieval Commune and Internal Violence: Police Power and Public Safety in Siena, 1287–1355." *American Historical Review* 73 (1967): 1–17.

Boyd, Brian. *On the Origin of Stories*. Cambridge, MA: Belknap, 2009.

Bragantini, Renzo. "Dialogo." In Bragantini and Forni, *Lessico critico decameroniano*, 93–115.

– "Premesse sull'ascolto decameroniano (con primi appunti sul codice biblico nel *Decameron*)." *Filologia e critica* 28 (2003): 23–40.

Bragantini, Renzo, and Pier Massimo Forni, eds. *Lessico critico decameroniano*. Turin: Bollati Boringhieri, 1995.

Branca, Vittore. *Boccaccio medievale*. Milan: Sansoni, 1956, 1996.

– *Giovanni Boccaccio: Profilo biografico*. Florence: Sansoni, 1977.

– "Il paessaggio nel Boccaccio: Descrittivismo, calligrafismo, allusivismo, espressivismo." In *Klaniczay-emlékkönyv: Tanulmányok Klaniczay Tibor emlékezetére*, edited by József Jankovics, 32–47. Budapest: Balassi Kiadó, 1994.

– "Studi sugli *exempla* e il *Decameron*." *Studi sul Boccaccio* 14 (1983–4): 179–89.
– *Tradizione delle opere di Giovanni Bocaccio*. 2 vols. Rome: Edizioni di Storia e Letteratura, 1958.
Branca, Vittore, ed. *Boccaccio visualizzato: Narrare per parole e per immagini fra Medioevo e Rinascimento*. 3 vols. Turin: Einaudi, 1999.
Braudel, Fernand. *The Mediterranean and the Mediterranean World in the Age of Philip II*. Translated by Siân Reynolds. London: Collins, 1972.
Bremond, Claude, Jacques Le Goff, and Jean-Claude Schmitt, eds. *L'exemplum*. Turnhout: Brepols, 1982.
Brilli, Elisa. *Firenze e il profeta: Dante fra teologia e politica*. Rome: Carocci, 2012.
– "The Making of a New *Auctoritas*: The *Dialogus miraculorum* Read and Rewritten by the Dominican Arnold of Liège." In *The Art of Cistercian Persuasion in the Middle Ages and Beyond*, edited by Victoria Smirnova, Marie Anne Polo de Beaulieu, and Jacques Berlioz, 163–82. Leiden: Brill, 2015.
Brown, Katherine A. *Boccaccio's Fabliaux: Medieval Short Stories and the Function of Reversal*. Gainesville: University Press of Florida, 2014.
– "Splitting Pants and Pigs: The Fabliau *Barat et Haimet* and Narrative Strategies in *Decameron* 8.5 and 8.6." In *Reconsidering Boccaccio: Medieval Contexts and Global Intertexts*, edited by Olivia Holmes and Dana E. Stewart, 344–64. Toronto: University of Toronto Press, 2018.
Brucker, Gene A. *Florentine Politics and Society 1343–1378*. Princeton: Princeton University Press, 1962.
Bruni, Francesco. *Boccaccio: L'invenzione della letteratura mezzana*. Bologna: Il Mulino, 1990.
Bruscagli, Riccardo. "Ribi buffone tra *Decameron* e *Trecentonovelle*." In *Studi di filologia e letteratura italiana in onore di Gianvito Resta*, edited by Vitielo Masiello, 249–68. Rome: Salerno, 2000.
Budini Gattai, Niccolò. "La percezione del mondo greco del XIV secolo tra incomprensioni culturali e *topoi* letterari." In Morosini, *Boccaccio geografo*, 103–31.
Burnett, Charles. "Michael Scot and the Transmission of Scientific Culture from Toledo to Bologna via the Court of Frederick II Hohenstaufen." *Micrologus* 6 (1994): 101–26.
Cachey, Theodore J. "Between Text and Territory." In Kirkham, Sherberg, and Smarr, *Boccaccio: A Critical Guide*, 273–9.
Caferro, William. *Petrarch's War: Florence and the Black Death in Context*. Cambridge: Cambridge University Press, 2018.
Camille, Michael. "Manuscript Illumination and the Art of Copulation." In *Constructing Medieval Sexuality*, edited by Karma Lochrie, Peggy McCracken, and James A. Schultz, 58–90. Minneapolis: University of Minnesota Press, 1997.

Cardini, Franco. "Le mura di Firenze: Un profilo storico." In *Su e giù per le antiche mura: Analisi storica per il recupero della cinta muraria di Firenze e progetto di percorso attrezzato*, edited by Francesco Bandini, 15–27. Florence: Alinari, 1983.

Carocci, Guido. "Le antiche divisioni della città di Firenze in quartieri e gonfaloni." In *L'Illustratore fiorentino: Calendario storico per l'anno 1909*, 81–9. Florence: Tipografia Arcivescovile, 1908.

Casagrande, Carla, and Gianfranco Fioravanti, eds. *La filosofia in Italia al tempo di Dante*. Bologna: Il Mulino, 2016.

Case, Mary Anne. "Feminist Fundamentalism." *Chicago's Best Ideas* 86 (2008). http://chicagounbound.uchicago.edu/chicagos_best_ideas/86.

– "Feminist Fundamentalism as an Individual and Constitutional Commitment." *American University Journal of Gender, Social Policy and the Law* 19 (2011): 549–76.

– "What Turns on Whether Women Are Human for Boccaccio and Christine de Pizan?" In *Reconsidering Boccaccio: Medieval Contexts and Global Intertexts*, edited by Olivia Holmes and Dana Stewart, 189–216. Toronto: University of Toronto Press, 2018.

Cazalé Bérard, Claude. "Filoginia/misoginia." In Bragantini and Forni, *Lessico critico decameroniano*, 116–41.

– *Stratégie du jeu narratif: Le Decameron, une poétique du récit*. Nanterre: Université de Paris X, 1985.

Celli-Olivagnoli, Franca. "Spazialità nel *Decameron*." *Stanford Italian Review* 3 (1983): 91–106.

Ceruti Burgio, Anna. "Annotazioni in margine all'ottava giornata del *Decameron*." In *Scritti in onore di Caterina Vassalini*, edited by Luigi Barbesi, 168–79. Verona: Fiorini, 1974.

Cesari, Anna Maria. "L'*Etica* di Aristotele del codice Ambrosiano A 204 inf.: Un autografo del Boccaccio." *Archivio storico lombardo* 93–4 (1966–7): 69–100.

Chandelier, Joël, and Aurélien Robert. *Frontières des savoirs en Italie à l'époque des premières universités (XIIIe–XVe siècles)*. Rome: École Française de Rome, 2015.

Cherchi, Paolo. *L'onestade e l'onesto raccontare del Decameron*. Fiesole: Cadmo, 2004.

Ciavolella, Massimo. "La tradizione della *aegritudo amoris* nel *Decameron*." *Giornale Storico della Letteratura Italiana* 147 (1970): 496–517.

Ciccuto, Marcello. "Il novelliere *en artiste*: Strategie della dissimiglianza fra Boccaccio e Bandello." In Ciccuto, *L'immagine del testo: Episodi di cultura figurativa nella letteratura italiana*, 113–55. Rome: Bonacci, 1990.

Citroni Marchetti, Sandra. "*Iuvare mortalem*: L'ideale programmatico della *Naturalis Historia* di Plinio nei rapporti con il moralismo stocio-diatribico." *Atene e Roma* 27 (1982): 133–4.

– *Plinio il Vecchio e la tradizione del moralismo romano*. Pisa: Giardini, 1991.

Clarke, K.P. "Author-Text-Reader: Boccaccio's *Decameron* in 1384." *Heliotropia* 14 (2017): 101–15.

– "Boccaccio and the Poetics of the Paratext: Rubricating the Vernacular." *Le Tre Corone* 6 (2019): 69–106.

– *Chaucer and Italian Textuality*. Oxford: Oxford University Press, 2011.

– "Leggere il *Decameron* a margine del codice Mannelli." In *Boccaccio e i suoi lettori: Una lunga ricezione*, edited by Gian Mario Anselmi, Giovanni Baffetti, Carlo Delcorno, and Sebastiana Nobili, 195–207. Bologna: Il Mulino, 2013.

– "Marrying Word and Image: Visualizing Boccaccio at the Spannocchi Wedding, Siena, 1494." *Studi sul Boccaccio* 40 (2012): 315–90.

– "*Sotto la quale rubrica*: Pre-reading the *Comedìa*." *Dante Studies* 133 (2015): 147–76.

– "Taking the Proverbial: Reading (at) the Margins of Boccaccio's *Corbaccio*." *Studi sul Boccaccio* 38 (2010): 105–44.

Cochin, Henry. *Boccace: Études italiennes*. Paris: Plon, 1890.

Cohen, Walter. *Drama of a Nation: Public Theatre in Renaissance England and Spain*. Ithaca: Cornell University Press, 1985.

Cohn, Norman. *Europe's Inner Demons: The Demonization of Christians in Medieval Christendom*. London: Pimlico, 1993.

Cohn, Samuel, Jr. "Criminality and the State in Renaissance Florence, 1344–1466." *Journal of Social History* 14 (1980): 211–33.

Coleman, Edward. "Cities and Comunes." In *Italy in the Central Middle Ages*, edited by David Abulafia, 27–57. Oxford: Oxford University Press, 2004.

Constable, Olivia Remie. *Housing the Stranger in the Mediterranean World: Lodging, Trade, and Travel in Late Antiquity and the Middle Ages*. Cambridge: Cambridge University Press, 2003.

Cooper, Helen. *The Canterbury Tales*. 2nd ed. Oxford: Oxford University Press, 1996.

Cottino-Jones, Marga. "The City/Country Conflict in the *Decameron*." *Studi sul Boccaccio* 8 (1974): 147–84.

– "Comic Modalities in the *Decameron*." In *Versions of Medieval Comedy*, edited by Paul D. Ruggiers, 151–71. Norman: University of Oklahoma Press, 1977.

– "Magic and Superstition in Boccaccio's *Decameron*." *Italian Quarterly* 72 (1975): 5–32.

– *Order from Chaos: Social and Aesthetic Harmonies in Boccaccio's Decameron*. Washington, DC: University Press of America, 1982.

Courcelle, Pierre. *"Connais-toi toi-même": De Socrate à saint Bernard*. 3 vols. Paris: Études Augustiniennes, 1975.

Crisiciani, Chiara. "Medici e filosofia." In *La filosofia in Italia al tempo di Dante*, edited by Carla Casagrande and Gianfranco Fioravanti, 37–64. Bologna: Il Mulino, 2016.

Crisicani, Chiara, and Agostino Paravicini Bagliani, eds. *Alchimia e medicina nel Medioevo*. Florence: SISMEL edizioni del Galluzzo, 2013.

Crum, Roger J., and John T. Paoletti, eds. *Renaissance Florence: A Social History*. New York: Cambridge University Press, 2006.

Cursi, Marco. *Il Decameron: Scritture, scriventi, lettori; Storia di un testo*. Rome: Viella, 2007.

– "Il Parigino Italiano 482: Un *Decameron* allo scrittoio del Boccaccio." In *Boccaccio e la Francia/Boccace et la France*, edited by Philippe Guérin and Anne Robin, 117–51. Florence: Franco Cesati Editore, 2017.

– *La scrittura e i libri di Giovanni Boccaccio*. Rome: Viella, 2013.

D'Andrea, Antonio. "Le rubriche del *Decameron*." In *Il nome della storia: Studi e ricerche di storia e letteratura*, edited by Antonio D'Andrea, 98–125. Naples: Liguori, 1982.

Daniels, Rhiannon. *Boccaccio and the Book: Production and Reading in Italy 1340–1520*. London: Legenda, 2009.

– "Where Does the *Decameron* Begin? Editorial Practice and Tables of Rubrics." *Modern Language Review* 114 (2019): 52–78.

Davidsohn, Robert. *Storia di Firenze*. 8 vols. Florence: Sansoni, 1956–68.

Dean, Trevor. "Marriage and Mutilation: *Vendetta* in Late Medieval Italy." *Past & Present* 157 (1997): 3–36.

Degani, Chiara. "Riflessi quasi sconosciuti di *exempla* nel *Decameron*." *Studi sul Boccaccio* 14 (1983–4): 189–208.

Degl'Innocenti, Luca, Brian Richardson, and Chiara Sbordoni, eds. *Interactions between Orality and Writing in Early Modern Italian Culture*. London: Routledge, 2016.

Delcorno, Carlo. *Exemplum e letteratura: Tra Medioevo e Rinascimento*. Bologna: Il Mulino, 1989.

– *La predicazione nell'età comunale*. Florence: Sansoni, 1974.

– "Studi sugli *exempla* e il *Decameron*, II: Modelli esemplari in tre novelle (I 1, III 8, II 2)." *Studi sul Boccaccio* 15 (1985–6): 189–214.

Delcorno Branca, Daniela. "'Cognominato Prencipe Galeotto': Il sottotitolo illustrato del Parigino It. 482." *Studi sul Boccaccio* 23 (1995): 79–88.

Del Popolo, Concetto. "Un'espressione di Calandrino (*Decameron*, IX 3.21, 24; 5.64)." *Studi sul Boccaccio* 27 (1999): 107–12.

De Robertis, Teresa, Carla Maria Monti, Marco Petoletti, Giuliano Tanturli, and Stefano Zamponi, eds. *Boccaccio: Autore e copista*. Florence: Mandragola, 2013.

Desmond, Marilynn. *Ovid's Art and the Wife of Bath: The Ethics of Erotic Violence*. Ithaca: Cornell University Press, 2006.

Di Girolamo, Costanzo, and Charmaine Lee. "Fonti." In Bragantini and Forni, *Lessico critico decameroniano*, 142–61.

Di Maria, Salvatore. "Structure of the Early Form of the *Beffa* in Italian Literature." *Canadian Journal of Italian Studies* 4 (1981): 227–39.

di Simone, Paolo. "Giotto, Petrarca e il tema degli uomini illustri tra Napoli, Milano, e Padova: Prolegomeni a un'indagine." *Rivista D'Arte*, fifth series, 2 (2012): 39–76, and 3 (2013): 35–56.

Doniger, Wendy. "Pregnant Riddles and Clever Wives." In Doniger, *The Ring of Truth and Other Myths of Sex and Jewelry*, 137–69. New York: Oxford University Press, 2017.

Dorini, Ugo. "Contributi alla biografia di Boccaccio." *Miscellanea storica della Valdelsa* 22 (1914): 73–91.

Duby, Georges. *Love and Marriage in the Middle Ages*. Translated by Jane Dunnett. Cambridge: Polity Press, 1994.

Dunton-Downer, Leslie. "Poetic Language and the Obscene." In *Obscenity: Social Control and Artistic Creation in the European Middle Ages*, edited by Jan Ziolkowski, 19–37. Boston: Brill, 1998.

Duranti, Alessandro. "Le novelle di Dioneo." In *Studi di filologia e critica offerti dagli allievi a Lanfranco Caretti*, 1:1–38. Rome: Salerno, 1985.

Durling, Robert M. "A Long Day in the Sun: *Decameron* 8.7." In *Shakespeare's Rough Magic: Renaissance Essays in Honor of C.L. Barber*, edited by Peter Erickson and Coppélia Kahn, 269–75. Newark: University of Delaware Press, 1985.

Eckstein, Nicholas. "The Neighbourhood as Microcosm of the Social Order." In Crum and Paoletti, *Renaissance Florence: A Social History*, 219–39.

Farber, Lianna. *An Anatomy of Trade in Medieval Writing: Value, Consent, and Community*. Ithaca: Cornell University Press, 2006.

Federici Vescovini, Graziella. *Medioevo magico: La magia tra religione e scienza nei secoli XIII e XIV*. Turin: UTET, 2008.

Fera, Vincenzo. "I *fragmenta de viris illustribus* di Francesco Petrarca." In *Caro Vitto: Essays in Memory of Vittore Branca*, edited by Jill Kraye and Laura Lepschy, 118–23. The Italianist 27. London: Warburg Institute, 2007.

Ferme, Valerio. "*Ingegno* and Morality in the New Social Order: The Role of the *Beffa* in Boccaccio's *Decameron*." *Romance Languages Annual* 4 (1992): 248–53.

Ferreri, Rosario. "Madonna Ambruogia e l'amore prezzolato (*Decameron* VIII 1)." *Studi sul Boccaccio* 21 (1993): 199–206.

Ferroni, Giulio. "Sulla struttura della beffa." In *Ambiguità del comico*, edited by Giulio Ferroni, 72–9. Palermo: Sellerio, 1983.

Filosa, Elsa, and Luisa Flora. "Tracce di Seneca (e Giovenale) nel *Decameron*." *Giornale Storico della Letteratura Italiana* 175 (1998): 210–19.

Flesch, William. *Comeuppance: Costly Signaling, Altruistic Punishment, and Other Biological Components of Fiction*. Cambridge, MA: Harvard University Press, 2007.

Fonio, Filippo. "Dalla legenda alla novella: Continuità di moduli e variazioni di genere; Il caso di Boccaccio." *Cahiers d'études italiennes* 6 (2007): 127–81.

Fontes-Baratto, Anna. "Le thème de la *beffa* dans le *Decameron*." In *Formes et significations de la beffa dans la littérature italienne de la Renaissance*, edited by André Rochon, 11–44. Paris: Publications de la Sorbonne Nouvelle, 1972.

Forni, Pier Massimo. *Adventures in Speech: Rhetoric and Narration in Boccaccio's Decameron*. Philadelphia: University of Pennsylvania Press, 1996.

– *Forme complesse nel Decameron*. Florence: Olschki, 1992.

– "Realtà/verità." In Bragantini and Forni, *Lessico critico decameroniano*, 300–19.

Forno, Carla. "L'amaro riso della beffa (VIII giornata)." In *Prospettive sul Decameron*, edited by Giorgio Bárberi Squarotti, 131–47. Turin: Tirrenia, 1989.

Franceschi, Franco. "Medici Economic Policy." In *The Medici: Citizens and Masters*, edited by Robert Black and John Law, 129–54. Florence: Villa I Tatti, 2015.

Franceschini, Fabrizio. "'Salabaetto' e i nomi di tipo arabo ed ebraico nel *Decameron*." *Italianistica* 42 (2013): 107–25.

Fryde, Edmund. "The Bankruptcy of the Scali of Florence in England 1326–1328." In *Progress and Problems in Medieval England: Essays in Honor of E. Miller*, edited by Richard Britnell and John Hatcher, 107–20. Cambridge: Cambridge University Press, 1996.

Geninasca, Jacques. "I contratti e la beffa." In *Eloquio del senso: Dialoghi semiotici per Paolo Fabbri*, edited by Pierluigi Basso and Lucia Corrain, 308–23. Milan: Costa & Nolan, 1999.

Getto, Giovanni. *Vita di forme e forme di vita nel Decameron*. 4th ed. Turin: Petrini, 1986.

Giardini, Maria Pia. *Tradizioni popolari nel Decameron*. Florence: Olschki, 1965.

Gilbert, Creighton. "Boccaccio's Devotion to Artists and Art." In Gilbert, *Poets Seeing Artists' Work: Instances in the Italian Renaissance*, 49–65. Florence: Olschki, 1991.

– "La devozione di Giovanni Boccaccio per gli artisti e l'arte." In Branca, *Boccaccio Visualizzatto*, 1:145–63.

Gittes, Tobias Foster. "Boccaccio's 'Valley of Women': Fetishized Foreplay in *Decameron* VI." *Italica* 76 (1999): 147–74.

Giusti, Eugenio. *Dall'amore cortese alla comprensione: Il viaggio ideologico di Giovanni Boccaccio dalla Caccia di Diana al Decameron*. Milan: LED, 1999.

Graf, Fritz. *Magic in the Ancient World*. Translated by Franklin Philip. Cambridge, MA: Harvard University Press, 1997.

Green, Monica. *The Trotula: A Medieval Compendium of Women's Medicine*. Philadelphia: University of Pennsylvania Press, 2002.

Gregory, Chris A. *Gifts and Commodities.* London: Academic Press, 1982.
Grimaldi, Emma. *Il privilegio di Dioneo: L'eccezione e la regola nel sistema Decameron.* Naples: Edizioni Scientifiche Italiane, 1987.
Gualtieri, Piero. *Il comune di Firenze tra Due e Trecento. Partecipazione politica e assetto istituzionale.* Florence: Olschki, 2009.
Guerin, Philippe. "De l'image au texte et du texte à l'image: Sur les puissances de la peinture chez Boccace." In *Boccace à la Renaissance: Lectures, traductions, influences en Italie et en France,* edited by Johannes Bartuschat, 13–39. Grenoble: Ellug, 2008.
Guidi, Guidubaldo. *Il governo della città-repubblica di Firenze del primo Quattrocento.* 2 vols. Florence: Olschki, 1981.
Heers, Jacques. *Esclaves et domestiques dans le monde méditerranéen.* Paris: Fayard, 1981.
Heyse, Paul. "Einleitung." In *Deutscher Novellenschatz,* edited by Paul Heyse and Hermann Kurz, 1:v–xxiv. Munich: Rudolph Oldenburg, 1871.
Hinnebusch, John Frederick. "Extant Manuscripts of the Writings of Jacques de Vitry." *Scriptorium* 51 (1997): 162–3.
Hollander, Robert. *Boccaccio's Last Fiction: Il Corbaccio.* Philadelphia: University of Pennsylvania Press, 1988.
– "*Utilità* in Boccaccio's *Decameron.*" *Studi sul Boccaccio* 15 (1985–6): 215–33.
Holmes, Oliver Wendell, Jr. *The Path of the Law and The Common Law.* Foreword by J. Craig Williams. New York: Kaplan, 2009.
Holmes, Olivia. "Trial by *Beffa*: Retributive Justice and In-Group Formation in Day Eight." *Annali d'Italianistica* 31 (2013): 355–79.
Howard, Donald R. *The Idea of the Canterbury Tales.* Berkeley: University of California Press, 1976.
Isenmann, Moritz. "From Rule of Law to Emergency Rule in Renaissance Florence." In Armstrong and Kirshner, *The Politics of Law in Late Medieval and Renaissance Italy,* 55–76.
Iser, Wolfgang. *The Implied Reader: Patterns of Communication in Prose Fiction from Bunyan to Beckett.* Baltimore: Johns Hopkins University Press, 1974.
Janowitz, Naomi. *Magic in the Roman World: Pagans, Jews, and Christians.* New York: Routledge, 2001.
Kantorowicz, Ernst Hartwig. *The King's Two Bodies: A Study in Mediaeval Political Theology.* Princeton: Princeton University Press, 1957.
– "The Sovereignty of the Artist: A Note on Legal Maxims and Renaissance Theories of Art." In Kantorowicz, *Selected Studies,* 352–65. Locust Valley, NY: Augustin, 1965.
Kinoshita, Sharon, and Jason Jacobs. "Ports of Call: Boccaccio's Alatiel in the Medieval Mediterranean." *Journal of Medieval and Early Modern Studies* 37 (2007): 163–95.

Kirkham, Victoria. "Painters at Play on the Judgement Day (*Dec.* VIII, 9)." *Studi sul Boccaccio* 14 (1983–4): 256–77. Reprinted in Kirkham, *The Sign of Reason in Boccaccio's Fiction*, 215–35.

– *The Sign of Reason in Boccaccio's Fiction*. Florence: Olschki, 1993.

– "A Visual Legacy: Boccaccio as Artist." In Kirkham, Sherberg, and Smarr, *Boccaccio: A Critical Guide*, 321–40.

Kirkham, Victoria, Michael Sherberg, and Janet Levarie Smarr, eds. *Boccaccio: A Critical Guide*. Chicago: University of Chicago Press, 2013.

Kirshner, Julius. "Ars Imitatur Naturam: A Consilium of Baldus on Naturalization in Florence." *Viator* 5 (1974): 289–332.

– "Civitas Sibi Faciat Civem: Bartolus of Sassoferrato's Doctrine on the Making of a Citizen." *Speculum* 48 (1973): 694–713.

– "A Critical Appreciation of Lawyers and Statecraft." In Armstrong and Kirshner, *The Politics of Law in Late Medieval and Renaissance Italy*, 7–39.

Klapisch-Zuber, Christiane. *Women, Family, and Ritual in Renaissance Italy*. Translated by Lydia G. Cochrane. Chicago: University of Chicago Press, 1985.

Kuhns, Richard. "The Creation of a Total Work of Art." In Kuhns, *Decameron and the Philosophy of Storytelling: Author as Midwife and Pimp*, 123–41. New York: Columbia University Press, 2005.

Land, Norman. "Calandrino as Viewer." *Notes in the History of Art* 23 (2004): 1–6.

Larner, John. *Culture and Society in Italy, 1290–1420*. London, Batsford, 1971.

Lee, A. Collingwood. *The Decameron: Its Sources and Analogues*. 1909. New York: Haskell House, 1972.

Legassie, Shayne Aaron. "The Lies of the Painters: Artisan Trickery and the Labor of Painting in Boccaccio's *Decameron* and Sacchetti's *Trecentonovelle*." *Journal of Medieval and Early Modern Studies* 43 (2013): 487–519.

Lehmann, Paul, Johannes Stroux, Otto Prinz, Johannes Schneider, and Heinz Antony, eds. *Mittellateinisches Wörterbuch bis zum ausgehenden 13. Jahrhundert*. 3 vols. Munich: Beck, 1959–67.

Leone, Michael. "Tra autobiografismo reale e ideale in *Decameron* VIII, 7." *Italica* 50 (1973): 242–65.

Louis, Nicolas. *L'exemplum en pratiques: Production, diffusion et usages des recueils d'exempla latins aux XIIIe–XVe siècles*. PhD dissertation. École des Hautes Études en Sciences Sociales, Facultés Universitaires Notre Dame de la Paix, 2013.

Lupo, Michele Angelo. "Elementi carnevaleschi nel *Decameron*." *Critica letteraria* 20 (1992): 775–807.

Maire Vigueur, Jean-Claude. "Flussi, circuiti e profili." In Maire Vigueur, *I Podestà dell'Italia comunale*, 2:897–1099.

– "Nello Stato della Chiesa: Da una pluralità di circuiti al trionfo del guelfismo." In Maire Vigueur, *I Podestà dell'Itaia comunale*, 2:741–814.

Maire Vigueur, Jean-Claude, ed. *I Podestà dell'Italia comunale, Parte I: Reclutamento e circolazione degli ufficiali forestieri (fine XII sec.–metà XIV sec.).* 2 vols. Rome: Istituto Storico Italiano per il Medio Evo, 2000.

Maire Vigueur, Jean-Claude, and Enrico Faini. *Il sistema politico dei comuni italiani (secoli XII–XIV).* Milan: Mondadori, 2010.

Makowski, Elizabeth M. "The Conjugal Debt and Medieval Canon Law." In *Equally in God's Image: Women in the Middle Ages*, edited by Julia Bolton Holloway, Constance S. Wright, and Joan Bechtold, 129–43. New York: Peter Lang, 1990.

Mallett, Michael. "Canigiani, Piero." In *Dizionario biografico degli italiani*, 18:94–5. Rome: Istituto della Enciclopedia Italiana, 1975.

Manetti, Renzo, and Maria Chiara Pozzana. *Firenze, le porte dell'ultima cerchia di mura*. Florence: Clusf, 1979.

Manikowska, Halina. "Il controllo sulle città: Le istituzioni dell'ordine pubblico nelle città italiane dei secoli XIV e XV." In *Città e servizi sociali nell'Italia dei secoli XII–XV*, 481–511. Pistoia: Centro Italiano di Studi di Storia e d'Arte, 1990.

– "Polizia e servizi d'ordine a Firenze nella seconda metà del XIV secolo." *Ricerche Storiche* 16 (1986): 17–38.

Mantini, Silvia. "Un recinto di identificazione: Le mura sacre della città; Firenze dall'età classica al medioevo." *Archivio storico italiano* 153 (1995): 211–61.

Marchesi, Simone. *Stratigrafie decameroniane*. Florence: Olschki, 2004.

Marcozzi, Luca. "Raccontare il viaggio: Tra itineraria ultramarina e dimensione dell'imaginario." In Morosini, *Boccaccio geografo*, 159–78.

Marcus, Millicent Joy. *An Allegory of Form: Literary Self-Consciousness in the Decameron*. Saratoga, CA: Anma Libri, 1979.

– "Mischief and Misbelief: The First Tale of Calandrino (VIII,3)." In Marcus, *An Allegory of Form*, 79–92.

– "Misogyny as Misreading: A Gloss on *Decameron* VIII, 7." *Stanford Italian Review* 4 (1984): 23–40.

– "The Tale of Maestro Alberto (I.10)." In Weaver, *The Decameron First Day in Perspective*, 222–40.

Markulin, Joseph. "Emilia and the Case for Openness in the *Decameron*." *Stanford Italian Review* 3 (1983): 183–99.

Martines, Lauro. *Lawyers and Statecraft in Renaissance Florence*. Princeton: Princeton University Press, 1968.

Martines, Lauro, ed. *Violence and Civil Disorder in Italian Cities, 1200–1500*. Berkeley: University of California Press, 1972.

Martinez, Ronald, L. "Calandrino and the Powers of the Stone: Rhetoric, Belief, and the Progress of *Ingegno* in *Decameron* VIII.3." *Heliotropia* 1 (2003): 1–32.

Masi, Gino. "Il sindicato delle magistrature communali nel sec. XIV (con particolare riferimento a Firenze)." *Rivista Italiana per le Scienze Giuridiche* 5 (1930): 43–115, 331–411.

Mauss, Marcel. *The Gift: The Form and Reason for Exchange in Archaic Societies.* Translated by W.D. Halls. London: Routledge, 1990.

Mazzetti, Martina. "Boccaccio e l'invenzione del libro illustrabile: Dal *Teseida* al *Decameron*." *Per Leggere* 21 (2011): 135–61.

Mazzoni, Francesco. "Tematiche politiche fra Guittone e Dante." In *Guittone d'Arezzo, nel settimo centenario della morte*, edited by Michelangelo Picone, 351–83. Florence: Cesati, 1995.

Mazzotta, Giuseppe. "Games of Laughter." *Romanic Review* 69 (1978): 115–31. Reprinted in Mazzotta, *The World at Play in Boccaccio's Decameron*, 186–212.

– *The World at Play in Boccaccio's Decameron*. Princeton: Princeton University Press, 1986, 2014.

McHam, Sarah. *Pliny and the Artistic Culture of the Italian Renaissance.* New Haven: Yale University Press, 2013.

Menzinger, Sara. "Mura e identità civica in Italia e in Francia meridionale (secc. XII–XIV)." In *Cittadinanze medievali: Dinamiche di appartenenza a un corpo comunitario*, edited by Sara Menzinger, 65–109. Rome: Viella, 2007.

– "Verso la costruzione di un diritto publico cittadino." In *La Summa Trium Librorum Di Rolando Da Lucca (1195–1234): Fisco, politica, scientia iuris*, edited by Emanuele Conte and Sara Menzinger, cxxv–ccxviii. Rome: Viella, 2012.

Migiel, Marilyn. *The Ethical Dimension of the Decameron.* Toronto: University of Toronto Press, 2015.

– "Figurative Language and Sex Wars in the *Decameron*." *Heliotropia* 2.2 (2004): 1–12.

– *A Rhetoric of the Decameron*. Toronto: University of Toronto Press, 2003.

– "The Untidy Business of Gender Studies: Or, Why It's Almost Useless to Ask If the *Decameron* Is Feminist." In *Boccaccio and Feminist Criticism*, edited by F. Regina Psaki and Thomas C. Stillinger, 217–33. Chapel Hill, NC: Annali d'Italianistica, 2006.

Milanese, Angela. "Affinità e contraddizioni tra rubriche e novelle del *Decameron*." *Studi sul Boccaccio* 23 (1995): 89–111.

Milani, Giuliano. *L'uomo con la borsa al collo: Genealogia e uso di un'immagine medievale*. Rome: Viella, 2017.

Milner, Stephen. "The Florentine Piazza della Signoria as Practiced Place." In Crum and Paoletti, *Renaissance Florence: A Social History*, 83–103.

Minnis, Alastair. "From *Coilles* to *Bel Chose*: Discourses of Obscenity in Jean de Meun and Chaucer." In *Medieval Obscenities*, edited by Nicola McDonald, 156–78. Rochester, NY: Boydell and Brewer, 2006.

Molho, Anthony. "Communal Income: Taxes on the Contado and the Gabelles." In Molho, *Florentine Public Finances in the Early Renaissance, 1400–1433*, 22–59. Cambridge, MA: Harvard University Press, 1971.

Montefusco, Antonio. "Dall'Università di Parigi a Frate Alberto: Immaginario antimendicante ed ecclesiologia vernacolare in Giovanni Boccaccio." *Studi sul Boccaccio* 43 (2015): 177–232.

Moravia, Alberto. "Boccaccio." In *Il Trecento*, 121–43. Florence: Sansoni, 1953. Reprinted in *L'uomo come fine e altri saggi*, 135–58. Milan: Bompiani, 1964.

Morosini, Roberta. "From the Garden to the Liquid City: Notes on 2.10, 3.4, 3.10 and 4.6/7, for a *Decameron* Poetic of the Erotico-Political Based on Useful Work ('civanza')." *Heliotropia* 12–13 (2015–16): 46–89.

– *Il mare salato: Il Mediterraneo di Dante, Petrarca e Boccaccio*. Rome: Viella, 2020.

– "The Merchant and the Siren: Commercial Networks and 'Connectivity' in Mediterranean 'Space-Movement,' from Jacopo da Cessole's *De ludo scachorum* to *Decameron* VIII 10." *Studi sul Boccaccio* 46 (2018): 95–131.

Morosini, Roberta, ed. *Boccaccio geografo: Un viaggio nel Mediterraneo tra le città, i Giardini, e … il mondo di Giovanni Boccaccio*. Florence: Pagliai, 2010.

Morpurgo, Piero. "Michele Scoto." In *Federico II: Enciclopedia fridericiana*, 2:316–23. Rome: Enciclopedia Italiana Treccani, 2005.

Mosetti Casaretto, Francesco, ed. *La scena assente: Realtà e leggenda sul teatro nel Medioevo*. Alessandria: Edizioni dell'Orso, 2006.

Muir, Edward. *Mad Blood Stirring: Vendetta in Renaissance Italy*. Baltimore: Johns Hopkins University Press, 1998.

Muscetta, Carlo. "Boccaccio e la commedia dei cafoni." In Muscetta, *Letteratura militante*, 163–7. Florence: Parenti, 1953.

– *Giovanni Boccaccio*. Bari: Laterza, 1972.

Najemy, John. *Corporatism and Consensus in Florentine Electoral Politics*. Chapel Hill: University of North Carolina Press, 1982.

– *A History of Florence, 1200–1575*. Malden, MA: Blackwell, 2006.

Neri Lusanna, Enrica. "L'antico arredo presbiteriale e il fonte del Battistero: Vestigia e ipotesi." In *Il Battistero di San Giovanni a Firenze/The Baptistery of San Giovanni, Florence*, edited by Antonio Paolucci, 2:189–201. 2 vols. Modena: Panini, 1994.

Nissen, Christopher. *The Ethics of Retribution in the Decameron and the Late Medieval Italian Novella: Beyond the Circle*. Lewiston, NY: Mellen University Press, 1993.

Nussbaum, Martha C. *Political Emotions: Why Love Matters for Justice*. Cambridge, MA: Belknap, 2013.

Ober, Josiah. *Democracy and Knowledge: Innovation and Learning in Classical Athens*. Princeton: Princeton University Press, 2008.

Ó'Cuilleanáin, Cormac. *Religion and the Clergy in Boccaccio's Decameron*. Rome: Edizioni di Storia e Letteratura, 1984.

Olson, Glending. *Literature as Recreation in the Later Middle Ages*. Ithaca: Cornell University Press, 1982.

Ong, Walter J. *Orality and Literacy: The Technologizing of the Word*. London: Routledge, 1988.

Opera del Vocabolario Italiano. https://artfl-project.uchicago.edu/content/ovi.

Ortalli, Gherardo. *Pingatur in Palatio: La pittura infamante nei secoli XIII–XVI*. Rome: Jouvence, 1979.

Paden, Michael. "Elissa: La ghibellina del *Decameron*." *Studi sul Boccaccio* 21 (1993): 139–50.

Panigiani, Ottorino. *Vocabolario etimologico della lingua italiana*. 2 vols. Milan: Sonzogno, 1937. Available online at www.etimo.it/.

Papio, Michael. "Geospatial Visualizations for the Study of Boccaccio." *Humanist Studies & the Digital Age* 5.1 (2017): 24–45.

– "An Intimate Self-Portrait." In Kirkham, Sherberg, and Smarr, *Boccaccio: A Critical Guide*, 341–51.

– "'Merus phylosophie succus': Neoplatonic Influences on Boccaccio's Hermeneutics." *Medioevo letterario d'Italia* 12 (2015): 97–127.

– "'Non meno di compassion piena che dilettevole': Notes on Compassion in Boccaccio." *Italian Quarterly* 37 (2000): 107–25.

Pastore Stocchi, Manlio. "Altre annotazioni." *Studi sul Boccaccio* 7 (1973): 189–211.

– "Taide." In *Enciclopedia dantesca*, edited by Umberto Bosco, 5:509–10. 2nd ed. Rome: Istituto dell a Enciclopedia Italiana, 1984.

Patterson, Lee. *Chaucer and the Subject of History*. Madison: University of Wisconsin Press, 1991.

Pearsall, Derek. *The Canterbury Tales*. London: Allen & Unwin, 1985.

Perrus, Claude. "La nouvelle V, 8, du *Décaméron*: Deux expériences de lecture." *Revue des études italiennes* n.s. 21 (1975): 249–83.

Perruso, Richard. "The Development of the Doctrine of *Res Communes* in Medieval and Early Modern Europe." *Tijdschrift Voor Rechtsgeschiedenis/ Revue d'Histoire du Droit/The Legal History Review* 70 (2002): 69–93.

Pertile, Lino. "Contrapasso." In *The Dante Encyclopedia*, edited by Richard Lansing, 219–22. New York: Garland, 2000.

– "Dante, Boccaccio, e l'intelligenza." *Italian Studies* 43 (1988): 60–74.

Perucchi, Giulia. "Boccaccio geografo lettore del Plinio petrarchesco." *Italia medioevale e umanistica* 54 (2013): 153–211.

– *Petrarca e le arti figurative: De remediis utriusque Fortunae*. Florence: Le Lettere, 2014.

Peters, Edward. "*Pars, Parte*: Dante and an Urban Contribution to Political Thought." In *The Medieval City*, edited by Harry A. Miskimin, David Herlihy, and A.L. Udovitch, 113–40. New Haven: Yale University Press, 1977.

Petoletti, Marco. "Boccaccio e Plinio il vecchio: Gli estratti dello Zibaldone Magliabechiano." *Studi sul Boccaccio* 41 (2013): 257–82.

Petralia, Giuseppe. "Sicilia e Mediterraneo nel Trecento." In *Spazi economici e circuiti commerciali nel Mediterraneo del Trecento*, edited by Bruno Figliuolo, Giuseppe Petralia, and Pinuccia F. Simbula, 1–16. Amalfi: Centro di Studi Amalfitano, 2017.

Pianigiani, Ottorino, ed. *Vocabolario etimologico della lingua italiana*. Milan: Sonzogno, 1937. Available online at www.etimo.it/.

Picone, Michelangelo. "L'arte della beffa: L'ottava giornata." In Picone and Mesirca, *Introduzione al Decameron*, 203–25.

– "Gioco e/o letteratura." In *Boccaccio e la codificazione della novella: Letture del Decameron*, 51–66. Ravenna: Longo, 2008.

– "The Tale of Bergamino (I.7)." In Weaver, *The Decameron First Day in Perspective*, 160–78.

Picone, Michelangelo, and Margherita Mesirca, eds. *Introduzione al Decameron*. Florence: Cesati, 2004.

Pietrini, Sandra. *I giullari nell'immaginario medievale*. Rome: Bulzoni, 2011.

– *Spettacoli e immaginario teatrale nel Medioevo*. Rome: Bulzoni, 2001.

Pinto, Giuliano. "Matrimonio e sessualità coniugale nella Toscana del Basso Medioevo: Una rilettura delle fonti." In Pinto, *Firenze medievale e dintorni*, 143–62. Rome: Viella, 2016.

Porcelli, Bruno. "*Dec.* VIII.2: Un amorazzo contadino da ridere." *Studi e problemi di critica testuale* 50 (1995): 85–94.

Posner, Richard. *Law and Literature*. Rev. ed. Cambridge, MA: Harvard University Press, 1998.

Quondam, Amedeo. "Le cose (e le parole) del mondo." In Boccaccio, *Decameron*, edited by Quondam, Fiorilla, and Alfano, 1669–1802.

Rait, Robert S. *Life in the Medieval University*. 1912. Cambridge: Cambridge University Press, 2011.

Rajna, Pio. "L'episodio delle questioni d'amore nel *Filocolo* di Boccaccio." *Romania* 31.121 (1902): 28–81.

Rea, Domenico. "Boccaccio a Napoli." In Rea, *Il re e il lustrascarpe*, 252–74. Milan: Mondadori, 1960.

Rebhorn, Wayne. "Redefining the *Beffa*: Boccaccio's Challenge to the Reader in *Decameron* VIII, 7." *Forum Italicum* 22 (1988): 204–22.

Reeve, Michael D. "The Text of Boccaccio's Excerpts from Pliny's *Natural History*." *Italia medioevale e umanistica* 54 (2013): 135–52.

Regnicoli, Laura. "Codice diplomatico di Giovanni Boccaccio, 1: I documenti fiscali." *Italia medioevale e umanistica* 54 (2013): 1–80.

– "Documenti su Giovanni Boccaccio." In De Robertis et al., *Boccaccio: Autore e copista*, 382–402.

Rico, Francisco. *Ritratti allo specchio (Boccaccio, Petrarca).* Padua: Antenore, 2012.

Rimmon-Kenan, Shlomith. *Narrative Fiction: Contemporary Poetics.* London: Methuen, 1983.

Robbe, Udalbo. *La differenza sostanziale tra "res nullius" e "res nullius in bonis" e la distinzione della "res" pseudo-marcianee.* Milan: Giuffrè, 1979.

Robert, Aurélien. "Médicine et théologie à la cour des angevins de Naples." In Chandelier and Robert, *Frontières des savoirs en Italie,* 295–349.

Robin, Anne. "Una modalità di conservazione della vita: *Il regimen sanitatis* della brigata del *Decameron.*" In *Humeurs,* edited by Giancarlo Alfano et al., 53–66. Bern: Peter Lang, 2016.

Robins, William. "The Case of the Court Entertainer: Popular Culture, Intertextual Dialogue, and the Early Circulation of Boccaccio's *Decameron.*" *Speculum* 92 (2017): 1–35.

Ronciere, Charles M. "Florence in the Fourteenth Century: The Evolution of Tariffs and Problems of Collection." In *Florentine Studies: Politics and Society in Renaissance Florence,* edited by Nicolai Rubinstein, 140–92. Evanston: Northwestern University Press, 1968.

Rossi, Luciano. "Sercambi e Boccaccio." *Studi sul Boccaccio* 6 (1971): 145–79.

Rotunda, Dominic Peter. *Motif-Index of the Italian Novella in Prose.* Bloomington: Indiana University Publications, 1942.

Russo, Luigi. *Letture critiche del Decameron.* Bari: Laterza, 1956.

Sanguineti White, Laura. *Seduzione e privazione: Il cibo nel Decameron.* Lucca: Maria Pacini Fazzi Editore, 2016.

Sanguinetti, Edoardo. *Lettura del Decameron.* Edited by Emma Grimaldi. Salerno: Edizioni 10/17, 1989.

Santagata, Marco. *Per moderne carte: La biblioteca volgare di Petrarca.* Bologna: Il Mulino, 1990.

Sapori, Armando. "La gabella delle porte di Firenze." In *Miscellanea in onore di Roberto Cessi,* 1:321–48. Rome: Edizioni di Storia e Letteratura, 1958.

– *Una compagnia di Calimala ai primi del Trecento.* Florence: Olschki, 1932.

Savelli, Giulio. "Riso." In Bragantini and Forni, *Lessico critico decameroniano,* 344–71.

Scanlon, Larry. *Narrative, Authority, and Power: The Medieval Exemplum and the Chaucerian Tradition.* Cambridge: Cambridge University Press, 1994.

Scattergood, John. "The Shipman's Tale." In *Sources and Analogues of the Canterbury Tales,* edited by Robert M. Correale and Mary Hamel, 2:565–81. Cambridge: D.S. Brewer, 2005.

Scionti, Francesca. *Capitalisti di faida: La vendetta da paradigma morale a strategia d'impresa.* Rome: Carocci, 2011.

Segre, Cesare. "La beffa e il comico nella novellistica del Due e Trecento." In *Passare il tempo: La letteratura del gioco e dell'intrattenimento dal XII al XVI secolo,* 13–28. Rome: Salerno, 1993.

– "Funzioni, opposizioni e simmetrie nella giornata VII del *Decameron*." *Studi sul Boccaccio* 6 (1971): 81–108.

Sherberg, Michael. *The Governance of Friendship: Law and Gender in the Decameron*. Columbus: Ohio State University Press, 2011.

Singer, Peter. *A Darwinian Left: Politics, Evolution and Cooperation*. New Haven: Yale University Press, 1999.

Smarr, Janet Levarie. *Boccaccio and Fiammetta: The Narrator as Lover*. Urbana: University of Illinois Press, 1986.

– "Clergy in the *Decameron*: Another Look?" *Heliotropia* 11.1–2 (2014): 55–64.

Sober, Elliott, and David Sloan Wilson. *Unto Others: The Evolution and Psychology of Unselfish Behavior*. Cambridge, MA: Harvard University Press, 1998.

Sorcha, Carey. "Imaging Memory." In Sorcha, *Pliny's Catalogue of Culture: Art and Empire in the Natural History*, 138–78. Oxford: Oxford University Press, 2006.

Steinberg, Justin. *Dante and the Limits of the Law*. Chicago: University of Chicago Press, 2013.

– "Dante's Justice: A Reappraisal of the Contrapasso." *L'Alighieri* 44 (2014): 59–74.

Stern, Laura Ikins. *The Criminal Law System of Medieval and Renaissance Florence*. Baltimore: Johns Hopkins University Press, 1994.

Stewart, Pamela D. "La novella di Madonna Oretta e le due parti del *Decameron*." *Yearbook of Italian Studies* (1973–5): 27–40. Reprinted in *Retorica e mimica nel Decameron e nella commedia del Cinquecento*, 19–38. Florence: Olschki, 1986.

Struever, Nancy. "Petrarch's *Invective contra medicum*: An Early Confrontation of Rhetoric and Medicine." *MLN* 108 (1993): 659–79.

Surdich, Luigi. *Boccaccio*. Rome: Laterza, 2001.

– "Tra Dante e Boccaccio: Qualche appunto sulla 'compassione.'" In *Le passoni tra ostensione e riserbo*, edited by Romana Rutelli and Luisa Villa, 35–50. Pisa: ETS, 2000.

– "La 'varietà delle cose' e le 'frondi di quercia': La nona giornata." In Picone and Mesirca, *Introduzione al Decameron*, 227–65.

Sznura, Franek. "Appunti sull'urbanistica fiorentina tra XIII e XIV secolo." In *Arnolfo: Alle origini del Rinascimento fiorentino*, edited by Enrica Neri Lusanna, 87–97. Florence: Paliai Polistampa, 2005.

Tabarroni, Andrea. "Notizie biografiche su alcuni maestri di arti e medicina attivi nello *Studium* bolognese nel XIV secolo." In *L'insegnamento della logica a Bologna nel XIV secolo*, edited by Dino Buzzetti, Maurizio Ferriani, and Andrea Tabarroni, 607–16. Bologna: Istituto Per la Storia dell'Università di Bologna, 1992.

Tabarroni, Andrea. "La nascita dello Studio di Medicina e Arte a Bologna." In Casagrande and Fioravante, *La filosofia in Italia al tempo di Dante*, 25–36.

Tanturli, Giuliano, and Stefano Zamponi. "Biografia e cronologia delle opere." In De Robertis et al., *Boccaccio: Autore e copista*, 61–4.

Tanzini, Lorenzo. *A consiglio: La vita politica nell'Italia dei comuni*. Bari: Laterza, 2014.

– *Firenze*. Spoleto: Fondazione Centro Italiano di Studi sull'Alto Medioevo, 2016.

– "I forestieri e il debito pubblico di Firenze nel Quattrocento." *Quaderni Storici* 147 (2014): 775–808.

Tesoro della lingua Italiana delle Origini. http://tlio.ovi.cnr.it/TLIO/.

Thomas, Yan. *Fictio legis: L'empire de la fiction romaine et ses limites médiévales*. Paris: Presses Universitaires de France, 1995.

– "La valeur des choses: Le droit romain hors la religion." *Annales, Histoire et Droit* 6 (2002): 1431–62.

Todorov, Tzvetan. *Grammaire du Decameron*. The Hague: Mouton, 1969.

Toldo, Pietro. "Dall'*Alphabetum narrationum*." *Archiv für das Studium der neueren Sprachen und Literatur* 117 (1906): 68–85, 287–303; 118 (1907): 69–81, 329–51; 119 (1908): 86–100, 351–71.

Tonelli, Natascia. *Fisiologia della passione: Poesia d'amore e medicina da Cavalcanti a Boccaccio*. Florence: SISMEL, 2015.

Trabalza, Ciro. "La coerenza estestica del personaggio di Calandrino nel *Decameron*." In Trabalza, *Studi sul Boccaccio: Preceduti da saggi di storia della critica e stilistica*, 235–64. Città di Castello: Lapi, 1906.

Trachtenberg, Marvin. *Dominion of the Eye: Urbanism, Art, and Power in Early Modern Florence*. Cambridge: Cambridge University Press, 1997.

Trexler, Richard. *Public Life in Renaissance Florence*. New York: Academic Press, 1980.

Trottmann, Christian. "Philosophie, médecine et rhétorique dans l'*Invective contre un médecin* et le *De sui ipsius et multorum ignorantia*." In Chandelier and Robert, *Frontières des savoirs en Italie*, 351–85.

Tubach, Frederic C. *Index exemplorum: A Handbook of Medieval Religious Tales*. Helsinki: Suomalainen Tiedeakatemia, 1969.

Uberman, George Didi. "The Molding Image: Genealogy and the Truth of Resemblance in Pliny's *Natural History*, Book 35, 1–7." In *Law and the Image: The Authority of Art and the Aesthetics of Law*, edited by Costas Douzinas and Lynda Nead, 71–88. Chicago: University of Chicago Press, 1999.

Usher, Jonathan. "Le rubriche del *Decameron*." *Medioevo romanzo* 10 (1985): 391–418.

Valentier, Wilhelm R. "Tino di Camaino in Florence." *Art Quarterly* 17 (1954): 116–34.

Vallerani, Massimo. "La cittadinanaza pragmatica: Attribuzione e limitazione della *civilitas* nei comuni italiani fra XIII e XV secolo." In *Cittadinanze medievali: Dinamiche di appartenenza a un corpo comunitario*, edited by Sara Menzinger, 113–43. Rome: Viella, 2017.

– "Fiscalità e limiti dell'appartenenza alla città in età comunale." *Quaderni Storici* 147 (2014): 709–42.

Velli, Giuseppe. *Petrarca e Boccaccio: Tradizione, memoria, scrittura*. Padua: Antenore, 1979.

– "La poesia volgare del Boccaccio e i *Rerum vulgarium fragmenta*: Primi appunti." *Giornale Storico della Letteratura Italiana* 169 (1992): 183–99.

– "Il rapporto Petrarca-Boccaccio: A proposito (anche) della Griselda." *Levia Gravia* 6 (2004): 215–25.

– "Seneca nel *Decameron*." *Giornale Storico della Letteratura Italiana* 168 (1991): 321–34.

Véronèse, Julien. "La magie divinatoire à la fin du Moyen Âge." *Cahiers de recherches médiévales et humanistes* 21 (2011): 311–41.

Vitale, Maurizio, and Vittore Branca. *Il capolavoro del Boccaccio e due diverse redazioni*. 2 vols. Venice: Istituto Veneto di Scienze, Lettere ed Arti, 2002.

Vocabolario degli accademici della Crusca. 4th ed. Florence: Domenico Maria Manni, 1729–38. Available online at: www.lessicografia.it/.

von Balthasar, Hans Urs. "The Tamar Motif: The Church in the Form of a Harlot." *Spouse of the Word: Explorations in Theology*. Vol. 2. San Francisco: Ignatius Press, 1993.

Waley, Daniel. *The Italian City-Republics*. 3rd ed. London: Longman, 1988.

– *Siena and the Sienese in the Thirteenth Century*. Cambridge: Cambridge University Press, 1991.

Wallace, David. *Chaucerian Polity: Absolutist Lineages and Associational Forms in England and Italy*. Stanford: Stanford University Press, 1997.

– *Giovanni Boccaccio: Decameron*. Cambridge: Cambridge University Press, 1991.

Watson, Paul. "The Cement of Fiction: Giovanni Boccaccio and the Painters of Florence." *MLN* 99 (1984): 43–64.

Weaver, Elissa B., ed. *The Decameron First Day in Perspective*. Toronto: University of Toronto Press, 2004.

Wilkins, Ernest H. *Studies on Petrarch and Boccaccio*, edited by Aldo S. Bernardo. Padua: Antenore, 1978.

Williams, Alison. *Tricksters and Pranksters: Roguery in French and German Literature of the Middle Ages and the Renaissance*. Amsterdam: Rodopi, 2000.

Wilson, David Sloan. *Darwin's Cathedral: Evolution, Religion, and the Nature of Society*. Chicago: University of Chicago Press, 2002.

Yun, Aimee. *The Bargello Palace: The Invention of Civic Architecture in Florence*. London: Harvey Miller Publishers, 2015.

Zak, Gur. "Boccaccio and Petrarch." In Armstrong, Daniels, and Milner, *The Cambridge Companion to Boccaccio*, 139–54.

Zamponi, Stefano, Martina Pantarotto, and Antonella Tomiello. "Stratigrafia dello Zibaldone e della Miscellanea Laurenziani." In *Gli zibaldoni di Boccaccio: Memoria, scrittura, riscrittura; Atti del seminario internazionale di Firenze-Certaldo, 26–28 aprile 1996*, edited by Michelangelo Picone and Claude Cazalé Bérard, 181–258. Florence: F. Cesati, 1998.

Ziolkowski, Jan M. "The Latin Grammatical and Rhetorical Tradition." In *Obscenity: Social Control and Artistic Creation in the European Middle Ages*, edited by Jan Ziolkowski, 41–59. Boston: Brill, 1998.

Zorzi, Andrea. "The Judicial System in Florence in the Fourteenth and Fifteenth Centuries." In *Crime, Society and Law in Renaissance Florence*, edited by Trevor Dean and K.J.P. Lowe, 40–58. Cambridge: Cambridge University Press, 1994.

– "Ordine pubblico e amministrazione della giustizia nelle formazioni politiche toscane tra Tre e Quattrocento." In *Italia 1350–1450: Tra crisi, trasformazione, sviluppo; Tredicesimo convegno di studi, Pistoia, 10–13 maggio 1991*, 419–74. Pistoia: Centro Italiano di Studi di Storia e d'Arte, 1993.

– "I rettori di Firenze: Reclutamento, flussi, scambi (1193–1313)." In Maire Vigueur, *I Podestà dell'Italia comunale*, 1:453–594.

Zunino, Estelle. "*Florentini, trufatores maximi*: De la *beffa* à l'identité florentine dans le *Décaméron*." In *La città nel Decameron*, edited by Alessandro Vettori, 95–110. Paris: Quaderni dell'Hotel de Galliffet, 2010.

Contributors

Teodolinda Barolini is Lorenzo Da Ponte Professor of Italian at Columbia University. A fellow of the Accademia Nazionale dei Lincei and the American Academy of Arts and Sciences, she has written extensively on Dante, Boccaccio, Petrarch, and the lyric tradition. Her books include *Dante's Poets* (1984; Italian 1993), *The Undivine Comedy: Detheologizing Dante* (1992; Italian 2003), *Dante and the Origins of Italian Literary Culture* (2006; Italian 2012), and a commentary on Dante's lyric poetry (Italian 2009, English 2014). Her online commentary on the *Divine Comedy* appears on Digital Dante: https://digitaldante.columbia.edu/.

Elisa Brilli is Assistant Professor of Medieval Italian Literature at the University of Toronto. Her recent publications include the monograph *Firenze e il Profeta* (2012), a critical edition of Arnold of Liège's *Alphabetum Narrationum* (2015), and the edition of the collective volumes *Faire l'anthropologie historique du Moyen Age* (2010), *Images and Words in Exile* (2015), and *Agostino, agostiniani e agostinismi nel Trecento Italiano* (2018).

Katherine A. Brown teaches in the Department of Romance Languages and Literatures at the University of Notre Dame. She is the author of *Boccaccio's Fabliaux* (2014, rpt. 2020) and several articles comparing the French and Italian traditions of the medieval period. She is also the editor of *Dialogues on the Decameron*, a special issue of *Quaderni d'Italianistica* (2017).

K.P. Clarke was the Sykes Research Fellow in Italian Studies at Pembroke College, Cambridge, and teaches medieval literature at the University of York. He is the author of *Chaucer and Italian Textuality* (2011), as well as numerous articles on Dante and Boccaccio in *Dante Studies, Studi sul Boccaccio, Modern Language Notes*, and *Le Tre Corone*. His current project is a monograph on the poetic lexicon of Dante's *Comedy*.

Rhiannon Daniels is Senior Lecturer in Italian Studies and co-director of the Centre for Material Texts at the University of Bristol. Her research focuses on the reception of Boccaccio in the Middle Ages and Renaissance, and in particular the history of the *Decameron* in early print culture. She is the author of *Boccaccio and the Book: Production and Reading in Italy 1340–1520* (2009) and a co-editor of *The Cambridge Companion to Boccaccio* (2015).

Leah Faibisoff is a visiting post-doctoral researcher at the Scuola Normale Superiore in Pisa. She has studied the bureaucracy of the Florentine chancery with special focus on the fourteenth century and the chancellors Ventura and Niccolò Monachi. Her current research explores the concept of Fortune in the political thought of everyday bureaucrats and administrators working in medieval and early modern Italian governments.

Maggie Fritz-Morkin is Assistant Professor of Italian at the University of North Carolina – Chapel Hill, and taught previously at Sewanee: The University of the South. She is a scholar of medieval Italian literature, specializing in the history of rhetoric, obscenity, and visceral speech, especially in the works of Dante, Petrarch, and Boccaccio. Her further interests include theories of debt, sanitation and urban studies, the rhetoric of medieval medicine, and literary translation.

Olivia Holmes is Professor of Medieval Studies at Binghamton University and director of Binghamton's Center for Medieval and Renaissance Studies, as well as editor of the journal *Mediaevalia*. She has published two monographs: *Assembling the Lyric Self: Authorship from Troubadour Song to Italian Poetry Book* (2000) and *Dante's Two Beloveds: Ethics and Erotics in the "Divine Comedy"* (2008). Her current book project is entitled *Boccaccio and Exemplarity: Setting a Bad Example in the "Decameron."*

Roberta Morosini is Professor of Romance Languages and Literatures at Wake Forest University. She has written extensively on Christian-Muslim relationships and the medieval Mediterranean, and has edited volumes on geography and cartography, including *Boccaccio geografo* (2010) and *Paolino Veneto: Narratore, storico e geografo* (2019). She is the author of *Per difetto rintegrare: Una lettura del Filocolo di G. Boccaccio* (2004), *Dante, il Profeta e il Libro* (2018), and *Il mare salato: Il Mediterraneo di Dante, Petrarca e Boccaccio* (2020).

William Robins is President of Victoria University and Associate Professor of Medieval Studies and English at the University of Toronto.

His studies of Trecento literature include a critical edition of Antonio Pucci's *Cantari della Reina d'Oriente* (2007, with Attilio Motta), the edited collection *Textual Cultures of Medieval Italy* (2011), and articles in venues such as *Speculum, Italian Studies, Exemplaria, Heliotropia,* and *Studi sul Boccaccio.* He is currently working on a critical edition of the *Historia Apollonii regis Tyri.*

Justin Steinberg is Professor of Italian Literature in the Department of Romance Languages and Literatures at the University of Chicago and Editor-in-Chief of the journal *Dante Studies.* He is the author of *Dante and the Limits of the Law* (2013) and *Accounting for Dante: Urban Readers and Writers in Late Medieval Italy* (2007). He is currently writing a book on Boccaccio and the law.

Index

www.ingramcontent.com/pod-product-compliance
Lightning Source LLC
LaVergne TN
LVHW090153080826
844660LV00013B/790/J

* 9 7 8 1 4 8 7 5 0 6 9 0 2 *